Beyond Virtue and Vice

PENNSYLVANIA STUDIES IN HUMAN RIGHTS

Bert B. Lockwood, *Series Editor*

A complete list of books in the series is available
from the publisher.

BEYOND VIRTUE AND VICE

Rethinking Human Rights and Criminal Law

Edited by

Alice M. Miller

and

Mindy Jane Roseman

PENN

UNIVERSITY OF PENNSYLVANIA PRESS

PHILADELPHIA

Published by
University of Pennsylvania Press
Philadelphia, Pennsylvania 19104-4112
www.upenn.edu/pennpress

Printed in the United States of America on acid-free paper

10 9 8 7 6 5 4 3 2 1

A catalogue record for this book is available from the Library of Congress.

ISBN 978-0-8122-5108-1

CONTENTS

Introduction   1
Alice M. Miller and Mindy Jane Roseman with Zain Rizvi

PART I. TRANSNATIONAL THEORY AND PRACTICE

1. Janet Halley in Conversation with Aziza Ahmed: Interview   17

2. Seismic Shifts: How Prosecution Became the Go-To Tool
   to Vindicate Rights   39
   Alice M. Miller with Tara Zivkovic

3. The Harm Principle Meets Morality Offenses: Human Rights,
   Criminal Law, and the Regulation of Sex and Gender   54
   Alli Jernow

4. Reflections of a Human Rights Activist   75
   Widney Brown

PART II. NATIONAL HISTORICAL PERSPECTIVES

5. Virtuous Rights: On Prostitution Exceptionalism in South Korea   93
   Sealing Cheng and Ae-Ryung Kim

6. Brazilian Sex Laws: Continuities, Ruptures, and Paradoxes   114
   Sonia Corrêa and Maria Lucia Karam

7. The Reach of a Skirt in Southern Africa: Claims to
   Law and Custom in Protecting and Patrolling Relations
   of Gender and Sexuality   134
   Oliver Phillips

8. Abortion as Treason: Sexuality and Nationalism in France   158
   Mindy Jane Roseman

PART III. CONTEMPORARY NATIONAL CONCERNS

9. Wanja Muguongo in Conversation with
   Alice M. Miller: Interview   173

10. Criminal Law, Activism, and Sexual and Reproductive Justice:
    What We Can Learn from the Sex Selection Campaign in India   185
    Geetanjali Misra and Vrinda Marwah

11. Poisoned Gifts: Old Moralities under New Clothes?   199
    Esteban Restrepo Saldarriaga

12. The Filth They Bring: Sex Panics and Racial Others in Lebanon   220
    Rasha Moumneh

13. Objects in Political Mirrors May Not Be What They Appear   233
    Scott Long

14. Harm Production: An Argument for Decriminalization   248
    Joanna N. Erdman

   Notes   269

   List of Contributors   335

   Index   337

   Acknowledgments   353

Introduction

Alice M. Miller and Mindy Jane Roseman with Zain Rizvi

Human rights is interested in power: identifying it, distrusting it, assessing its operation for good and ill in human interactions. Human rights as doctrine and practice initially preoccupied itself with the abuse of state authority, and predominant areas of focus in the field have been constraining this abuse and conducting critiques of the administration of criminal justice. Criminal law as theory and practice is one of the most visible, material forms of state police power—and, along with military capacity, one of the state's privileged uses of coercive force.[1]

Yet human rights as rhetoric and practice also seek to harness state power in more affirmative ways. Over the last two decades, human rights advocates have made claims to state power in fields of health, housing, and education, calling for the state to fulfill its duties in these social, economic, and political realms. Rights groups have increasingly invoked the use of state power as a remedy for harm, with some taking a more definitively prosecutorial turn. There may be no essential contradiction between advocates' engagement with and attempts to limit the use of criminal law; human rights, after all, may function as both "shield and sword" regarding penal powers of the state.[2] However, in both advocacy and scholarship, there is a remarkable lack of attention to and assessment of these two approaches as deeply interconnected. Those involved in rights work have tended to focus on criminal law as either friend or foe in their subfield, rather than recognize its instrumentalization in different ways across various subfields.

This bifurcation of attention suggests an unresolved and deep vexation in human rights theory and practice as it engages the criminal law. This book seeks to respond to this silence by exploring contestations, lacunae, and contradictions at the borders of decriminalization and criminalization in local and transnational rights theory and practice, particularly in work on sexuality, gender, and reproduction. As the engagement between rights and penal law in these domains is deepening, producing troubling dilemmas in almost every regime (national and transnational), debate is necessary. We need to begin to stake out a thoughtful framework and principles of engagement for analyzing the rather fraught relationship between human rights and criminal law.[3]

The use of criminal law to regulate sex, gender, and reproduction is decidedly not new; such regulation has been the hallmark of the modern state. As a taxonomic matter, "criminal law" is simply the doctrinal designation given to laws that define the content of crimes and their punishments. It also encompasses the procedures surrounding how crimes are investigated, how evidence is collected, and how suspects are charged, tried, and treated on conviction or exoneration. Criminal law is the regime that allows the state to use force (for example, deprive liberty, fine, punish corporally, or execute) as a response to a certain set of acts deemed in that time and place as sufficiently "harmful" to justify the infliction of this pain.[4] That which constitutes a crime both invites and limits the state's ability to punish, and the mode by which the state inflicts such punishment is endlessly in flux. Many foundational works in the field of criminology and criminal jurisprudence demonstrate that the definition of crime and punishment is a matter of ideology and politics; of concept, norm, and tactic; of morality and economics.[5] These ideologies and moralities are judgments on conduct and persons. It is not new, therefore, to acknowledge that almost all aspects of the definition of a "good" person in society are bound up in constituting crime, criminal law, and the criminal.

What is new, in the past two decades or so, is the expansion of human rights into the regulation of sexual, reproductive, and gender practices and expressions. Claims around sexual and reproductive rights come with their respective social movements, sometimes working at cross-purposes vis-à-vis the role of the criminal law. It is at this advocacy-driven inflection point that this volume's interrogation of the relationship between human rights and criminal law begins. The current inflection point at once encompasses rights-based calls to liberalize previously penalized practices (for example, decriminalization of sex outside of marriage, whether heterosexual sex, homosexual sex, or sex for money) and rights-based calls to penalize previously unsanctioned practices (for example, coerced sex within marriage).

Today, human rights' presentation of itself is as an emancipatory and power-contesting practice and, at the same time, a prosecutorial and carceral one.[6] Human rights vindication is of course not the only motivation for penal law. In national and international settings, harsh criminal penalties are invoked simultaneously to defend "traditional values" as much as to promote "modern human rights." These diverse impulses are visible in the recent calls to impose the death penalty for homosexuals (in Uganda and elsewhere)[7] and persons who kill homosexuals (in the United States).[8] Draconian practices trail avowedly progressive impulses to punish in service of some higher ethic, as in the global calls to "end impunity" for violence against women (VAW) through the prosecution of rapists in contexts as diverse as the conflicts of the eastern Democratic Republic of Congo and ex-Yugoslavia and the recent "notorious" rapes in India. The fact that the worldwide calls to punish rape are part of an international rights regime that explicitly excludes capital punishment seems lost in the call by some groups to execute rapists at the national level. Sometimes the liberalization of the criminal law in one aspect of sexuality is literally offset elsewhere in the penal code, such as in Nicaragua, where abortion became criminalized in all cases just as same-sex sexual conduct was decriminalized, both in the name of human rights.[9]

Other examples illustrate the synergies and disjunctures within and between criminal law and rights claiming, as the regulation of sex, gender, and reproduction becomes more apparent and extensive. In 2004, representatives from several West African nations met in N'Djamena, Chad, to develop model legislation to address a persistent HIV epidemic.[10] Articles 1 and 36 of this model law called for nations to criminalize the risk of transmission of HIV.[11] Women's rights advocates were on both sides of the appeal. Some were convinced that the criminal law would give them leverage over their philandering partners; others were concerned that the criminal law would only stigmatize and disempower women.[12] Many countries criminalize HIV with radically different local contexts: Canada is at the forefront of nations that criminally prosecute practices associated with the transmission of HIV; Uganda joined the ranks in 2014.[13]

Prostitution law is a particularly contradictory and tense site for criminal law and rights claims. Since the nineteenth century, exacerbated under anti-trafficking conventions, prostitution law in many countries served to punish sex enacted "merely" to gratify the passions of another; it marked (mostly) women as tainted vectors of lust and disease. Now, criminal prostitution laws have been revarnished with the language of women's rights, in part through the conflation of prostitution and trafficking, harnessing overlapping nineteenth-, twentieth-, and twenty-first-century legal doctrines on criminal trafficking in persons.[14] Those rights advocates recuperating prostitution law claim to protect women's autonomy by criminalizing the buying (and sometimes selling) of sex. This is in direct tension with claims by other human rights advocates that decriminalization best protects sexual autonomy. Canada, for example, recently emerged from a fierce parliamentary fight over the appropriate approach to reforming its criminal law after its Constitutional Court struck down key aspects of its law regulating the sale of sex, on the grounds that the law itself promoted violence against those in sex work.[15] Despite a firestorm of criticism, Amnesty International passed a resolution in 2015 authorizing its board to develop and adopt a policy that supports the full decriminalization of all aspects of consensual sex work.[16]

Contestations regarding the use of criminal law in service of women's rights continue to erupt in the Global North and Global South, whether over prosecutions for female genital cutting/mutilation or penalties against the wearing of headscarves.[17] As of 2017, some intersex advocates have also joined the "prosecution as human rights tool" approach, campaigning for criminal penalties against medical practitioners carrying out non–medically necessary genital cutting and surgeries.[18]

Despite the ubiquity of these eruptions from rights toward the use (and abuse) of the criminal law today, formal legal systems based on human rights, as well as the constellation of organized rights-based advocacy movements, are relative newcomers to the realms of sex, gender, and reproduction—at least as compared to criminal law, its procedures, and its practitioners. The deployment of human rights arguments to advocate for the decriminalization of abortion or sex outside of marriage, or for the criminalization of sexual assault as a vindication of human autonomy and rights, is of even more recent vintage.[19] As noted, the regulation of sexuality, gender, and reproduction by criminal law has a varied but deep connection to the emergence of the modern state. The relative newness of the dynamic between the recognition of gender, sexual, and reproductive rights and the centrality of their control to the modern state may explain the range of positions and norms generated.

The time is ripe to revisit the junctures and disjunctures of human rights and criminal law—between and among claims in sexuality, reproduction, and gender. In so doing, we can identify some guiding conditions and rules of engagement for human rights advocacy and practice in expanding or limiting recourse to criminal law. We need a method and an ethic here, and we must consider the meaning of such rules for a diverse range of people. Notably, we admit the perils of simultaneous over- and underregulation in some moves to promote decriminalization, given the realities of the inaccessibility of access to justice for many marginalized populations who are often unrecognized as victims of crimes.

This book is offered as an entrée into such conversations and debates. In the chapters that follow, well-known scholars and advocates located around the world write from their diverse disciplines (history, law, public health, anthropology) and sites of action (women's rights, gay rights, sex worker rights, constitutional law, HIV activism, mainstream human rights) on the issues and conundrums of their work at the intersection of criminal law, human rights, and sexuality, gender, and reproduction.

All of the contributors, as well as the editors, share diverse connections to the human rights movement and consider themselves friendly critics of it to varying degrees. Many have been active in opposing the overexercise of police power and promoting decriminalization overall, while others have participated in campaigns to expand criminal law's response to specific violations (for example, VAW). Still others are more agnostic about the use of criminal law to advance human rights. We asked them all to write in English, although English is not necessarily the first language of all contributors. At this point in their lives, and whatever their origins, most would be counted as part of a global, cosmopolitan community that shares many values. One of us is clearly identifiable as an abolitionist of the penal state, while several of the rest of us take a skeptical view of the state's deployment of criminal law but are accepting of its (possibly much reduced and always more accountable) role in marshaling some coercive power to punish.

We have organized the book into three sections: chapters in the first part focus on the international and transnational aspects of human rights and criminal law; the second, on nationally bounded questions from a historical perspective; and the third, on national rights debates in the contemporary moment. Of course, the local informs the global, and historical struggles seep constantly into the present. Law is a common thread running through the chapters, but legal discourse—judicial opinions and legislation—is not always their site of inquiry. This is due to the different disciplinary and theoretical locations of the contributing authors; historian Mindy Jane Roseman, for example, focuses on a few specific cases, while human rights attorney Widney Brown reflects on the arc of her career.

The authors had latitude to write in a manner that best suited their voices, as well as to reach beyond the usual audience for an academic publication. For that reason, the chapters, while they treat similar subjects, are not uniformly expository essays. Some chapters take the form of interviews (for example, between Aziza Ahmed and Janet Halley and between Alice M. Miller and Wanja Muguongo) and first-person accounts (for example, the chapters by Brown and Scott Long), while others are situated, self-reflective critiques (for example, the chapter by Geeta Misra and Vrinda Marweh and that by Oliver Phillips). We believe this approach maintains the conceptual integrity of this book and underscores that no one genre of discourse need dominate scholarship. Moreover, the choice to embrace and integrate interviews and self-reflection with essays recognizes that human rights scholarship does not solely emanate from the exclusive bastion of academe.

The book's organization is meant to enact our primary message: meaningful human rights commonalities can only be derived from a diversity of perspectives and experiences across time and place. Therefore, we proceed from grounded methodologies, inspired by nominalist tradition that honors the disparate detail in crafting a larger account. There is no privileged vantage point from which to discern the whole of lived, complicated, and extemporized experiences.

As for the book's content, we asked our authors to address two questions. First, how does invoking the criminal law to prevent or remediate human rights violations matter to the projects of justice and emancipation of diverse people? Second, and conversely, how does human rights doctrine and practice constrain (or enable) the legitimacy and administration of criminal law and its pretensions to serve justice? Many authors incorporate perspectives from feminist, critical race, and queer studies in order to investigate power and its indeterminate creations in the realm of inquiry regarding criminal law.

The contributors to in this volume investigate contradictions, flag conflations and assumptions, analyze "unholy" alliances, and call out inadvertent repressions. They examine the relationships between local histories and contemporary politics oriented around criminal law, organized around ideas of sexualized and gendered citizenship. Many of the chapters tell stories about states or governments using the criminal law in service of nation building, or in the social construction of a certain kind of citizen. They investigate prevailing raced and gendered behavioral expectations in various states at various political moments, with due deference to class and other privileges in selective enforcement. A few chapters weave in tales of moral and sex panics that diverted attention away from misrule (or enabled the rulers to consolidate power). Several of the chapters examine the challenges of advocacy, especially calls for criminalization by advocates who know full well its risks and its costs to the innocent and to the guilty. Though some of the chapters make fewer references to international human rights than do others, they nevertheless refer to constitutions, which have in turn been informed and enriched by modern human rights doctrines.

Human rights, as the last common global project standing,[20] uses languages and methods that seduce us into a problematic of eternal universality.[21] We wish to confront that problematic in context. In the chapters that follow, we observe that the universalizing language of human rights (in this case, regarding sexuality, gender, and reproduction and their entanglement with criminality) must always be understood in relation to specific context, which is at once local and global (and, within the latter, both transnational and international). In other

words, discourse and institutions (of which criminalization and human rights
are both) are in dialogue across jurisdictional and temporal boundaries yet re-
tain a certain fidelity to their locations.[22] This is borne out in each chapter. The
abstractions of the criminal law yield to specific operations and ideologies within
in and between national struggles over race, age, and gender in these stories.

The chapters' authors were encouraged to make connections between topics that are often treated in advocacy silos. We asked them to think through how
the reform of a rape law, for instance, might be tied to the reform of a sodomy
law, or how abortion politics might be positioned as a kindred neighbor of queer
politics through scandals or reforms of the criminal law. Our reasons for this
derive from frustrations in our own experiences as advocates and scholars.[23]
Human rights advocacy often isolates sexuality, gender, and reproduction from
one another. "Sexuality" in rights work tends toward issues relating to sexual
orientation, sex work, sexual exploitation, and HIV transmission; "gender" gets
amalgamated with women's equality and discrimination, including gender-
based and sexual violence; and "reproduction" in rights work is often reduced
to abortion, although it sometimes includes contraception, assisted reproductive technologies or surrogacy, and maternal mortality.[24] From the human rights
perspective, although the same rights are marshaled to support advocacy in each
domain (for example, privacy, nondiscrimination, health, freedom from torture,
and other bodily integrity rights), the actual practice and development of rights
in these areas are greatly disconnected.

This, no doubt, is an artifact of the political economy of advocacy. Large
international human rights organizations, such as Amnesty International and
Human Rights Watch, are divided by populations and topics (for example,
women, children, arms, international crime) or by geographic area; smaller nongovernmental organizations often address a single topic (forced marriage, female
genital cutting/mutilation, business, information). All compete for a limited
pool of resources and public attention. Endeavors that work across issues and
join human and financial wherewithal are the exception that proves the rule—
despite the obvious benefit of integration. The creation of siloes is, we believe,
a central cause of the remarkable lack of human rights theorization around
prosecution and defense. Rarely does a report on VAW take up the question of
how the defendant's rights are best protected. Notably, formal legal classifications of these very same issues do not always fall into the same silo. For example,
sometimes the criminalization of sexual conduct is in sections of the penal code
addressing crimes against the body, sometimes crimes against honor and public
offenses. As Roseman notes in her chapter, abortion crimes have been cataloged
as crimes against the state and as crimes against a person.

Moreover, the tendency to categorize rights advocacy thematically also works against the recognition that so many human rights matters are intersectional;[25] the discrete taxonomy of social difference—race or ethnicity, gender, sexuality, socioeconomic status, able-bodiedness, and so on—is artificial and false. Rather, these social categories confer degrees of privilege and marginalization that in turn vary within and across categories. For human rights advocacy to be effective, it must take account of the ways in which these categories intersect, particularly when invoking the power of criminal law. As several authors emphasize (Ahmed and Halley, Miller and Tara Zivkovic, Sonia Corrêa and Maria Lucia Karam, Brown, and Long, among others in this volume), the administration of criminal justice is selective; politics and prejudice that pluck out one aspect of a person play a key role in how they are treated. Individuals, due to their race or ethnicity, sexual orientation, nonconforming gender expression or behavior, age, or class, may be more or less vulnerable to harassment, arrest, prosecution, and punishment for sexual conduct.[26] Importantly, however, while some of the logics of penalization are interconnected and reinforcing, there are asymmetries and discontinuities, as Roseman's and Misra and Marwah's chapters make clear. The criminal regulation of pregnancy and its termination, for instance, has its own very specific logic, sometimes linked but often distinct from the regulation of sexual conduct, including prostitution laws, sexual orientation and gender identity or expression, and nondisclosure of HIV. Although pregnancy is most often but not always connected to sexual conduct, the legal regimes and political maneuvers to address the two are historically very separate.[27] These paths diverged even before the claims surrounding fetal life seemingly hived off abortion from other nonconforming gender and sexual practices in the rights advocacy world. The criminalization of abortion is often a story of nationalism, imperialism, patriarchy, and anticlericalism. Its decriminalization is yet another chapter in the tale of modernization and feminism, but all women do not face equal penalties under its criminalization.

The chapters highlight the challenges to connect as we work across sex-, gender-, and reproduction-related practices; in some important ways, (de)criminalization of sex work, decriminalization of same-sex behaviors or gender expressions, and prosecutions against sexual assault tend to generate focused, category-exclusionary analysis. Very few reports on refugee women, for example, note that this population might include gay-identified cisgender women, trans women, or cisgender heterosexual women, or that this population might include women of all kinds who are coerced into selling sex, as well as those making the decision to sell sex strategically.[28] Moreover, while LGBTI may be a useful political signifier of difference and diversity across gender and sexuality in some settings, it is almost never the correct grouping to understand how the law actually functions for the sets of people affected. The *L* (lesbian) is not treated like the *T* (trans*), which is not treated the same as either the *G* (gay) or the *B* (bisexual) in the hands of either the police or the courts, and the *I* (intersex) is even more distinct in terms of needs and issues. (Trans* is an umbrella term denoting someone who does not identify with, or necessarily always conform to, the gender identity they were assigned at birth. See https://www.urban-dictionary.com/define.php?term=trans*.) The different way that gender stereotypes work for persons deemed women versus those deemed men matters when understanding what is at stake in decriminalizing same-sex conduct: the underlying rules for "men" and "women" reflect historical disjunctions for their treatment under the criminal sanctions for same-sex sexual conduct. Clarifying points of gendered difference even in unified campaigns for coalitions across sexuality and gender diversity is a vital step toward thoughtful advocacy surrounding state mechanisms of power and both corporal and carceral control.

Throughout this book, the contributors reveal and interrogate the particular and distinct logics of criminal law's role in ordering gender privilege and sexual and reproductive practices through their analyses of time and place. This ordering, of course, intersects with other hierarchies such as race, age, class, and citizenship. Ahmed's interview with Halley is clear in claiming an essential predictability of this effect as Halley borrows from critical legal theory's calculus on who bears the surplus of (mistaken) penal violence by the state.[29] Brown also calls out the racist impacts of criminal law tolerated by some rights activists. Hierarchies and exclusionary connections are evident in the chapters of Corrêa and Karam, Long, Rasha Moumneh, and Phillips in their recounting of panic and sexual crises[30] across race, migration, nation-building, and urbanization. They can also be seen in the populist discourse of contemporary nationalisms found in Sealing Cheng and Ae-Ryung Kim's and Roseman's chapters.

In current advocacy and academic climates, we see more clearly another kind of connection across criminal regulation of sex, gender, and reproduction. The calls for, and fact of, the recriminalization of abortion in the United States and elsewhere can be understood as instances of resistance to the neoliberal political individualism and globalization that are so visible in the emergence of gender equality and gay rights claims.[31] The contributors to this book ask us to confront the fact that modern human rights doctrine is a part of the liberal and neoliberal international order that primarily structures relationships between individuals and states, although it offers language, values, and tools to contest it as well. Sexual self-determination and sex equality are what motivated, in part, the liberalization of criminal laws relating to same-sex sexual practices, contraception, and abortion; these notions sound in the registers of international human rights, inter alia, as equality, nondiscrimination, autonomy, and privacy in family life. Finally, what all these stories have in common is recourse to rights talk, with support from criminal law or human rights norms, as a means of establishing and regulating normative behavior in changing times.

Some Caveats

Both the vast potential scope and the more modest actual frame of our book bear some explanation. First, indebted as we are to theories that emerge from grand fields of critique, such as queer, postcolonial, and critical legal studies, we make no claim to narrate a unified theory of human rights, sexuality, gender, and criminal law. Second, we rely on, but do not present, a review of the literature on the changing nature of the state, especially the scholarship on the forces operating to shore up or undermine the state as an apparatus of control.[32] Third, we fully acknowledge the pitfalls of treating law as a unitary or stable category of study or engagement. We hope the work here both justifies being called legal studies and demonstrates the expanse and diversity of this effort. We do not here address all the varieties of law found globally, but we recognize the need to do so as this work evolves. Distinct national legal traditions shape the domestication of international human rights, especially in the manner those rights are expressed; these traditions equally reflect the diversity of criminal codes. What figures in this volume is a search for commonalities across differences, as well as a search for ways to ensure that all forms of this thing called criminal law can nonetheless be tested in regard to the things called human rights.

We note that in our focus on criminal law, most of our authors address its expressive claims and doctrinal and political functions, rather than studying criminal law empirically in its full application. These chapters are not social-science-based studies of health impacts of law, or accounts of demographic shifts correlated with the imposition of criminal law.

In this book, we treat the universe of human rights as both something that can be called on and something that cannot be called one thing. Human rights bestows on time an eternal present. As critical practitioners, we understand that this is something of a (dis)guise. "Human rights" is a historical artifact of its own; its universality is in fact a political assertion, which, when explored, is at once polyvocal and multipositional. Its meanings and effects are contingent. Yet it does not follow that they are without content or purpose. All the concepts of criminal law, sex, gender, and reproduction have histories that root them in time and place and limit them in scope and scale, yet at the same time they escape the local. International human rights, with its hortatory assertions to be universal, interdependent, and indivisible, seems to efface history and context:[33] in the imagination of modern human rights, if women have a right to abortion, they ought to have had claims to one in the past (although tacit or unexpressed) and have claims to one in the future, whether or not the country in which any particular woman lives recognizes one, or in the absence of any abortion rights movement (historical or contemporaneous). Situated as we are now, with the political commitments we represent, human rights are a fiction, but a materially functional fiction. They operate as a set of standards against which to *challenge* state power and practice, and they provide a set of standards to *guide* state power and practice, including that which is exercised through criminal laws and policies.

Finally, a note about morality: within a human rights call to reform the penal law concerning gender, sexuality, and reproduction, it is commonly claimed that rights is about removing the vestiges of an outdated morality. Human rights, as a product of liberal theory, are premised on equality of all for all, and they would employ the logic of the harm principle to discern the justification for criminal punishment, rather than some traditional notion of "morality"—as glossed by states claiming certain forms of religious or traditional justifications. As numerous commentators on this project, and chapter authors themselves, have noted, *morality* is a freighted word. Morality is more accurately a plural—moralities—neither ahistorical nor decontexual. Yet to recognize this, and regard various faiths' scriptural prohibitions as a handful of moral sources among many, is not to concede that anything goes, or to jettison an ethical base. But we are mindful of discourses that accept "morality" as the terrain of only some claims (as when Alli Jernow writes of "harms-based" versus "morals-based" regulation, or when Joanna N. Erdman interrogates how morals harms reenter as if physical harms in Canadian jurisprudence). Whenever possible, we highlight this linguistic moment to ensure that we do not appear to denote "secular regulation" of sexuality, gender, and reproduction as without ethics, as a form of tolerance of sexual abuse, or as unresponsive to an ethic of care between persons. In his chapter, Esteban Restrepo Saldarriaga holds out the promise for constitutionalism to be the reference point for such a morality at the same time that he recognizes its shortcomings.[34]

The chapters in *Beyond Virtue and Vice* provide a contextual account of how, at the national and international levels, across time and space, criminal law has been used to produce normative models of sexuality, gender, and reproduction—and, conversely, how human rights have been and might be used to alter that norm. At the same time, many of the chapters demonstrate how human rights actors—who often have been involved in decriminalization advocacy in other sites—have pushed for, and succeeded in, enlarging the reach of criminal law, despite the knowledge that its application frequently falls on already-marginalized people and communities. This book calls attention to the way in which a powerful fantasy of criminal law's operation currently drives some human rights work in the domains of sexuality, gender, and reproduction, which ultimately portends danger and produces paradoxes of line drawing around narrow forms of virtue, even as it rhetorically seeks freedom from regulation.

Conclusion

Does human rights doctrine have within its corpus principles that are both starting and ending points,[35] and can we secure this notion of criminalization as "the last resort" with an additional ethic of practice? As we have not found anything intrinsic to criminal law and theory that limits its content, application, or reach, how can human rights serve as the standard of review in determining the reach and use of criminal law? Our fealty to understanding human rights as an evolving and contested field suggests the need for skepticism of certainty, even or especially when we call on criminal law to do rights work. We think skepticism is a framework with which human rights practitioners and scholars will find historical resonance because it involves a general distrust of state power and a turn to the least restrictive options in cases in which that power is invoked. Some may recognize this as a variant of "narrow tailoring" and "strict scrutiny" for state action, a posture that is anchored in many legal traditions, including human rights doctrine.[36] The process of justifying or critiquing the use of criminal law is also very open-textured. This double potential for contestation in justification suggests why the human rights field has had, in practice, much more to say about the application of criminal law than about its justifications.

Here, we turn from looking for doctrinal rules arising from within human rights to articulating what we call rules of engagement to guide advocates when flirting with criminal and punitive laws. Our proposed rules of engagement start with an embrace of the indeterminacy of rights as a practice: their goals may be universal certainty, but their practice must be more iterative and reflective.

We start with *empathy*, given our understanding that human rights have something to say about pain and should attend to the intended pain of penalization. Although we have seen that rights have taken a strong turn toward the expressive mode of criminal law, in fact, the application of criminal law has material consequences: criminal law condemns by inflicting actual pain (for example, through the deprivation of freedom at minimum, life at maximum). As one advocate passionately noted (paraphrased here), "We the feminists send men to prisons that are hell holes—haven't we some obligation to ensure that prisons are just if we invoke them?" As many of our authors demonstrate, concern for the impact of law on the least powerful, as played out in hierarchies of race (Corrêa and Karam), nationality (Moumneh), or respectability (Muguongo and Miller), must enter into the proposals at the beginning of policy reform concerning suffering, not the end. In other words, where matters of gender, sexual, and reproductive practices and behaviors are concerned, there is nearly always discriminatory application and enforcement across different hierarchies of power affecting both victim and violator.[37]

Empathy for the suffering intended by criminal law is closely related to *solidarity*, which involves attending to the application of criminal law across differently situated groups more generally. Moumneh's chapter on discordances and silences between gay and women's rights groups in some recent sex panics in Lebanon demonstrates the threats to rights where solidarities are not present. Brown's reflections on the tendency of prosecutions under criminal law in the United States to fall on the groups already most racially marginalized also reflects this, as does Corrêa and Karam's historical investigation of revisions of the criminal laws regulating sex work, adultery, and rape in Brazil. These chapters all reiterate that silos, not solidarity, currently dominate the practice of rights advocacy concerning gender, sexuality, and reproduction. Cheng and Kim detail the failures of practical solidarity among (women) sex workers and women's groups in South Korea; their analysis makes clear the tendency of rights groups to embrace the logics of sexual respectability when paired with autonomy in ways that generate more jail time for women on the "wrong" side of virtue. The practice of solidarity can have bold objectives.

Finally, empathetic practices and self-aware solidarities together mandate *a politics of accountability*, which addresses the material effects of criminal law. By *materiality*, we mean the need for human rights practices to engage not solely with the expressive features of penal law (such as campaigning on the notion that "the worst crimes deserve an international court") but also with the material deprivations it entails: the intentional infliction of the pain, at a minimum, caused by deprivation of liberty. Decriminalization campaigns for abortion, sex work, and HIV regularly produce empirical studies of who gets policed or goes to prison under these laws, with the factual evidence of the failure of intended effects and discrimination enlisted as part of the law reform efforts.[38] Our calls to use criminal law for our own ends require a similar commitment to empiricism—solidarity and empathy, at least rhetorically, open a path toward accountability: the obligation to know and respond to the distributional and proportional consequences of criminalization for all (Ahmed and Halley).

It is a tall order: the cultivation of solidarity, empathy, and accountability, informed by an awareness of indeterminacy and the knowledge that if we hold back on revenge, some may well suffer unfairly through failure to redress. This is why we premise our rules of engagement on a cautious, even ambivalent regard for both criminal justice and human rights. Our position, however, raises an important question: If criminal law is the last resort in responding to foul abuses and systemic violations, what should be the first resort? How do we mesh prevention and remedial programs, such as distributional policies for assistance to remove people from at-risk situations, treatment for mental health issues, and restorative work for both victims and perpetrators, with our calls to end impunity as a violation in itself? This is unknown territory: the gateway for protection against gendered violence, for instance, has been through the door of criminal law. But we want to encourage advocates and scholars to consider how to put criminal responses in relationship to other forms of state action that fully recognize wrongs done but do not solely or exclusive rely on penal sanctions in the process.

Skepticism is not nihilism, nor is it a refusal to engage with the state. Empathy, solidarity, and accountability could structure a kind of humility and minimalism in the penal force of the state, while acknowledging a role for the state's productive powers of administration and material support (without which the entire range of human rights enjoyment would not be possible). Skepticism focuses on the state's nature as a collective good and seeks to think about the practices of meaningful participatory democracy as also being internal to both rights and criminal law. It is an embrace of ambivalence, with equal measures of wariness and hope.[39] It notices the very specific ways that contemporary anxieties regarding gender, reproduction, and sexuality are both allayed and exacerbated by the recourse to rights talk, as well as criminal law. The task is at once simple and difficult. We must be alert that the call to "end impunity" might be working at cross-purposes with human rights, and remain committed to engaged practice and a belief in the emancipatory possibilities of conjoined movements concerning sexual, gender, and reproductive justice. The mode demands robust debate, combined with action-oriented engagement. The time is now.

PART I

Transnational Theory and Practice

CHAPTER 1

Janet Halley in Conversation with Aziza Ahmed: Interview

Aziza Ahmed is a leading feminist legal theorist, and a former student of Janet Halley. Ahmed engaged Halley in an open-ended discussion touching on feminism, sexuality, legal regimes, and human rights during 2014. The following is an edited version of their encounter.

AZIZA AHMED [AA]. Let's start with a bit of background to your work and approach to law first; then, I will focus on insights from your masterful intervention into our thinking about law, feminism, sex, injury, and politics in *Split Decisions: How and Why to Take a Break from Feminism*[1] and close with some reflections on current and breaking challenges to feminism as an emancipatory project, particularly in regard to the role of criminal law. To begin: What was your path to feminism?

JANET HALLEY [JH]. I have been engaged with feminism since the late 1970s. In fact, the first form of feminism that moved me deeply was radical feminism of the kind with which I now don't see eye to eye. A big change happened in my relationship with feminism around the time of the sex wars in the U.S. in the early to mid-1980s. I wasn't directly involved in the conflict within feminism over pornography and sexual liberation that broke out so dramatically in the confrontation between dominance feminists and "Pleasure and Danger" feminists around the Barnard Sexuality Conference in 1982, but watching it shook my confidence in the evolution of radical feminism into dominance feminism at that time.[2] For many of us that was a time of real rethinking about basics. And at the same time, there was gay liberation and then HIV, a suite of political events, which caused many of us in the

U.S. to move further from radical feminism and further from feminism itself.

For example, I went to law school in the mid- to late 1980s (Yale Law School, JD, 1988), and early on in my time there, a self-identified gay woman, in the closet, came up to me and said, "We don't need to worry about this [AIDS] epidemic because we're just medically not in line for it." I wanted to slug her. I was with the lesbians who took the death of gay men as our own issue. But much of their politics around sexuality was not—and I agreed with Eve Sedgwick, didn't need to be—feminist. So even then, my identification with gay men made it difficult for me to see feminism as the total explanation of all things related to sexuality.

In 1990, out came Judith Butler with *Gender Trouble*[3] and Eve Kosofsky Sedgwick with *Epistemology of the Closet*,[4] two huge interventions simultaneously exploring a critique of the pervasive feminist perception of the world as divided along an m/f frontier: men/women, masculinity/femininity, male/female. They both objected to this orientation of feminism to an m/f distinction that made it persistently central no matter which form it took. Both saw the centrality of this concern as a privileging of a heterosexual presumption. To be sure, Butler and Sedgwick went in different directions with that insight, as I show in *Split Decisions*. Sedgwick's idea was to extend Gayle Rubin's hypothesis that the big explosion of work on sexuality—work that became known as queer theory—wouldn't necessarily want to start from feminist premises, and I was on board with that.[5] So I've had many different phases, different political moments, different career settings, different political strategies, different goals, in the general domain of feminism, not just one.

AA. Was your early engagement with feminism an activist engagement?

JH. My engagement has always felt activist, even when I'm doing intellectual work. I don't myself treasure the theory/practice distinction very much because working on ideas feels very muscular and difficult to me.

AA. Your career has moved from the study of literature to law—how did you move from humanities into the law?

JH. I was a Miltonist, a student of seventeenth-century English literature. I got my PhD in English in 1980 and went to teach at Hamilton College, a small liberal arts college in upstate New York. My scholarship very quickly took a turn that was quite widespread at the time among left and critically oriented literary people, which was toward the cultural text. This means that we had the idea that the textual practices of, say, a book or a poem, or of either the censorship or staging of theatrical performances, or even aesthetic judgment were quite continuous with the culture, broadly speaking, and that the literary critic could reach beyond literature while still doing literary criticism.

A big influence on me at that time was Christopher Hill's *Milton and the English Revolution*, which was a Marxist history;[6] Hill interpreted Milton as a revolutionary. Hill's approach was pushing me further and further toward law as a subject matter. This tangle with law would be totally paradoxical from the perspective of Hill's Marxism, but it made sense to me. I was unhappy as a teacher at a small college where the internal politics were very intense and, for me, very dysphoric. But also at that time I thought I didn't like teaching. I later learned better. Both experiences (small college teaching and reading Hill) were teaching me that attending to "expression under conditions of political pressure" was a very interesting way to see language and literary production and that *law* was often in the mix when political pressure became real enough to cause people to need special expressive resources. Long story short, it made sense to jump to law and to legal studies. So it was an effort to extend something that was coming directly out of my approach to literature.

AA. Do you consider yourself someone who works in "law and humanities"? How does your training in literature impact your work now? "Rape in Berlin" (which takes an anonymous World War II German woman's diary as its starting point) is one of my favorite articles that you've written.[7] And each time I read it, I imagine the two parts of your training—literature and law—aligning to make a powerful critique of the way feminists are engaging with the law of rape.

JH. Until recently I have not thought of myself as a law and humanities person, but other people seem to see me that way. I have been trained in two disciplines, in literature and in law. They don't seem to me to overlap very much. But at the same time, I think I probably read law as a text more than somebody without my literary background would do, and I see the powerful interventions that texts (both literary and legal) make in our lives and in our social environment, possibly in a more political way than some literary people do. I'm very chary about this intersection in part because the two professional fields—law and literature as academic institutions—suffer an acute case of mutual unrequited love and can be very uncharitable about efforts to build the "interdiscipline." It's a dangerous space, and I approach it guardedly.

"Rape in Berlin" was an unusual development in my whole approach to this because I was at that time quite at an impasse about how to write about rape. It seemed to me that rape was such holy territory and that you just couldn't rethink it. Rape was known, and yet I was having more and more misgivings with feminist law reform around rape.[8] But I didn't know how to talk about my discomfort.

So, I thought, why don't I really jump back into my literary self and get out of my own legal and political contexts, and specifically that feminist context, and read something that is a really good literary treatment of the problem, of what is rape and how bad is it compared to other things, like death? "Rape in Berlin" was an attempt to use literature to escape from some of the constraints that I felt were binding me in the law school context, in the legal context, and in the world created by the feminist legal politics that I was embedded in.

Well, I was so lucky. My brother tipped me off to the existence of this diary of a woman who'd been in Berlin when it fell to the Soviets in 1945, and it very quickly became clear to me that it was a fabulous piece of art, which oddly enough was a reason to discredit it as "a fabrication" in some German political circles. But it seemed to me to be a rich opportunity to think about how rape is *representation* as well as *event*. What I mean is that rape happens, but even while rape is happening the participants in any "rape event" know a whole array of cultural tropes and narratives about it.

The assembly of these narratives and tropes are what Sharon Marcus, in "Fighting Bodies, Fighting Words," called the rape script.[9] Marcus argues that rape, even as an event, is scripted. It is not one big bang. It happens temporally, over time, between people who have various understandings of what the event must mean. So that a feminist approach to thinking about reducing rape or reducing the harm of rape or reducing the danger of particular rapes might be to think of it as a literary event that we know about and have a role in, like a play that we can participate in and try to tilt toward different endings. This nonreductionist approach to rape seems to me to be a very important political point to make about this particular form of violation, even though—no, instead, *because*—rape has this deep literary dimension.

AA. Let's turn to your book, *Split Decisions: How and Why to Take a Break from Feminism*. The book's publication has had several consequences. First, it produced a predictable "splitting of the room" for feminists and still continues to upset feminist conversations. Second, it provided some key frameworks for critiquing current feminist engagements with the law. Third, it cleared the way for bringing queer theoretical frames into debates within feminism. And fourth, it helped make way for acknowledging intrafeminist contestation as a key driver of feminist legal advocacy.

So I thought we could discuss these consequences of *Split Decisions*, in turn, as they relate to our current topic of criminalization and international and human rights.

But first, in *Split Decisions* and in the section called "Queer Theory by Men," you lay out a framework for understanding feminism as a very particular analytic. I was hoping that we could start there. What are the elements and shape of this "feminist analytic"? Why did you develop your critique with this focus, and what cautions does it raise for you?

JH. The argument in *Split Decisions* is framed around events in American feminism during my lifetime—feminist "idea events," if you will—that I've been part of. What I found in years of reading both text and practices was that American feminism quite consistently frames sex, sexuality, gender, and the family around m/f. And I do want to emphasize, because this has been I think misunderstood, that this pivotal element of American feminism didn't have to be that way. I'm not declaring a Platonic essence or a central committee's command. I just found that every book or article I read that professed to be feminist also turned, often at the crucial, normative moment—at the moment of envisioning the problem and/or the solution—on m/f.

I think there can be many forms of feminism that don't turn on what is basically the heterosexual difference, and troubling those ways into existence is the preeminent project of Judith Butler's *Gender Trouble*. But Butler's feminism never really does break out of the m/f distinction either. In all the reading that I did getting ready to write *Split Decisions*, I asked myself, does this article, does this book break out of the m/f distinction? The thing that struck me, again and again, was that it didn't.

AA. And you mean Butler's book in particular?

JH. I think the beauty of *Gender Trouble* is the mighty struggle Butler put forth to make m/f optional. But so much other feminist work just caves in. Let me put it this way. The intersectionality effort is, as I say in my book, an effort to find ways of putting other frames of social difference next to the feminist project to figure out their interactions in the world, in politics, and in thinking. Critical race theorists (or race crits)[10] and postcolonial or subaltern feminist work[11] often take a departure from m/f. I called this the divergentist strand in hybrid feminism, and I thought it had so much promise. People do a lot of remarkably inventive things in the key of gender when they make that departure. But what I saw again and again was that, at the moment the author needed to reaffirm his or her feminism, the text would revert to m/f. As I went around asking about this, I often heard scholars complaining that feminist journal editors were insisting on this affirmation: "My editor made me do it!" I felt that so much energy was being held in check.

Gayatri Spivak's "Can the Subaltern Speak?" is classic example.[12] She pushed the presumption that m/f is the key to sex, sexuality, gender, and the family into a *very* small space in this remarkable essay. In legal studies, the productivity of divergentist work is remarkable: Angela Harris's "Race and Essentialism" and Regina Austin's "The 'Black Community'" are classic examples.[13] Both of them entertain the idea of a conflicted, multiple, and internally riven reality that their antiracism and their feminism grapple with directly: harmony from the start is clearly not the goal. This is so obviously productive in intersectional work. Why wouldn't it be just as productive in work entirely within the bounds of sex, sexuality, gender, and the family?

By contrast, in what I called convergentist feminist work, the moral of the story is determined in advance. At some point, m/f morphs into m>f, and with that move comes the idea that something about *m*—men, maleness, masculinity—has some kind of conceptual, political, material advantage over *f* that is seen as not a good thing but as, a priori, a problem, a thing to be worried about, a normative crisis for which we need feminism as a solution.

It wasn't that feminism had to attend to power only as m/f or m>f, but I noticed that it persistently did, unless a feminist was pursuing an ancillary end or intersectional project that caused her to diverge. And once you went looking for it, divergentist feminist work in the intersectional domain was not just a rivulet—it was more like a river.

Another branch of the river started for me with Sedgwick's *Epistemology of the Closet*, in her Axiom 1, "People are different from one another."[14] It would be impossible to summarize that amazing essay here, but there are lines that completely arrested me when I first read them and that animate the idea of taking a break from feminism—or TABFF. Sedgwick was just as concerned as Butler was that pitching sexuality perpetually on m/f was tethering it to heterosexual difference in a way that would make it incapable of a fully affirmative embrace of "homo" anything. Thus far her argument maps onto Butler's project in *Gender Trouble*. But Sedgwick was also concerned that making m/f central also precluded from view the vast dimensions of sexuality/power that have nothing to do with m/f. This is an extension, actually, of Gayle Rubin's conclusion in "Thinking Sex," that feminism could not be the complete source for all theoretical or social or political work on sexuality.[15] Butler's agonistic relationship in *Gender Trouble* to m/f within feminism is just *skipped over* by Sedgwick and Rubin, who see the problem and keep moving. They have *other* work to do and proceed to do it. That seemed to me a highly promising branch of the river to follow, just as promising as the divergentist intersectional branch.

AA. You have suggested that when you say, "take a break from feminism," you just mean a something like taking a "cigarette break." So you're not saying we should abandon feminism altogether?

JH. When I propose that it might be okay for some people to take a break from feminism, I'm doing so on an assumption that feminism, which is an indispensable part of our political repertoire, is alive and well and is doing a lot of good things, has done a lot of good things, and needs to do more good things in many, many places on the planet where feminism is exactly the right tool to be using. I'm not saying that everybody needs to take a break from feminism. I think that would be a disaster; if that started happening, then I would start arguing *against* taking a break from feminism because we need feminism.

What we don't need is to commit ourselves to an idea that only feminism, feminism 24/7, sublime transcendent feminism, is the only tool we have for thinking about sex, sexuality, gender, and the family, or the workplace, or war, or anything. And you're right; I've started to try to remind people that "taking a break" has a very temporary connotation, like taking a cigarette break. A person can be a feminist all day long and then take a break. I myself was doing that—taking a break—because I thought it was valuable to have somebody holding open the alternative possibility. Since then I've reentered feminism and suspended it many times.[16]

So basically, I'm seeking what I call in *Split Decisions* a politics of theoretical incommensurability—a proliferation of left-wing theories about power that we could then walk around with almost as if we were switching one pair of eyeglasses for another, putting on one theory and then putting on another theory to see which one makes the world more intelligible. Which one makes the world make more sense? If you're only wearing your feminist glasses all the time, you'll only see the things that those feminist glasses let you see, and they may blind you to things that the feminist idea set doesn't already include.

AA. You have been describing your own voyage into the space known as queer theory. Of course, we know that this postmodernist turn in work on sexuality has been resisted very vigorously by feminists committed to the "dominance" model—that is, the idea that male domination and female subordination are so ubiquitous that feminism should pay attention to nothing else.[17] The ideas that the intelligibility of the world is contingent on our theories about it and that we have some kind of control over that were endemic in the radical feminism of the 1960s and 70s but have kind of gone missing, dating possibly back to the sex wars. What is your assessment of the queer return to it?

JH. I'm not quite sure that I would say that queer work as we see it in America and globally is always sympathetic with this "lens switching" approach. There's a lot of very dogmatic queer theory that matches the sound and feel of dominance feminism, albeit in the key of sexual minorities. And there's a lot of queer theory that exemplifies the kind of mobility project that I think you've said your work exemplifies.

So the queer project that I would like to see, which is neither commensurate with nor identical to all queer rights work, would be an effort to enrich the theoretical vocabulary of the Left so that it would be open to *seeing otherwise*. That is, seeing not only sex, sexuality, gender, and the family in experimentally new ways, but having that kind of epistemic openness about a lot of things.

AA. How might your m/f critique take on reproduction as well as sex? One could argue that attending to the politics of reproduction makes it even more difficult for feminism to move away from the m/f framing.

JH. Great question. In a way, the feminist politics of reproduction took the queer turn when it supplemented an American civil rights–based vision centered on abortion rights secured through constitutional adjudication with a public health approach. You know much more about this than I do, Aziza, but it seems clear to me that the civil rights approach foregrounds abortion as a *women's* issue, and it's centered on a woman's need to control the consequences, for her, of heterosexual intercourse. It is definitely the kind of feminism that is grounded in "m/f, m>f" analytics, if only in the minimal sense that the consequences of heterosexual intercourse can be saliently different for women than they are for men. Moreover, the constitutionalized civil rights framing is m>f feminism in that it is carrying a brief for women: we are seeking *women's* access to abortion and contraception, freedom from forced sterilization and abortion, etc. The Supreme Court seems bent on making sure we spend a *lot* of energy maintaining the rights we have, such as they are.[18] Many of us experience the official privacy frame for all this work as slightly askew for a number of reasons: we see rights to reproductive decisions *for women* as a cornerstone of any plausible equality project.

But the public health framing, even just of reproduction but far more if you extend it to sexuality and sexual health, makes the same move in practice that Sedgwick and Rubin did at the level of theory. Sexuality and reproduction understood as health issues led to a project that is now so much bigger, includes so many different aspects of human experience, appeals to so many different legal and political tools, and envisions human well-being in so many, many different ways. I see it as the queer turn in the key of reproduction.[19]

Just follow HIV around, for example, and add it to the issues of reproductive rights. HIV is a tracer of the myriad events of moist-tissue contact between humans. It doesn't respect the m/m frame in which we first noticed it, or the m/f frame in which so many rights approaches seem to want to contain it. It's both everyone's problem and the problem of an infinitely extended series of human-to-human intimacies. I've learned this from you, Aziza![20]

Of course, that's no guarantee of real divergence. As your work shows, Aziza, it's possible to fall back to a minority-rights model, and we see it happen all the time. But again and again, people come back to me from the field, where this vision has been reduced to a list of "affected minorities," asking ruefully, "Why did we do that, when what I saw out there in people's erotic and reproductive lives spans across identity in so many ways?"

AA. You align yourself with a school of thought called critical legal studies or CLS. CLS often engages with a "distributional analysis." This analysis is also central to another critique you offer as a way of understanding the turns m/f feminism has made: you use the CLS tool of distributional analysis to point out the particular forms of power that m>f or dominance feminism has called forth, the legal tools it prefers to use, and the ways it imagines law operating in the world. Maybe the first small question we can tackle concerns explaining what you consider a distributional analysis to be? Then, we can ask how you situate your understanding of the law inside the various understandings presented by CLS. And finally, how can we connect this set of tools and debates in CLS to feminism or to "taking a break"?

JH. CLS is alive and well, despite all the efforts of so many people to declare it dead and over. I find a continuing need among my students for critical approaches to law and a huge appetite for basic training in the tools developed for emancipatory thought and action in CLS.

Many, many different things and ways of thinking poured into critical legal studies, coming in at historically different moments and then kind of held in the tradition. It really goes back to American legal realism; then, it embraced a lot of ideas from Marx and American socialism; took a sharp postmodernizing turn with the rest of the American left intelligentsia in the 1980s and 1990s; absorbed the political experiences of the civil rights and Black Power movements, the anti–Vietnam War movement, the feminist movement, and related left social movements but diverged from their identitarian base; and received massive postcolonial influence from the sheer number of postcolonial intellectuals who came to CLS for help understanding the flood of American legal ideas into the global space and created a whole body of new critical work on the colony and postcolony.

By a "distributional analysis" we mean "trying to see a how a legal intervention, existing or possible, might redistribute social benefits and social costs."[21] You may look at the current distribution and think, "I don't like what I'm seeing. What I'm seeing feels like injustice to me, feels unjust." Well, CLS in its distributional analysis mode asks, "How does law sustain this? And what could law *really* do to change it?"

It therefore starts with a normative impulse. It's often quite inchoate: "I'm not liking what I'm seeing." It can also be very learned: "I know everything I can learn about public housing policy, microfinance, parental leave—and I think it is unjust." But the next few steps, inspired by legal realism, are not ethical steps, excepting that the general project is an ethical project or a justice-seeking project. It involves saying, "Okay, what is the field in which this legal thing operates? Who are the players or the stakeholders in that field?" Multiply them out, figure out who they are. Maybe go do some ethnographic work or maybe read a lot about it, and figure out who they are.

The next step in a distributional analysis is to identify the differences among the stakeholders. And here taking a break is really crucial for our conversation, Aziza, because multiplying the stakeholders means that you're not looking just at what happens to women. You're looking at what happens to the men, you're looking at what happens to the old people, you're looking at what happens to the environment, you're looking at what happens to the literary tradition in which the story is being told. You're looking at a lot of different interests, not even necessarily limited to human ones, and a lot of different rhetorical and representational forces.

Then step number three is to figure out, in a Marxist sense, what is the "surplus" (more power, more access to goods, higher status, and so forth) that is being distributed among these players as they interact with each other. That is, we follow Marx's emphasis on the capitalist's ability to extract surplus value from the worker's labor *rather than* identity politics' tendency to focus on the harm suffered by those in a subordinate position. The basic intuition here is that remedying the harm makes it exceptional and tilts us to remedies that accept the nonexceptional baseline; whereas focusing on the surplus calls into question *all* the gains that a particular social field distributes. They can *all* now be—at least in imagination—redistributed. The perfect example is workplace discrimination. Win your discrimination lawsuit and you are entitled to the nondiscriminatory wage, the wage everyone else has been getting. You have not challenged the employer's profit even a little.

In any single social game, we imagine the players or the stakeholders to be "bargaining in the shadow of the law."[22] That is to say, they are dealing with each other in all kinds of ways—in a self-interested way, in an altruistic way, in a totally indifferent, "I don't even see you" way—to distribute a surplus that is generated in the game. This capacity to negotiate is structured by many things, and one of them that we might be able to change is the background web of legal rules.

Once you've identified the players and identified the surplus and figured out how the players bargain in the shadow of which legal rules, you can see how the players consolidate or fragment the surplus, trade it among themselves, grow it, shrink it, benefit from it, and suffer its loss. Sometimes even suffer its gain. Some games are very rigid and top-down; others are more mobile than they look from an identity-political stance. It can be a huge strategic and tactical advantage to identify mobilities.

To give a quick example: American feminists have decried the huge amount of uncompensated labor that women perform in the home and have framed the legal and social norms that force and persuade women to accept this disproportional share of household labor as "the problem." But framing this in m/f, m>f, carrying-a-brief-for-feminism terms, and as a harm, has tempted many legal feminists to identify the husband/father as the sole beneficiary of the wife/mother's sacrifice and to seek remedies that recoup his gains at the time of divorce or death. Alimony and joint property reform in family law. But taking a broader look at the

economic trades that go on in any ongoing household can pinpoint bargaining between household members that distributes a wide variety
of social costs and benefits among parents, children, relatives living
elsewhere, friends, even ancestors. The surplus is the wealth of the entire household and encompasses many more kinds of resources than
the money that can be squeezed out of the husband at the time of the
household's existential crisis at divorce or death. Suddenly you can see
the benefits that flow to women because they do the lion's share of
household labor and the costs that men shoulder because they are expected to bring home the big paycheck. The men may be winning out
overall, but you have a more complex and adequate picture of the moving parts. And identifying the background rules against which households generate and distribute this surplus reveals a huge number of legal
rules that condition the bargaining power of husbands, fathers, wives,
mothers, and children of various ages. Of course, some households will
follow a male-exploiter model, but now that you are not presuming that
they *all* do or that male exploitation is not the *only* thing going on even
in households where it is happening, you can see a lot of the distributional stakes "otherwise."

Now it's time to think in terms of justice again, very late. This is what
we call the "is/ought" distinction.[23] We try to put off the moment of thinking ethically or thinking in terms of justice, partly to reduce the inevitably
large impact of our a priori commitments on what we will notice.

This "temporary suspension" of the ethical lets you see the legal order
as it actually functions—a mesh of tools with many small levers and some
large levers that help achieve distributions of power and resources and
other things people want to have. Once you see them, you can ask, Is this
just? And if your answer is no, you can go back to the levers and work
on emancipatory projects.

AA. How does this work in the domain of feminists' engagement with criminal law? With your coauthors Prabha Kotiswaran, Chantal Thomas,
Hila Shamir, and Rachel Rebouché, you've observed feminism making
the turn to criminalization for many wrongs that men commit against
women.[24] In "Rape in Berlin" and "Rape at Rome," you have challenged
feminists to rethink the effort to make rape and sexual violence committed in armed conflict international crimes on a par with torture and
genocide. Many feminists ask, How can it be a bad idea to reform the
law so that it takes the harms suffered by women as seriously as those
suffered by men?

JH. When we use the levers of prosecution, conviction, incarceration, and even death as a penalty, we engage the state (or the international criminal system) at the apex of its self-understanding as the entity enjoying a monopoly over legitimate force. The state and the international criminal system like to promise us that they will use that force to eliminate the most serious wrongs that humans inflict on one another. And feminists have picked up that language: they have spoken of ending rape, ending trafficking, ending impunity, zero tolerance—all the slogans of would-be totalitarian-style social control. But that's not how criminal law as we know it—and especially international criminal law—works. We've bought into a magic realist image of punishment.

Seen instead as a complex package of legal levers that human beings use and from which they derive bargaining power and manage ideological conflict, criminal law doesn't end much of anything. There are so many ways to discuss this, I hardly know where to start. Let's take just one aspect of it: the decision to sweep more wrongdoing of a particular kind into the criminal system. Feminists object to the high rate of impunity for rape and call for more prosecutions, easier prosecutions, more convictions, and more certain and more onerous punishments. They are objecting to what Duncan Kennedy has called the tolerated residuum of sexual abuse, and what you could also call the "false negatives" of the criminal system.[25] And rightly so: that tolerated residuum of abuse (may I call it the TRA?) not only lets individual men who have raped walk free in society, directly constraining the safety and well-being of the women they have raped, it also tells all the other women that they are at risk and that, if they want to lead safer lives, they also have to lead more constrained, less free lives. Expanding the definition of rape, subjecting it to lower burdens of proof, eliminating forms of evidence that can be used to persuade juries to acquit, taking away discretion in sentencing, allowing the death penalty for rape: all of these and many more are rule shifts that feminists have advocated for to reduce the TRA. They are intended to—and plausibly *do*—ensure that the system achieves more true positives: guilty men incapacitated and punished by incarceration. And that will, we believe, deter some men who might rape from trying it. Women come out safer, less constrained, more free. Good.

But in the real world, you can't do this without also generating more false positives: innocent men in jail. This is a real cost of women's increased safety and freedom through the reduction of the rate of false negatives. Why should feminists care about this? The cost falls on men, and all men benefit from male privilege. Let them be afraid of being charged with and convicted of crimes that they did not commit: we'll get even more deterrence and more safety and freedom for women.

But the distributive effects of a system with a smaller TRA and therefore a higher rate of false positives are very complex, and my sense is that feminists need to have a richer analysis of them. Let me list just some:

First, many women love the innocent men who go to jail. They are their sons, lovers, husbands, friends. Sometimes they were dependent on them for support, and now that support is gone. Jailing innocent men hurts women.

Second, the spectacle of innocent men going to jail delegitimizes the system.

Third, many cases are close and/or ideologically contested, making it possible to have large controversies over whether particular convictions or acquittals were false or true. These controversies produce clear results only for those who are ideologically committed to the justice of those outcomes ahead of time. The jailing of innocent men does not solve—rather it makes more possible—this entrenchment.

Fourth, many of the rules that feminists have advocated for have the effect of turning women not into freer social agents but into more thoroughly protected ones. Think, for instance, of mandatory arrest and no-drop prosecution in the domestic violence or DV setting in the U.S.: these rules treat the women in DV cases like children who cannot decide for themselves.

Fifth, many of the arguments that justify stricter punishment depend on a language of victimhood that some (by no means all) feminists find disempowering. To them, it is a cost. But try arguing for increased criminalization without using it. The substitution of *survivor* for *victim* in U.S. rape politics is motivated by precisely this feminist resistance against describing women as helpless and ruined when in fact they are often highly resilient; but the new term is just as problematic, implying as it does—that old Victorian saw again—that rape is the fate worse than death.

Sixth, and here I'll stop, intensifying punishment for sexual wrongs can have consequences that register only on an intersectional analysis. It is easy to demonize a national enemy or colonized population by charging its men with rape and other sexual atrocities; it is impossible then to convict enemy or colonized men without reiterating

and vindicating the ethnic, national, religious, or racial demoniza-
tion. Black women in the U.S. suffer a far higher rate of rape and sexual assault than white women, but decreasing the TRA in this context
will ensure that more black men—both guilty and innocent—will go
to prison; and it will enable more white women to levy false or unsupported charges of rape (often in perfectly good faith) against
black men to evade responsibility for their sexual liaisons with them.
This is a highly complex social negotiation with lots of costs and
benefits on all sides. Pretending it's simple seems, to me anyway,
irresponsible.

In short, the criminal system distributes not only acquittals and
convictions but social powers and social costs of many kinds in highly
complex ways. Doing a distributional analysis of how these costs and
benefits circulate seems to me a necessary first step before deciding to
criminalize.

AA. What is at stake in this shift from feminist neoformalism to a distributional analysis?

JH. To take one of the many dimensions: What should feminists do about
Elizabeth Bernstein's term *carceral feminism*?[26] It sounds like a per se
condemnation. But the CLS preference for distributional analysis arises
from a sense that the *outcomes*, not the *tools*, should ground our normative thinking. In our 2006 article introducing the concept of "governance
feminism," Hila Shamir, Prabha Kotiswaran, Chantal Thomas, and I did
say that governance feminism (GF) was primarily penal in attitude.[27]
Further work on GF has decisively shown that feminists use many legal
tools besides criminal law.[28] I think that, in our *resentissement* of the success of dominance feminism in the carceral feminist and GF project, we
overestimated its ubiquity. Take domestic violence as an example. The
criminal focus there seems almost overwhelming (e.g., all acts of violence against women should be prosecuted), but it also comes with a
gender-specific search for immunity from prosecution, an argument that
women should get meaningful defenses if they kill their abusers. It's
both carceral and anticarceral if by carceral we mean to indicate the
prison-industrial complex, mass incarceration, and the like. Of course it
is highly punitive: women who kill their abusers essentially impose
the death penalty through private action. But let's keep going: DV
feminists have built large institutional components, from the shelter
movement to the restraining order complex, which are not—or are not

primarily—criminal in approach. The restraining order is civil legally but highly punitive socially, and if you violate your order, you can go to jail for that alone. Meanwhile, the shelter movement has resulted in a social-work component that has managed, so far, in the U.S. at least, to stay at arm's length from the state. There's even a vast pedagogical element, reaching from elementary school curricula to the World Bank's development programming, that makes the cessation of domestic violence a core priority for the *assujettissement* (subjectification) of men and women: it's deep cultural work. If we are interested in the relationship between feminism and criminal enforcement, we should pay attention to the *non*criminal forms of GF. And if we want to move from is to ought here, we need to think in quite granular ways about the distributional effects of these many elements of the feminist-built DV system.

AA. So, we shouldn't imagine governance feminism to encompass only criminal law tools or only dominance feminist aspirations.

JH. Dominance feminism is pretty consistently punishment-oriented, but even there it faces feminist contestation.[29] For example, building the new anti-trafficking system, from a feminist point of view, was pervasively a struggle between dominance feminists, who view all sex work as exploitation and think of trafficking and prostitution as coterminous categories, and feminists inspired by very different strands of feminist thought and action and who oppose what they see as a dangerous conflation of prostitution with trafficking. In this context, the antidominance feminists varied a lot—some of them were liberal "autonomy" feminists, some were "Pleasure and Danger" postmodernists, and some were postcolonial feminists with a critique of Western hegemony over what we used to call the third world. Liberal feminists brought their freedom, equality and democratic participation projects, while labor feminists used legal levers to promote worker bargaining power at the bottom of the pay scale.[30] Even in anti-trafficking, there's no one feminism and there's no one governance.

AA. Surely you're not deemphasizing the role of dominance feminism in turning feminism toward crime. We see it with the war on terror. We see it with rape, and we see it with trafficking.

JH. I'm not sure what the right level of emphasis is, but I'm very glad that the project is coming in for extended treatment in this book. In the process, let's recall that feminism never gets much traction in governance unless it can "fit in" to existing powers-that-be and that criminalization is a keynote feature of the contemporary, neoliberal political economy. Consider, for instance, the lesson offered to us in the fascinating dissertation by Allegra McLeod.[31] She demonstrates, to my satisfaction anyway, that the recent rise of international criminal law and transnational cooperation in state-based criminal enforcement preceded 9/11 by quite a bit. Instead, a major force behind the build out of the international criminal law that we see today started with the Clinton administration's idea about how to make the United States perpetually relevant at the international level after the fall of the wall. One of the main arrows in Clinton's quiver, McLeod convincingly argues, was to strengthen networks of criminal enforcement that would be both international and deeply integrated into national systems and then tightly coordinated with each other. The American influence part of it was that this newly interoperable international criminal system would be subject to American direct and indirect control as much as was possible, consistent with the ambition to secure international cooperation. Which is what we have now.

The new anti-trafficking system was forged in this crucible. It was a project of the United Nations Office for Drugs and Crime, not of any human rights body! When, in the late 1990s, as part of the wider effort described by McLeod, the countries of the Global North identified transnational organized crime as a challenge to this new institutional legal order, it came with a rising interest in translating illegal labor migration into trafficking. I don't think I can emphasize enough that this was about building a post–Cold War global market economy in which international exchange in goods and services, in money and guns, would be capitalist and internationally transparent, while the international flow of labor would be under tight control and bounded by national frontiers. It followed a contract/crime doctrinal paradigm in which markets would be "free" to the extent that coercive trade was criminally barred—and in which the Trafficking Protocol and the Smuggling Protocol would ensure that international labor migration came under new criminal control.[32] And after 9/11, this system became part of an intensified securitization of the international and state orders.

And here came the opening for dominance feminists: trafficking had previously been defined in international law in the context of trafficking in women and children for the purposes of prostitution. That's how the international conventions from the early and mid-twentieth century defined it.[33] A large governance feminist push came from dominance feminists to make sure that, if trafficking was to be incorporated into this new bulking up of an international criminal enforcement system, anti-prostitution as envisioned by them would be a prominent part. They were smart. They showed up at the Vienna meetings leading to the Palermo Protocols knowing exactly what they wanted. They wanted prostitution to become an international crime for everyone involved, except the prostitute.[34]

Luckily for everyone who disagrees with the dominance feminist take on prostitution, Mary Robinson, the then UN high commissioner for human rights, sent Anne Gallagher to Vienna, and the feminist human rights world sent a lot of savvy activists, setting in place a contest for influence at the Vienna meetings *among feminists.* This somewhat disparate group was determined that the Vienna meetings would not degrade or displace the rights of refugees, would focus on the needs of vulnerable migrants, and would not victimize the very sex workers whom the dominance feminists aimed to "rescue." These human rights feminists won a lot. For instance, very early in the Vienna process they helped to ensure that anti-trafficking would focus not only on women and children but on labor exploitation more generally. The very name of the protocol—"*human* trafficking," not "trafficking *in women and children*"—signals a victory for this alternate corps of feminist advocacy.

But the dominance feminists still wanted to equate trafficking with prostitution, and the human rights feminists had a kind of ambivalent role to play here because they shared the civil libertarian tradition of American progressives. On the one hand, they knew that criminalizing everything can be really scary, especially in states with criminal law systems in which the rights of the accused are meaningless. But they also felt that now was the time to use criminal enforcement to get leverage over exploitative actors in industries well beyond the sex sector—in agriculture, and construction, and domestic work, wherever vulnerable workers go, and are sometimes forced to go, for vulnerable work. This feminist ambivalence about criminalization emerged again in their agenda.

The human rights feminists in Vienna managed to reduce the exposure of sex work from mandatory criminalization to circumstances involving force and exploitation: prostitution is explicitly included as an example, but so are other forms of forced labor.[35] But just before the Palermo Protocol was adopted, the U.S.-based dominance feminists (unsurprisingly) managed to achieve much more in the U.S. Congress, where the human rights voice was muted at best and where the dominance feminists could fall in with their classic allies—religious and social conservatives. The resulting U.S. Trafficking Victims Protection Act (TVPA) includes a special category of "sex trafficking" under which dominance feminists are producing ideologically simpatico governance feminists.[36] On the one hand, prostitution (of over-eighteen-year-olds), by itself, is not a *severe* form of trafficking and therefore not subject to mandated criminal prosecution under the TVPA: for that, it must be obtained through force, fraud, or coercion, like all other severe forms of trafficking in all other sectors of the economy. On the other hand, sex trafficking is now named as such in a federal statute and, domestically, the federal criminal enforcement enterprise is strong-arming states into making it an actual crime. In Massachusetts, for instance, kicking a prostitution charge against a john or pimp up from prostitution to sex trafficking doubles the minimum penalty.

One of the fascinating elements of this process of feminists creating the story of "trafficking" is what you could call its conditions of audibility, its conditions of intelligibility. Dominance feminism had undergone its carceral turn years earlier. In the rise of anti-trafficking, its advocates spoke convincingly in terms of social control to people who wanted to control south–north migration in the post–Cold War world. Their audibility was very high. Whereas the human rights people spoke a language that was utterly foreign to those who convened the Vienna meetings that led to the trafficking protocol. Remember, this was the UNODC's baby. The paradigm tools on the table were international drug and arms trafficking control. I think the drug/arms control people looked at the human rights feminists and just thought, "What? Who are you and what are you talking about? We want to punish transnational organized crime and you're talking about shelters? You're talking about protecting refugees? We don't get it—we don't get *you*." So, I think there was an interaction between vigorous feminist activists on both sides, with an audibility advantage on the side of feminists who were already penal minded, shall we say?

AA. We see a similar dynamic in the international criminal law of rape, where feminists with a range of feminist ideologies went international together. Did the conflict that arose in anti-trafficking play out there, too?

JH. You are referring to the intrafeminist politics in the establishment and administration of the new International Criminal Court (ICC). The human rights establishment, from what I can tell from the outside, has lain dormant when it comes to resisting the rise of an international criminal court.[37] And even academically, the critique of the International Criminal Court is in its infancy. There is a crying need for distributional analyses of the ICC. In "Rape at Rome," I examine the work of feminists in the negotiations leading to the Rome Statute, which established the ICC, and it's no coincidence that those meetings were virtually simultaneous with the Vienna process for trafficking, although somewhat different genealogically. Here, the precedents are recently established ad hoc tribunals: the International Criminal Tribunal for the Former Yugoslavia (ICTY), the International Criminal Tribunal for Rwanda (ICTR), and a few others.[38] By the time the Rome Conference convened, international feminist activists had already determined to take rape as "high up" the hierarchy of crimes in armed conflict as they could and to ensure as many rape prosecutions and convictions as they could. And where anti-trafficking could have taken the form of victim empowerment rather than criminalization, the ICC was predetermined to be a criminal system.

Here is where the interaction among feminists was so different at Rome, for the ICC—and at Vienna, for the trafficking protocol. In Vienna feminists were engaged in outright intra-feminist conflict, whereas at Rome, there was a broad range of feminist ideologies on site, but they carried a common line, and that line was dominance feminism. It's a very puzzling thing, and I think it calls for explanation. How could liberal and sex work feminists, who were unquestionably involved, fall in with an overall strategy and a host of rule reforms animated by a feminist ideology they would normally find so problematic?

I think there are a lot of reasons this happened, and I think they provide danger signs that nondominance feminists could look for when they engage in reform processes in which dominance feminists have an audibility advantage. Feminists were invited to the table—indeed, onto the central committee running the pro-court NGO coalition at the conference—on the condition that they pull a single coalitional line. The effort to find a single rubric for the object of feminist reform—which evolved from rape to sexual violence to gender violence—privileged the dominance feminist impulse to inflate the scope of prohibitions and to conflate very different social circumstances. Dominance feminists *already* collapse the continuum.[39] This meant that counterweights against the criminalization impulse and differences among severe and less severe harms were hard, possibly even *incorrect*, to articulate. And the ground on which everyone was operating was not markets, where many nondominance feminists seek women's autonomy and/or agency, but rather crime, precisely the strongest turf for dominance feminists. They know how to discipline and punish.

But another factor was an emerging common sense within international feminism that was specifically *designed* to evade internal feminist critique: the idea that sexual violence was the common problem of all women across the globe and a nondivisive, unproblematic priority for feminists everywhere. North or South, rich or poor, in or out of the battle space, religious or not, modern or traditional, Left or Right—no one could take a stance against taking a stance against sexual violence. As one feminist activist put it, sexual violence gave feminists the hope of finding "languages that cannot be rejected."[40]

But a distributional and intersectional analysis of this framework should give at least some feminists pause. For a brief while, for instance, the ICTY had a feminist-inspired rule that there could be no consent defense to a charge of rape: sexual contact between a man on one side of armed conflict and a woman on the other would be rape. Karen Engle has argued that this and other reforms sought by feminists in the ICTs confirmed nationalist framings of the conflict,[41] and once I really understood her argument, this rule effort has continued to deeply shock me. Enforced in the context of nationalist armed conflict, this rule would allow nationalist factions to promote rape prosecutions *where there was consent and even mutual enthusiasm*, as part of the nationalist project. The ICTY could have actually prosecuted such a case. Don't forget that the ICTY started its work while the conflict was still ongoing. All of this could then have sent the message to the dwindling multiethnic social groups and families in the region that they had to back off of sexual relations across ethnic lines.

I wonder how feminists got to this point. Certainly they knew that collusion with nationalist projects was a big danger: Engle tells the story of their explicit debate about it. But unlike the sex-trafficking context, where some feminists can identify distributional advantages that some women actively seek in sex work, the rape context did not include a debate about the social value of the sex itself. It was condemnation and prohibition all around. I got a chance to ask one of the leading feminists in the ICTY process what she thought about this, and what she thought of the feminist activist intervention ramping down from no-consent-defense to accepting a rule requiring the accused to present his evidence to the judge first to make sure it was sound. She agreed that retreat from the no-consent-defense rule was a good thing, not because of the official feminist line that it would make the resulting international law easier to download into domestic laws, but because she acknowledged that some women would flout the nationalist demand to shun alliances across ethnic lines and would have sex they really wanted with men they were otherwise presumed to loathe and oppose. But as far as I know, she never included that reason in her published work. She was silent on the subject.

At the Rome Conference, feminists were coalitioned into a single voice and spoke to the conference via the officially approved feminist NGO.[42] The agenda was to criminalize at the highest possible level and with the greatest intensity possible, and the wrong that this effort aimed at was framed as sexual or gender violence. The result was a profound depoliticization of feminism that I find quite troubling, especially because not all the women who carried that line believed it. We can expect more of this as the NGO-ization of international feminism proceeds, with its reliance on donors with strong ideological commitments that they are willing to treat as conditions and with its transformation of a feminist political and emancipatory voice into an expert one.

AA. What are some of the breaking developments in feminist engagement with international criminal law? What should people concerned about this nexus be looking for?

JH. Overall, I'd suggest that the essays collected here have been written after the crossing of a certain Rubicon in feminist legal experience, from strictly outside legal power to a well-established, if partial and necessarily compromised, place within it. *Owning* that shift will enable feminists and their allies to come to a new stance in the perpetual juggle of reconstruction and critique and hopefully will open a whole new era of feminist critique.

CHAPTER 2

Seismic Shifts: How Prosecution Became the Go-To Tool to Vindicate Rights

Alice M. Miller with Tara Zivkovic

For almost two decades, rights advocates have argued for the use of international rights standards to govern the criminal regulation of gender, reproduction, and sexuality, seeking to constrain and shape the criminal law toward a more rational, progressive, and just posture. Advocates argued that a rights basis would redirect criminal law away from repressive and tradition-captured (often called morality-based) regulation, and toward a harms-based, more globally justifiable use in service of rights protection. As gay- and lesbian-rights advocates joined women's rights advocates in this focus, their expanded arguments averred that this way of deploying harm as rights violation supported a conjoined liberty-and-equality project for previously stigmatized or subordinated persons.[1]

The call by advocates to use human rights to guide and limit the use of the criminal law in the spheres of gender, sexuality, and reproduction has had some apparent successes—in legislative reform efforts, in judicial decisions, in public understandings in local and global fora. One need only think of the constitutional court decisions striking down laws criminalizing consensual same-sex sexual activity, or international criminal or regional human rights court decisions refocusing sexual violence laws away from female chastity and toward bodily integrity and autonomy for all persons.[2]

The intervention into criminal law pushed in the 1990s by rights advocates was focused on a specific approach under the "harm" principle: criminal law's use was limited to those actions and behaviors that actually resulted in a distinct *harm to* individuals, property, or material social goods, as opposed to actions that shocked, offended, or harmed ideas of the so-called proper roles for women and men, or about the correct way to have sex.[3] In adopting the harm principle, global rights advocacy was thereby asserting that it could link and limit "harm" to serve its own figurations of human rights abuses. The reformed criminal law would be rights-based in two directions—a limited use of coercive state power (itself a potential site of "harms") *and* a purposeful use of this power toward protecting people against harm or rights abuses (see Brown and Jernow, this volume).

However, the last twenty years of reform of criminal law tell a different story. Many scholars have noted that the rationale of focusing on harm tends to explode, creating apparently limitless grounds for new, modern crimes even as some crimes are removed.[4] Human rights advocacy itself has been paradoxically central to this explosion of new harms and expanding penalizations; while praiseworthy at times, as when prosecutions are called on to remedy previously unattended-to suffering, rights advocates' reliance on criminal law also comes with some dangerous effects, sometimes increasing, rather than decreasing, criminal regulation in the context of gender, sexuality, and reproduction. The rights-based expansion of criminalizing harms works through policing and punishment as an element of equal access to justice, and because this operates through often unaccountable and unreformed state power, criminal law's operation often reproduces hierarchies of existing power. Moreover, while each of these expansions of national penal power emerges in a distinct historical context, one of the perverse synergies is a tendency toward penal state aggrandizement (even as other parts of the state diminish).

In this chapter, we call attention to three areas of rights work as particularly potent sites for the tectonic shift of human rights advocacy from primarily defensive vis-à-vis the punitive state to primarily offensive (that is, in expanding harms). First, we address the human rights–based campaigns at the global level for the International Criminal Court (ICC); second, women's rights, with a focus on sexual violence against women; and finally, and more recently, a new (and mostly sexually focused) attention to children's rights, an area that has a tendency to tip toward punishment in the name of protecting the innocence of the imagined child.

Three other facets of rights work bear noting as we explore the complicated conditions of the pro-ICC, women's rights, and child rights movements' turns to prosecution. First, we highlight the ad hoc and unfinished theorizing of substantive core principles within human rights regarding the legitimate reach of criminal law and the state. While rights work had stressed defense against overreach by the state, much of its application was regarding excessive or abusive punishment, not what can be made a crime. Second, we call attention to the way that time and timing matters: different ideologies and practices associated with "rights" are more salient and acceptable in different global epochs. Finally, running through all three sites is a concern with the way in which claims arising within them can be so easily instrumentalized by other actors.

The three sites of human rights that this chapter focuses on have different relationships to the expansion of criminal law, yet their histories overlap in time. The period bookended by the world conferences (1990–2000) produced defining rhetorics for contemporary rights, as initially "dissident" rights like women's rights stormed the citadel of mainstream human rights and in turn became mainstreamed. Because many of the pledges to apply human rights doctrines to these new subjects were devoid of specificities, advocates analogized and borrowed from other areas of law, and we see in the early 1990s a convergence of international human rights, criminal law, and humanitarian law in matters relating to sex, gender, and reproduction. Human rights practice was engaging with criminal law reform at the very moment that human rights was both the new "moral language of humanity,"[5] expanding in rhetorical use, and ripe for a crisis within itself.[6]

Transitions, Justice, and the Human Rights Campaign for the ICC

In the case of the transitional justice (TJ) movement, some advocates turned to criminal law in post-totalitarian or postconflict settings as a means to redress multiple harms: the harm to victims who would otherwise go without remedies, the harm to democratic society if these crimes weren't prosecuted, and the harm to future at-risk populations. The receptivity of human rights groups to incorporating humanitarian law into the human rights framework in the 1990s allowed for the emergence of individual criminal culpability of both previous government actors and nongovernmental insurgent groups.[7] With "Ending Impunity" as their slogan, human rights actors translated prosecution into respect for rights and deterrence of rights violations. While the processes associated with TJ work on both domestic and international planes, and go far beyond mere prosecution,[8] the legitimacy of TJ globally is largely shaped by international norms.

The question here is how major human rights groups, originally distrustful of penal power, came to be its greatest champion. We focus here on one stream of advocacy arising in relationship with TJ but having a distinctly different orientation to postconflict or postauthoritarian justice: that of international criminal prosecution. How, and with what effects, did the creation of the ICC, which involved calls to states to prosecute or turn persons suspected of gross human rights violations over to the ICC, become a core rallying cry of human rights?

The key innovation in this period was to hold that violations of "fundamental bodily integrity rights" (for example, torture, extrajudicial executions, forced disappearance, and arbitrary detention) must be prosecuted by successor governments after conflict.[9] These claims arose in the late 1980s and early 1990s, when abusive dictatorships—many in the Americas, Eastern Europe, and Southeast Asia—began to disintegrate. While state abusive practices had been documented and protested as part of the mainstream human rights movements' work, in the Americas during the 1990s the unique claim that criminal prosecution would serve to "redress" *both* individual and democratic harms gained traction.[10] Prosecutions based on human rights advocates' denunciations of massive bodily integrity violations form the basis of what is "justly" made criminal.

What emerges is a human rights advocacy that offers justifications for the use of criminal justice. Thus, in the lead-up to the ICC in the mid-1990s, we see one of the major shifts in the human rights field's engagement with criminal law—a general turn toward criminal law as a tool of rights. This pivot required a rights-oriented justification to overcome the historical wariness of the state's prosecutorial powers by many human rights actors.[11] The newly forming (and newly funded) TJ movement imputed to the state an affirmative duty to prosecute gross human rights violations of previous regimes.[12]

It is in this era that "ending impunity" emerged as the preferred rhetoric for ensuring justice. Moreover, pessimism toward the possibility of effective prosecutions in domestic courts triggered advocates to begin demanding international criminal accountability. In global criminal justice, recourse to criminal law as a social (reordering) tool merges with a lack of faith in unreliable states.[13] The distrust of particular nation-states by human rights advocates (because their court systems were either corrupt or lacked capacity) in turn generates support for the ICC.[14] Although its principle of complementarity fortifies the duty of the state to prosecute domestically, the ICC as a "court of last resort" is celebrated by human rights advocates for its unique role in being able to supersede timid, ineffectual states. In the Balkans, in Rwanda, and in their ad hoc courts, as well as the various hybrid tribunals of Sierra Leone, East Timor, and Cambodia, to name some of the most established, the state is pushed toward justice through supranational forces.

We note a second shift here too, more philosophical and absolutist. The criminal law became, rather than a tool among many, the sole mechanism for bringing about "justice" after a change in regime, pushing land reform, social welfare shifts, or other interventions out of view.[15] Turns to prosecution are treated as treated what Samuel Moyn describes as "a rhetorical strategy that celebrates the 'justice cascade' as so self-evidently good as to need no defense."[16] As discussed more later, the global women's antiviolence movement took up this goal of ending impunity and moved the duty to prosecute up the hierarchy of state duties in the triumvirate of "respect, protect and fulfill rights," elevating it in policy terms over other kinds of state work for equality.

In an Amnesty International policy statement on impunity from 1995, the persistent human rights abuses of the early 1990s are framed as arising from the "phenomenon of impunity." Prosecution is vital not only for the individual case but also as a deterrent, as anything less leads to a "self-perpetuating cycle of violence" that will unquestionably lead to more violations.[17] In terms of the severity of the punishment, Amnesty International urged serious sentences in the name of deterring further violations.[18] Evidence of this turn can also be seen in the reaction of the nongovernmental organizations (NGOs) in the Coalition for the International Criminal Court (CICC) after the ICC's first acquittal in 2012.[19] Rather than celebrate the unanimous decision as an indicator of judicial independence and fair procedure, the NGOs were furious: as Tor Krever describes, "Human Rights Watch announced that the judgment left the victims of Bogoro 'without justice for their suffering'; other groups spoke of the 'abandonment of victims.' Organizations once known for championing the rights of defendants to fair trials now lamented judges' failure to convict when there was patently insufficient evidence to do so."[20]

Mahmood Mamdani, among others, has written extensively about the neo-colonial turn of international courts as governance, but we now see a critique arising from within a concern for the principles of rights.[21] Karen Engle warns that criminal law produces "changes in the movement in negative ways" and "reinforces pre-existing biases within the human rights system," by which she means not just the focus of prosecution on the Global South but also the way that national habits of prosecution tend to follow preexisting inequalities; rights work that focuses on "innocent victims" tends to miss these dynamics.[22] Engle calls attention to the danger of treating the carceral state as a rights avenger: exemplary human rights prosecution of ex–political leaders serves as cover for the ongoing policing of already stigmatized populations (see also Brown, this volume).

Whether a more cautious, less absolutist posture toward the goods of global criminal prosecution would have resulted in the creation of an ICC is an important tactical question. But here tactics became ontology, and what may have begun as a campaign strategy became a normative position. These shifts in rights (from shield to sword, toward ending impunity as the primary engine of justice) are echoed, amplified, and altered in the work we turn to next—that of advocacy for women's human rights.

Women's Rights: The Call to Prosecution to "End" Violence against Women, and Its Paradoxical Diminishment of Autonomy and Consent

Women's human rights advocacy encompasses many subfields and dimensions, but here we focus on advocacy toward the state's obligation to end violence against women (VAW) and more particularly sexual violence against women.[23] Women's rights advocates sought the attention of the mainstream human rights system by proliferating evidence of unremediated harms, thus confounding the limiting principle of "harm" for criminal law. Additionally, a focus on sexual violence led the VAW movement into a very particular quagmire around consent and the vexed role of criminal law in promoting "consent." These twinned moves (the production of harm stories and a deracinated consent story) are central to our claim about the role of the women's movement in dangerously expanding the penal reach of the state.

Any consideration of women's rights as a key site for expansionist penal states must also recognize that, like TJ, it is a multilayered site. In the formative years of the early to mid-1990s, some feminist advocates highlighted attention to bodily violence while others strove to highlight global markets and structural policies. Some advocates resented their exclusion from the "big boy" tent of TJ and ICC campaigning, while others decried as "unfeminist" any reliance on the UN Security Council or penal power. Recognizing this diversity sharpens the paradoxes of campaigners seeking to both shrink and expand the role of the penal state in the context of sex and gender equality. It also cautions against totalizing statements regarding "women's rights advocacy": reviewing some of the canonical texts[24] on global "women's rights as human rights" in the early 1990s, it is clear that engagement with the penal state was neither the sole initial move of women's human rights nor foreordained as the dominant claim.

Yet the work on VAW did come to drive most of the global recognition of women's rights as worthy of inclusion in the canon of human rights.[25] In the lead-up to the 1993 World Conference on Human Rights in Vienna, women's groups initially coalesced around demands for a new, special mechanism to address discrimination against women. By the time the petition reached the

UN, the demand had shifted to ending "violence against women,"[26] with violence articulated as both a "cause and consequence of discrimination."[27] In this harnessing of rights to respond to inequality, advocates held that national criminal law mischaracterized or missed entirely the nature of "harms to women"—for example, by characterizing sexual assault as a crime against family and honor. Advocates called for attention to human rights principles of bodily integrity, health, autonomy, and equality to recharacterize the violations, moving away from the focus on harms to chastity and family. It is, of course, a classic move of rights work to "shine a light" on previously unseen abuses and thereby gain moral outrage and compel action.[28] What was new was the use of gender-specific violence, and especially sexual violation, as the site of attention.

Women's rights advocates documented and campaigned against previously "tolerated" practices around sexuality (for example, female genital cutting or marital rape) as new and undeniable harms.[29] Because it was about sexuality—a relatively new topic for human rights—the need to redefine the borders of right and wrong within the universe of sexual conduct was paramount.[30] At this time, the penal state became the rights-protecting state.[31] This approach was drafted in the wake of the TJ movements' call to prosecution as vindication.[32] Criminal prosecution was further naturalized as the most doctrinally supportable way of invoking state responsibility and state action (under the "due diligence" framework), which was understood as a critical "desiderata" for the use of human rights. As Janet Halley (this volume) states, voices within transnational feminist advocacy linked "ending impunity" for human rights violations to prevention as well. While this turn may have begun as an invocation of prosecution as one tool among many in a gender equality project, over time, ending VAW became entirely a project of criminal justice, with prosecution used as key evidence of commitments to equality.[33]

It was not just violence, but sexual violence, that took the lead as the most successful claim on media, international NGOs, and intergovernmental attention.[34] VAW campaigning relied on sexual violence in two ways: the atrocity overwhelmed any "cultural" objections, and sexual violence rendered the gender of the cis women victims particularly visible.[35] This campaigning over time tracked ICC crimes, seeking to alter their content in more gender-specific ways. The newly formed Women's Caucus for Gender Justice worked to ensure that the statute anchoring the jurisdiction of the ICC included both gendered and explicitly sexual crimes, including "sexual slavery" and rape.[36]

In the defining of rape, the centrality of the role of "consent" came to the fore. *Consent* emerged as the term garnering consensus among sexual rights advocates as the dividing line between "good" and "bad" sex in the modern regime of human rights.[37] Promoting consent was meant to extract "good," voluntary sexual behavior from regulation by criminal law. It allowed for same- and different-sex sexuality to be judged under the same standard, freed of "immorality." Moreover, the search for *meaningful* consent among feminist and women's human rights groups became the holy grail of "good sex." Many feminists distrust "consent" as a shibboleth of a liberal state, a legal fiction behind which unequal power flows; feminists thus seek to fill its content with more than "mere agreement" in order to counteract the tolerance for so much unwanted, but consented to, sex.[38]

But fewer and fewer actions by women and girls, or anyone in constrained circumstances, will meet this new standard of meaningful consent, as the circle of meaningful consent draws tight, producing even more criminalization. In NGO advocacy and documentation literatures, as well as a range of court decisions, one finds an expanding array of things and conditions postulated to vitiate meaningful consent. Poverty, discursively attributed to all women selling sex, negates meaningful consent,[39] as does lack of information about health or, more particularly, HIV status. Age differentials, discussed in the next section, are also used to determine the boundaries of consent, with varying rationales for bright lines across hetero- and homosexual sex, and with insidious race and class implications.[40] Other key kinds of information whose denial or misapprehension can remove consent are, according to a British court, confusion about the gender of one's sexual partner.[41] As Carole S. Vance notes, the role of information in consent is vexed: while more information on sexuality in general, and the sexual health and status of a partner in particular, *is* valuable, information's wholesale incorporation into criminal law as part of the standard ("informed consent") for sex is a serious mistake.[42] Overall, criminal law remains the default regulator of sex, rendering women (and men) vulnerable to overprosecution.

Children's Rights, Criminal Law, and the Expanding Penal Regimes for the Management of Innocence

As we turn to this final section on children's rights, the persistent assimilation of "women" to "children" tugs at the story. Inability to give meaningful consent is connected—perhaps rightly but usually quite rigidly—to younger ages, sutured to feminine gender. Thus, the "women and children" style of discourse reappears, rendering women *as if* children, and all children *as if* female, and all females *as if* weak. There are, as Joseph Fischel observes in the United States, many power differences in negotiating sex that need attention, but today rape prosecution is the sole mode in which the dense, contradictory questions of "consent," age, and gender power differentials are evaluated.[43]

In the preceding discussion, the wrong of sexual activity begins to be enveloped by the question of age as a specific vulnerability.[44] Therefore, it is to the specific international law regime addressing the human rights of those of "young age," defined in international law as those under eighteen years of age, that we turn to next to explain human rights movements' prosecutorial turn. Although we suggest in the end that the international child rights regime may also help us constrain the carceral state, in practice it has been an enabling environment for the penal state in at least three ways. First, the idea of the child as "at risk," immature, even "innocent," and made legible globally as a feature of *age*, has been created in part by the international regime. Second, this globalization of the child includes with it a now "scientific" international ideology equating the future of the child with the future of the nation, a strong claim tying child welfare to national security and the need for fierce measures by the state. Finally, the incomplete development around children's affirmative sexual, gender, and reproductive rights—coupled with the high saliency of child harms—has allowed the ubiquitous invocation of punishment to protect the globally sympathetic, pseudouniversal category of "children."

Currently, the child rights regime seeks to inform but not to facilitate action, a fascinating inversion of the general rights idea that "information is power" around action. The most robust aspects of sexual and reproductive rights are rights to information and services—produced in their most instrumental form, not as ideas but as facts (about sexual health, disease, and services to ameliorate harm).[45] Sexual conduct and reproductive conduct are in themselves deemed harm for the young, so that sexual and reproductive health information rights are "harm reduction rights"—not enabling rights. Modern rights regimes seek to both empower girls and young women (and, to a lesser extent, boys and young men) vis-à-vis their sexual and reproductive lives and at the same time remove them from exposure to sexual conduct and reproduction. Rights today are often deployed in local contexts where early ages of marriage and childbearing are the norm, and criminalization is posited as a national intervention into "local culture."

A few examples of the many, and by now notorious, national and transnational claims around protecting children follow. In May 2013, the Moldovan Parliament passed amendments to its code punishing "propagation of any other relations than those related to marriage and the family in accordance with the

Constitution and Family Code," which the UN Office of the High Commissioner for Human Rights states is a "coded reference to LGBT."[46] In the United States, there has been an eruption of state-level laws seeking to limit trans* persons' access to single-sex public toilets, under the claim of protecting children from predatory harms of "fake women," and in resistance to a now-rescinded U.S. federal government policy that required schools receiving federal money to allow access to toilets according to a person's presentation of his or her gender.[47] Notably, when Amnesty International adopted its then-groundbreaking 1991 policy on supporting decriminalization of same-sex sexual behavior, it led with language on the "rights of consenting adults, in private."[48] Then as now, clarifying the power of individuals under eighteen years of age to determine sexual activity was a bridge too far.

The very use of the term *child* is both problematic and dictated by international human rights law. The international treaty regime set up for infants, toddlers, young children, adolescents, and teens covers all (born) persons under eighteen and is called the Convention on the Rights of the Child (CRC), so the term *child* is mandated (Article 1). Yet the CRC itself stresses the differences among persons under eighteen. One of its core principles of interpretation is that of attending to "evolving capacity," which is meant to provide for distinct and changing claims on rights and protection for differently aged persons.[49]

Many advocates seek to capitalize on the sympathies evoked by the term *child* and deliberately apply the word to older adolescents. The recent U.S. campaign "Stop Killing Kids" did this to great effect, ending the juvenile death penalty.[50] The current transnational campaigns to end child early and forced marriage mobilize repulsion at the specter of a prepubescent girl wed to a middle-aged man; often, this is a descriptive misnomer, as the age of early marriage varies greatly across regions, with most marriages of girls under eighteen involving fourteen-, fifteen-, and sixteen-year-old adolescents.[51] A similar dynamic is visible in campaigns to end "child sex trafficking," which rely on the same horror regarding the little girl sold into sexual slavery. Each of these invocations (capital punishment, marriage, and trafficking) relies on the idea of "the child"—hovering in our mind's eye at around seven or nine. Yet these invocations fail to allow for the youth with a beard and a gun, or the young woman selling sex because she herself has a child to support.[52] Notably, when these modifiers are added to the putative child, he or she becomes a possible perpetrator—child solider, super predator, or prostitute—and thus subject to the criminal law.[53]

The bright line of eighteen has also naturalized the metric of chronological age as a defining feature of both childhood and the regime of child rights itself, even as very few clear age metrics are provided in the text of the treaty. It is worth remembering that calibrating age from day of birth in order to delineate a specific moment of maturity of legal relevance is relatively recent.[54] Most cultural systems around the world distinguished people and their duties and entitlements by a set of developmental and physiological capacities and associated rituals, which were linked to, but not measured precisely by, chronology and were also often differentiated by gender and caste or class. Marriage, sexuality, and reproduction were coconstructing aspects of this process of adulthood, but not independent variables—one came of age by doing these things.

Robyn Linde, in her investigation of the "invention of the "global child," notes that chronological age for the first time became a marker of legal status as part of the formation of the modern state. By the nineteenth century, much of Europe, the United States, and independent and colonial regimes in the Americas, Africa, and Asia had instituted age-sensitive legal regimes, albeit with huge variability as to what age was salient for what regime, with duties and entitlements also varying across gender or race.[55] Uniformity on the scope of the "global child" came late in the game: it was in the 1989 CRC when all persons eighteen and younger were defined as "children." The convergence on eighteen deserves more attention than given here, as it is its own complicated and important story.[56]

In modern, biopolitically regulating states, Linde writes, the welfare of the nation was joined to the welfare of the child in the 1890s, as the emerging scientific method of epidemiology helped create the category of "child"—distinct from adults by virtue of scientifically demonstrated vulnerability and immaturity (for example, "childhood morbidity"). The vulnerability of the child also enabled a new claim by the state, such that state responsibility for national welfare justified the state in supplanting the authority of the family (especially the father). These ideas moved relatively seamlessly into the globalization of the child in international law, as epitomized by the drafting of the UN Declaration of the Rights of the Child in 1959 and then, thirty years later, the CRC. The state's strong interest in the child underpins the elaboration of child rights and state duties under the treaty, alongside but not trumped by parental rights.[57]

The drafters of the text of the CRC in the late 1980s sought to both create a universal category of "child" and provide for differentiation within childhood. They focused on the "best interests of the child," coupled with the core idea of "evolving capacity," all governed by a norm of nondiscrimination: this was meant to install a flexible idea of a growing agentic child.[58] The CRC set up a sliding power relationship between the child, the state, and family, but it did not initially imagine the child as having an interest in holding the power to determine its gendered or sexual life.[59] The CRC is one of the first treaties to speak of sexuality, but its Article 34 specifies it as a site of danger. Through the evolving practices of treaty interpretation, the committee that monitors the CRC has begun to characterize children's rights as including their right to affirmatively seek and receive information about sexuality, gender, and reproduction. In 2003, for example, the committee issued two groundbreaking interpretive comments obligating states to guarantee access to age-appropriate, accurate information about HIV, as well as about diversity of sexual orientation, sexuality, and reproduction—including contraception.[60] These information rights are good rights, as are the rights to sexual and reproductive health services. Yet there was—and still is—much less clarity, for example, around the age at which an adolescent can act on his or her sexual or gender identity desires.[61] The international and regional regimes emphasize equality in standard setting on consent between girls and boys and in same-sex and heterosexual conduct, but they leave discretion when setting a minimum age for sex. The interplay and tolerance of gaps and silences within and between the international and regional or transnational child rights regimes are notable. The CRC was adopted in 1989 *after* the establishment of nearly all binding regional regimes—European, inter-American, and African.[62] These regimes, which have subsequently developed child-specific protocols or principles, nonetheless can best be characterized as inconsistent and mostly cautionary about child rights in the domains of gender and sexuality.[63]

The lack of coherence in the approach to the questions, "What can a child do?" and "From what should the child be protected?" makes historical sense, given the global diversity of understandings about the meaning of youth. But in a globalizing regime, it is particularly tricky to determine the right age (metric) for various rights when young ages can encompass both agency and vulnerability: the right of young persons to determine their gender, including how to match their gender ideas and their body, exemplifies this issue, not only within the international system but also within and between global and local sites.[64] The issues, decisions, and lifelong implications for trans* and intersex young people are very different, but what is common is the incomplete theorization of rights for younger people around embodiment, gender, and sexuality. This fogginess about what youth can do stands in clear contrast to the full-throated embrace of penalization of the conduct of "the other" toward those under eighteen, reminding us, as Matthew Waites has written, that penal regimes (such as in statutory rape law) do not create a zone of empowered decision-making for underage young people but rather create zones of prohibition for others.[65]

It is the production of (sexual) innocence that most privileges the use of criminal law as a tool in human rights advancement for those under eighteen.

Innocence designates a child as being "free from guilty knowledge" and as the marker of one who ought to be "free from the harm" such knowledge entails. What children might want to know or need to know to develop their gender, determine the shape of their body, or consider their sexuality—normative or nonnormative—as desired is barely addressed.[66] Fischel calls the work to create, maintain, and distinguish this feature of children "managed innocence."[67] Innocence understood this way makes agentic action suspect: for those under eighteen, in the international and the regional regimes, the most robust aspects of sexual and reproductive rights are rights to information (mostly limned as "sexuality education") and services.[68] These are mostly robust but inconsistently articulated, particularly vis-à-vis parents and guardians.

The fact that the modern international rights regimes engage simultaneously with several local regimes, some of which espouse traditions of early marriage— and hence early sexual activity and childbirth—and some of which prohibit early marriage but tolerate sex outside of marriage for young people, helps explain the fractured, incomplete thinking about age limits for sexual rights. Current rights regimes seek to both empower those girls and young women (and to some extent some boys, if of a minority gender or sexuality) in their sexual and reproductive lives and at the same time remove them from mandated exposure to sexual conduct and reproduction.

Examining the discourses around not just the innocence but also the guilt of children is revelatory—for instance, children portrayed as perpetrators of crimes and horrific acts, kids who bully kids for being gay or trans*, kids convicted of sexual offenses and placed on "sexual predator registries," and "child soldiers" carrying out horrendous acts of cruelty in conflict.[69] Clearly, race and gender (in the United States, a 1990s discourse created the idea of "the super predator," figured as a black, teenage male) play a huge role in how some kids can be stripped of their innocence by the very same nations that are so insistent elsewhere on childhood's innocence. We note here, as a corrective to the protectionist, prosecutor state, that the CRC regime also pushes the opposite way for "guilty children": it not only prohibits the execution of those under eighteen, but also asserts that they cannot be handed to adult prisons and courts, and that *rehabilitation* (not retribution) is the only accepted rationale for juvenile justice.[70] At the very least, when kids are the perpetrators of sexualized conduct toward other kids (whether bullying or other assaults), remembering the CRC would keep rights advocates from invoking the punitive state as the first and best response. We close with the figure of the guilty child deliberately, using the very treaty (the CRC) that we have condemned as an enabler of the punitive state as the modern stance protecting children.[71] The CRC can be a defense against the punitive state, but under what conditions and with what claim of personhood can a child engage both responsibility and protection?

Conclusion

In examining the ways that human rights practices themselves have generated more attention to pain, by overreliance on narratives of harm, which invoked the state's punitive powers, we suggest the need to revisit our theories of punishment and rights vindication as elements of human rights' commitment to "what is human." Moyn has argued that it is the refusal of contemporary human rights to designate a solid vision of "the good life" that constitutes its greatest political strength but also accounts for its moral thinness.[72] It appears that some TJ movements, women's groups, and child rights advocates are moving toward thicker, more moral calls to rights: toward using prosecutions to restore democracy, deploying stronger rape law to promote an idea of substantive equality for women, or managing the production of the "right kind of child" for the nation, even as rights advocates are also calling for removal of penalties from other forms of sexual conduct, at least for adults. The resulting moves reveal opposing tendencies and as yet unarticulated ideologies vis-à-vis dismantling and reempowering a sovereign, yet responsive, state, one charged with creating the conditions for democracy and "becoming human."

Should the state be built up so?[73] The debates over what makes "good enough sex" (and for whom) are where rights advocacy densely engages the state normatively in both sword and shield practices. Absent more agreement on limiting principles for state prosecution, human rights here create some of the preconditions for the easy turn to state control and prosecution as the mode of rights promotion, rather than state liberation. Looking at how human rights advocacy has simultaneously asserted, expanded, and thus eviscerated the eighteenth-century idea of the harm principle articulated by John Stuart Mill as a *limiting principle* to overprosecution demonstrates the extent to which human rights as doctrine and practice has not yet enunciated a theory of criminal law as part of the role of the state: Is it the tool of last resort, as civil law doctrine insists (Corrêa and Karam, this volume), or a tool of first resort for rights? Women's groups and sexually and gender-diverse persons are just stepping up to claim state attention.[74] Arguably, it is the wonderful porousness of rights claims to new victims, whether they be cis women or trans* adolescents, that contributes to its potential to expand the state as it expands state obligations. Yet human rights, on its other edge, retains a strong sense that that state is not to be trusted too much with the rights of persons under its control, especially in regard to detention.[75] Given this, how can deploying human rights be most beneficial to sexual, gender, and reproductive diversity, power, and freedom?[76]

We think a more honest assessment by rights advocates of our own role in expanding the penal state is a prerequisite to a more rights-worthy renegotiation. The contentiousness of the fights over justice in postauthoritarian regimes, as well as sexual and reproductive rights, makes honest self-evaluation imperative and tricky. But this should not distress us: unsticking ought to be conceived of as a hard but worthy collective process. If human rights can be a justice-oriented process of contestation for the modern era, then we very much need to agree to keep asking these and many other questions within the hearing of others.

CHAPTER 3

The Harm Principle Meets Morality Offenses: Human Rights, Criminal Law, and the Regulation of Sex and Gender

Alli Jernow

Law regulates sexual activity and the body in a variety of ways. It condones or condemns certain forms of sexual activity. At the same time, what one does with one's own body, and whom (or what) one does it with, would seem to be among the most quintessential of private behaviors, at the core of the personal domain of an individual. Where sex and the law meet is the realm of morality, specifically the set of offenses known as "morals offenses."[1]

The conventional foundation for almost all discussions of privacy, morality, and the law is John Stuart Mill's *On Liberty*, published in 1859, in which he argued that the state may properly restrain someone's liberty only to prevent harm to others.[2] That harm, moreover, had to be tangible and concrete. Although commonly referred to as the "harm principle," Mill's thesis is actually a striking assertion of autonomy. He wrote, "The only part of the conduct of anyone for which he is amenable to society is that which concerns others. In the part which merely concerns himself, his independence is, of right, absolute. Over himself, over his own body and mind, the individual is sovereign."[3] While privacy or autonomy is not the only way to conceive of human sexuality, Mill's ideas have so powerfully shaped the debate that they still echo in common law courts today.[4]

"Morals offenses" are typically certain forms of sexual activity that, although consensual, are condemned by the law, including sex outside or before marriage (adultery and fornication), nonprocreative sex (anal sex, oral sex, sadomasochistic sex, commercial sex), incest, and bigamy.[5] Louis Schwartz, defending the newly adopted American Model Penal Code (MPC) in 1963, wrote that what "truly distinguishes the offenses commonly thought of as 'against morals' is not their relation to morality but the absence of ordinary justification for punishment by a non-theocratic state"—namely, preservation of public order and security.[6] Moral offenses, he continued, seek the "restraint of conduct by others that is regarded as offensive."[7]

Unease about the role of moral judgments in law stems from the belief that, in a pluralist society, individuals hold divergent moral beliefs and "the role of law and government is to equally and adequately safeguard the rights necessary for each individual to pursue his or her own normative view of 'the good life'— not to affirmatively advance one moral, normative view of 'the good' over others," writes Chai Feldblum.[8] In classic liberal theory, the state should be neutral among these varying conceptions of the good life.[9] At the same time, normative judgments are embedded in every aspect of criminal law. The harm principle itself is not neutral. As Joel Feinberg has explained, even a penal code based "exclusively on the harm principle" is meant to "vindicate the morality of preventing harm and respecting autonomy."[10]

In this chapter, I use the term *morals offenses* to refer to those offenses that are explicitly justified with reference to "morality" or "public morality," terms that most often are used simultaneously to describe and to equate traditional views on sexual behavior and majority opinion. *Morality jurisprudence*, then, refers to how courts assess government assertions of justifications based on this kind of morality.

Although the contours of the modern right to privacy are not coextensive with the harm principle, Mill's treatise is generally viewed as the philosophical source of the right to privacy. Courts may use the term *privacy*, but, as Feinberg observes, "philosophers, reading between the lines of the leading judicial opinions, have had no difficulty identifying it as the concept we have often called personal autonomy."[11] Discussions of privacy and the state's power to regulate or prohibit sexual behavior are almost always simultaneously discussions of whether the state's rationale is a sufficient justification for interfering in acts that cause no harm to others.

A century after it was published, *On Liberty* resulted in a sea-change in Anglo-American thinking about the nature and purpose of criminal law. The harm principle migrated from philosophical texts to legislative and parliamentary guidance and eventually to the courts. This chapter traces the paradigm shift of mid-twentieth-century legal thought from its British origins to its reception and impact in the European Court of Human Rights and in national courts in the United States, South Africa, and India.[12] The harm principle has been most frequently cited in cases decriminalizing sodomy. One might assume that the harm principle and the related assertion of the right to individual autonomy—whether construed as liberty or privacy—would appear to make a wide range of morals offenses suspect. Yet the harm principle consistently fails as a general limitation on the criminalization of private conduct. This chapter asks why courts appear ready to jettison so-called morality-based justifications in some contexts—specifically, same-sex sexual conduct—while the overall application of the harm principle remains quite limited.

From Philosophy to Lawmaking: The Harm Principle and the Function of Criminal Law

The mid-twentieth century is the starting point for much of the current debate on regulating sexuality through criminal law. In September 1957, the Committee on Homosexual Offenses and Prostitution in Great Britain, appointed by the home secretary in 1954 and better known as the Wolfenden Committee, after its chairman, John Wolfenden, published the result of a three-year inquiry. The Wolfenden Report recommended the decriminalization of male homosexuality (sex between women had never been a penal offense). With regard to prostitution, the Wolfenden Committee recommended increasing the penalties for some "street offenses" but leaving private acts of commercial sex unregulated. The report described the function of criminal law:

> [To] preserve public order and decency, to protect the citizen from what is offensive or injurious, and to provide sufficient safeguards against exploitation and corruption of others, particularly those who are especially vulnerable because they are young, weak in body or mind, inexperienced, or in a state of special physical, official or economic dependence. It is not, in our view, the function of the law to intervene in the private lives of citizens, or to seek to enforce any particular pattern of behavior, further than is necessary to carry out the purposes we have outlined.[13]

The Wolfenden Report featured the oft-quoted line, "Unless a deliberate attempt is to be made by society, acting through the agency of the law, to equate the sphere of crime with that of sin, there must remain a realm of private morality and immorality which is in brief and crude terms, not the law's business."[14]

These recommendations were not implemented in the United Kingdom until ten years later.[15] However, the Wolfenden Report had considerable influence on judicial thinking and lawmaking around the world, both in terms of shaping the jurisprudence of common law countries and, more generally, in terms of how privacy and autonomy are treated in international human rights law and specifically under the International Covenant on Civil and Political Rights. The Wolfenden Report touched off the Hart-Devlin debate, with H.L.A. Hart taking the position that the harm principle limits criminal law and Patrick Devlin defending the right of states to enact laws to protect common moral views, a position known as legal moralism. Devlin accused the Wolfenden Committee of misunderstanding the reason for the very existence of law.[16] He wrote, "The law must protect also the institutions and the community of ideas, political and moral, without which people cannot live together. Society cannot ignore the morality of the individual any more than it can his loyalty: it flourishes on both and without either it dies."[17] In other words, Devlin's view was that society is bound by shared moral beliefs and that criminal law can legitimately prohibit violations of these beliefs. Hart responded with the classical liberal argument that the criminal law should not be used as a means of enforcing public morality in the absence of more specific harms. He modified Mill's thesis to argue that the prevention of harm to others *or to oneself* is the only principled basis for criminal laws. Among legal scholars, Hart is generally believed to have emerged victorious.

During the same time period in the United States, the American Law Institute narrowly approved Tentative Draft No. 4 of the Model Penal Code (MPC) (the entire official MPC was not adopted by the American Law Institute until 1962).[18] Tentative Draft No. 4 was revolutionary in that it did not criminalize fornication, adultery, or sodomy, conduct that was at the time prohibited in almost all American states. The drafters, invoking Mill, explained, "The Code does not attempt to use the power of the state to enforce purely moral or religious standards. We deem it inappropriate for the government to attempt to control behavior that has no substantial significance except as to the morality of the actor."[19] The animating philosophy was thus "the idea of immunity from regulation of private morality."[20]

There was also a scientific basis for the thinking behind the new MPC. Alfred Kinsey's research on sexual behavior, published in 1948 and 1953, revealed that "Americans were no longer conforming their private behavior to the natural law ideal reflected in the criminal law; that is, the law channeled sexual activities into procreative marriage, but Americans derived much of their sexual satisfaction from nonprocreative or nonmarital activities."[21] The comments in Tentative Draft No. 4 cited the Kinsey studies "to show that sexual derelictions are widespread and that the incidence of sexual dereliction varies among social groups."[22]

At the time Tentative Draft No. 4 was adopted, the "exclusion of criminal penalties for consensual sodomy was without precedent in this country."[23] Illinois adopted the MPC in 1961, thus repealing its sodomy law.[24] The pace of change quickened in 1969, which was marked by the Stonewall riots and the birth of a more visible gay liberation movement. As William Eskridge reports, "Between 1969 and 1975, twelve state legislatures followed Illinois to repeal their consensual sodomy laws. . . . By the beginning of 1981, eleven more states had revoked all criminal penalties for private sodomy between consenting adults."[25]

For commercial sex, the MPC took some steps toward reform of the existing laws. While sex for hire was still criminalized, living off the proceeds of sex work was not a crime unless it was shown that the person was involved in commercial exploitation of the sex worker. Promoters—pimps, procurers, brothel keepers—were penalized more heavily than sex workers. Clients were subject to fines but not imprisonment.[26]

As for abortion, the MPC added additional avenues to obtain legal abortions, including risk of a physical or mental defect in the fetus, as well as pregnancies that resulted from rape, incest, or sex with a girl under sixteen.[27] Nevertheless, the comments on the abortion provision supported an even "more radical revision of prevailing abortion law than [was] embodied in the text."[28] State legislatures began adopting the expanded list of circumstances justifying abortions in 1967, and by 1969 fourteen states had passed statutes based on the MPC.[29] By the end of 1970, four other states had repealed criminal penalties for abortions performed by a licensed physician.[30]

Harm, Morality, and Autonomy in the Courts

The Wolfenden Report and the MPC used the harm principle to characterize the primary function of criminal law as preventing harm. While much of criminal law is devoted to deterring or punishing obvious injuries to others—murder, assault, kidnapping, and so forth—this focus on harm enabled both the Wolfenden Committee and the MPC drafters to undermine widely prevalent justifications for laws that criminalized private sexual behavior. In other words, laws should be designed to prevent harm to others and should not concern themselves with actions that do not cause such harm. Both documents were intended to guide legislators, not judges, in the drafting of laws. Yet the use of the harm principle and the resurrection of Mill in thinking about how laws should be justified with reference to their purpose have become commonplace in judicial challenges to existing laws. Parties before the court and courts themselves have asked whether the harm principle could or should be used as a substantive limit on the state's authority to criminalize conduct. In essence, the question, What is the *function* of criminal law? has become instead, What are the *constitutional limits* on criminal law?

This section reviews the application of harm, morality, and autonomy in those jurisdictions where same-sex sexual conduct was decriminalized through the use of the harm principle. Thus the inquiry begins with the Wolfenden Committee's premise that private, consensual same-sex sexual conduct should be beyond the reach of the criminal law, sometimes referred to as the beginning of the separation of "crime" from "sin." Adherence to the harm principle should have an impact on other forms of private, often but not always sexual, behavior. Throughout this chapter, the focus is on harm, autonomy, and morality rather than any single issue. Same-sex sexual conduct, commercial sex, incest, sadomasochism, assisted suicide, polygamy, adultery, and drug use are some of the fact patterns in which these issues arise. Although some abortion cases are included for their discussion of individual autonomy, abortion has generally not been treated under the harm principle analysis. Instead, the harm to the "life" of the fetus is balanced against the harm to the woman's health, bodily integrity, or privacy.

The European Court of Human Rights

The European Convention for the Protection of Human Rights and Fundamental Freedoms accords specific protection to "private life" under Article 8.[31] There are, however, a number of legitimate aims for legislation that interfere with private life, one of which is the protection of morals. Legislation aimed at the protection of morals must still pass the tests of being necessary in a democratic society, meaning that it must be both responsive to a pressing social need and proportionate. Through cases concerning same-sex sexual conduct, assisted suicide, and sadomasochism, the European Court of Human Rights has construed Article 8 to protect some degree of personal autonomy and development.

The harm principle made its first appearance in the European Court in the case of *Dudgeon v. United Kingdom*.[32] The Sexual Offences Act 1967 gave effect to the recommendations of the Wolfenden Committee in England and Wales, but in Northern Ireland, the law had remained unchanged.[33] Jeffrey Dudgeon filed a complaint before the European Commission of Human Rights in 1976, which found a violation and referred the case to the Court. The Court, in its 1981 judgment, held that Northern Ireland's laws criminalizing sodomy violated the guarantee of respect for private life under Article 8 of the European Convention.

The Court quoted with approval the Wolfenden Committee's description of the function of criminal law.[34] It concluded that there was no such "pressing social need" for the interference with private life, given that there was "no sufficient justification provided by the risk of harm to vulnerable sections of society requiring protection or by the effects on the public."[35] The Court then stated that the public view of homosexuality as "immoral" could not justify "the application of penal sanctions when it is consenting adults alone who are involved."[36]

Dudgeon and the later cases of *Norris v. Ireland* and *Modinos v. Cyprus* directly influenced the development of international human rights law. In 1994 the United Nations Human Rights Committee, the expert body that hears allegations of violations brought under the International Covenant on Civil and Political Rights, in *Toonen v. Australia* ruled that a sodomy law in Tasmania violated the right to privacy guaranteed by Article 17 of the ICCPR.[37] The Human Rights Committee found it "undisputed that adult consensual sexual activity in private is covered by the concept of 'privacy,'" and it rejected the argument that the law could be justified on moral grounds.[38]

Following *Dudgeon*, however, the European Court disavowed any broad notion of sexual autonomy in cases involving sadomasochistic sex and adult consensual incest. In the sadomasochism case of *Laskey v. United Kingdom*, it recognized that the conduct at issue implicated the right to privacy but found the interference justified by either actual or potential harm.[39] Here, the harm was supplied by the injuries, apparently minor, experienced by the willing participants.[40] In *Stübing v. Germany*, the criminal sentence imposed on a brother for a long-term sexual relationship with his sister was found to be a justifiable intrusion into privacy, especially in order to protect the sexual self-determination of siblings, just as the national courts had concluded.

Outside the realm of sexual activity, the Court fleshed out the notion of individual autonomy in the assisted suicide case of *Pretty v. United Kingdom* (2002). The Court found that criminalizing assisted suicide did not violate the right to respect for one's private life, yet recognized that "the notion of personal autonomy" was central to the concept of privacy and that personal autonomy included "the right to make choices about one's own body." Nevertheless, the ban on assisted suicide was necessary in order to "safeguard life by protecting the weak and vulnerable and especially those who are not in a condition to take informed decisions against acts intended to end life or to assist in ending life."[41]

The Court's most expansive proclamation of autonomy as undergirding the right to respect for private life came in the 2005 case of *K. A. and A. D. v. Belgium*, which concerned sadomasochistic sex between opposite-sex partners. The Court reaffirmed that "personal autonomy" was an important principle in interpreting Article 8 and that the right to have sex derived from the right to have control over one's own body.[42] This right included the right to engage in activities perceived as being "physically or morally harmful or dangerous to one's person."[43] Since consensual sexual relationships were a part of an individual's free will, criminal law could only interfere if there were "particularly serious reasons."[44] Here, however, the Court found the interference justified by the fact that videotapes of the sex acts revealed that the stop command of the "victim" was not heeded by the other participants. In other words, at a certain point, the criminal law was necessary to safeguard the victim's own right to free choice in expressing her sexuality.[45] Thus, the harm that justified the application of the criminal law was a harm to the other participants' autonomy.[46] Although, as in *Laskey*, the Court found no violation of Article 8, *K. A. and A. D.* is actually a stronger assertion of the right to privacy. It rests not on moral disapproval as a justification, or at least not exclusively, but rather on the permissibility of government action to prevent harm by protecting one of the participants' right to withdraw consent.

In its abortion case law, the European Court has reaffirmed that the decision whether to have a child falls within the notion of private life. However, a woman's "right to respect for her private life must be weighed against other competing rights and freedoms invoked, including those of the unborn child."[47]

American Courts

The U.S. Constitution, like those of Canada and India, contains no explicit article articulating a right to privacy. Instead, the right to privacy has been developed through constitutional adjudication. Many of these cases, beginning with *Griswold v. Connecticut* in 1965, concerned access to contraceptives and abortion.[48] In *Roe v. Wade*, the Supreme Court made clear that it considered this right of privacy to be "founded in the Fourteenth Amendment's concept of personal liberty and restrictions upon state action."[49]

The Due Process Clause of the Fourteenth Amendment protects against the deprivation of liberty without due process of law. Under "substantive due process doctrine," this has become more than a guarantee of fair procedure. Instead, the right not to be deprived of liberty without due process of law has been construed to include a substantive right to privacy. The scope of this zone of privacy, however, is continually contested. Cases reflect a tension between viewing privacy as circumscribed to decisions about whether to reproduce and viewing it as something much closer to personal autonomy.[50]

The state of morals legislation in the United States has been much discussed since the Supreme Court decided *Lawrence v. Texas*, striking down a state sodomy law and reversing its earlier decision in *Bowers v. Hardwick*. The language on morality in these two cases is so strikingly different that each merits a close examination. In *Bowers*, the majority opinion by Justice Byron R. White flatly rejected the claim that "the Court's prior cases have construed the Constitution to confer a right of privacy that extends to homosexual sodomy."[51] Moreover, he wrote, "any claim that these cases nevertheless stand for the proposition that any kind of private sexual conduct between consenting adults is constitutionally insulated from state proscription is unsupportable."[52] As for the respondent's argument that the State of Georgia required a rational basis for its law "other than the presumed belief of a majority of the electorate in Georgia that homosexual sodomy is immoral and unacceptable," the Court stated, "The law, however, is constantly based on notions of morality, and if all laws representing essentially moral choices are to be invalidated under the Due Process Clause, the courts will be very busy indeed. Even respondent makes no such claim, but insists that majority sentiments about the morality of homosexuality should be declared inadequate. We do not agree, and are unpersuaded that the sodomy laws of some 25 States should be invalidated on this basis."[53]

Justices Harry A. Blackmun and John Paul Stevens dissented, with Justice Blackmun writing, "The concept of privacy embodies the 'moral fact that a person belongs to himself and not others nor to society as a whole.'"[54] He dismissed the asserted justification, writing that "a State can no more punish private behavior because of religious intolerance than it can punish such behavior because of racial animus."[55] Morality fared no better. Finding support in Hart, Justice Blackmun wrote that a law that "enforce[d] private morality" was entirely different from the regulation of public sexual activity. While public sexual activity might interfere with the rights of others, the present case involved no such interference, "for the mere knowledge that other individuals do not adhere to one's value system cannot be a legally cognizable interest . . . let alone an interest that can justify invading the houses, hearts, and minds of citizens who choose to live their lives differently."[56]

For Justice Stevens, *Loving v. Virginia* was operative; a majority belief in the immorality of a particular practice was "not a sufficient reason for upholding a law prohibiting the practice." Decisions by couples "concerning the intimacies of their physical relationship, even when not intended to produce offspring, are a form of 'liberty' protected by the Due Process Clause of the Fourteenth Amendment."[57]

The U.S. Supreme Court overturned *Bowers* in June 2003, when it decided *Lawrence v. Texas.* Writing the majority opinion, Justice Anthony M. Kennedy made clear that the case was about liberty writ large (Justice Sandra Day O'Connor wrote separately on equal protection grounds). He viewed liberty as presuming "an autonomy of self that includes freedom of thought, belief, expression, and certain intimate conduct."[58] He characterized the *Griswold* line of cases as establishing that "the right to make certain decisions regarding sexual conduct extends beyond the marital relationship."[59] In his reading, *Roe* was less about the specific right to terminate a pregnancy than about "the right of a woman to make certain fundamental decisions affecting her destiny."[60] By claiming a jurisprudential foundation for a decisional form of privacy, he realigned privacy with liberty.

According to Justice Kennedy, there was an "emerging awareness that liberty gives substantial protection to adult persons in deciding how to conduct their private lives in matters pertaining to sex."[61] As evidence, he cited to the 1955 Tentative Draft No. 4 of the MPC, the 1957 Wolfenden Report, and the 1981 *Dudgeon v. United Kingdom* decision by the European Court.[62]

Justice Kennedy also rejected the morality justification. He wrote, "The issue is whether the majority may use the power of the State to enforce these views on the whole society through operation of the criminal law. 'Our obligation is to define the liberty of all, not to mandate our own moral code.'"[63] Justice O'Connor returned to this theme in her concurrence. Moral disapproval of a group cannot be a legitimate governmental interest under the Equal Protection Clause because legal classifications must not be "drawn for the purpose of disadvantaging the group burdened by the law."[64]

Justice Kennedy carefully demarcated what was not at stake: "The present case does not involve minors. It does not involve persons who might be injured or coerced or who are situated in relationships where consent might not easily be refused. It does not involve public conduct or prostitution. It does not involve whether the government must give formal recognition to any relationship that homosexual persons seek to enter."[65] Although clearly dicta, Justice Kennedy's line-drawing paragraph indicated that most criminal laws concerning sex would remain untouched and signaled that the decision was not tantamount to formal recognition of same-sex relationships.

In a typically scathing dissent, Justice Antonin Scalia warned of the various catastrophes that would follow the overruling of *Bowers*.[66] Laws against "bigamy, same-sex marriage, adult incest, prostitution, masturbation, adultery, fornication, bestiality, and obscenity" were now called into question by the majority's repudiation of moral choices as a basis for legislation.[67] If the promotion of a "majoritarian sexual morality" was not a legitimate state interest, then "none of the above-mentioned laws can survive rational-basis review."[68]

Lawrence touched off a firestorm of commentary about its meaning. Did the decision announce a broad right of sexual autonomy? Was it about identity, stigma, and exclusion?[69] Or was it fundamentally about valuing personal and intimate relationships?[70] *Lawrence* left much unsaid—including the level of scrutiny applied—either deliberately or out of a certain sense of judicial squeamishness.[71] With *Lawrence* itself so indeterminate, its meaning has been produced by lower court interpretation.

Justice Scalia claimed that *Lawrence* decreed "the end of all morals legislation."[72] Fifteen years later, that outcome is far from settled.[73] *Lawrence* has been the basis of challenges in state and federal courts to laws criminalizing adultery, sex work, incest, polygamy, and the sale of sex toys.[74] As one commentator wrote, "The constitutional right to privacy is a mess."[75] On marriage, of course, Justice Scalia proved prescient.[76]

Post-*Lawrence* cases alleging a broad right to sexual autonomy have not been successful, although adultery and fornication statutes, which were in any event rarely used, proved easy targets. In *Martin v. Ziherl*, the Supreme Court of Virginia found "no relevant distinction" between *Lawrence* and a challenge to the state adultery law.[77] The Court read *Lawrence* as holding that "decisions by married or unmarried persons regarding their intimate physical relationship are elements of their personal relationships that are entitled to due process protection."[78] It concluded, "We find no principled way to conclude . . . the Virginia statute criminalizing intercourse between unmarried persons does not improperly abridge a personal relationship that is within the liberty interest of persons to choose."[79]

Sex work, bigamy, and adult consensual incest have fallen on the other side of the line.[80] There have been some notable *Lawrence*-inspired dissents. In *State v. Romano*, one justice disagreed with the majority opinion upholding the constitutionality of Hawaii's prostitution law. According to Justice Steven H. Levinson, *Lawrence* "announced a federal privacy interest in private consensual sex."[81] He also criticized the state's efforts at a harm-based rationale, noting that they were entirely unsupported by the evidence.[82]

The sale and possession of sex toys ("obscene devices") lies somewhere in the middle, with circuit courts split over the implications of *Lawrence*.[83] Litigation about Alabama's law prohibiting the commercial distribution of devices designed "primarily for the stimulation of human genital organs" spawned six federal court decisions and lasted eight years. After the trial court found the law unconstitutional, the Eleventh Circuit reversed, rejecting any fundamental right to sexual privacy and reaffirming the constitutionality of morals justifications. The Eleventh Circuit noted that the Supreme Court had "never indicated that the mere fact that an activity is sexual and private entitles it to protection as a fundamental right."[84] It described the trial court as applying "John Stuart Mill's celebrated 'harm principle'" and observed that "regardless of its force as a policy argument, however, it does not translate *ipse dixit* into a constitutionally cognizable standard."[85] The Eleventh Circuit also reaffirmed public morality as a legitimate state interest.[86] Referring to older Supreme Court jurisprudence upholding morality as a sufficient justification, the Eleventh Circuit complained, "One would expect the Supreme Court to be manifestly more specific and articulate than it was in *Lawrence* if now such a traditional and significant jurisprudential principal has been jettisoned wholesale."[87] By contrast, in *Reliable Consultants v. Earle*, the Fifth Circuit held that a Texas law that made it a crime to promote or sell sexual devices violated the right to privacy, thus reversing the trial court's finding that there was no Fourteenth Amendment violation.[88] The court found that the right recognized in *Lawrence* "was not simply a right to engage in the sexual act itself, but instead a right to be free from governmental intrusion regarding 'the most private human contact, sexual behavior.'"[89]

The Fifth Circuit rejected the morality-based justification, reasoning that "if in *Lawrence* public morality was an insufficient justification for a law that restricted 'adult consensual intimacy in the home,' then public morality also cannot serve as a rational basis for Texas's statute, which also regulates private sexual intimacy."[90] Although the petition for rehearing en banc was denied, five judges dissented, disagreeing with the panel opinion's "unwarranted extension" of *Lawrence*.[91]

How, then, to make sense of *Lawrence*? Shortly after *Lawrence* was decided, Katherine Franke, a scholar of gender and sexuality, criticized its "domesticated liberty," pointing out that it left lower courts free to "cabin protection of . . . nonnormative sexualities."[92] She wrote, "The price of the victory in Lawrence has been to trade sexuality for domesticity—a high price indeed, and a difficult spot from which to build a politics of sexuality."[93]

One of the readings proposed by Cass Sunstein was that "*Lawrence* is really a case about the social subordination of gays and lesbians, whatever the rhetoric about sexual freedom in general. *Lawrence*'s words sound in due process, but much of its music involves equal protection."[94] This was not the preferred reading at the time, but it appears to have gained credence. As Nan Hunter, comparing *Roe* and *Lawrence* on the tenth anniversary of the latter, observed, "If we measure the state of sexual freedom by the ending exclusions prong of the civil rights paradigm, it is in terrific shape. . . . If, however, we measure the state of sexual freedom in anti-hierarchy terms, the conclusion is far less optimistic."[95]

The legacy of *Lawrence*, it appears, has much more to do with Justice O'Connor's equal protection concurrence than with Justice Kennedy's paean to liberty. O'Connor, too, rejected morals justifications, but for the specific reason that they masked animus. The morality asserted by Texas as a justification was nothing more than hostility toward gay men. Indeed, the one area in which Justice Scalia has proved unwillingly prophetic is marriage equality. His dissent accused the majority of dismantling "the structure of constitutional law that has permitted a distinction to be made between heterosexual and homosexual unions, insofar as formal recognition in marriage is concerned. If moral disapprobation of homosexual conduct is no legitimate state interest for purposes of proscribing that conduct . . . what justification could there possibly be for denying the benefits of marriage to homosexual couples exercising '[t]he liberty protected by the Constitution?'"[96] Ten years to the day after *Lawrence* was handed down, marriage equality became the law of the land. *Lawrence* could have ushered in an era of substantive checks on criminal law. In retrospect, it led not to greater autonomy and privacy rights—sexual and otherwise—but rather to court clerks' offices and wedding bells—to the "domesticated liberty" of marriage.

South African Courts

In South Africa, issues of harm, privacy, and the role of morality have been explored in cases dealing with same-sex sexual conduct and commercial sex. In contrast with the United States, where the privacy/autonomy line of cases that culminated in *Lawrence* began with jurisprudence concerning reproductive choice, reproductive rights in South Africa have been much more focused on equality, a reflection of its postapartheid constitutional landscape.[97] The South African Constitution contains explicit guarantees of privacy, equality, and nondiscrimination, including on the basis of sexual orientation. In addition, Section 12(2) of the Constitution guarantees everyone "the right to physical and bodily integrity," which includes the right to "make decisions concerning reproduction" and to "security in and control over their body." Judicial challenges to the Choice on Termination of Pregnancy Act, providing for unconditional abortions in the first trimester and abortions in limited circumstances, including risk to physical or mental health or to social or economic circumstances, up until twenty weeks, have been unsuccessful.[98] In one case, the Transvaal High Court considered whether, like in the United States, the right to choose should be protected under the dignity and privacy guarantees of the South African Constitution. It concluded that it was "not necessary to resort to those general guarantees" because the provisions of Section 12(2) "were clearly designed specifically to protect the woman's right to reproductive self-determination."[99]

In 1998 the National Coalition for Gay and Lesbian Equality brought a constitutional challenge to the statutory and common law sodomy ban. The Constitutional Court of South Africa agreed that the laws violated constitutional guarantees of equality, dignity, and privacy. The Court elaborated on a concept of privacy that it had earlier described as "what is necessary to have one's own autonomous identity."[100] Justice Laurie Ackermann, writing the unanimous opinion, observed, "Privacy recognizes that we all have a right to a sphere of private intimacy and autonomy which allows us to establish and nurture human relationships without interference from the outside community. The way in which we give expression to our sexuality is at the core of this area of private intimacy. If, in expressing our sexuality, we act consensually and without harming one another, invasion of that precinct will be a breach of our privacy."[101] Weighing the proportionality of the interference, Justice Ackermann found no justification for the law: "The enforcement of the private moral views of a section of the community, which are based to a large extent on nothing more than prejudice, cannot qualify as such a legitimate purpose."[102]

Concurring, Justice Albie Sachs reaffirmed the applicability of the harm principle, writing, "The law may continue to proscribe what is acceptable and what is unacceptable even in relation to sexual expression and even in the sanctum of the home, and may, within justifiable limits, penalize what is harmful and regulate what is offensive."[103] As for "prostitution and sado-masochistic and dangerous fetishistic sex," Justice Sachs simply noted that there was "controversy."[104] Finally, he recalled the moral nature of the Constitution. "What is central to the character and functioning of the state . . . is that the dictates of the morality which it enforces, and the limits to which it may go, are to be found in the text and spirit of the Constitution itself."[105]

Since *National Coalition* was decided in 1998, an ongoing debate about the scope of privacy has played out in arguments over the criminalization of sex work, producing, inter alia, several court cases.[106]

Sex workers and advocacy organizations have been litigating in court with mixed success. In 2002 the Pretoria High Court ruled in *Jordan v. State* that a

provision of the Sexual Offences Act, Section 20(1)(a), was unconstitutional because it distinguished between the seller and buyer of sex. On appeal to the Constitutional Court, however, a six-to-five majority reversed the high court decision
on discrimination and also found the right to privacy inapplicable.[107] Writing
for the majority, Justice Ngcobo distinguished *National Coalition* on the ground
that striking down the sodomy law protected the rights to dignity and nondiscrimination of gay men. In other words, the sodomy case should be understood to be about equality and not about a right to sexual autonomy per se.[108]

In their minority opinion, Justices O'Regan and Sachs disagreed, arguing
that the law *did* limit a sex worker's right to privacy, but found that her privacy
right was "attenuated" by "making her sexual services available for hire to strangers in the marketplace."[109] They distinguished the kind of sex at issue in *National Coalition* by emphasizing that there "the protected sphere of private
intimacy and autonomy relates to establishing and nurturing human relationships."[110] Commercial sex, by contrast, was "indiscriminate and loveless."[111] Although there was a form of privacy at issue, it fell "far short of deep attachment
and commitments to the necessarily few other individuals with whom one
shares . . . distinctly personal aspects of one's life."[112] The sex worker was not
"nurturing relationships" but rather making money. She had thus emptied the
sex act of its private character. Because the privacy right was weak at best, the
justifications for restricting the right were sufficient. The state, acknowledging
that "the suppression of sex cannot be justified merely on the basis of enforcing
a particular view of morality," listed eight reasons to uphold the provision, including the risks of abuse, the spread of HIV/AIDS, and the connection of sex
work to other crimes, such as drug abuse and trafficking.[113] Many of these evils
had been called into question by the report of the law reform commission, but
Justices O'Regan and Sachs held that the resolution of such factual questions
was best left to the legislature. Thus the prohibition of sex work was a "constitutionally permissible legislative choice."[114]

In two more recent cases, however, sex workers have successfully argued that
they were entitled to effective protection for other constitutional rights, not related to the right to privacy. In *Kylie v. Commission for Conciliation, Mediation
and Arbitration*, a case of alleged unfair dismissal of a sex worker by a brothel
owner, the Labour Appeal Court drew heavily on the minority judgment by
O'Regan and Sachs in support of its holding that the "illegal activity of a sex
worker does not per se prevent the latter from enjoying a range of constitutional
rights."[115] In *SWEAT v. Minister of Safety and Security*, the Western Cape High
Court accepted the applicant's contention that arrests of sex workers were targeting "not the illegality of sex work *per se*, but rather the public manifestations

of it."[116] Arrests with no reasonable expectation of prosecution infringed on "sex workers' rights to dignity and freedom, as enshrined in Sections 10 and 12 of the Constitution." The court interdicted police in the Cape Town area from arresting sex workers "while knowing with a high degree of probability that no prosecution will follow such arrests."[117]

The *National Coalition* and *Jordan* courts viewed the sexual activity at issue very differently. Nicole Fritz has accurately described this distinction between the forms of sex in *National Coalition* and *Jordan* as the difference between "civil" and "uncivil" sex.[118] Only sex in service of certain relationships—long-term, emotional ones that the court can assimilate to marriage—is worthy of full constitutional protection. Three years after *Jordan*, in *Fourie v. Minister of Home Affairs*, the Constitutional Court held that the exclusion of same-sex couples from the marriage laws constituted prohibited discrimination.[119] In this sense *National Coalition*, like *Lawrence*, has proved to be much more about relationships than about sex. However, the more recent cases of *Kylie* and *SWEAT* demonstrate the ability to claim protection for other constitutional rights, if not protection for sexual autonomy itself.

India

As in the United States, the Constitution of India has no explicit protection for privacy. There had been very few decisions on sex or privacy in India until the Delhi High Court made news around the world when it read down Section 377 of the Indian Penal Code in July 2009 in *Naz Foundation v. Union of India*.[120] "Indian Court Overturns Gay Sex Ban" was a typical headline.[121]

One of many revolutionary aspects of the opinion was the manner in which the court construed Article 21 of the Indian Constitution to include the unenumerated right to privacy. Article 21 provides, "No person shall be deprived of his life or personal liberty except according to procedure established by law."[122] Previous Supreme Court decisions had read the Constitution to protect "personal liberty" in the context of decisions about police visits to the houses of people considered to be habitual offenders or the authority of revenue officials to search and seize documents.[123] Although these earlier decisions had cited to American substantive due process jurisprudence, including *Griswold* and *Roe*, there were no Indian cases on whether this right to privacy included sexual autonomy.[124] As Vikram Raghavan put it, "*Naz Foundation* dodges through the Supreme Court's line of inconsistent decisions on privacy to forcefully assert that the Constitution protects a fundamental right to privacy."[125]

According to the Delhi High Court, any infringement of the fundamental right to privacy requires a compelling state interest to survive.[126] It then stated that "enforcement of public morality does not amount to a 'compelling state interest' to justify invasion of the zone of privacy of adult homosexuals who engage in consensual sex in private without intending to cause harm to each other or others." The court found support for the dismissal of public morality as a compelling state interest in *Lawrence* and *Dudgeon*.[127] The court concluded, "Thus popular morality or public disapproval of certain acts is not a valid justification for restriction of the fundamental rights under Article 21. Popular morality, as distinct from a constitutional morality derived from constitutional values, is based on shifting and subjecting notions of right and wrong. If there is any type of 'morality' that can pass the test of compelling state interest, it must be 'constitutional' morality and not public morality."[128] The court cited with approval the Wolfenden Report's description of the function of criminal law.[129]

Since *Naz*, a number of commentators have suggested that the court did not in fact repudiate all morals justifications.[130] For example, Raghavan writes that the decision did no more than suggest that "mere public disapproval of a practice or behavior is an inadequate reason to restrict it."[131] Justice J. S. Verma, shortly after the decision was handed down, argued that the outcome could and should have been reached based solely on the right to health and that the debate about constitutional morality was unnecessary.[132]

Perhaps most significantly, the author of the opinion, Chief Justice Ajit Prakash Shah, elaborated on the reasoning behind *Naz* after retiring from the bench. He framed the government arguments in support of Section 377 as a recap of the position of Devlin in the Hart-Devlin debate.[133] However, he did not fully embrace Hart's position either. Instead he stated, "Nobody can argue that criminal law has no role to play in regulating individual liberty in order to protect public morality. What the court holds in *Naz* is that it is the 'constitutional morality' rather than popular morality that is the controlling benchmark. It must be noted however that a distinction between public morality and constitutional morality does not lead one to the conclusion that they are mutually exclusive. They only have significant departure points."[134]

As examples of departure points, he cited the prohibition of discrimination on the grounds of caste or religion. By contrast, laws concerning gambling were an example of convergence. In the eyes of Chief Justice Shah, public morality could still be a valid basis for legislation.

Naz was overturned by the Supreme Court of India in December 2013 in *Suresh Kumar Koushal v. Naz Foundation*.[135] In an opinion notable for both the thinness of its reasoning and its deference to majority opinion, the Supreme

Court ignored substantial evidence in the record detailing discrimination against sexual minorities and instead emphasized that they were only a "miniscule fraction of the country's population."[136] It rejected the characterization of Section 377 as criminalizing identities—an important point for the court below—and instead held that it "merely identifies certain acts which if committed would constitute an offence."[137] Although the government had not appealed the Delhi High Court decision, the Supreme Court observed that Parliament had not yet moved to amend the law. To many commentators, *Koushal* signaled that the Supreme Court had become a "majoritarian" institution, one that deferred to the will of the public and the Parliament rather than protecting individual rights.[138]

Koushal stands out even more as an anomaly when compared with a decision handed down by an earlier, different bench of the Supreme Court, *National Legal Services Authority v. Union of India*. In this constitutional writ petition, the Supreme Court recognized the diversity of gender identities and affirmed the constitutional rights of transgender persons to be free from discrimination. The Court, relying on Article 21's protection of "personal autonomy," wrote that "self-determination of gender is an integral part of personal autonomy and expression and falls within the realm of personal liberty guaranteed under Article 21."[139] The contrast with *Koushal* is striking.

There are signs that *Koushal* will not last long. In an unrelated case challenging the Aadhaar program, a mandatory biometric ID system that assigns every Indian resident a unique identity number, a nine-judge Constitution bench of the Supreme Court considered whether there was a constitutionally protected right to privacy.[140] In a unanimous decision, the Court held that the right to privacy was protected "as an intrinsic part of the right to life and personal liberty under Article 21."[141] This was not rule-making by judicial fiat, the Court explained, since "a panoply of protections governing different facets of a dignified existence" had already been held to fall within the protection of Article 21.[142] "The sanctity of privacy lies in its functional relationship with dignity. Privacy ensures that a human being can lead a life of dignity by securing the inner recesses of the human personality from unwanted intrusion. Privacy recognizes the autonomy of the individual and the right of every person to make essential choices which affect the course of life."[143]

In its comprehensive review of regional and international privacy cases, as well as jurisprudence from the United Kingdom, Canada, South Africa, and the United States, the court cited to not only search-and-seizure and surveillance decisions but also to a number of cases involving sexual orientation and same-sex relationships, including the American and South African marriage equality cases. The Court reviewed two Indian cases that it viewed as outliers, one of which was *Koushal*. It rejected *Koushal*'s reliance on the supposedly "miniscule" number of sexual minorities, stating,

> The purpose of elevating certain rights to the stature of guaranteed fundamental rights is to insulate their exercise from the disdain of majorities, whether legislative or popular. The guarantee of constitutional rights does not depend upon their exercise being favorably regarded by majoritarian opinion. The test of popular acceptance does not furnish a valid basis to disregard rights which are conferred with the sanctity of constitutional protection. Discrete and insular minorities face grave dangers of discrimination for the simple reason that their views, beliefs or way of life does not accord with the "mainstream." Yet in a democratic Constitution founded on the rule of law, their rights are as sacred as those conferred on other citizens to protect their freedoms and liberties.[144]

Although the Court clearly signaled that *Koushal* would be overturned, noting that the "right to privacy and the protection of sexual orientation lie at the core of the fundamental rights guaranteed by Articles 14, 15 and 21 of the Constitution," it deferred the ultimate decision on "constitutional validity to be decided in an appropriate proceeding."[145]

Following *Aadhaar*, the Supreme Court issued notice that a series of public interest cases, including the challenge to Section 377, would be heard by a five-judge Constitution bench.[146] Having found a right to privacy in the Constitution, the Supreme Court appears set to rewrite its privacy jurisprudence. Given the language of *Aadhaar* on sexual orientation as a facet of privacy and the reopening of the curative petitions challenging *Koushal*, it seems that it is only a matter of time before *Koushal* is overruled.

Conclusion

Around the world, courts striking down laws criminalizing gay sex have trumpeted the absence of harm in consensual adult sexual behavior. They appear to be closely following a Mill-Wolfenden-Hart playbook. But the rejection of morals as a valid justification for laws criminalizing or prohibiting other "self-regarding conduct"—essentially acts of individual autonomy—is much less consistent. After *Lawrence*, for example, commentators in the United States expected a wide range of criminal laws to fall. That simply has not happened, and *Lawrence*, while celebrated, is not now perceived as a substantive limit on criminal law.[147]

One explanation is the use and abuse of the notion of harm. For example, governments paying lip service to the harm principle routinely offer unsupported assertions of the harms associated with commercial sex work.[148] In *Romano*, the lone dissenting justice objected that the claimed ills of sex work were "speculative and attenuated" and did not "constitute evidence at all."[149] In the dissenting opinion in *Jordan*, Justices O'Regan and Sachs queried some of these assertions and yet ultimately decided the issue was one for the legislature.[150] As Dan Kahan writes, "There may be some who will take offense at the idea that the Fourteenth Amendment enacts John Stuart Mill's *On Liberty*, but a great many who are just fine with that idea will still be motivated by identity-protective cognition to impute secular harms to 'private conduct' (from unconventional sexual behavior to recreational drug use to smoking to generation of nuclear power) that transgresses their religious or cultural values."[151]

Thus the harm principle is accepted everywhere and yet is so plastic as to be without any real power to challenge state regulation of private behavior. One example is a line of marijuana cases in Canada.[152] There, the Supreme Court still identified potential harms in private marijuana use, even though the majority rejected the harm principle and even the dissent found it only a brake on the state's power to imprison. Furthermore, as Bernard Harcourt describes, there may even be a new trend toward an "illiberal" use of the harm principle to justify a variety of new criminal laws.[153]

There are at least two other readings of the dynamics at play here. It is likely that at the time that many of the cases decriminalizing same-sex sexual conduct were decided, the harm principle was a more secure intellectual footing for courts reluctant to assert seemingly radical notions of equality. When Canada reformed its criminal code, the justice minister took pains to emphasize that decriminalization of homosexual sex did not imply approval.[154] The European Court of Human Rights used similar wording in *Dudgeon*.[155] In other words, the use of the harm principle was itself more instrumental than principled. It did the work of rejecting the criminalization of activities that did not cause harm to others, while falling far short of an endorsement.

The other strand that connects these cases is the importance of constitutional as opposed to "conventional" morality. In *R v. Butler*, Canadian Supreme Court justice John Sopinka wrote, "I cannot agree with the suggestion of the appellant that Parliament does not have the right to legislate on the basis of some fundamental conception of morality for the purposes of safeguarding the values which are integral to a free and democratic society."[156] Both the Delhi High Court

and the South African Constitutional Court affirmed that constitutional morality outweighed popular morality. These courts hark back to Ronald Dworkin's
views of morality. In his analysis of homophobia, Dworkin rejected Lord Devlin's
morality as based merely on public opinion. He maintained that "the principles
of democracy we follow do not call for the enforcement of the consensus, for
the belief that prejudices, personal aversions and rationalizations do not justify
restricting another's freedom itself occupies a critical and fundamental position in our popular morality."[157]

   With this perspective, it is easy to understand how *Lawrence*'s "most powerful social message has been legitimation of equality for gay people";[158] why the
South African Constitutional Court, looking back on *National Coalition*, described it as being a case about the "right of gay people not to be discriminated
against unfairly";[159] and the Delhi High Court's emphasis on the importance of
guaranteeing rights regardless of the traditional stigmatization of sex workers.[160]
The use of the harm principle in the sodomy cases served less as a vindication
of Mill than as a jurisprudential device to expose majoritarian discrimination
as irrational. Cases involving same-sex sexuality may then represent the harm
principle's high-water mark. Where this work has been completed—at least in
the sense that criminal laws have been struck down—the harm principle now
lies discarded.

CHAPTER 4

Reflections of a Human Rights Activist

Widney Brown

I am going to start with a caveat. As a former criminal defense attorney who practiced in New York City and as a human rights activist who has worked around the world at leading international organizations, such as Amnesty International and Human Rights Watch, I find it difficult to maintain my objectivity regarding the criminal justice system, whether we are discussing those systems in developed countries, in war-torn countries, in deeply corrupt countries, or in profoundly impoverished countries. My bias is simple: when the justice system works, it largely works for those who are privileged. Mostly, criminal justice systems fail victims, violate the rights of the accused, reflect and entrench the prejudices of the larger society, and are instruments of injustice.

To be clear, I believe in justice for victims of crime and accountability for those who perpetrate crimes. When I first moved to New York City, I joined the New York Women Against Rape. Advocating for victims and survivors of rape, intimate partner violence, and incest, I became aware of how the criminal justice system failed most victims. Put simply, most cases were not taken seriously, and when women understood what they were required to demonstrate and what was deemed probative, many simply gave up on justice.

I was part of a group of activists who campaigned to reform the laws and rules of evidence governing these cases. We advocated to repeal the statutory requirements that a woman prove that she "earnestly resisted" the rape; that allowed prior sexual history to be introduced; and that provided for a reduced sentence if a woman was killed in the "heat of passion." But what I saw during that time was not just the way many victims were revictimized in the criminal justice system, but also the privileging of some victims vis-à-vis the rights of defendants. For example, if the victim was a white, educated woman and the defendant an African American man, then the tables turned, and the defendant was presumed to be guilty.

I believed that both of these injustices spawned further failures of the system. Anyone perusing the record of convictions involving crimes of sexual violence got the message that only white girls are raped and that rapists are predominantly black men.

Fast-forward several years and I was a lawyer who had stumbled into doing criminal defense. I represented victims of bias-related violence based on sexual orientation, gender identity, and HIV status. Some of my cases involved the legitimate arrests of my clients, followed by their beating. Many more cases involved the abuse of my clients by the police, followed by an arrest based on some pretext. In the 1990s, when I was doing this work, my trans clients were so routinely subjected to police abuse and arrest that I coined the phrase "walking while trans."

Advocating for these victims, I understood how the concept of "equal protection of the law" is unrealized—even unreal—for the vast majority of people who come into contact with the criminal justice system, regardless of whether they are victims, witnesses, or defendants.

(De)Constructing Criminality

In many cases, the positionality of the affected person, victim or defendant, is either not clear or altogether perverted. Take the example of the girls and women I interviewed in a Saudi Arabian prison. I went to Saudi in early 2003 and was able to visit a women's prison in Riyadh—one of the largest prisons in the country. I spoke with the warden, staff, and numerous prisoners. Every woman and girl in the prison was a migrant who had traveled to the country to do domestic work. As females, they were not allowed to leave the home of their employer without permission and without being escorted. In fact, many I spoke with never left the home. If they were caught outside their workplace without their *iqamas* (residency permits), which their employers held, they could be detained and deported.[1]

In the prison, woman after woman told a strikingly similar story of isolation and exploitation by her employer. I would estimate that 90 percent of the girls and women in the prison had been charged with the crime of "illegal pregnancy" and were serving two-year sentences. These were women and girls who were virtually prisoners in their workplaces, yet in none of their cases was there an investigation to ascertain whether the sex that resulted in the pregnancy was consensual. When I asked these questions, it became evident that most of the girls and women were treated as property, and the men in the house felt entitled to demand sexual access. After hearing their stories, it was not difficult to conclude that the victims of violence were imprisoned, while their perpetrators went free.

After they had served their sentence, they would be deported to their country of origin, typically without receiving the wages they earned before being detained. As I asked them about their experiences in the Saudi criminal justice system, I found that they had no legal representation and that the few who actually attended any court hearings were not supplied with an interpreter. They knew the charges against them, but because being pregnant was sufficient evidence of the crime, there simply was no due process through which they could challenge the charges. Most important, there was no mechanism for contesting the very concept of "illegal pregnancy."

I left the prison feeling rage that these girls and women who had risked so much to try to find economic opportunity would instead go home impoverished and stigmatized, even as their employers got away with exploitation and sexual violence.

Later, I attended numerous meetings with Saudi government officials, including the minister of interior, to discuss the Human Rights Watch investigators' findings. Initially, I had planned to bring up the situation and ask for investigations into sexual violence against migrant workers. The meeting was held in a cavernous room drenched in gold leaf. The minister met with us, accompanied by an entourage of young men. As one of only two women in the room, I was virtually invisible. I struggled with whether to raise the issue of the migrant workers' cases when the minister lectured us on the guilt of those in the criminal justice system. As he explained it, people confess because they are guilty. And if they refuse to confess, this is also evidence of their guilt. Given the inevitable guilt of those who are detained, the minister explained that torture simply helps those who are guilty come to terms with their guilt. In refusing to confess initially, they were responsible for the torture.

I remained silent rather than demand the government investigate whether any of these women were raped. I made this decision because as I listened to justifications for the rampant abuses within the system, I feared that raising the issue would likely lead to further abuses of women. The subsequently published report was edited to protect those we had interviewed.

My silence in that meeting goes to the heart of what I believe is the uneasy, even vexed, relationship many human rights activists have with the criminal justice system. On the one hand, the state holds the duty of respecting, protecting, and fulfilling the human rights of the people it governs. On the other hand, the worst violations often happen in the context of the criminal justice system—in part because it is where the policing power of the state is at its strongest and thus where abuse of power is most likely to occur and where the severity of the abuses is so profound. Adding to the problem is the often sweeping scope of the penal law that effectively captures and criminalizes behaviors that cause no harm. In many cases, the law reflects the morality of the elite, and the law is a tool used to effectively control those who are less privileged or outsiders.

Knowing that a criminal justice system is deeply flawed and the source of systematic violations, how can human rights activists demand that the state bring those who perpetrate crimes to justice without appearing naïve or even dangerous?

The Role of the State

This quandary is particularly painful for me because I became a human rights activist precisely because I wanted to advocate for diligent state action that addressed nonstate actor violence against people based on their gender, gender identity, or sexual orientation. But by engaging the state as an "ally," the human rights movement, myself included, has lost some of the distance it once had when it saw the state primarily as the source of violations.

This is exacerbated by the difference between how behaviors in the public sphere versus those in the private sphere are analyzed under human rights principles and addressed by the state. This difference has caused tension between women's rights activists and some mainstream human rights actors. For example, in my experience, when individuals promote political and religious views that undermine women's rights or gender equality, and consequently face persecution by the state, some mainstream human rights activists have defended their rights to free speech and freedom of expression.[2] Yet when individuals or groups spurred on by these beliefs attack women (for example, raping women who dare to take to the streets to demand equality and justice), in many cases in the past, what I saw was mainstream activists limiting their demands to effective remedies and instead issuing vague recommendations about prevention. To be clear: violating freedom of expression can never be justified. But the indifference of most states to the routine violence that leaves people in marginalized communities living with profound insecurity is reprehensible.

There is nothing simple about this quandary. Defending freedom of expression—even when the content of that expression is anathema to human rights principles—goes to the very heart of the human rights movement. In short, no one should be imprisoned for the exercise of the right to free expression, so long as that expression does not amount to an incitement of violence.

But to those fighting to protect individuals and groups who are already desperately marginalized within their communities and states, it is small comfort that discrimination, violence, and exclusion at the hands of nonstate actors only requires the state to act with due diligence. This is particularly the case since the line between official (state) and nonstate actors in many cases is not as clear-cut as many assume. Death squads, militias, and defenders of morality may all technically qualify as nonstate actors but are nonetheless often shielded by the state because of their positions. Whether we are talking about killing doctors who perform abortions, raping women who dare to demand equality, killing queers, or beating indigenous rights activists, in practice the law too often sides with the perpetrators rather than the survivors.

What systems should be put in place to restrain the policing power of the state in such a manner that the violations that flow from the abuse of that power are stopped? And how can such systems be designed such that the police and criminal justice system can fulfill their responsibilities of convicting and punishing the guilty and helping them to stop offending, while protecting the innocent? As a human rights activist, I have seen how the criminal justice system's failure to fulfill this mandate is devastating. Fear, anger, and vigilantism are the obvious outcomes of a failed criminal justice system. But the harm goes more deeply. The threat of violence in societies in which the criminal justice system has failed comes both from nonstate actors who are free to commit crimes with impunity and from police and security forces who—sometimes in a desperate attempt to demonstrate they are able to exercise their authority—shoot to kill and otherwise engage in unlawful behavior. Those who are victims of crime feel that the lack of justice somehow calls into question both the harm they have experienced and the truth of their story.

This issue is not relegated to criminal justice systems in developing countries. These same problems haunt the justice systems in many developed countries as well. Human rights advocates have tended to take on faith that developed countries are largely able to deliver justice and that egregious abuses within a criminal justice system are a function only of poverty and corruption. The stories of injustice even in countries where resources are not a problem belie that narrative. Two examples, among the many that come to mind, are the cases of the Central Park Five and Sara Reedy.

Ken Burns's documentary *The Central Park Five* details the arrest of five young black and Latino men for the rape and near-deadly beating of a white woman in New York City's Central Park.[3] They confessed, were convicted in 1990, and served between seven and thirteen years in prison before their conviction was overturned and the person who was actually responsible for the crime was found years later.[4] It became apparent that the police, eager to reassure a public alarmed by the attack, had both coerced the teens into confessing and ignored exculpatory evidence.[5] This did not happen in a country where the police had few resources. It happened in a city with the resources to use the most powerful forensic techniques to analyze the evidence. However, the need for a quick fix to assuage the fears of the mostly privileged people who go running in Central Park trumped the need to do an impartial and thorough investigation that followed facts and evidence, not headlines about "wilding" gangs of kids of color.[6]

The rush to judgment that resulted in the wrongful conviction of five black and Latino youths stands in contrast to the case of Sara Reedy, a rape victim in Pittsburgh, Pennsylvania, whom the police accused of fabricating the story of her sexual assault. Reedy, a white woman, had been working at a gas station to pay her way through college when one night a man entered the station, stole hundreds of dollars from the cash register, assaulted her, and left. She was arrested and jailed after the detective who interviewed her concluded that she had not only lied but also stolen the money, and she was released on bail. A year later, the man who raped her was caught because of another rape and confessed to raping Reedy.[7] Reedy received a settlement of $1.5 million as compensation for the violation of her rights.

As a human rights activist, the jarring difference in state and public reactions to these two incidents (both victim narratives, but with shifting victims) is the greatest challenge to my faith in the human rights paradigm. I found that because human rights organizations in the United States were often fearful of taking on the systemic failure of the criminal justice system, the response of organizations was often to question individual failures of specific detectives, rather than challenging the systematic bias of the system.

In the United States, there is a popular belief, even a mantra, among those who probably believe that they will never face arrest or prosecution that "justice is blind," meaning courts do not unfairly mete out justice according to status of person but treat all equally; in my experience, the criminal justice system is blind (that is, ignores the harms) when it comes to those who are poor, demonized, or marginalized, but this is the opposite of what "blind justice" is intended to mean. While certain high-profile cases, like the Central Park Five case, sometimes lead to demands for change, effective oversight and scrutiny of the system are rare. Stories of false convictions, lives destroyed, and decades lost are all too common in the United States. But any soul-searching about what justice means lasts only until the next headline about some horrific crime is published. The Innocence Project, with its focus on reexamining evidence and bringing forensic skills to bear to help exculpate wrongly convicted defendants, is one of the few long-term positive outcomes from these predictable bouts of public hand-wringing over miscarriages of justice and empty mea culpas.[8]

This brings me back to one of my key points: states protect the citizens they care about—namely, those who wield political and economic power. States demonize and abuse and make "other" those who don't belong. The same people who don't belong are ironically those who are most in need of the state's protection because their outsider status means that they are more likely to be targeted for exploitation or abuses by nonstate and state actors alike.

Reconciling the Thirst for Justice with the Need to Exercise Rights

There is overwhelming evidence that criminal justice systems around the world are flawed. This is a challenge to human rights advocates: they cannot ignore how justice is failing both victims and suspects alike.

In order to build justice systems that truly reflect the principle that all people should enjoy the equal protection of the law, there are a range of questions that we must ask and debate within our communities. Let me pose a few of these that have been particularly salient for me as I worked to promote the rights of individuals criminalized for their sexuality, gender identity, sexual orientation, expression, beliefs, and work. Some are substantive and some are procedural; any meaningful reform of the criminal justice system must address both.

Some substantive questions are as follows: What is defined as a crime? What are the patterns and practices of the police? How is prosecutorial discretion exercised? Are all defendants ensured legal representation, and how is adequate defense defined? Are there disparities in sentencing for comparable crimes? Is the appeals process driven by considerations of efficiencies or truth-seeking? Who is in the countries' prisons?

As for procedural questions, the following should be considered: Do any rules of evidence or procedure undermine due process and fair trial protections? Do any rules of evidence or procedure undermine or discount the testimony of victims or witnesses? Is the presumption of innocence reflected in all parts of the system? Is there judicial independence?

Let's examine some of these questions in order to see what insights a human rights lens can and cannot provide in analyzing the flaws in criminal justice systems.

First, with regard to what is considered a crime, the human rights movement is quick to decry the criminalization of certain actions that fall squarely within the exercise of a right—for example, the criminalization of dissent or the crime of apostasy. However, it has taken time for the human rights movement to challenge the criminalization of actions that have not yet been deemed rights, such as sexual conduct, especially when they involve choices that society may deem immoral, such as adultery, homosexuality, or sex work. Yet "morality"[9]—rather than "harm," the criterion many liberal democracies use as a touchstone—too often drives what is deemed a crime. Drug and alcohol use or buying and selling sex are often criminalized, while corruption and some forms of economic exploitation or even torture are not outlawed. Returning to my experience in Saudi Arabia, possession of alcohol is illegal, and it was a crime for women to drive a car, but there is no law explicitly prohibiting the use of torture. A small number of European countries have made it unlawful for women to wear full-face veils. In the United States, the Department of Justice has tried to rewrite the definition of torture, turning waterboarding into an "enhanced interrogation technique."

The overreach of the criminal justice system, often defended in the name of cultural mores, can create substantial risk for some victims. For example, in countries that have crimes based on morality, reporting a rape that is then deemed "unsubstantiated" can lead to charges of adultery or fornication. Sex workers who are victims of violent crimes or property crimes often fear reporting the crime for fear they will be charged with prostitution or related offenses while their complaints will go unaddressed. The recent trend in developed countries of making it a crime to be in a country while holding irregular immigration status means that people who may be targeted for exploitation and violence are simply unable to access the criminal justice system.

Other biases in criminal law can exclude people from protection. If a Native American woman living on a reservation is raped by someone who is not also Native American, even if the police can identify a suspect, the Native American courts do not have jurisdiction over the suspect, and the U.S. court often will not take jurisdiction over the case.

Undercriminalization also creates a risk for victims. Victims of torture whose allegations are typically against police or security forces find that even if their report is taken seriously, it can only be prosecuted under the common crime of battery.[10] Throughout Central Asia, where torture-driven confessions define the criminal justice system, the penal codes largely do not include the crime of torture. In the rare case that there is even an attempt to address the violation, the only law available to the prosecutor is that of "harm to health."

The substance of criminalization is only part of the equation of whether a criminal justice system is fair. Equally important are issues related to process and practice. Let's start with policing practices. An individual is likely to get a summons for drinking alcohol from an open container in a poor neighborhood in New York but has nothing to fear for drinking wine in Central Park, which is bordered by some of the wealthiest neighborhoods in Manhattan. Young black men are often subjected to "stop and frisk" routines in New York City, a police practice of detaining, questioning, or searching individuals for contraband, and then charged for possession of minor amounts of marijuana. But smoking a joint in an upscale brownstone is practically a protected activity.

This is a form of profiling. There are two dimensions to profiling: whose behavior is scrutinized and what neighborhoods are policed for what crimes. Working as a lawyer in New York City, I learned that police assume that transgender women, especially trans women of color, are sex workers and that being recognizably transgender was sufficient for an arrest. These same police are not nearly as diligent in identifying high-price sex workers servicing high-profile clients in five-star hotels in the very same borough. Setting aside the obvious point of whether sex work should be criminalized, current police practice serves to reinforce the marginalized status of transgender women and protect, if not high-priced sex workers, then at least their powerful clients.

But it is not just police who profile and manipulate. Prosecutors in search of high conviction rates that serve their careers may profile both victims and defendants before deciding whether or how to proceed. Such actors may abuse their prosecutorial discretion and a wide range of expansive criminal laws. In the United States, prosecutors in pursuit of drug dealers sometimes employ the Racketeer Influenced and Corrupt Organizations Statute, which holds all defendants responsible for all the criminal acts of an organization, regardless of the individual's role or status in the supposed organization.

In one particularly well-known case in the United States on which I worked, Kemba Smith, an African American college student, was intimately involved with a drug dealer. The relationship quickly turned abusive, and Smith was unable to extricate herself. When her boyfriend was murdered, the prosecutor moved in to shut down the operation. Smith was arrested and charged with criminal conspiracy related to her abusive boyfriend's drug dealings, even though the prosecutor acknowledged that she had not used, handled, or sold any drugs. Smith, who had no record, was sentenced to twenty-four and a half years in prison.

Overcharging and punishing those who are more victimized than culpable is evidence of prosecutors abusing their discretion. And nowhere is this abuse and the racism in the U.S. criminal justice system more apparent than in the so-called war on drugs—a war initiated by President Richard Nixon in 1971 that has sent countless people to prison whose only crime was addiction or, as in Smith's case, getting involved with the wrong man. If you are poor or otherwise marginalized on account of your race, immigration status, sexual orientation, and so on and you use drugs, you will end up in prison. However, if you are white or otherwise privileged, with a few exceptions, you will end up in a rehab center. Given the centrality of drug laws as a means of social control, not unlike the U.S. government's prohibition on the production and sale of alcohol in the 1920s, the war on drugs has led to overcrowded prisons and a complete loss of faith in the fairness of the criminal justice system in the United States. Additionally, the focus on criminalizing people who use and abuse drugs has diverted resources from crimes in which someone is harmed. Human Rights Watch has done extensive research about the failure to process hundreds of rape evidence kits in numerous jurisdictions, not only in the United States but globally, meaning that people who committed acts of sexual violence and could possibly have been identified and prosecuted remain free and that their victims are denied justice.

Rights-based rhetoric regarding the rule of law in criminal justice systems emphasizes that rules of evidence and procedure should protect both defendants and witnesses. Nonetheless, there remain examples of rules of evidence that are clearly prejudicial to victims and witnesses or, conversely, that place an unfair burden on the defendant. In cases of sexual violence, rules of evidence such as those that allow defendants to bring up a victim's prior sexual history often discourage victims from even reporting the crime. Perhaps in response to concerns about the criminal justice system's failure to investigate crimes of sexual violence, there is a growing trend in the United States of defining people convicted of these crimes as monsters. Sex offender registries are now commonplace and sometimes lead to retaliation against people who have already served their sentences. These people live their lives in constant fear of being attacked under the belief that "once a rapist, always a rapist." This violates the very principles of legality, as does the indefinite administrative detention of people convicted of crimes of sexual violence (deemed sexual offenders or sexual predators) after they have served their sentences.

Many of the most invidious elements of the United States' criminal justice practices foreshadowed the systematic violations of international human rights law evident in the United States' Guantanamo Bay Detention Center. It is not a great leap to go from a three-strikes law (in which offenders convicted of two or more violent crimes or serious felonies are likely to receive life imprisonment, regardless of the severity of the crimes) to indefinite detention without a trial or conviction, which largely characterizes the experiences of those imprisoned at this infamous military prison. The treatment of people convicted of crimes of sexual violence, and the move from constitutional rights protection into the world of "predicting" future dangerousness, has powerful likenesses to a wide variety of practices used by colonial and dictatorial regimes (preventive detention, administrative detention), which function on the belief that the government can predict who will commit crimes.

Increasingly, we are seeing the use of secrecy laws, including the use of secret evidence, in a manner that effectively creates an undue burden on defendants. In cases involving whistle-blowers, national security is used to defend lack of transparency, even when the secrecy is related to hiding evidence of crimes and violations. This leaves whistle-blowers facing prosecutions for violating laws that are suspect (but this issue requires an article unto itself).

The concept of the "presumption of innocence" of defendants is not as widely contested, though it is routinely ignored and is another side of profiling. Attributing criminality to classes of people based on their age, race, ethnicity, or immigration status has devastating consequences for people in these communities and undermines justice. In countries where homosexuality is a crime, those who are so identified are treated as putative criminals. If the criminal law makes same-sex sexual conduct a crime, then for those who are perceived to have same-sex sexual relations, not only have they committed a crime, they are chronic offenders. The increasing criminalization of people based on their immigration status leads to the marginalization of people who may be constructed as "outsiders" within a country and to presumptions about their criminality.

A survey of who is disproportionately incarcerated in any country almost always reveals who is marginalized in that country. In Saudi Arabia, it is migrant workers. In India, it is Dalits and indigenous or tribal peoples who are on the lowest rung of a birth- and descent-based social hierarchy. In Australia, it is aboriginal people. In the United States, it is African Americans. In Europe, it is Roma. But understanding profiling is not as simple as tracking a society's hierarchy of power and privilege—it is about understanding how those individuals and communities whose experiences are least recognized are also those that live at the intersection of multiple forms of discrimination and exclusion. Commitment by states to the human rights principle that all people are born free and equal in dignity and rights should underpin any criminal justice system. Instead, we see those living at the intersection of multiple forms of discrimination also living in the crosshairs of the police.

My experience has taught me that there are two aspects of sentencing that are important to scrutinize: (1) inherently harsh or lenient sentences for crimes of comparable severity and (2) harsh or lenient sentences based on underlying bias, meaning that two defendants convicted of the same crime get widely divergent sentences.

An example of the former is the practice in many states of providing lenient sentences for torture. Police officers who abuse their power and intentionally harm detainees are often given token sentences. Under Chinese law, the punishment for torture to gain a confession is three years. In contrast, Australia has a law making it unlawful for more than three bikers to congregate, and those who break the law are subject to sentences ranging from fifteen to twenty-five years.

An example of the latter in the United States is the disparity in sentencing for possession of crack cocaine versus powder cocaine. Even though the drugs are virtually identical, there is a presumption that white people of privilege use powder cocaine, while poor people of color use crack—a cheap, rock version of cocaine. For more than two decades, possession of one gram of crack was charged as the equivalent of 100 grams of cocaine, leading to largely race-based disparate punishment. Race and class also appear to play a role in determining who is deemed eligible for alternatives to incarceration. In short, white people go to rehab; black people go to prison. The race of the victim plays a crucial role in determining whether someone convicted of murder will face the death penalty in the United States, sending the not too subtle message that the life of a white person is more precious than the life of a person of color. Punishment for crimes of sexual violence also seem to be driven more by the judge's or jury's perception of the victim's sexual purity—in my review of many national practices, actual doctrine and individual judgments made it clear that the sexual status of the victim mattered as much to the court as evidence of violence: raping a good girl (that is, a girl with sexual purity or high moral status) could get a defendant into trouble, whereas raping a woman deemed a whore might be ignored.[11]

It is critically important that the criminal justice system serve the needs of the people, not political parties, military powers, or economic interests. This means that actors within the criminal justice system must have the scope to act independently in the service of truth and justice. Corruption among police destroys any faith in the criminal justice system. Prosecutors who wield their discretion as a political ax also undermine the system. But judicial independence is the last check against abuses and is absolutely critical to the integrity of the criminal justice system. Independence is both about whether judges are subject to undue influence from political or military actors and also about whether they are beholden to other entrenched interests such as corporations or other powerful economic actors. In some countries, judges who maintain their independence may be subject to overt threats, impeachment, and violence.

A final question for judging a criminal justice system that I will consider here relates to the existence of a meaningful appeals process and review of lower court decisions. One principle is that the end of the justice process should create a sense of certainty and finality and should contribute to the system being seen as consistent, rather than error prone or arbitrary. This is at odds with the principle that justice is about seeking the truth and recognizing the harm of finding someone guilty of a crime he or she did not commit. Errors are inevitable, even in well-functioning systems. Our understanding of the reliability of evidence is constantly changing. Eyewitness testimony was once considered virtually definitive. Increasingly, there is a strong body of evidence that, in fact, eyewitness accounts may be deeply flawed.

Constantly improving standards for analyzing evidence and gaining a better understanding of the reliability of that evidence are slowly opening a window into understanding elements that contribute to wrongful convictions. Given the inevitability of error, the appeals process must be robust.

Moving from Denial to Action

For most human rights advocates, it is untenable to ignore the failures within the criminal justice system, and it is equally untenable to give up on the criminal justice system. While rampant abuses and overincarceration in the United States have spawned an abolitionist movement, human rights principles demand justice and accountability for actual harms.

I propose that there are four key demands that the human rights movement can make to begin to address the vexed relationship of the human rights movement with the state and its policing powers.

First, the human rights movement could campaign to strictly limit the scope of criminal law. It is widely accepted within the human rights movement that penal codes must, at a minimum, exclude crimes that are the exercise of rights, unless that exercise undermines the rights of another person. In short, I may take to the streets to protest the price of rice or wheat, but I may not steal my neighbor's rice or wheat.

In determining the limitations on the exercise of the right to freedom of expression, the right to freedom of association, and so forth, it is imperative that governments limit these restrictions to those cases in which there is a demonstrable harm rather than relying on vague and overbroad concepts like public morals. When the "public morals" exception was included in permissible limitations on some rights within human rights law, drafters may have believed that societies were safely homogenous (or that "morality" was an unassailable basis for state interference), but in today's diverse and globalized world, this concept seems an anachronism (see Erdman, Jernow, and Miller and Zivkovic in this volume).

A determining factor in what may legitimately constitute a crime would be to define what constitutes a real harm. Although a simple scan of the penal code using this principle would eliminate many crimes that offend but do not harm a person, the larger task of defining harm is not easy. While physical and economic harm may be easy to assess and define, there are other harms that are less tangible, such as psychological harm. Some of this can be mitigated through common sense. Anyone who has had a broken heart can attest to real pain but understands that turning to the criminal justice system to remedy the pain is ill advised. However, some of the hammering out of the definition of harm will require public debate and discussion informed in part by sociological studies. This process can only be legitimate if voices from all sectors of society are heard. Ideally, this would entail a *de novo* review of the penal code. The key point of such a campaign would be to ensure that penal codes are never used as tools to maintain the power of the privileged, but rather that they are used as tools for challenging those who abuse that privilege to exploit others and to cause harm.

This raises the question of how to address penal codes built around religious laws. In fact, many penal codes have their roots in some religious tradition. Principles within human rights, such as freedom of conscience, religion, and belief, might be explored to limit the reach of (elements in) such religiously derived codes, in addition to the harm principle.

Additionally, any review of the penal code should include a review of the rules of evidence and procedure, as well as of laws or guidelines on sentencing, so that those rules that reflect the biases and prejudices of the larger society can be identified and eliminated.

The second key demand that the human rights movement can make is that states provide for an independent, civilian oversight mechanism to scrutinize how the criminal law is enforced. The composition of such an oversight mechanism must reflect the diversity of the community and, in particular, ensure that those communities who are most scrutinized by the police have strongest representation. Civilian oversight should include access to records, subpoena powers, and the ability to hear complaints against the police. All arrests should be recorded and reported, indicating the basis for the arrest, the location of the alleged crime and the arrest, details of the defendant, and the resolution of the case. By aggregating and disaggregating this data, it should be possible to identify patterns of policing that may be discriminatory or abusive.

Third, while prosecutorial discretion is important because it allows compassion to overrule the demands for justice when exceptional circumstances are in play, it must be exercised transparently and in good faith. Identifying "good faith" is not simple, but collecting and analyzing data about which cases were taken and which were dropped or pleaded out should provide some evidence of how the discretion is being exercised. To that end, the office of the prosecutor should publish on an annual basis what cases reached the office; initial, interim, and final charges; the resolution of the case; and details of the sentencing, charge by charge.

Fourth, the prison system needs transparency. Only those people convicted of serious offenses and deemed a threat to others should be imprisoned. Furthermore, every effort should be made to find alternatives to incarceration that are not exploitive and that allow the person to remain engaged with his or her family and community through, for example, education and work. Every state should ensure that a key principle driving the administration of the prison system is rehabilitation. Every judge who has the power to sentence a person to prison or rule on a related case should be required to visit prisons regularly. Media freedom should include access to all forms of detention and prison facilities.

Conclusion

It is imperative that human rights activists not allow the serious flaws within the criminal justice system to pit one group of human rights activists against another. It is not simply that justice for victims and accountability for perpetrators is necessary to build a rights-respecting society; there is a deep thirst for justice that runs through every society. Rather than arguing internally, the human rights movement must acknowledge the immense challenges it faces and take seriously the need for change.

To advocate a rebuilding and reimagining of the criminal justice system, including the wholesale review of criminal codes, may seem naïve. Admittedly, defining harm—harm that demands the attention of the state—is not simple. However, until the human rights movement tackles the criminal justice system and the ways it protects the privileged and marginalizes and criminalizes people who are powerless or impoverished, the aspiration of all people being treated as free and equal in dignity and rights will remain beyond our grasp.

PART II

National Historical Perspectives

Virtuous Rights: On Prostitution Exceptionalism in South Korea

Sealing Cheng and Ae-Ryung Kim

This chapter addresses a paradox in the stream of legal changes regulating sexuality in South Korea (henceforth Korea) since the 1990s, locating such tensions within a particular formation of neoliberalism that we shall refer to as the "neoliberal sex hierarchy." Gayle Rubin, in her proposal of the idea of the sex hierarchy, said, "Sex is always political. But there are also historical periods in which sexuality is more sharply contested and more overtly politicized. In such periods, the domain of erotic life is, in effect, renegotiated."[1]

We propose that the expansion of the criminal apparatus around prostitution and trafficking in Korea constitutes part of one such renegotiation. Most relevant to our discussion here is how the new legal paradigm of liberalization in Korea since the 1990s, in particular recent reforms of the Korean Criminal Code, has made room for, first, the recognition of "women's right to sexual self-determination," as witnessed in laws on sexual violence and rape; and second, the decriminalization of most private sexual behavior between consenting adults, as in the repeal of laws on seduction and adultery. Yet this liberal understanding of sexual autonomy—promoted by some women's rights activists—is absent when it comes to sex work. In fact, the criminalization of prostitution and its related activities has increased in scope and intensity in the name of antitrafficking efforts and the protection of women's human rights. And a 2016 constitutional review of the antiprostitution laws reaffirmed that "the act of selling and buying sex could not be accepted or justified" and that the protection of moral values in this case justified the violation of individual rights.[2] Thus, despite the gender- and equality-encompassing claims of a vibrant new social movement, we believe that the definition of women by their sexual purity has been retained in the current "renegotiation" of sexuality.

A particularly poignant example of the clash between women's sexual agency and sexual victimhood arose in 2013, in the case of a forty-one-year-old woman (surnamed Kim) who was indicted under the 2004 antiprostitution laws for providing sexual activity in exchange for 130,000 won (approximately U.S.$120) in Seoul in 2012. She was arrested pursuant to two 2004 acts that criminalized the purchase and sale of sex, and any form of mediation thereof, and particularly singled out prostitution "trafficking." In her petition for judicial review, Kim claimed that the laws infringed on her "rights of self-determination and equal rights."[3] In accepting the petition for review, criminal law judge Oh Won-Chan said that "providing sex in exchange for money is still a private matter," and it is "impossible to know clearly the consensus on whether private sexual exchange causes grave harm to social norms." He went on to say that "sexual contact between adults, unless it involves coercion or extortion, should be left for the parties to decide in view of their *right to self-determination*. . . . The current law does not reflect a change in social views that the state should not interfere in such matters" (our emphasis).[4]

This statement, coupled with the agreement to review Kim's conviction, caused an outcry from the mainstream women's movement: protesters insisted that "sexual self-determination" did not apply to women in prostitution. Notably, many of those protesting were activists and scholars who had lobbied tirelessly for the recognition of women's right to sexual self-determination (*seong-jeok ja-gi-gyeol-jeong-gwon*) for over two decades.[5] Their movement's landmark success in 1994, in the form of the Special Act on Sexual Violence, launched the idea of "women's sexual self-determination" first and foremost as freedom from violence engendered by Korean patriarchy.[6] In the 1994 framework, prostitution was viewed as part of this patriarchal violence from which women needed protection. The 2013 decision, the movement claimed, threatened to legalize prostitution, thereby legitimizing the sexual exploitation of women and expanding the scale of the sex trade, flying in the face of the recent 2004 reforms.[7]

This tendency of women's rights activists to promote sexual self-determination while simultaneously policing its boundaries is the starting point of our analysis of gender and sexual purity politics in contemporary Korea. Key additional aspects include the movement's grappling with the legacy of Confucianism, colonialism, postdictatorship marketization and globalization of Korea, and the redefined Korean state. For many female activists and academics, women are not only victims of individual acts of violence but also victims of a patriarchal structure rooted in Confucianism. Ever since the political liberalization process that took place after the removal of military dictatorship in 1987, the women's movement has made concerted efforts to lobby for both criminal and civil legal reforms addressing sexual violence, domestic violence, sexual harassment, and the household registration system in order to challenge "Korea's strong patriarchal culture, which sees women/wives as the property of men/their husbands."[8] Sexual violence is a form of gender violence committed by men against women under this frame. The 2004 reforms of the laws governing the selling and buying of sex, the antiprostitution acts, in part a response to the global anti-trafficking drive that started in the new millennium, were seen as another milestone in Korean women's fight against Korean patriarchy (see Miller and Roseman with Rizvi, Halley and Ahmed, and Miller with Zivkovic, this volume).

This moment may be the mark of "governance feminism" in South Korea.[9] We see it also as the mark of the "sexual limits of neoliberalism."[10] The government in which women activists found partnership and that was receptive to arguments for women's human rights was also the government that was pushed into neoliberal reforms in the late 1990s. Both the Ministry of Gender Equality and the National Human Rights Commission were founded under President Kim Dae-jung (1998–2003). It was also in this period that structural readjustments were made as responses to the 1997 historic financial crisis. South Korea received the largest-ever bailout in the history of the International Monetary Fund—$55 billion. The restructuring increased the trend toward flexible employment relations and weakened labor rights and trade unions, forcing many into precarious lives of underemployment or unemployment.[11] Concomitant with the forces of privatization, deregulation, and "flexibilization," this period saw an increasing partnership between the state and civil society in the promotion of the ideals of self-managing, self-sufficient, and self-advancing subjects.[12] Thus, the new discourses of human development have focused on personal ability, responsibility, style, and consumption as indexes of success, all in line with neoliberal discourses. Social critics have noted that a newfound sense of personal freedom and responsibility has come to "obscure escalating structural inequality in South Korea."[13]

In this chapter, we look at how this discourse of *liberal selfhood* has come to inform the new sexual ideals manifest in criminal legal reforms in the last two decades, as well as in the work of the women's movement more generally. We believe this convergence of neoliberal thinking explains the simultaneous expansion and contraction of criminal law regulating sexuality across different sites of women's (presumably heterosexual) sexual activity.

With insights drawn from a wide variety of texts, we ask the following questions throughout this chapter: What kind of sexuality does the criminal code endorse, ignore, or penalize? What are the content, scope, and limits of the right of sexual self-determination? In what ways does this right conflict with the feminine ideal of chastity embedded in the legal term "women with no habitual debauchery"? Why, in particular, are the state and the women's movement so resistant to applying the notion of a right to sexual self-determination for women in sex work? In this work, we posit that a certain "modern but controlled" women's sexuality functions to maintain not only intimate but also social, political, and economic relations in neoliberalizing Korea.

"Women with No Habitual Debauchery": The Historic Gendering of Sexual Virtue and the Korean Criminal Code

Until the penal reforms of June 2013, female chastity (exemplified by the term "women with no habitual debauchery") had been an operative concept in the Korean Criminal Code. This persisted even with the emergence of the rhetoric of human rights and feminism as part of the twentieth-century modernization project.

The ideal of chastity as feminine virtue can be traced to the founding of Confucianism as the ruling political and social ideology during the Korean Choson dynasty (1392–1910 A.D.). The Chosun court adopted Confucianism to rebuild the law and order purportedly destroyed by Buddhism during the Koryo dynasty (918–1392 A.D.). Confucianism sharply separated the domestic, private sphere from the public and subordinated the female to the male. The ritual role of women was key to transmitting rights in the patrilineal descent group, and a law in 1413 clearly distinguished between the primary wife and other wives.[14] A chaste woman was a woman sexually accessible only to her husband for the proper continuation of the lineage system—the very cornerstone of social hierarchy. Chastity was therefore the most valuable virtue of women and was institutionalized in the *yollyo* (virtuous women) system that canonized women who defended their chastity with death, bringing honor to both their natal and conjugal families. These ideas have persisted in postwar Korea, such that the "idealized image of a good mother and virtuous wife was held up to be the highest goal to be aspired for by all women."[15] The pervasiveness of these feminine ideals has functioned to silence the experiences of women whose chastity was questionable—such as those who experienced sexual slavery under Japanese colonial rule but did not share their stories until the 1990s (also known as the comfort women),[16] as well as women in prostitution, who were legally classified as "fallen women" in the 1961 Act to Prevent Immoral Behavior.

Discursively, the ideal of chastity was expressed at one end by the term "women with no habitual debauchery" and at the other by the prostitute.[17] The crime of mediating debauchery (Article 242, chapter 22) addressed soliciting or forcing "chaste" (married or unmarried) women to sell sex. The legalized system of prostitution under colonial law made it necessary to distinguish between legal prostitutes and "women with no habitual debauchery": only the latter could be authentic victims of the "crime of mediating debauchery."[18] Although prostitution was made illegal following the end of Japanese colonialism in 1945, the term "women with no habitual debauchery" was retained in the Korean Criminal Code adopted in 1953. The Korean legal system thus continued to police the divide between the debauched and the virtuous within its prostitution laws.[19]

Even though Korean law had defined neither "habitual" nor "debauchery," legal scholar Yeong-geun Oh explains that the term was understood to circumscribe women's sexuality strictly within the marital context.[20] The criminal law thus helps buttress the institution of marriage—and therefore makes a full vehicle of heteronormativity and patriarchy in that a woman is licensed to have sex only with her spouse.

This discourse reinforces—and, we argue, still supports—a double standard: both men and women are subject to sexual legal prohibitions, yet only women are targets of "protection" and only a woman's history of debauchery is relevant. Park Jeong-Mi's study of the litigation process under the "crime of obtaining sex under false promises of marriage"[21] (also known as the Seduction Law) between 1953 and 1960 suggested that the term "women with no habitual debauchery" operated as the standard under which "women's sense of virtues" was judged.[22] Court records revealed that this "amounted to proving the victim's *virginity*, beyond [the] *habit* of lewd acts."[23] In the immediate aftermath of the Korean War (1950–53), seduction trials "functioned as the 'public sphere' to verify a sense of chastity of Korean women, to establish a new standard of it, and to socially punish the women who fell short of such a standard."[24] The focus on chastity in prosecuting the crime of seduction was therefore part of a project to rebuild the patriarchal gender order that had been destroyed by the war.[25]

As a legal concept, "women with no habitual debauchery" thus divided women into two groups: the virtuous, protected by the law, and the debauched, punished by it. The figure of the prostitute, in contrast to that of the *yollyo*, has come to embody the antithesis of feminine virtues. The postcolonial women's movement considered legalized prostitution a remnant of Japanese colonialism and therefore something that should be purged. As conservative women's groups dominated under Park Chung-hee's military dictatorship (1961–79), their hostility toward prostitution prevailed: prostitution was "an existence that destroys families and corrodes the foundation of nation-building" and "a blemish and a cancerous presence amongst women," and prostitutes were "hollow and vain women" who "shatter female chastity and ethics."[26] In other words, the movement for the abolition of prostitution, and the state regulation that it called for, took shape within the postcolonial context of eliminating Japanese influence and restoring Korean virtues and morality for nation building.

Therefore, "women with no habitual debauchery" must be read not as strictly legal but rather as indicative of a larger state project to discipline sexuality—and women's chastity in particular—in order to restore and maintain the social order in postcolonial and postwar Korea. Such a regulatory regime further served the needs of the developmental state under the military dictatorship of Park Chung-hee. The nation-building project that brought global economic success to Korea by the late 1980s deployed Confucian ideals of social hierarchy and gender distinctions to maintain a stable and subordinate population of citizen-workers. Notions of militarized masculinity mobilized Korean men as "industrial soldiers," and feminine ideals of the good mother and wife became key to keeping a docile and disposable female labor force.[27]

In this period, criminal law regulating both male and female sexuality buttressed the ideal of chastity and the patriarchal family order: only men who sexually violated "virtuous" women were punished, only women who were virtuous could command the law's protection, and all women straying outside their prescribed realm of virtues were punished.[28]

It was only in the 1990s that a more autonomous women's movement came to significantly influence criminal law reform, flipping the logic with the concept of a "right to sexual self-determination." Women activists called for criminal law reforms to protect women from sexual coercion and sexual violence, rather than debauchery: it is widely noted that "the anti-sexual violence movement in Korea can be claimed to be the kernel of the women's movement."[29]

Much as sexual violence became the rallying point for the formation of a transnational women's human rights movement,[30] in Korea, the fight against sexual violence also fostered the independence of the women's movement from its original home in the democracy movement.[31]

For women activists, reforming the criminal code—"a symbol of authoritarian rule in Korea"[32]—was key to bringing about a paradigm shift in Korean society after the success of the democratization struggle in 1987. As the military government had used criminal special acts for the oppression of dissidents, the National Assembly introduced various amendments to the criminal code to reduce security surveillance, protective detention, and other state violations of individual rights. However, the "moralist and male-centered biases" of the criminal code remained in the early democratizing moment.[33] Against this background, women's organizations took up legal advocacy in the early 1990s.

The turn to law was prompted by both the need to better protect women activists' own work and the desire to broaden the impact of women's advocacy on the state and society in general. The women's rights movement was prompted to lobby for legal reforms when a women's rights group became a target of criminal prosecution for human trafficking by a man whose wife was sheltered by the Women's Hotline.[34] Furthermore, during this time, the activists came to see the inadequate and unsatisfactory definition of crimes of sexual violence, punishment of offenders, and treatment of victims by the police and legal profession as central to the problem of male-oriented law.[35]

The 1994 Special Act on Sexual Violence marked the first significant legal success of the Korean women's movement. It not only put forward a new and broader definition of sexual violence but also further marked a major paradigm shift on women's sexuality, recognizing sexual violence as an infringement of women's right to sexual self-determination.[36] Worth noting is that the right of sexual self-determination is not in the criminal code. Activists and scholars, as well as judges, have often interpreted its basis as being in Article 10 of the Constitution, which assures citizens of human dignity and their right to pursue happiness, and in Article 17, which reads, "The privacy of no citizen shall be infringed."[37] We observe that women's rights advocates mobilized the "right to sexual self-determination" as a proscription against violence, rather than a broader reconceptualization of sexuality.

Feminist scholars have nonetheless expressed concerns about the limits of the right to sexual self-determination for women in general and for Korean women in particular. First, they raise concerns that "sexual self-determination [as a] right" is largely understood as a passive right from restraints and interference.[38] It arises as a claim only when it is violated, as opposed to being a right to be asserted—such as an active right to sell sex, perform an abortion, or enjoy sex.[39] Second, some argued that the language of "self-determination" has worked negatively for women in cases of sexual violence. Their autonomous will is sometimes equated with the assertion, "You should know (and do?) better," making women responsible for preventing and eliminating such violence.[40] Extending this logic to understand the heavier penalization of women who sell sex without coercion under the 2004 laws, we can also see how women, now more than ever, "should know better" than to sell sex.[41] Finally, Park Hye-jin shows convincingly in her study of court rulings that the concept of sexual self-determination poses a number of dilemmas in the interpretation of the criminal law.[42] Specifically, Park found a distinction between sexual violence crimes and sex crimes. Sexual violence crimes are crimes against individual legal good (*bop-ik*) and are therefore recognized as violations of sexual self-determination. Sex crimes, such as seduction, adultery, and prostitution, are crimes against sexual customs and are therefore violations of society's legal good.

This distinction raised a pertinent question in various attempts to review sex laws: Does the individual right of sexual self-determination outweigh society's need for morality and order? The scope of behaviors considered outside the protection of the right of sexual self-determination has been changing. The gender of the offender and the victim also has a significant bearing on the mapping of such rights. Therefore, even though the crime of sexual offense under false pretense of marriage and the adultery law were found unconstitutional in 2009 and 2014, respectively, prostitution has been reinscribed as the antithesis of women's right to sexual self-determination, as we show in the following discussion.

Sex in the Laws: Reforms toward Sexual Autonomy

Crimes of Rape and Sexual Abuse

The rape law underwent dramatic revisions between 1995 and 2013, shifting from valorizing a woman's chastity to recognizing a married woman's sexual autonomy. The debate over marital rape in particular marked both marriage and rape as key sites of struggle over the limits of women's right to sexual self-determination.

Before 1995, rape was prosecuted under Chapter 32 of the criminal code, "Crimes against Chastity." It was a crime that could only be committed against a "chaste" woman by a man who was not her husband. In 1995, Chapter 32 was renamed "Crimes of Rape and Sexual Abuse." A person who "through violence or intimidation has sexual intercourse with a female" was guilty of rape. Together with the 1994 Special Act on Sexual Violence, this change reconfigured women's sexuality, transforming it from a symbol of women's honor (chastity) to an aspect of her rights as a human being.

These legal changes may be celebrated as emancipatory but are in fact complex. Until the penal reforms of sexual violence crimes in June 2013, Korean jurisprudence and procedures on the (historically gender-specific) crime of rape offered limited protection (deemed "under-protection" by Kuk Cho) to women[43] but no protection to men or trans persons (trans*).[44] The (female) victim had to file a complaint—unlike other crimes, for which the legal process is initiated by prosecutors—in order for any prosecution of rape to be carried out; this was supposedly to protect the victim's privacy and honor, but it had the effect of deterring women from reporting rape.[45] The rape law recognized only penile-vaginal penetration, not other rape-like (*yusaganggan*) penetrative assaults such as penile-anal or object rapes. Men and transgender people also could only be victims of sexual assault, not rape. This rendered rape a gender-specific crime committed only against women by men, thereby equating ultimate sexual victimhood with femininity. Such laws and their practice thus constructed women as "suffering bodies in need of protection by the law and by the State."[46]

It was also in 2013 that the Supreme Court overturned the marital exemption to rape, which women activists and legal scholars had been lobbying for since the 1990s. The 2013 Supreme Court decision turned on a redefinition of the scope of the term *women*: the Court held that "the term 'women' [*bunyeo* in Korean] refers to all females, whether they are adults or minors, married or unmarried."[47] For the first time in Korean history, the sexual self-determination of wives was recognized. Its existence served to remove rape from the consideration of wifely chastity.

These changes have played a role in constructing the crucial case for the right of women to sexual self-determination and fundamentally challenging the notion of women as men's property. Yet they are by no means complete. A key example is that the requirement that a woman prove the defendant used "utmost force/threat" and that she exhibited "resistance to the utmost" for a criminal charge of rape has persisted, against demands by women activists and legal scholars. Not only does the need to demonstrate "utmost force" reproduce an ideal of female chastity reminiscent of the historical figure of the *yollyo*, who defended her chastity to the death, it also implies that the right to sexual self-determination for women (from sexual violence) needs to be earned with "utmost resistance."

The Seduction Law

The Seduction Law,[48] discussed earlier, policed the divide separating "virtuous" from "debauched" women by formally punishing men who violated chaste women with false pretenses of marriage, while also reaffirming the importance of "woman's sense of virtues."[49] Reform of the Seduction Law provided the public space for debating the need for regulating women's sexuality and for pushing back against state intervention into the lives of private citizens. The Constitutional Court's 2009 decision that the law was unconstitutional marked a formal—but incomplete—recognition of women's sexuality outside the patriarchal family.

The scope of the right to have one's sexual self-determination protected from state intervention was expanded in the 2009 constitutional review of the law. The review was initiated by the petitions of two men who had been convicted of the crime of sexual intercourse under pretense of marriage, and the majority opinion asserted the scope and importance of the right to sexual self-determination.[50]

Even though the petition was submitted by two men, the majority opinion found that the law was unconstitutional on principles of gender equality and privacy and highlighted the need to value "women's dignity and values." Public debates about the law also served as an important rallying point for those who wanted to bring women's sexuality within a human rights framework. Women activists argued that the law protected women's chastity rather than their human rights.[51] The Ministry of Gender Equality supported the law's rescission, stating that it "discriminates against women by emphasizing chastity," and it further claimed in its 2015 report to the Committee on the Elimination of Discrimination against Women that the law was abolished on the grounds that it "impairs women's sexual self-determination."[52]

Invoking discourses of equality and rights simultaneously with the more conventional language of women's dignity, this decision articulated some of the major tensions in Korean society over women's sexuality outside marriage. Previous decisions upholding the constitutionality of the law rested on the assumption that protection of women's chastity preserved society's moral values, but the 2009 decision anchored women's dignity (and social stability) in their right to sexual self-determination rather than in their chastity. This change pushed forward an idea introduced by the rape law reforms—that women's sexuality was not just about male honor but rather was integral to being autonomous and thus on par with men. The Constitutional Court decision also recognized that women are not necessarily victims in nonmarital sexual relationships, indicating women's sexual capacity outside marriage. Yet, as we shall examine later, this decision is far from holding that women have the right to engage in any consensual sexual relationship.

The Adultery Law

Article 241 of the criminal code criminalized sexual relations with anyone other than one's spouse, with a maximum prison sentence of two years. As such, the law enforces marital fidelity. Since 1990 there have been five constitutional challenges to the adultery law, all raising essentially the same question: whether the state should regulate sexual morality through criminal law.[53] In the past, women activists and supporters of the adultery law viewed this criminal sanction as preventing a husband's infidelity and thereby protecting the financial security of wives. But since the fourth judicial review of the law in 2008, involving a female celebrity indicted for having an extramarital affair, legal scholars and women's organizations increasingly have criticized the law for its suppression in the context of women's rising socioeconomic status, as well as their vulnerability to criminal charges.

Despite waning support, the Constitutional Court resisted attacking the adultery law on the basis that it protected marital relationships, even as it limited the right of individuals to privacy and sexual self-determination.[54] Curiously, however, in 2011 the Constitutional Court proposed "that lawmakers seriously consider whether or not to abolish Article 241 as a criminal offense in view of the legal codes in other countries and changes in Korea's attitudes toward sex."[55]

Therefore, the 2015 Constitutional Court's seven-to-two decision to condemn the law was significant in marking a shift in the Court's role in circumscribing the power of criminal law to regulate sexuality. The majority opinion stated, "It should be left to the free will and love of people to decide whether to maintain marriage, and the matter should not be externally forced through a criminal code." The dissenting opinion, in contrast, warned that abolishing the law could lead to "disorder in sexual morality," encourage extramarital affairs, and undermine family life. The decision marked a triumph of individual autonomy and gender equality, expressed through the language of love and free will, over normative notions of sexual morality.[56]

We see these criminal code reforms concerning marital rape, seduction, and adultery as reflecting three key currents in the reconfiguration of gender and sexuality in Korea. First, on the basis of gender equality, the law recognizes women as sexual subjects, deemed capable of giving or withholding consent to sex with men, regardless of the nature of the relationship. *Chastity* is no longer an operative term in the criminal code, and the phrase "women with no history of debauchery" disappeared with the penal reforms adopted in June 2013. Nonmarital sexuality no longer translates automatically into women's victimhood.

Second, on the basis of privacy, certain ideas have come to formally construct sex as a matter of free will and consent, leading to a growing rejection of state interference in private sexual life. There is a mounting challenge to the use of criminal law for the moral regulation of individual sexual behaviors. Constitutional reviews of the adultery law and the Seduction Law have overturned the constitutionality of these criminal statutes in the context of changing sexual mores and increasing demand for personal freedom and gender equality.

Third, the locus of control over sexuality has shifted from the institution of the patriarchal family to individuals. Men's sexual self-determination has been established, as premised on the personal right to pursue happiness and privacy (as in the 2009 decision that the Seduction Law was unconstitutional). Yet the right to sexual self-determination as a concept has remained primarily a negative right of women invoked against male violence. In other words, sexual self-determination remains marked as gender specific and tethered to women's protection from sexual violence and men's freedom to exercise their sexuality.

Love (mentioned in the 2015 adultery law decision) has entered legal discussions of sex, whereas *debauchery* and *chastity* are no longer legally operative terms.[57] While these changes resonate with "modern" notions of the state and privacy, we also see tensions. These developments echo with the neoliberal focus on the person as a self-generating agent of her own life—without regard for material conditions. Moreover, concern about the sanctity of marriage and family has persisted (contributing to the long-standing support for maintaining the penal adultery law). We see these tensions and ideas emerging in the support for and debate over the prostitution laws examined shortly; moreover, a strong resistance to sex outside marriage for women remains. The unprecedented compulsion to equate sex work with women's sexual victimhood, discussed next, though not without challenge, needs to be understood in relation to these limits and preconditions and to the newfound ideals of consent, privacy, and freedom.

Prostitution Laws: Antiprostitution Laws and Anti-trafficking Campaigns

The 2004 antiprostitution laws were enacted partly as the Korean response to the global anti-trafficking initiatives in the new millennium, with reference to a range of legal instruments such as the UN Protocol to Prevent, Suppress and Punish Trafficking in Persons, as well as the externally powerful U.S. Trafficking Victims Protection Act.[58] Shaped by the global anti-trafficking campaign and a domestic women's movement that took up the issue of prostitution in this context, South Korea adopted Act 7196 on the Punishment of Sexual Traffic and Associated Acts (or the Punishment Act) and Act 7212 on the Prevention of Sexual Traffic and Protection of Victims Thereof (or the Protection Act) in March 2004. The purpose of the Punishment Act is "to eliminate prostitution, procuring prostitution and associated acts, and human trafficking for the purpose of prostitution, and to protect the human rights of *victims of prostitution*" (our emphasis) (Act 7196, Art.1). The purpose of the Protection Act is to "prevent prostitution and to support the protection and *self-reliance* of victims of prostitution and those who sell sex" (our emphasis) (Act 7212, Art.1).

Scholars and legal professionals have long critiqued the conflation of prostitution with human trafficking in the Trafficking Victims Protection Act[59] and the "cooptation of trafficking as a tool for the criminalization of prostitution."[60] As Sealing Cheng found in her analysis of the 2004 laws in Korea, "International norms about trafficking in persons and women's human rights . . . become appropriated and translated into anti-prostitution policies in South Korea," facilitating "the re-articulation of what authentic Korean culture and society is, and what Korean womanhood should be."[61]

In our introduction, we noted the incongruities in the tendency of women's rights activists to promote sexual self-determination while simultaneously policing its boundaries; here we explore this curious contradiction, which we term *prostitution exceptionalism*. This stance undermines many of the apparent paradigm shifts visible in the new rape law and the affirmation of privacy and individual choice seen in the growing acceptance of sex outside the marital (conjugal) relationship, as well as in the aversion to state intervention manifest in the repeal of the Seduction Law and the adultery law. In prostitution exceptionalism, the moment a woman asserts her neoliberal (market-inflected) "self" and chooses to sell sex, her presumed (material and legal) poverty as a woman in sex work is advanced as sufficient grounds to distrust her self-determination.[62] The exceptionalism concerning sex work demonstrates that the women's movement's claim to promote women's sexual self-determination and fealty to neoliberalism goes only so far. A brief history of the evolution of Korean laws concerning prostitution and recent engagements with law reform in this area makes both prostitution exceptionalism and its links to the legacy of sexual purity more visible.

Sex work, as previously mentioned, has been regulated in the criminal code as an issue of sexual morals (beginning with the old Article 242, "crime of mediating debauchery"). Prostitution has been criminalized since the provisional government took over control from the Japanese colonialists in 1945. The interim government outlawed licensed prostitution with the 1948 Act on the Abolition of State-Sanctioned Prostitution Systems, also known as the Abolition Act. Selling sex was criminalized in the criminal code (adopted in 1953) and in subsequent special acts: the 1961 Act to Prevent Immoral Behavior and the 2004 Punishment Act and Protection Act. These laws reflected the prevailing conceptualization of women as either sexually pure or debauched. According to Chapter 22, "Crimes concerning Sexual Morals," Article 242, of the criminal code, "A person who, for the purpose of profit, induces a minor female or *a woman with no habitual debauchery*, to engage in sexual intercourse, shall be punished by imprisonment for not more than three years or by a fine not exceeding fifteen million won" (our emphasis).[63]

While this clause punished the crime of mediating debauchery with "women with no habitual debauchery" and minor females, the 1961 Act to Prevent Immoral Behavior also introduced the term *fallen women* (*yullak yeoseong*) to denote women who sold sex. Even as the 1961 act criminalized both men and women for sexual commerce, it was (the presumed) women who sold sex rather than (the presumed) men who bought sex who were the primary targets of arrests and punishment.[64]

The reformed 2004 antiprostitution laws, therefore, mark a significant paradigm shift, framing sex work as a problem of women's human rights rather than of sexual morals. For the first time in Korea's history, the laws asserted the state's responsibility to protect rights and introduced human rights language into the legal regulation of sex work. The laws no longer presumed women in prostitution to be "debauched," recognizing that they could be victims trafficked into prostitution. It thus empowers nongovernmental organizations (NGOs) and women to pursue cases of abuse through legal channels.[65] Since 2004 there has been an increase in the number of class-action suits, as well as individual lawsuits, brought against brothel owners for forced prostitution.[66] The Protection Act makes provisions for education to prevent prostitution in high schools and middle schools, as well as the establishment of assistance centers, counseling services, self-reliance programs, and welfare service provision for victims.[67]

The prostitution law reform (layered over preexisting ideas and criminal law) produced a hierarchy of deserving and undeserving women. "Victims of prostitution"—referring to anyone who has been forced, drugged, or trafficked into prostitution and any juveniles or seriously disabled people found in prostitution[68]—are entitled to state protection, with women's organizations acting as the main mediator between the state and the victims. Men and women suspected of the *uncoerced* selling or buying of sex, or of profiting from such transactions ("prostitutes," "brothel owners," or "pimps"), are liable to be prosecuted. In addition, the Punishment Act newly defines coercion, deception, and trafficking for the purpose of prostitution as punishable and dramatically increases the penalty with a minimum of three years' imprisonment. Even though the Protection Act states that its purpose is "to support the protection and self-reliance of victims of prostitution and those who sell sex," the distinction between victims and those who sell sex (uncoerced) is actually one between protection and punishment. While the range and duration of state assistance provided to "prostituted women" in "self-sufficiency" (*jawal*) programs are much lauded—though limited in effect—those who fail to prove their victimhood are now more heavily penalized (for example, the cap on the penalty for selling sex was raised from 100,000 won to 3 million won).[69]

"Prostituted women" and "prostitutes who are willing to quit prostitution" deserve protection, as do "women with no habitual debauchery."[70] Police, together with NGO workers, identify "authentic victims" of prostitution who can access state welfare provisions. The state and women's NGOs collaborate in restoring "prostituted women" as properly gendered citizens through rehabilitation programs. This echoes Jesook Song's 2006 analysis of the neoliberal welfare policy that identified the "deserving" homeless based on their employability and their desire to be "normal"—functionally narrowing the focus of these laws to male breadwinners.[71] The self-sufficiency programs aim at channeling women's labor out of sex work and into gender- and class-appropriate realms.

We find that the discourse of victimization in Korean antiprostitution policies in effect marks the sexual limits of productive citizenship, thereby reinscribing sexuality in the "private" realm and buttressing the moral hierarchy that marginalizes sex workers in the first place. Under these rational, universalist, and well-meaning initiatives, such as policies for homeless people and women's human rights, runs a moral undercurrent that shores up the legitimacy of the family, the market, and the state. Debates about how sex work should be regulated are entangled in the nationalist historiography of foreign intrusions. As Cho Youngsook, one of the key women leaders lobbying for the 2004 laws and subsequent director of the state-sponsored national organization to coordinate prostitution-related NGOs, suggested, prostitution is a product of Japanese colonialism (1910–1945), and then of US military occupation since 1945, subsequently proliferating with the globalization of western sexual mores and capitalism.[72]

In the fierce objection to judicial review of the antiprostitution laws in 2013, noted at the beginning of this chapter, we see how the unique impossibility of sexual self-determination for sex workers has become obvious to some women activists, scholars, and lawmakers. While women's right to sexual self-determination is seen to be *violated* in sexual violence or *exercised* in private, consensual sexual relations (as seen in the repealing of the Seduction Law), it is simply silenced when it comes to prostitution. Sexual self-determination for women in sex work is the only site where this self-determination is conditional on freedom from socioeconomic vulnerabilities: lawmaker Cho Bae-sook, one of the initiators of the 2004 antiprostitution laws, pointed out that most of the women engaged in prostitution are "living under exploitative conditions at the very bottom of the food chain."[73]

The National Alliance to Solve the Problem of Prostitution further argued that the 2013 request for judicial review "ignores the tremendous scale of exploitation in the sex industry, the human rights infringements against women, the social stigma that women who sell sexual services endure, and the reality of the low socioeconomic status of women with limited freedom to choose."[74] In April 2015, when the Constitutional Court held the hearing on the laws, Kim Hye-sook, a philosophy professor at Ewha Women's University, stated, "I would be willing to consider legalization of prostitution in a positive light if Korea was a more just and fair society. . . . Yet there is still a lot of discrimination (against women) at workplaces and the glass ceiling is still pervasive. We need to examine what pushes the women into prostitution first before considering giving them freedom to choose prostitution as their job."[75]

So until Korea becomes a utopia, free from gender discrimination, women would not be "given" the freedom to engage in sex work. The argument in short form is as follows: sex work is inherently and uniquely exploitative and enslaving for women; women enter sex work only because they have no choice due to their low socioeconomic status; and women's social and economic vulnerability translates *automatically* into sexual victimhood only in sex work and not in other forms of sexual relationships. While a few feminists have claimed that marriage and prostitution are both products of patriarchal subordination, mainstream understanding among women advocates and in Korean society is that marriage and prostitution are socially and morally distinct spheres. The distinction between commercial and noncommercial sex is one between slavery and freedom, premised on the assumption that money abrogates sexual self-determination in sex.

Sex Work and the Neoliberal State

Sex work, newly framed in the language of trafficking, is relocated as part of a *critique* of the neoliberal circuit of sexuality, the market, crimes, and nationalism.[76] In a dramatic retelling of the story of women in prostitution through the anti-trafficking discourse, women activists and the state echo each other in their attention to the victimhood of "prostituted women," but differ slightly in their focus.[77] While the state focuses on prostitution as a violation of women's human rights (by pimps, brothel owners, and clients), women's groups further argue that women are victims of their socioeconomic vulnerabilities. As such, the prostitute is transformed from the quintessential "debauched woman" to a "woman with no habitual debauchery" who ends up in prostitution not due to her own moral depravity but rather because she is a victim of socioeconomic circumstances. By this logic, she deserves to be rescued and restored through state-provided services and support to become a "self-sufficient" citizen again. However, such protection and support are only available to "authentic victims." Prostitution exceptionalism undergirds the movement's paradoxical need to both defend the market within Korea, as an engine of development, and condemn it as destructive to Korea in the context of the global market for women. This contestation produces the need for the "coerced" victim of trafficking—note here, however, that the rhetoric driving the women's movement is poverty, but the law recognizes only force. Moreover, the condition of (sexual) innocence for protection also means that sexual self-determination is circumscribed as a negative right at best, if not irrelevant, and is unable to be claimed if the motive to do so arises from the market rather than force.

We see the growth of three significant features of the neoliberal state in the 2004 antiprostitution law: the criminal control apparatus, the welfare-as-surveillance apparatus, and state incorporation of NGOs. The first produces an ever-increasing population of criminals, including sex workers, clients, and mediators of transactional sex. The second entangles women in "an increasingly value-laden welfare program" tied to the promotion of the nuclear family, gender order, and class structure.[78] And the final feature creates the fraught partnership between Korean women's organizations, the criminal law, and the Korean state.

The women's movement has been key to this growth, despite having had a hostile relationship with the state before the 1990s.[79] Starting with the 1994 Special Act on Sexual Violence, women advocates have framed sexual violence as gendered violence by men against women and have focused on the institutional and symbolic powers of criminal codes to transform patriarchal values in Korean society.[80] Yet these efforts, together with the expansion of the welfare-as-surveillance apparatus, have incorporated the women's movement into the state project and expanded the regulatory powers of the latter. This inscription of sexual violence as gender violence into the criminal code risks mobilizing the larger crime-control apparatus to perform expressive justice and to affirm the law's capacity to maintain order, as Kristin Bumiller also found in the United States.[81] Some women's groups in the anti–sexual violence movement, however, have come to realize the limits of legal reforms and to question the growth of the crime-control apparatus and of state control over the lives of women and children, as well as offenders.[82]

Thus, there is a notable structural aspect to the exceptionalism of sex work when it comes to women's right to sexual self-determination. As long as a woman stays out of sex work, she belongs to the generalized group of women who are adequately empowered socioeconomically to exercise their right to sexual self-determination in having marital, premarital, and maybe even extramarital sex. However, when a woman engages in commercial sexual exchange, structural inequalities and poverty suffered by women constitute the only valid lens to predetermine her lack of agency. Such structural coercion is presumed to be the only reason for women's engagement in sex work, and therefore sexual self-determination is irrelevant. A polarization of worlds is created: commercial sex has come to bear the burden of all that is wrong with gender inequalities, capitalism, and foreign intrusions, while noncommercial sex now bears the mark of freedom, independence, and self-determination. The sovereignty of the zone of privacy—as opposed to the public and commercial spheres—now serves as "a model for freedom or liberty."[83]

In Korean criminal law, sex for money has come to capture the legal imagination of what Gayle Rubin called "bad sex," regardless of consent.[84] Consent is impossible in prostitution because it involves sex for money, and a "debauched" woman's consent does not count. Rubin has pointed out that "within the law, consent is a privilege enjoyed only by those who engage in the highest-status sexual behavior. Those who enjoy low status sexual behavior do not have the legal right to engage in it."[85] In the neoliberal sex hierarchy, sex between consensual partners means sex free from monetary exchange, and it is therefore private and an expression of self-determination. Sex for money violates the ideal of free will and love, immediately qualifying it as a public issue because it is the epitome of unfreedom.[86]

This exceptionalism perhaps marks the limits of the 2013 penal reforms that removed all gender-specific terms in a range of sexually related crimes. The overhaul of the concept of gender-specific sexual victimhood is built on the two-decade-long struggle by the women's movement for the recognition of women as sexual subjects on par with men, as well as a liberalization of discussions about gender and sexual diversity. The reforms replaced the term *women* with *persons* in defining the victims of various sexual crimes, including the crime of rape

(Article 297), "human trafficking" (Article 289), and "sexual intercourse or in-decent act with minor" (Article 305).[87] These changes address a long-standing problem of the criminal code, its defining sexual violence as a crime against women, though in reality such violence has been perpetrated against people regardless of gender and sexual orientation.[88] In other words, men and transgender persons could also be recognized as victims of rape, as well as of a range of other sexual crimes. While social opinions about and the actual enforcement of these legal changes remain to be seen, these reforms testify to the way criminal laws can serve as a site for promoting the principles of gender equality and recognition of gender diversity. The celebration of liberal ideas of equality and inclusion in these reforms takes place alongside the increased criminalization of sex work as violent, immoral, and un-Korean.

Conclusion: Virtuous Rights

In the context of Korea's globalization processes (first initiated by the state in the 1990s) and the rise of the women's movement in the 1990s, a major shift in the organization of sexuality has taken place. The challenges to the criminal code in the past twenty years attest to a liberalization of sexuality. Both women and (some) men are now considered capable of exercising their rights to sexual self-determination. The Constitutional Court recognized "free will and love" as the basis of sexual relationships. These developments are cause for celebration for the women's and LGBT movements. Against this wave of apparent liberalization, however, is the increased criminalization of sex work as victimizing women (particularly through "sex trafficking" laws) in the 2004 antiprostitution laws, as well as the continued criminalization of abortion. We examined how these contradictions have come about and found that the sex law reforms since the 1990s embody many of the paradoxes found between sexuality, criminal law, and neoliberal governance, on the one hand, and the continual instrumentalization of women's sexuality, on the other.

Understanding criminal law as a site for the legitimization and contestation of a particular sexual order[89] and locating the law within a continuum of apparatuses for neoliberal governance,[90] we close this piece by asking, Is the apparent liberalization of sex laws in the name of human rights, equality, and privacy a neoliberal reconfiguration of governance and discipline?

We note that criminal law's regulation of female chastity has shifted to a policing of the "rigid moral boundaries between market and intimate domains" through a more elaborate apparatus of criminal justice, social welfare, and the media.[91] Through the global language of human trafficking and human rights, criminal law also introduced "prostituted women" (perhaps all women) as victims and therefore justified the expansion of state powers—especially the power over criminalization—as necessary and modern. We argued earlier that the legal category of "women with no habitual debauchery" and its reincarnation in the "prostituted woman" illuminate the operation of biopower as both governance and discipline. Both terms throw light on the operation of the law on the direction of lives rather than on isolated transgressive acts (despite the claim that the law regulates conduct). The failure to lead a chaste life labels a woman as "debauched," outside the norm of chastity, or as a "prostitute" who willingly debauches herself—in contradistinction to "the prostituted woman"—not only unfit to call on the protective power of the state but also subjected to its punitive powers. Whether as the protected or the penalized, one becomes a subject of and to state discipline.

Our examination demonstrates how the language of victimization in the women's movement has embedded women sex workers in a gendered nationalist discourse that inscribes women's sexuality in this circumstance as an object of protection, symbolic of the nation's honor. While women activists have claimed that sex work is a product of "violence," both sexual and structural, the only measures taken focus on the expansion of the criminal apparatus and rehabilitation of women into gender- and class-appropriate positions. Activists have narrowly contained the claims of rights and self-determination within their vision of ideal, middle-class heterosexuality, rather than recognizing the fundamental citizenship rights of Korean women by "removing the economic and social obstacles they regularly encounter."[92] Victimization circumscribes women's right to self-determination as a negative right emerging from violence, marginalizes women who engage in nonnormative forms of sexuality, and prevents an effective approach to the multiple systems of domination that have shaped women's experiences.

The set of legal changes discussed here is evidence that the role of criminal law has been shifting from safeguarding sexual morals to "being a catalyst for democracy."[93] The removal of the term "women with no habitual debauchery" from the Korean Criminal Code in 2013 is a logical development of democratization, but also of neoliberalization: the recognition of formal equality before the law, regardless of gender identity and sexual orientation, shores up the autonomous liberal self. The idea of the right to sexual self-determination that has become part of the legal language is intimately intertwined with the newfound sense of personal freedom.[94] Together, they operate as part of the neoliberal morality, encouraging citizens to assume responsibility for risks in their public and intimate lives and to know what they should strive for and how they should do so within state-prescribed parameters, as the state organizes its resource redistribution and retribution among its citizens according to "the direction of the lives of individuals, groups and the population as a whole."[95]

In spite of the apparent liberalization of sex laws in Korea, we agree with Victor Tadros that "liberation from the blunt technology of the juridical does not prevent the individual being subjected to the loving force of bio-power."[96] The "direction of lives"—with specific reference to sexuality—that neoliberal governance demands is premised on a "hostile worlds" view of sexuality and the market,[97] generating a neoliberal sex hierarchy[98] that delineates the divide between "legitimate" and "illegitimate" sexuality according to its perceived distance from commercial transactions. In a neoliberal economy in which every citizen is encouraged to be an entrepreneur of and for oneself (*homo economicus*), sex has been constructed as the last private domain for the realization of self and must steer clear of economic transactions. Sex work—the explicit exchange of sex for money—is seen as, at best, a "coerced" choice and, at its worst, a bad choice that needs to be punished, while other forms of labor and life trajectories such as marriage are imagined to be "free" choices. As such, sex work marks the sexual limits of neoliberalism.

CHAPTER 6

Brazilian Sex Laws: Continuities, Ruptures, and Paradoxes

Sonia Corrêa and Maria Lucia Karam

Brazil presents a compelling case to examine the trajectories of criminal laws in relation to sex over time. Sexuality is indelibly fused with the constructs and cultural imagination of Brazilian society.[1] From the 1980s on, under the spell of democratization, the country experienced intense struggles surrounding citizenship and human rights, including issues such as gender equality, abortion, LGBTQI rights, HIV/AIDS, and prostitution. After a new constitution was approved in 1988 that established the principles of equality, freedom, and nondiscrimination domestically, Brazil soon became known around the world as a "friendly country" for the sexual rights claims forwarded in the transnational circuits of sexual politics.[2] However, when more closely examined through the critical lens of its domestic criminal sex laws, Brazil's position as a sexual rights champion is more dubious and is fraught with contradictions.

This history of a more sexually repressive Brazil is reflected in the evolution of its criminal codes; reforms of Brazilian criminal laws were enacted precisely at defining moments in the reconfiguration of its state and social relations. Since its independence in 1822, Brazil has had three criminal codes that corresponded to major state reorganizations. The first was promulgated in 1830, seven years after the first Brazilian Constitution defined the system of government as a constitutional monarchy (the Brazilian Empire). A second code was approved in 1890, immediately after the transition from the monarchy to the republic (1889). The third complete revision of the criminal code took place fifty years later, in 1940, in an era of both political authoritarianism and crucial modernization known as the Estado Novo (the New State), following the 1930 Revolution.

Since then, there have been piecemeal reforms. In 1984 the chapters containing its general provisions (*Parte Geral*) were overhauled; the 1990s, and more substantially the 2000s, witnessed partial reforms to the chapters containing the definitions of crimes and penalties (*Parte Especial*), as well as reforms to other penal laws not included in the code. Some of these are significant because they have substantively altered criminal provisions specifically concerning sexuality.

This chapter traces the genealogy of sex crimes under Brazilian law in its relation to broader elements of the political economy. It offers descriptive snapshots of each moment of criminal law reform to identify ruptures and, above all, lines of continuity in terms of the criminal regulation of sexuality and the persistence of punitive legal ideologies in Brazil. It argues that despite constitutional reforms toward equality, normative assumptions around gender and sexuality reproduced inequality through criminal law. The final section examines the forces and processes still at play in the context of democratization that have helped maintain these ideational imaginaries that, in turn, fail to problematize the effects of criminalization.[3]

The 1830 and 1890 Penal Codes: The "Liberalism" of Slave Owners and Positivist Republicanism

The 1830 and 1890 penal codes reflect the contradictions at work in Brazil's achievement of independence. Unlike in other Latin American nations, Brazilian independence was not the outcome of hard-fought anticolonial struggles; instead, it resulted from an economic pact between elites and the Portuguese royal family. Thus, from the beginning, basic inequality was entrenched in Brazil's foundation. In 1822, of Brazil's 3.6 million inhabitants, 1.9 million were slaves. This number doubled by 1850, a time when slavery had already been abolished in most of the Americas (except the United States). Slave labor sustained plantations and gold mining, as well as the livelihoods of many working-class urban dwellers.[4] In this predominantly agrarian and slave-based economy, patriarchal norms predominated and governed a mostly illiterate population. Even the nonslave population, including the elites, had very low levels of education.

In contrast to these underlying and sharp social inequalities, the legal architecture of the empire took its inspiration from the liberal and egalitarian ideals of the Enlightenment. The 1824 Constitution, combining principles of the French and Spanish Constitutions of 1791 and 1812, respectively, promoted the principle of jus soli (citizenship birthright by place), thereby eliminating the colonial notion of a rigid social hierarchy on the basis of "blood," which drew distinctions between those whose blood was racially "pure" and those whose blood was "contaminated" or "defective." Electoral rules enfranchised all men twenty-five years and older whose annual income was at least 100,000 reis (the Brazilian national currency). Slavery was nonetheless preserved in the name of property rights, and women and slaves were excluded from voting.[5]

While abolishing the death penalty for ordinary crimes, the 1824 Constitution upheld its use for crimes of aggravated homicide, robbery, and slave uprisings. It abolished colonial-era punishments (at least for free citizens), delineating the principles that guided the drafting of the 1830 Penal Code. Inspired by European political liberalism, the 1830 code sought to precisely define crimes and proclaimed the equality of all before the criminal law and the individuality of punishment and sentencing. The writ of habeas corpus was also explicitly introduced in the 1832 Code of Criminal Procedure. At the same time, a host of specific crimes and penalties were directed at slaves alone—notably, punishment by flogging and death for the leaders of slave insurrections.

With regard to sexuality, the most salient legacy of the liberal spirit of 1830 was the omission from the Brazilian Penal Code of the crime of sodomy, making Brazil the fifth country in the world—and the first south of the equator—to decriminalize so-called crimes against nature.[6] As in France, this modernizing approach nevertheless coexisted with blatant gender biases. For example, the penal code's chapter titled "Crimes against the Safety of Honor" (Dos crimes contra a segurança da honra), which included rape and other crimes, recognized only women—and in some cases only some women—as potential "victims." Section I of this chapter defined rape (estupro) as forced vaginal intercourse, establishing different penalties accordingly to whether the "victim" was an "honest woman" (mulher honesta) or a "whore" (prostituta). The same section differentiated modalities of rape: vaginal intercourse with a virgin (defloramento); seduction (sedução); and indecent assault (atentado violento ao pudor). Violent abduction (rapto violento) and consensual abduction (rapto consensual) were defined in Section II of the same chapter. Vaginal intercourse with a virgin, seduction, and consensual abduction were defined as offenses only against women younger than seventeen years of age, thereby establishing the first so-called age of sexual consent in Brazilian penal law. Except for the crime of indecent assault (atentado violento ao pudor), which did not imply vaginal intercourse, for all other crimes defined in this chapter, the law established an accessory penalty to be added to the main penalties of imprisonment or exile. The accessory penalty consisted of providing a dowry to the "victim" if she was a virgin or "modest" (*honesta*). However, no punishment at all would be imposed if the perpetrator married the "victim."

The conservative assumptions regarding gender and sexuality are reflected in the next chapter of the penal code, "Crimes against the Safety of the Civil and Domestic State" (Dos crimes contra a segurança do estado civil e doméstico). It defined the crime of adultery (*adultério*). In cases involving married women, penalties were one to three years' imprisonment with forced labor for both parties, regardless of whether the man was married. Except for this case, married men could commit adultery only when they maintained a mistress. Polygamy (*poligamia*) was also criminalized for both women and men. Abortion was considered in the chapter "Crimes against the Security of the Person and Life" (Dos crimes contra a segurança da pessoa e da vida). Abortion, with or without the consent of the pregnant woman, was criminalized, as was the provision of drugs or other means to induce it. Yet self-induction of abortion was not criminalized. Completing the compendium of sex crimes was Part IV of the penal code, titled "Crimes of Police" (Dos crimes policiaes),[7] which punished the display or distribution of written papers or images offensive to "morality and good customs," as well as any action performed in public spaces that could clearly offend "morality and good customs." These vaguely defined infractions, as well as the infractions of vagrancy and panhandling, also included in Part IV, were often employed indirectly as a means to curtail and punish sexual behaviors considered deviant, such as prostitution and same-sex relations, even though sodomy was not a crime.[8] Thus, the 1830 Penal Code inched toward establishing the notion of equal protection under the law while retaining certain patriarchal inequalities in defining crimes and punishments. This code, and those that would be issued in the future, preserved gender hierarchies and masculine and race privileges in the face of democratizing pressures.

The 1830 Penal Code was reformed in 1890, right after the Proclamation of the Republic (1889), which immediately followed the abolition of slavery in 1888.[9] The new 1891 regime under the Republican Constitution included additional guarantees of individual rights. However, it continued to exclude the illiterate and women from the franchise, although it did extend it to (male) beggars, soldiers, and members of religious orders. The First Republic also had scant concern for social rights. Various specters haunted the republican elites, "from the fear of blacks that after the abolition came to mean fear of the people, to gender and sexual anxieties that threatened the project of a nation that was being built on the basis of an idealized image of Europe . . . based on a paradigm of whitening and reproductive compulsory heterosexuality."[10]

The 1890 Penal Code, approved a year before the 1891 Constitution, reflected these ideological anxieties. The new code, as well as the laws on penal procedures, preserved core liberal premises of 1830. In a few cases, it even extended them, such as when it increased the margins of defense for those accused of common crimes and restricted some forms of detention. However, in line with novel theories of "social order," the 1890 code multiplied the number of misdemeanors (listed in the preceding code under the already mentioned title "Crimes of Police"). Besides begging, vagrancy, and drunkenness, the list of misdemeanors included the practice of capoeira (the martial art developed by Brazilian slaves), openly reflecting the elite's panic with respect to the potential violence of Afro-Brazilians after abolition.

The specific definitions of the 1890 Penal Code in relation to sexuality remained partly unchanged; however, in some cases, subtle alterations were made that pointed toward new parameters of sexual disciplining. For example, the title that included most sex crimes was altered to "Crimes against the Security of the Honor and Dignity of Families and the Public Outcry for Decency" (*Dos crimes contra a segurança da honra e honestidade das famílias e do ultraje público ao pudor*), a semantic change indicating that both the family and public spaces would become more strictly subject to criminal law—the guarantor of moral order, honesty, and good behavior.

With regard to adultery, the different treatment of female and male adulterous spouses was maintained; moreover, charges against the sexual partner of an adulterous woman could only be based on material evidence—that is to say, his in flagrante delicto arrest or a self-incriminating document. More significantly, the new code made voluntarily induced abortions performed by women on themselves a crime, with the same penalty as that of consensual abortion performed by others (imprisonment for one to five years). The law allowed for a reduced penalty if the pregnant woman committed the crime to hide her own "dishonor," an exception that was clearly aimed at protecting the "honor" of fathers, brothers, and husbands, rather than women's dignity.

The new logic of sexual disciplining can also be seen in the definitions of crimes of sexual violence. The crime of indecent assault—defined as "harming the modesty of either sex, by means of violence for the purposes of satisfying lustful passions or moral depravity" (*atentar contra o pudor de pessoa de um, ou de outro sexo, por meio de violência ou ameaças, com o fim de saciar paixões lascivas ou por depravação moral*)—inaugurated the victimization of persons of both sexes under the criminal law. This intriguing shift toward the inclusion of men in the category of potential victims appears to have been motivated by a transformation in thinking about homosexuality. By the end of the nineteenth century, the conception of homosexuality as a perversion or deviation became widely diffused by European thinkers in the realms of public health and criminology. Brazil's physicians were quite receptive to this thinking.[11] In contrast to indecent assault, rape continued to be defined as a crime that could only be perpetrated against women. Yet the crucial distinction between a virgin and a nonvirgin but "modest woman" was introduced, while the distinctions in all cases between these women and prostitutes was maintained. In relation to rape, defloration, indecent assault, and abduction, a number of aggravating circumstances implied increased punishment, as was the case when the perpetrator was a minister of any religious faith. This novelty reveals much about the mind-set of lawmakers in the First Republic, where strong anticlerical feelings intersected with unshaken patriarchal views.

While during the empire period (1822–89) concerns about premature sexuality mainly focused on women under seventeen years of age, the first republican Penal Code (1890) introduced a novel type of crime: the corruption of minors (corrupção de menores) (of both sexes) through "acts of lewdness . . . with or against these [persons]." It also redefined the victims of the crimes of seduction and consensual abduction to be women under the age of twenty-one. In addition to defining a new age of sexual consent, the new code also established the concept of "presumption of violence" whenever the victim (man or woman) was under sixteen years old. By adopting a presumption of violence, the code established that a minor was presumed to be incapable of consent, thus transforming sexual acts with minors into rape or other violent sex crimes.

Prostitution, tolerated in the 1830 code although morally condemned, was now considered part of the pantheon of modern social evils to be addressed and prevented by the state. Consequently, the 1890 Penal Code included a full chapter on "pimping" (do lenocínio). The legislators did not go so far as to criminalize soliciting, but they delineated the harm as "the facilitation of or induction into prostitution"; the "exploitation of misery to lead women to sex work"; and later (in an amendment made in 1915) the "provision of assistance and lodging for sexual services to take place." These definitions were broad and vague enough to allow for constant police harassment of prostitutes and brothels.[12] In addition, the 1890 code changed the 1830 definitions on "moral and good customs" (moral e bons costumes) and created the new crime of "public outrage on decency" (ultraje público ao pudor), which also permitted arbitrary police investigation and prosecution of certain behaviors, including soliciting and feminine behavior by men, even though this conduct was not explicitly criminal.

As various authors observe, the 1890 code was just the beginning of regulating conduct that the republican elites considered repugnant or that challenged its perceived privileges.[13] For instance, the 1892 Decree Number 1034-A, which specified rules on the organization of the Federal District Police, gave the police a very broad mandate to maintain urban order. Article 22, paragraph 21, of the decree stipulated that close surveillance should be performed over "women of bad behavior,"[14] who offended "public morals and good customs." These rules of police procedure created more opportunities to treat the unequal more unequally, especially with regard to sexual behavior. Similar ordinances were adopted in other cities.

The First Republic's ideology, moral stances, social anxieties, conceptions, and practices of criminal justice—as reflected in the gendered, sexualized, and class-based criminal code—would cast a long shadow over Brazilian twentieth-century social and political history, even as the country experienced fundamental transformations in the course of the 1920s and 1930s.

The 1940 Penal Code: Conservative Modernization

The First Republic reached its end with the so-called 1930 Revolution, led by Getulio Vargas. Although Brazil as it was in 1930 is not comparable to France in 1789, Mexico in 1910, or Russia in 1917, the political movement that would leave behind the First Republic involved sectors of the elite, the middle class, and the Catholic Church, as well as wide participation of the popular classes. The revolution was preceded by a series of urban strikes in the 1910s, the creation of the Communist Party in 1922, and the long-standing rebellion of young social military reformers—a movement known as Tenentismo—who opposed the agrarian oligarchies that controlled the Old Republic with their vices of corruption, cronyism, and electoral manipulation. During those years, various reformist initiatives arose in education and public health. Fascism also emerged, as illustrated by the Brazilian Integralist Action (Ação Integralista Brasileira). The 1930s' upheaval was part of the worldwide reaction to the 1929 financial crisis, which took its toll on the Brazilian economy and its exports.[15] The post-1937 authoritarian period known as Estado Novo, on which the upheaval of the 1930s had extended influence, was the most widely scrutinized moment of Brazilian history in the twentieth century.

Vargas led the disparate forces, gathering them together as the National Liberation Alliance. They did not necessarily share the same ideological projects, but they were united in their common disgust with the oligarchic federalism of the First Republic. Most of them called for strengthening centralized state powers. Under these forces, between 1930 and 1934, the new government established the eight-hour workday for commercial and industrial laborers and regulated women's labor—setting equal pay for men and women—as well as the work of minors. The 1932 electoral reform secured women's suffrage and the anonymous ballot for persons older than eighteen, while preserving the old voting restrictions for the illiterate.

Yet there were marked differences between the interests at work in the revolution. If the Communists were guided by class contradictions and struggles, other reformers were influenced by Auguste Comte's theory of positivism or by the Catholic Church's vision on harmonious relations between capital and labor. At the same time, fascist groups, which were part of the National Alliance, made totalitarian appeals. There were fierce disputes between the old agrarian elite and the emerging industrial bourgeoisie, and many regional tensions erupted.[16] Despite this tense atmosphere, the 1934 Constitution reaffirmed labor rights and women's suffrage, created the Electoral Justice and Labor Justice systems, and nationalized a number of economic sectors. But this constitution was also heavily criticized by the conservative sectors for not establishing strong institutions to contain political insurgencies.

Regardless, a 1935 Communist military uprising was brutally suppressed, and in 1937 Vargas closed Congress and decreed a new constitution by presidential fiat.[17] Elections were suspended, censorship was imposed, and political power was completely centralized until 1945, when Vargas was pushed out of power.[18] The period of 1930–45 came to be known for its sharply etched illustration of "conservative modernization."[19] The modernizing legacy of the Vargas era was, nonetheless, unequivocal. It encompassed the definitive industrialization of Brazil and the related rural-urban migration, as well as the proletarianization of workers and the expansion of the urban middle class. Economic, educational, and health infrastructures were established; the state apparatus was rationalized; and, most importantly, a solid labor rights and social protection legal frame was approved and has mostly endured.

That said, after 1937, the political vision that had originally coalesced around the new industrial bourgeoisie and the state's social progressive sectors gradually shifted back toward controlling agrarian elites and other conservative sectors. In the words of Sandra Carvalho, "[This was] a revolution that started liberal and anti-oligarchic and that modernized the economy and social rights, but under the effect of tensions between ideologies and interests it became an authoritarian regime. . . . A modernizing authoritarianism."[20] Consequently, the concepts and norms related to sexuality and gender adopted and propagated between 1930 and 1945 also became marked by sharp dissonance between modernizing ideas and practices, on the one hand, and the disciplinary appeals of the positivists, hygienists, and criminologists whose influence on political elites persisted, on the other.

There also remained the persistence of Catholic doctrine. Vargas, though strongly attached to secularism and *laicité*,[21] relied on political relations with the church to mediate social and political tensions. In 1931 the new government, in partnership with the Catholic hierarchy, unveiled the famous statue of Christ in Rio and promoted the enthronement of Our Lady of Aparecida, the Black Virgin, as the patroness of Brazil. The 1934 charter included various amendments proposed by political forces linked to the church, such as the inclusion of religious education in the public education system. Having been sidelined by the voices of secular positivism in the late nineteenth century, the church was once again positioned to influence the state, and even after 1937, relations remained cordial.[22]

In terms of gender-related laws and policies, the right to vote and the regulation of women's work meant the recognition of women as citizens and contributors to the economic modernization of the country. On the other hand, the requirements of a massive labor force to power industrialization mobilized pronatalist and maternalist ideologies that envisioned women as the wives and mothers of healthy workers.[23] With respect to sexuality, the contradictions in the 1940 Penal Code are also glaring expressions of the Vargas-era combination of "modernizing" drives and regressive features.

For example, the 1940 code encompassed positive changes, such as eliminating the accessory penalty of paying a dowry in cases involving the rape of a "modest woman," as well as the double standard between adulterous spouses. With regard to "sexual consent," the age at which sexual contact carried a "presumption of violence" was reduced to fourteen. This change was justified in the code's explanatory memorandum in terms that, even today, may sound rather liberal to many: "In the present time it would be abstractly hypocritical to deny the reality that a person who is fourteen (14) already has the theoretical notion, quite accurately, of the secrets of life and of the risks she undertakes by submitting to the lust of others." Those deemed to be mentally disabled, however, were still presumed to be unable to consent to sexual activity, no matter their age. The code also retained the crime of seduction when the victim was "a virgin woman, younger than 18 and older than 14," with whom the perpetrator had carnal intercourse, taking advantage of her "inexperience or justifiable trust." Moreover, it expanded the crime of corruption of minors to include inducing a person under eighteen and over fourteen to perform or witness a lewd act. Other crimes related to sexuality also incurred increased punishment when they involved the same age group (older than fourteen but under eighteen).

The logic of state paternalism and the sexual morality of the 1890 Penal Code were preserved in several other respects. The title "Crimes against the Security of the Honor and Dignity of Families and the Public Outcry for Decency" was replaced by the more generic "Crimes against Morals" (*Dos crimes contra os costumes*). Reaffirming that virginity and the sexual "untouchability" of women until marriage were the essential elements that made seduction and consensual abduction criminal acts; the 1940 code also created the crimes of sexual possession and indecent exposure by fraud (*posse sexual* and *atentado ao pudor mediante fraude*), once again emphasizing the victimization of "modest women." This iteration of the criminal code eliminated the distinction between the "modest woman" and the "public woman," or prostitute, for cases of rape. However, the code kept the differentiation between rape—still understood as forcing vaginal intercourse, or "carnal intercourse" (*conjunção carnal*), with a woman—and indecent assault, which encompassed other forms of coerced sexual intercourse through which both men and women could be victimized. In contrast to the 1890 code, which established a single punishment for both types of crimes (imprisonment of one to six years), the new law raised the penalties: three to eight years' imprisonment for rape and two to seven years for indecent assault, a differentiation that is to be explained by the ideological value given to the reproductive potential of penile-vaginal sexual acts, or "carnal intercourse."[24]

With respect to prostitution, the 1940 code changed various articles of the chapter on pimping ("*Do lenocínio e do tráfico de mulheres*"). Once again, persons who provided sexual services were not criminalized, but new crimes were created, and 1890 definitions were expanded so as to capture other conduct revolving around prostitution. For example, Article 231 was added to cover the crime of international trafficking of women for sexual exploitation. These changes mirrored the international agreements of the first half of the twentieth century, especially the definitions of the League of Nations' 1921 Convention for the Suppression of the Traffic in Women and Children and 1933 Convention for the Suppression of the Traffic in Women of Full Age, even though the ratification of the latter was compromised by the demise of the league.[25]

With regard to abortion, the 1940 code specifies one to four years of imprisonment for voluntarily induced abortions. Consent to these abortions is vitiated if the woman is fourteen years old or younger or mentally disabled, or if consent "is obtained by fraud, violence or serious threat," in which case the abortion is punishable by imprisonment of three to ten years for the perpetrator. Once again, a pregnant woman inducing her own abortion is subject to imprisonment for one to three years. The protection of her honor, however, was eliminated as a mitigating factor. On the other hand, the 1940 Penal Code established two exceptions to criminalization: (1) when abortion is the only way to save the life of the woman, and (2) when the pregnancy was due to rape and the woman or her legal representative (in case of her incapacity) agrees to have the abortion. The 1941 Law on Misdemeanors categorized advertising processes, substances, or objects intended to cause abortion as a misdemeanor. The original version of the law also included the advertisement of contraceptive methods.[26]

Most of the crimes related to sexuality remained on the books until the 1990s, when a series of partial reforms eliminated some, conceptually reframed others, and added new ones. Even so, a number of articles of the 1940 code have not been repealed, such as the articles that criminalize abortion.

The Dictatorship (1964–1985) and the Transition to Democracy

From 1964 to 1985, Brazil endured a dictatorial military regime and yet another cycle of "conservative modernization." The regime, politically supported by the elites and sectors of the middle class, implemented technocratically framed policies to enhance the industrialization of the country through heavy investment in infrastructure and technology in various areas, including telecommunications.[27] The regime's economic policy—while very successful in terms of growth and popularly referred to as the "Brazilian miracle"—also accentuated inequalities that only began to see reductions in the 2000s. Most importantly, the dictatorship resulted in the 1980s external debt crisis, which carried long-term negative economic consequences.[28] The dictatorship brutally repressed dissent, curtailed all forms of organization, and imposed strict censorship. Its leaders deployed systematic discourse on the internal enemies: the Communists, the guerilla groups, and the "anti-Brazilian voices," which sometimes included those deemed "morally vicious."[29]

The transition to democracy that began in the mid-1970s was slow and protracted. It was completed in 1989 with the first direct presidential election.[30] Democratization fully restored the rule of law, but it was achieved through a contradictory and complex pact of governability, reflecting the structural inequalities and paradoxes of the Brazilian national formation. The resistance against the dictatorship, which accelerated and intensified after the 1979 political amnesty, was broad based and heterogeneous in composition. It involved a wide cross section of society: urban and rural workers, the middle class, grassroots groups (many of which were mobilized by Catholic liberation theology), indigenous peoples, Afro-Brazilians, feminists, LGBTs, HIV activists, and organized sex workers.[31] Lawyers and jurists played a key role in these political processes. The fierce contestations of the "state of exception," or government outside regular legal principles, which had prevailed under the dictatorship, inspired many legal actors to develop a substantive critique of the criminal justice system and the state's power to punish.

Democratization enlarged, deepened, and diversified the aspirations of citizenship and rights claims. After the 1980s, citizenship claims were no longer confined to the upper and middle classes, which had always participated in state affairs, or contracted workers, whose rights had been recognized by the state during 1930–45. The vocabulary of citizenship rights was absorbed—and struggled for—by a wide range of "unexpected" individuals, groups, and movements that articulated new constitutional foundations.[32] As in other Latin American countries, both state institutions and organized civil society groups adopted human rights as their lingua franca and insisted that the "right to have rights" transcended the limits of national sovereignty.[33]

Brazilian Sexual Regulation and Rights in the Age of Global Neoliberalism: The Role of Criminal Law as the Vindicator of Human Rights

Although equality and freedom have grown in both the political imaginary and juridical norms, Brazil remains one of the most unequal countries in the world. A long-standing legacy of social authoritarianism continues to feed the conceptions, habitus, and practices of stratified citizenship.[34] If democracy was established in institutional terms by the 1988 Constitution, an abyssal gap remains between the institutional formality of law and lived access to rights. Furthermore, Brazilian democratization coincided with and was impacted by global forces and processes, including those concerning concepts and applications of criminal justice, the effects of which cannot be circumvented even today, as can be seen in matters of sexuality.

Over the last thirty years, Brazil has been swept by the forces of neoliberalism—that is to say, a set of practices and ideas tied to the contraction, if not crisis, of the welfare state in Europe and the United States. Simultaneously, this transformation has brought intensified ideologies that favor expanding the state's punitive power. These ideologies mobilized new social perceptions of risk and vulnerability, as well as bringing calls for increased security measures: a "securitization," or police state, whose central premises are anchored in the logic of "law and order."[35] Therefore, the concurrent collapse of socialism did not engender a critical review and repudiation of the totalitarian perversions of these regimes. Rather, the collapse of the state in the era of neoliberal ideologies allowed default doctrines of securitization and principles of risk management to be applied to many other dimensions of life: human security, food safety, and even HIV/AIDS.[36] The global war on terror waged from 2001 onward would further expand and legitimize states' justifications for surveillance, control, and punishment, to the detriment of constitutional and human rights.

Against this backdrop, it is productive to bear in mind the analyses developed in other chapters in this volume (for example, Brown, Halley and Ahmed, and Restrepo Saldarriaga)—all of which examine the double bind of the criminal justice system as both a source of human rights violations and their supposed antidote. This double bind is particularly evident in claims to women's rights and gender equality, children's rights, racial equality, and other forms of non-discrimination, as well as sex-related claims generally. These claims have pushed human rights to consider the state's responsibility to provide effective remedies, including with regard to private actors who commit acts of violence such as sexual violence. These calls to redress sexual, gendered, and racial harm more often than not have fueled the expansion of states' punitive capacities and tutelary and arbitrary power, though perhaps not intentionally.

The web of current and historical forces and ideologies around the state and risk, as well as equality and security, intersected with the shifting and complex internal social and political dynamics at work in Brazilian democratization. For example, in the course of the last thirty years, levels of urban criminality and violence have skyrocketed, mostly related to the effects of prohibition and its "war on drugs": between 1980 and 2012, the annual number of homicides in the country increased from 13,910 to 56,337, while the homicide rate rose from 11.7 to 29.0 per 100,000 inhabitants.[37] A large number of these homicides were related to the violence generated by the illegality of the drug trade.[38]

At the same time, there has been a proliferation of new forms of social conservatism, principally as manifested by religious dogmatism. While the end of dictatorship meant that the internal political enemies vanished, "criminals" or "potential criminals" now loom as the menace. There is no left-wing counterbalance to this trend, either, as democratic consolidation has, unfortunately, shifted the transformative political aspirations of the 1970s and 1980s back toward pragmatism, in terms of both gaining positions in the state apparatus and political-electoral stratagems. Today, both on the left and on the right, law reforms and public policy proposals are quite easily subordinated to the dictates of public opinion, which clamors for the punitive power of the state to be expanded. In Brazil, as elsewhere, public opinion is mostly formed by the impact of massive media spin-offs around the rise of crime in the last thirty years.[39]

It is therefore not a surprise that social movements engaged in the defense of children's rights, racial equality, and, more recently, LGBT rights, as well as against human trafficking and gender-based violence, are also demanding the protection of human rights through criminal prosecution as a presumptive measure of justice or as an instrument of social pedagogy—sometimes even of political transformation and emancipation. Consequently, the reforms of the 1940 Penal Code that took place after the 1990s, even with regard to sex-related crimes, actually are arguably instances of hypercriminalization (that is, repressive rather than emancipatory).[40] What we describe in the following discussion links not only the punitive, anxious security state to increased regulation of sexuality, even in the idiom of rights, but also reveals the ways in which domestic politics are continually pulling on and being pushed by international developments. The explosion of international criminal law, especially around children and trafficking, as will be discussed, is one such force.

An illustration of this paradoxical shift is found in the Statute of Children and Adolescents. It was inspired by Brazil's ratification of the 1989 Convention on the Rights of Children and reflects the strong influence of the Catholic hierarchy. On the progressive side, the statute establishes that childhood covers birth through eleven years old, and that adolescence covers between twelve and eighteen years old, providing a quite advanced view on the ability of young adolescents to make decisions and express their views. Moreover, the statute repealed the criminalizing approaches that had prevailed since the nineteenth century with regard to poor, abandoned children and adolescents. Despite these progressive views on children as rights holders, childhood and adolescent sexuality is addressed primarily in terms of risk and victimization, and the statute enumerates a host of new crimes, such as sexual exploitation and abuse associated with pedophilia and child pornography.

From the 1990s on, the issue of sexual abuse of children and adolescents was addressed by parliamentary committees of inquiry. These institutions must be situated in relation to the 2003 ratification of the Optional Protocol to the Convention on the Rights of the Child on the Sale of Children, Child Prostitution and Child Pornography and to the 2004 ratification of the Palermo Protocol to Prevent, Suppress and Punish Trafficking in Persons, Especially Women and Children, a supplement to the UN Convention against Organized Crime. In part legitimated by these international norms, over the course of the last ten years, pedophilia and the sexual exploitation of children have triggered highly visible police operations, media reports, and increasing societal anxieties.[41]

Similar tendencies are observed in the realm of gender-based laws. In 2001, Law Number 10224 introduced the new crime of sexual harassment, defined as "to constrain someone for the purpose of obtaining sexual advantage or favor, when the agents of the conduct benefit from their condition of higher hierarchy or ascendancy inherent to position of employment, post or function."[42] The criminalization of harassment in the workplace, it should be noted, is a step at odds with the well-established principle of proportionality, which requires criminalization to be avoided whenever milder alternatives exist to resolve conflict. For example, in the case of harassment, labor legislation to impose sanctions would be much more effective and less costly than criminal penalties.

In 2005, Law Number 11106 altered some provisions of the 1940 Penal Code, repealing the outdated crimes of consensual abduction, seduction, and adultery. It also amended crimes related to prostitution, as we will discuss in the following pages. The most comprehensive reform of the provisions concerning sexuality came in 2009 with Law Number 12015, the result of long-term, systematic feminist pressure on lawmakers. This pressure was reinforced by the ratification of the inter-American standard, the Belém do Pará Convention for the Eradication of Violence against Women; the ratification of the UN Convention on the Elimination of All Forms of Discrimination against Women in 1994; and approval of the outcome documents from the UN Vienna and Beijing Conferences in 1993 and 1995.

Among other modifications, Law Number 12015 changed the title "Crimes against Morals" (Dos crimes contra os costumes) to "Crimes against Sexual Dignity" (Dos crimes contra a dignidade sexual). It also eliminated the longstanding distinction between rape and indecent assault, putting an end to the traditional gender-specific understanding of the crime of rape. The new definition of rape is "[to] constrain someone, by means of violence or serious threat, to have carnal intercourse or to practice or allow the practice of other lewd acts with her or him." However, the law retained the punishment of six to ten years of imprisonment for rape, as defined by the 1990 "heinous crimes law." Furthermore, the 1940s' concern with the reproductive effects of sexual acts was not entirely removed: under the new law, if the rape results in pregnancy, it carries an aggravated penalty.[43] And twenty-first-century lawmakers reaffirmed the old belief that fraud might lead someone inadvertently to consent to sexual relations: the 2009 reform merely consolidated the crimes of "sexual possession by fraud" and "indecent exposure by fraud" under the name "sexual violation by fraud" (violação sexual mediante fraude), also eliminating the gender-specific nature of the crime. Once again, penalties were increased.

Regarding prostitution, Brazil has criminalized related activities, but not the people directly involved, keeping relative moral neutrality on the issue. Brazil, therefore, has been a welcome site for sex worker rights advocacy, particularly in response to HIV/AIDS and beyond, both nationally and internationally.[44] These conditions have, however, significantly changed since the 2000s, under the growing impact of media and policy debates around sexual exploitation of children and trafficking for sexual purposes.

As mentioned, Brazil ratified the Optional Protocol on the Sale of Children, Child Prostitution and Child Pornography in 2003 and the Palermo Protocol in 2004, two international treaties that combine human rights and criminal justice premises and measures. A series of parliamentary inquiry commissions led to the establishment of new policy structures and penal code reforms. The 2003 Inquiry Commission on Sexual Abuse and Exploitation of Children and Adolescents proposed a first reform (Law Number 11106 of 2005), which made crimes related to prostitution gender neutral, as indicated by the new title: "Pimping and Trafficking in Persons" (*Do lenocínio e do tráfico de pessoas*). On the one hand, this new neutrality is to be praised. On the other, the reform added to the existing crime of international trafficking for sexual exploitation (*tráfico internacional de pessoas*) the new crime of internal trafficking (*tráfico interno de pessoas*), which was defined as "to promote, intermediate, or facilitate, inside the national territory, the recruitment, transportation, transfer, lodging or reception of a person that will engage with prostitution,"[45] and which carried a penalty of three to eight years of imprisonment.

Four years later, Law Number 12015 changed the name of the title once more, this time to "Pimping and Trafficking in Person for Prostitution or Other Form of Sexual Exploitation" (*Do lenocínio e do tráfico de pessoa para fim de prostituição ou outra forma de exploração sexual*). It introduced a few changes in the definition of the crime of internal trafficking and reduced the penalties to two to six years of imprisonment, lower than the penalties for international trafficking. It also created another crime: "Encouragement of Prostitution or Other Form of Sexual Exploitation of Vulnerable Persons" (*Favorecimento da prostituição ou de outra forma de exploração sexual de criança ou adolescente ou de vulnerável*). This new criminal conduct was defined as "[to] subject, induce or attract to prostitution or other forms of sexual exploitation someone who, being under 18, or because of mental disability or other infirmity, lacks the necessary discernment to practice this act; also to facilitate [engagement with prostitution], impede or make it difficult for the person to abandon [the practice]."[46] The associated penalty is four to ten years of imprisonment. The same penalty attaches to the conduct of those who, under such circumstances, practice carnal intercourse or other lewd acts with persons between fourteen and eighteen years old, as well as to the owner, manager, or responsible party for the place where there is such a practice.[47]

These changes have problematic effects. For example, the crime labeled "internal trafficking" ends up criminalizing the act of assisting people to move for the purpose of prostitution. Law Number 12015 defines as crimes the promotion or facilitation of the movement of persons inside the national territory for the exercise of prostitution or other forms of sexual exploitation. It also defines the following behaviors as criminal: "to intermediate, encourage, sell or buy the trafficked person, or, being aware of this condition, transport, move or lodge them."[48] Therefore, the new law provides grounds for the agencies of the criminal justice system to interpret the mobility of people who offer sexual services as a crime, when mobility is often an important strategy for people in sex work. These new definitions also expand the possibilities of "justified" police operations and inspections in commercial sex areas and locations, as any sex worker who is found away from his or her place of residence may occasionally be seen as a trafficked person. Furthermore, in the name of protecting adolescent sexuality, the law actually criminalizes the conduct of clients of sexual services (when the person providing the service is over fourteen and under eighteen) by, as mentioned earlier, prohibiting the act of having carnal intercourse or engaging in other lewd acts with persons between fourteen and eighteen years old who are subjected, induced, or attracted to prostitution or to another form of sexual exploitation.[49]

It is also worth mentioning that, in 2008, an interministerial policy platform was established to deal with trafficking in persons, and from 2010 on, antitrafficking measures became a priority of the Dilma Rousseff administration before her impeachment in August 2016.[50] Importantly, it should also be mentioned that, since the ratification of the Palermo Protocol and even when policy guidelines already were broadly defined to include all forms of labor, Brazilian criminal trafficking law remained restricted to the punishment of trafficking for sexual purposes until Law 13344 was introduced in October 2016.[51]

In 2012 a radically distinct bill was presented to the House that proposed the decriminalization of commercial sex (in the case of persons over eighteen) and its related activities and the legalization of these services as labor rights.[52] This provision reflects the view, held by Brazilian civil society and political institutions, that sex work should be decriminalized. However, the trajectory of recent legal reforms in relation to sex work and trafficking and the prevailing political conditions in Congress after the 2014 elections—the House is the most conservative it has been since 1964—do not make us optimistic about the prospect of removing penal regimes from sex work in the near future. In Brazil, concerns about childhood and adolescent sexuality and the illusory belief that criminal justice could deter premature or consensual sex considered to be forced reached their culmination in the aforementioned Law Number 12015.

Law Number 12015 of 2009 repealed the 1940 Penal Code's original rules, which established the concept of "presumption of violence." This apparent step forward did not exactly constitute a breakthrough because lawmakers merely replaced the old conception (of presumption of violence) with a new type of crime: "the rape of vulnerable [persons]." This new crime is defined as the act of "having carnal intercourse or practicing other lewd acts with a person who is younger than 14 years" or with "someone who, due to mental disease or other mental disablement, lacks the necessary discernment to practice the act, or that for any other cause, cannot resist." The penalty is imprisonment for eight to fifteen years, which is higher than the penalty established for the core crime of rape. The minimum term is also higher than the minimum term for the basic type of homicide.

The current definition of "rape of vulnerable [persons]" has appeared more ideologically compelling than the previous definition of "presumption of violence." But when examined from a critical perspective, in the same manner as the 1940 definition, the reform kept intact a dominant sexual morality that condemns in advance the expression of the sexuality of persons under fourteen or mentally disabled persons, who are perceived to be naturally potential "victims" of sexual abuse. The law does not recognize any possibility of development or ability of these persons to decide on matters related to sexuality and leads to criminal cases that should be interrogated. For example, a thirteen-year-old girl who is willing to have sex with her eighteen-year-old boyfriend cannot freely exercise her sexuality, because her boyfriend is threatened by eight years of incarceration.

Conclusion

From the early days of the Brazilian nation-state, the development of criminal laws, including those regarding sexuality, has been complicated by paradoxical combinations of strong liberal views (particularly concerning property and privacy) and sharp social, racial, and gender inequalities, as well as the persistence and redeployment of punitive ideologies that more often than not have targeted and continue to target those who are viewed as less deserving citizens.

Criminal law reforms, including of sex laws, have occurred during moments of definitive and profound social, cultural, and political transformation. Coincident with those moments, the anxieties of those in power were somewhat assuaged through the criminal code's preservation of gender and sex hierarchies. The resulting reforms bring to mind the dilemma faced by the main character in the famous Italian novel *The Leopard*: "If we want things to stay as they are, things will have to change."[53] Changes and debates that have taken place in the past, as well as those that continue to unfold in this current era, have neither escaped blurring the boundaries between law and morality nor ripped off the curtains that hide the meanings, purposes, and effects of undemocratic punitive ideologies.

Against this backdrop and in light of our concern for how criminal law should be used in regulating sexual conduct and abortion, we go back to the classical distinction between law and morality. While values enshrined in law—specifically the values expressed in guaranteed fundamental rights—have an ethical basis (the democratic ethos), morality and law are entirely distinct. Moral dictates—be they from religious traditions, human nature, reason, or social mores—can be neither imposed nor coerced as legal rules. Rather, moral standards must be freely embraced.[54] To use a classical formula, virtue is the expression of freedom. There is no virtue where there is obligation or duty.

As Luigi Ferrajoli underlines, the confusion between law and morality does not do the law good because it leads to totalitarian, inquisitorial malfeasance and arbitrary decisions. And neither does it do morality good because moral standards can be more authentic, as argued by classical theorists such as Samuel von Pufendorf, Christian Thomasius, Ludwig Feuerbach, Jeremy Bentham, and Wilhelm von Humboldt, when not linked to coercion and expressing autonomous and unconditioned choices.[55] The recognition of the dignity and freedom inherent to every person guarantees the possibility to choose our own morals and prevents us from being coerced into moral transformation or changing how we think and feel. This recognition also requires democratic states to establish conditions that enable freedom of conscience, autonomy, and moral plurality to flourish and to create parameters of tolerance in relation to positions and behaviors that are not harmful to others, though the majority may judge them to be immoral. At least in theory, democratic states should not impose a particular moral conception on their citizens, much less so if it is enforced by a violent, harmful, and painful punitive power.

Today, in Brazil, as in other countries, punitive state obligations are derived from what we consider a distorted reading of the Constitution. The protection of fundamental rights, as enshrined in international human rights law and democratic constitutions, compels the state to implement positive interventions that create enabling conditions—economic, social, political, and cultural—for the effective realization of these rights. This cannot imply resorting to the criminal justice system. The criminal justice apparatus cannot effectively uphold the protection of fundamental rights—quite the contrary. For example, Brazil has the third-largest prison population in the world.[56] In December 1995 there were 173,104 Brazilian prisoners, a rate of 107 per 100,000 inhabitants.[57] In twenty years, the Brazilian prison population has more than tripled. In June 2016 more than 700,000 prisoners were in detention, a rate of 352.6 prison inmates per 100,000 inhabitants.[58] This rampant growth also affects women, as the female prison population more than quadrupled in the last fifteen years, from about 10,000 in 2000 to roughly 42,000 in 2016.[59] As elsewhere in the world, criminal law and incarceration policies are highly selective: the large majority of prison inmates are poor and, in various locations, predominantly black.

The inherent racism and classism of imprisonment suggests that criminal law can never be a means for promoting and protecting human rights. It is vital not to lose sight of this wider landscape when examining the application of criminal law to sexual matters. The redress of gender-based violence, the overcoming of remnants of a patriarchal power structure, the elimination of constraints to the free exercise of sexuality, and the eradication of all forms of discrimination cannot be attained through the criminal justice system without resulting in nefarious collateral social effects. The easy, simplistic, and merely symbolic appeal to the criminal justice system does not prevent crimes and does not resolve social, racial, or gender-based conflicts. Hypercriminalization engenders additional injustice, a great deal of suffering and pain, stigmatization and the deprivation of freedoms, and new forms of structural violence that arise from the selectivity inherent to the punitive power of the state. We must interrupt the arguments and ideologies embedded in conservative "law and order" arguments or deployed by supposedly progressive viewpoints that perpetuate inequalities and the patterns of exclusion that still characterize Brazilian society and its political institutions. Criminal repression, whatever its direction, contributes neither to the recognition nor to the guarantee of fundamental rights, because inequality, prejudice, and discrimination are at the core of the very idea of punishment and underpin the persistent logic of the criminal justice system.

CHAPTER 7

The Reach of a Skirt in Southern Africa: Claims to Law and Custom in Protecting and Patrolling Relations of Gender and Sexuality

Oliver Phillips

What's in a Skirt? The Visceral Reality of the Symbolic

In November 1992 a woman walking alone on campus at the University of Zimbabwe (UZ) was pursued and stripped naked by a mob of approximately one hundred male students. She was rescued by university personnel and members of the Student Representative Council by being bundled into the car of two female deans who happened to be passing, thus saving her from further violence. Male students claimed that their actions were justified because her skirt (a miniskirt) was too short.[1] The following Monday, the campus awoke to accounts of a second such attack that had taken place over the weekend in a nearby shopping center. Following this and a Students' Union meeting in which these incidents were not even mentioned,[2] women on campus began mobilizing a response through the Women's Studies Association. A few days later, they dressed in miniskirts and held a protest march to which about forty supporters came, including only six men (me among them).[3]

As soon as we gathered, we found ourselves surrounded by over five hundred taunting male students, who threatened the women with gang rape and threw missiles (stones, seed pods, sticks, and so on). The women managed to make their way around campus, accompanied all the time by the far larger mass of actively menacing and extremely threatening men. Of the men present in support of the women, four were impressively big and very well known; they commanded great physical respect and intimidated the threatening body of male students just enough to restrain them; their constant interventions were vital in keeping the attacking students at bay.

But there were still a number of scuffles, and a security guard who attempted to arrest a male student for throwing stones at the women was severely assaulted, reportedly ending up in intensive care. It was clear that the campus security guards had neither the authority nor the resources to impose themselves on the situation. The Zimbabwe Republic Police were not called because they had been such frequent and violent suppressors of student protests in the preceding months that their arrival on campus would likely have dramatically increased the violence.[4] Additionally, women walking in central Harare at night without proof of marriage had recently been subject to mass arrests in police sweeps to "clear up the streets" (discussed further later), and so the protesting women knew that the police were as unlikely to defend women in miniskirts as they were to defend the right to protest.

Immediately following the dispersal of the crowds, in an aggressive exchange with some of the male students who had been threatening the women, I was told that the woman who was attacked was a "temptress" who "got what she deserved" for "advertiz[ing] her goodies." These young men were forceful in making clear that they believed the miniskirt represented a "violation of our African norms and expectations." The letters that flourished in Harare's newspapers over the next few months were dominated by similar references to temptation, tradition, and "just deserts": "We do not want our streets and institutions to be transformed into pornographic localities by social outcasts who are suffering from the Loss of Self-Discipline Syndrome (LSDS) in a bid to emulate the decadence of the Western cultures."[5] The city was also said to be "the deathbed of Shona morals."[6] The male students I spoke to claimed that they were defending traditional values by demanding that women wear "decent" (that is, long) skirts, and they warned menacingly that women should "discipline themselves, or we shall do it for them."

It was of little concern that traditionally, precolonial Shona women had worn *nhembe*, a cloth considerably smaller than a miniskirt. Nor did it matter that the long skirt was introduced to Zimbabwe under the aegis of Victorian "decency" by British colonials, making it as much an importation of Western style as a miniskirt. My attempts to remind aggressive male students of this fact simply invited them to cast me as an imperialist who should not tell *them* about *their* culture but should rather "go back to England" and mind my own business. As a white Zimbabwean, this was not the first time such a suggestion had been made to me. However, as this chapter demonstrates, on this occasion these arguments struck me as vividly illustrating the extent to which tradition's reinvention and invocation are predicated on concerns about social relations in the *present* (disguised as a preoccupation with the past), in a way that demands a similarly artificial juxtaposition of modernity and "tradition."[7] The miniskirt becomes a vector of discipline or resistance in contesting the shape of contemporary national identities, highlighting how boundaries of sexuality and gender are mapped onto our bodies through our clothing; clothes come to reflect the way we present ourselves in relation to the commonly understood historiography of those boundaries. This becomes specifically complicated in a postcolonial context, where these boundaries of identity, sexuality, historiography, and representation are all so heavily invested. This explains why the 1992 incident at UZ is far from unique, even today.

On December 17, 2014, a young woman wearing a short skirt in downtown Harare was similarly attacked. While there had been numerous such attacks in the intervening decades, the proliferation of smartphones by 2014 meant that the entire incident was filmed and then posted on YouTube, where it quickly circulated to viral effect.[8] The incident took place at one of the major minibus and taxi ranks (Simon Muzenda) in central Harare, a crowded and lively space where sexual harassment of women is not uncommon.[9] In the video, a baying crowd of men shout "Hure!" (Whore!) at a young woman as they tear at her skirt and underwear. A male companion attempts to help her. He continues alone in this task, despite aggressive attempts to separate them, as they find one taxi after another shutting their doors firmly to deny her any shelter from the men persistently trying to grope her. Eventually, the driver and tout of a taxi do come to the aid of the woman and her friend, and they are bundled safely away.

As soon as the video was posted on YouTube, it went viral throughout the region, producing a particularly strong reaction from the members of Zimbabwean women's organizations who just two months earlier had marched in the hundreds in an attempt to draw attention to the need to address precisely this issue. While these marches had attracted scorn from more conservative quarters, this incident now served as undeniable proof and vindication of the women's complaints about the frequency of sexual assaults and the impunity enjoyed by perpetrators.[10] Because of this discursive context, but also because the video was so widely circulated and garnered such a vociferous reaction, police were quick to identify the men and publicly invite the woman assaulted to make a formal report so that they could proceed with criminal charges.[11] The trauma of such frightening and public humiliation caused the woman to wait another week to report the incident, but as soon as she did, the men were arrested and produced in court to be charged with indecent assault.[12] They were imprisoned on remand until March 2015, when a female magistrate convicted them both and sentenced them to twelve months of imprisonment each (with four months suspended for good behavior).[13] Key activists campaigning for the men's prosecution included women of significant public and political profile, such as the Member of Parliament Jessie Majome, previously deputy minister of justice and legal affairs. With the active and strong support of women wielding such clear political and judicial capital and the irrefutable evidence of the assault so widely broadcast and discussed, it is perhaps unsurprising that the law was enforced so swiftly, but it also seems likely that the visibility of the powerful women who declared their vociferous indignation and expressions of support was crucial in helping the complainant feel safe and supported enough to proceed with a prosecution.

In a striking difference to the reaction to the incident in 1992, the majority of the reports, letters, and comments published online and in the print media in 2014–15 focused their condemnation on the male aggressors and either asserted a woman's right to dress as she will or, at a minimum, insisted on her right to dignity and protection from harassment. This more progressive response may also reflect the visceral impact of the video, in which the young woman's fear is plain for all to see and utterly comprehensible: the raucous, menacing mob of men displays an undeniable lack of the "discipline" that underlies the most basic expectations of reasonable social interaction. These men behave in ways impossible to reconcile with any notions of the propriety so central to Shona culture (including "traditional" culture) or of the politesse so necessary for densely urban modernity. On top of this, the protest marches that had preceded the incident had clearly informed the perspective from which so many people viewed the video online, foregrounding the discursive frame that developed.

If one pays attention to the comments posted online by anonymous men, one still finds some appeal to the "tradition" that was cited to me by students in 1992 and that associates women's call for rights with foreign contamination—a strategy designed to discredit women's rights as "foreign," one that is very familiar to postcolonial feminists across continents and that has been so eloquently deconstructed and disabled by Uma Narayan.[14] But the comments posted after any online publication are invariably an amplified representation of indignant but marginal voices. It would seem that the voices defending such attacks on women as "in defense of tradition" were relegated to the rarer margins in 2014. Meanwhile, those voices demanding an end to men's impunity for these assaults appeared to have a firm purchase on the state apparatus that administers the criminal law, possibly as a result of women's increased access to the institutional power of governance and their realization of more constitutional rights in the public (as opposed to the private) realm. In other words, the platforms

supporting women's responses to this incident in 2014 offered far greater leverage for an effective response than those that were available in 1992. A key platform is that of social media, for access to live streaming and such broad and
instant circulation has provided women with a new and powerful instrument
through which to claim solidarity and call for action from supporters of either
gender. At the same time, access to constitutional rights and to the positions
that enable the exercising of those rights also appears to facilitate this.

On the men's initial appearance in court in 2014, Majome explained succinctly the relevance of these incidents for issues far beyond the length of a
skirt: "This is a fundamental women's rights issue. It violates all known basic
freedoms, freedom of movement and expression; it undermines everything and
even the right to the protection of the law and the right to equality. The conviction of the culprits would vindicate all these rights that I have mentioned. The
law must be enforced. It must come down hard on people who want to undermine the law."[15] These battles over miniskirts thus throw light on the law's role
as an instrument through which to patrol sexual expression and "appropriate"
gendered behavior, on the one hand, and as a means of support for the advances
in sexual autonomy and gender equality that are promised through international
and regional human rights conventions, on the other. But a fuller appreciation
of the contrasting expectations of law's disciplinary and productive impact requires us to consider the law's historical role in producing the relationships that
gave rise to these claims to tradition (for they are indeed historically located,
though perhaps not in the way that those making such claims would wish). It
also requires us to examine the specific political and sociocultural dynamics that
cohere to produce such a preoccupation with miniskirts in this way and at this
time.

The Reach of the Miniskirt across Time and Space

It is important to note that the men who participated in these attacks, whether
at UZ or at the Simon Muzenda bus rank, were far from representative of all
men, and in each case there were other men who gave significant help to the
women facing physical attack. This will be discussed in more detail later, but it
is also notable that these incidents have been and continue to be mirrored elsewhere in sub-Saharan Africa with surprising frequency. The specific act of men
stripping women in miniskirts, the content of their rationalizations, and the
courageous determination of the women who choose to protest despite the response they know it will invite are far from unique. The regularity with which

similar occurrences have been reported in many different parts of Africa during the intervening years is particularly striking, as the miniskirt repeatedly features as a catalyst for extraordinary hostility toward, and often violent conflict about, sexual propriety and gendered behavior. Evidently, the incident I witnessed reflects an issue that is not unique to Zimbabwe nor to the context prevailing in 1992. Rather, this was one moment in a continuing history of very similar incidents across the continent and even farther afield; readers from many African countries will instantly recognize that they have each had their "miniskirt moments," examples of which are detailed later.

From early on in the three decades that Hastings Kamuzu Banda ruled Malawi (1961–94), women were banned from wearing skirts above the knee or from wearing trousers.[16] Even though those laws were subsequently phased out, Malawian women have since been stripped naked for wearing trousers or miniskirts,[17] just as women in Kenya[18] and South Africa[19] have been similarly "disciplined" in recent years. In December 2012, authorities in Swaziland blocked women marching in miniskirts as they campaigned for equal rights and safety in a country where two-thirds of teenage girls have been victims of sexual assault; police later declared that they would thenceforth be using colonial-era laws to prosecute women for wearing "revealing or indecent" clothing.[20]

In Uganda, miniskirts were banned by Idi Amin in the 1970s, and though rarely enforced, the ban remained law until 2002.[21] In 2013 the minister for ethics and integrity, Father Simon Lokodo (an ordained Catholic), enthusiastically led determined attempts to revive this ban, countered by equally vociferous protest from women's groups and human rights defenders.[22] For them, social media served, as it did in Zimbabwe in 2014, as a strategic platform through which to reinforce appeals to law and to mobilize protest campaigns; the enormous technological and social developments of the past forty years also highlight the impervious purchase of the conflict over miniskirts.[23] In December 2013, the day before it passed the notorious and much contested Anti-homosexuality Act (since overturned by the constitutional court on a technicality), the Ugandan Parliament approved the Anti-pornography Act of 2014. The original bill had defined pornography so broadly as to include the revealing of thighs and buttocks in a manner considered "sexual."[24] The final act, signed into law by President Yoweri Museveni, does not make any reference to miniskirts or any clothes, nor even to "thighs, breasts, and buttocks," and is focused on the need to establish an intent to eroticize.[25] However, these substantive and definitional changes were obscured, as public debate of the act adopted the "miniskirt" framework, which greatly preoccupied Lokodo, the act's most energetic supporter. He repeatedly vowed (and even attempted)[26] to use the new law to arrest women for wearing skirts above the knee.[27] With Lokodo rendering the mini-skirt a symbol of the lewd immorality that the act was designed to eliminate, the media embedded the "anti-miniskirt bill" label in public consciousness.[28] However misleading this label may be regarding the act's final form, it was read and interpreted as licensing a violent repudiation of miniskirts, as well as au-thorizing attacks on women wearing them. There was a sudden and marked increase in violent attacks on women by groups of men in different parts of the country, attributable directly to the passage of the act and its specific associa-tion (however erroneous) with miniskirts.[29] With the number of sexual assaults committed by groups of men suddenly so high and with women responding with such vehement campaigns through media, both conventional and social, as well as through legal measures challenging the act, the Anti-pornography Act was recalled and remains under review at the time of writing.[30] Additionally, the police issued statements warning men that they would be arrested for such attacks, stressing that the act did not criminalize miniskirts.[31]

Similarly, in 2007–8 in Nigeria, concerns about the immorality of women's "indecent dressing" (including but not limited to the miniskirt) were serious enough to warrant the proposal of similar legislation prohibiting "sexual intim-idation," which was defined as dress "capable of sexually seducing the other person."[32] However, this national legislation was ultimately not enacted, and at-tempts to do the same in Lagos State produced rapid disaster. As the *Lawyer's Chronicle* noted, "The press and the public condemned the massive arrest of girls and women by the police on the streets of Lagos over what was termed as inde-cent dressing which resulted in victims illegally detained, allegedly raped and their money extorted. The law was eventually scrapped."[33] Then, in Novem-ber 2012, news reports made the shocking claim that twenty women had been killed in one night for nothing more than wearing miniskirts and trousers in the northern state of Borno, the site of Boko Haram's insurgency.[34]

However, it soon transpired that these reports were baseless and fabricated in order to spread "confusion . . . disaffection and crisis."[35] That this awful claim of such extreme action could have any plausibility or purchase is partly due to the fact that it was alleged to have occurred in Borno, where Boko Haram's vio-lent methods have actually given battles over gender and culture a bloody and extreme religious ferocity. But it is also clear that these fabricated claims owe their credibility to the familiarity of the miniskirt's symbolic power in conflicts over gender and culture throughout the region. Indeed, attacks on women (both physical and rhetorical) for being "improperly" dressed appear to traverse time and nationality—a cursory search suggests the miniskirt has also been the sub-ject of debate in Botswana,[36] Namibia,[37] and Zambia.[38]

Indeed, the tight stretch of the miniskirt's physical cloth seems to stand in direct contrast to the broad stretch of its metaphysical reach. This is even more the case when one considers that disputes about the miniskirt are not particular to Africa and that proposals to ban them have come from a variety of countries as diverse as (but not limited to) Chile,[39] Indonesia,[40] South Korea,[41] and Italy[42] (a country more commonly identified as a center for European fashion and often associated with far more explicit displays of overt sexuality). The miniskirt seems to court controversy wherever it appears. Its ready adoption by some seems to be inevitably accompanied by calls for greater propriety by others.[43] And there are certainly countries where far more extensive covering of women's bodies is expected and even enforced. It is important to recognize that concerns about women's dress appear integral to conflicts about the appropriate performance and expression of gender the world over.

In this sense, the miniskirt's symbolic reach is both broad (widespread) and short (direct). This dual dimension arises first from the fact that the dressed body inevitably represents a constructed mediation of the self and society: "Being personal, [the dressed body] is susceptible to individual manipulation. Being public, it has social import."[44] Thus, dress has long been a personal statement of the political, part of the normative reproduction of dominant mores (and hence a mechanism of discipline), while also providing a medium for the expression of individuality and difference (and hence a source of resistance or subcultural identity).[45] It signifies conformity or transgression and thus serves as an overt representation of the relationships among power, gender, class, race, and sexuality.

This has been particularly recognized in the work of such theorists as Judith Butler, whose advocacy of "gender trouble" is well reflected in the practice of drag—a direct challenge to the gender binary that defies the prescriptive conformity of specifically gendered clothing, thus disrupting the performativity of the normative gender binary.[46] Indeed, the symbolic power of dress in relation to the embodiment of gender is most vividly illustrated by the continued and violent persecution of transgender and transsexual people the world over.[47] The fact that transgressing such visibly coded representations of the gender binary leads not only to prosecution in law but also frequently to violent attack reflects the powerful threat that such transgressions are perceived to pose to the gendered relations of power so intrinsic to the heteronormative structures that undergird patriarchal societies.

Compared to most gender-specific clothing, the miniskirt offers a more uniquely invested (and hence more contested) articulation of the relationship between the female self and society. This is arguably because of the miniskirt's inherent ability to engage both desire and subversion: it simultaneously attracts the male gaze (through the heteronormative convention of sexualizing the female body) and disturbs the male gaze (challenging heteronormative conventions that deny women's sexual agency and that struggle to recognize women's sexuality outside reproduction and men's ownership). The miniskirt projects contradictory messages of autonomy and objectification, agency and vulnerability, independence and complicity, liberation and exploitation. As such, it elicits strong responses in a wide variety of geographical and social locales. It could be argued, for example, that far from being emancipatory, miniskirts make women accomplices in their own sexual objectification and oppression. Either way, what miniskirts do represent is a sexuality free from the association of maternity. Arising out of the 1960s Twiggy-thin fashion, the miniskirt "defined itself against the maternal body."[48] It represents an expression of sexuality beyond procreation and, implicitly, outside the conventional boundaries of marriage and the family. Such associations mean that the miniskirt resonates with very specific histories of gender and race in southern Africa (discussed later). Its symbolic value is only further understood in the context of the postcolonial era, where the legacy of colonial strictures continues to shape social relations and values.

What was of explicit concern to the male students at UZ in 1992 was that they associated the miniskirt with sex. In their eyes, it reached across what Ratna Kapur has characterized in another context as "the precipice of desire and subversion."[49] It was identifiable to the men as an explicitly sexual signifier, and whether the crowd read it as signifying a woman's sexual availability or as signifying her sexual independence and agency, it represented an implicit challenge to "traditional" gendered power dynamics. This generated a highly sexualized response that sought to reassert gendered roles and their asymmetrical restrictions on sexual desire. Sexuality was manifestly instrumental here, and, just as has been the case in so many other locales and times, this battle over women's dress reinforced the performativity of gender, recalling Butler's suggestion that women's bodies are "shaped by political forces with strategic interests in keeping that body bounded and constituted by the markers of sex."[50]

The men's comments and actions aimed to assert a specifically patriarchal African culture that precluded miniskirts, silencing women's demands for sexual autonomy, stripping away their claims to sexual agency, and restoring the disciplinary bounds of a phallocentric sexual hierarchy. Equally, the women recognized the extent to which their own actions could trouble these boundaries—performing gender anew, refuting men's control, and shifting hegemonic conceptions of sexual propriety. Thus, the miniskirt, so invested with sexual power, served as an instrument for both its proponents and its detractors; it became an instrument through which the women challenged gender hierarchies, and through which the men disciplined this gender transgression and attempted to reassert control over women's sexual behavior. Significantly, it is the miniskirt's contentious and contradictory representational characteristics that make it an ideal foil through which to both challenge and reinforce the hegemonic (predominantly polygynous) heteronormativity that is ascendant over definitions of gender in Zimbabwe and across the region.[51]

The extraordinarily violent reaction of some men to women wearing miniskirts may therefore relate to the fact that the miniskirt's challenge to notions of gendered propriety also disturbs, excites, and confuses, challenging men's comfortable presumptions on the unfamiliar "precipice of desire and subversion." This complex response elicits in some men the need to assert more simplistic and definitive boundaries of gender propriety through discipline, and it is possible to trace some transcontinental continuity in the rationalizations that inform their behavior and that underlie these attacks. One obvious example of this is the apparent universalism of the popular belief in "victim precipitation," specifically in relation to sexual assaults, in which a woman is blamed for being attacked because of the clothes she wore or the way she behaved or the place she was in. Her transgression of gender-appropriate behavior provides an "explanation" that works to supplant the responsibility of the attacker. This features prominently and repeatedly in the reasoning offered by authorities for their proposal of miniskirt bans in Uganda, Nigeria, and Swaziland, as well as in the reasons provided by male students for their attacks on women on the UZ campus in November 1992. Recent research in both the United Kingdom and the United States reminds us that these attitudes are also still popular in countries that endorse gender equality:[52] juries in rape trials commonly attribute the assault to the complainant's transgression of a convention of gendered or sexual propriety.[53] Blaming an "inappropriately dressed" woman for her own victimization is far from unique to any specific locale.

In these miniskirt incidents across the region, competing claims to law feature prominently: demands for criminal or other laws to ban or to patrol women's dress and sexual expression, discrimination claims from women and supporters, and the assertion of human rights as the basis for both protection and increasing sexual agency. "It's my right," asserted one Kenyan woman, just as the women demonstrating at UZ had claimed in 1992.[54] In December 2014, Zimbabwean member of Parliament Majome also grounded the miniskirt issue in allusions to more forthright and explicit claims to fundamental rights of equality and the rule of law. Similarly, the Malawian vice president (later president) Joyce Banda declared, "Some of us have spent our entire life fighting for the freedom of women. . . . It is shocking some men want to take us back to bondage."[55] In South Africa, the Women's League of the governing African National Congress called a march "to emphasize that women had the right to wear whatever they wanted without fear of victimization."[56] The competing calls to prohibit and punish the wearing of miniskirts, on the one hand, and to protect women's rights and prosecute their abuse and discrimination, on the other, reflect a shared faith and investment in the power of law to offer satisfactory resolution. They each position the law firmly as an appropriate terrain for this contest, presenting it as a "magical instrument of delivery,"[57] through which they expect to be granted a resolution they favor. Such evidently shared faith in law demands that we take a closer look at the historical context capable of generating this common investment by such different actors, and it requires us to consider the conditions and factors that shape the possibilities of law's response.

The Miniskirt's Postcolonial Reach in Southern Africa

In November 1992 the male students who attacked the protesting women refused bluntly to accept the accusation that they were colluding in their own colonization, that traditional *nhembe* cloths were far more revealing than the long, Victorian-era skirts in which they wanted women to be clothed. Instead, they labeled me a white imperialist, and the heat of the moment inhibited any more nuanced account of the relationships among tradition, the body, and clothing and the extent to which these have changed. All postindustrial cultures witnessed variable trends in styles of dress, shifts in the stylistic representation of gender difference, and changes in the symbolic power of how much or what flesh was exposed over the course of the twentieth century. This is particularly true for Zimbabwe, where the twentieth century witnessed colonization, settler government, revolution, and postcolonial independence. It is therefore useful to consider some key aspects of the changing structures of patriarchy that persisted throughout these grand shifts. The triumph of Christianity's "civilizing mission" (with its moral framework of individual sin, redemption, and righteousness) and the introduction of a legal framework that enabled the development of individual wage earners and governmental subjects were preconditions for colonization and were also fundamental to shifting notions of social and bodily propriety.[58]

There is a rich historiography that reveals African women's bodies as long-serving vectors of contestation and discipline through which can be mapped competing attempts to patrol the troubled intersections of race, culture, sexuality, and gender. A most notable early marker of this was Saartjie Baartman's exhibition as the Hottentot Venus in early nineteenth-century London and Paris. The exhibition presented the black body for display to white inspection and coincided with the emergence of new theories of eugenics and scientific racism, which both treated visual differences between people as significant markers of innate value and so served to license the British colonial expansion into the African interior that followed.[59] With colonization came innumerable laws, regulations, policies, and practices that ascribed differential values to bodies according to the confluence of their race and gender. The colonial social order was explicitly premised on white male subjectivity, and the hegemonic ascendancy of both whiteness and masculinity impacted all bodies in relation to their licensed productivity and the extent to which they merited protection or prosecution.[60] Thus, in Southern Rhodesia (later Zimbabwe), fears about interracial sex resulted in overzealous and heavy-handed punishments for mere indications of black men's sexual interest in white women, while white men's access to black women went unrestricted and unpunished.[61] Marginalized on account of both race and gender, black women were further ascribed a partial legal subjectivity in that they had no direct recourse to law (that was the prerogative of their male guardians), but they did have the ability to offend. In this way, their legal subjectivity was both incomplete and negative.[62]

A woman's assertion of an independent sexual agency directly challenges her status as the reproductive property of a man. Historically, African women's reproductive capacity was not something over which they had ownership as individuals. Instead, decisions about marriage, sex, and reproduction were vested in their fathers, husbands, brothers, or other male guardians. The exchange of *lobola* (bridewealth), the practice of polygyny, and marriages under customary law are still very common in Zimbabwe and throughout much of the region, and the sexual autonomy of those women under these regimes remains restricted. In Southern Rhodesia, colonial authorities had recognized the power of these structures when, in alliance with African men wishing to assert greater control over their wives, they made adultery an offense only when it involved married women. No man, married or unmarried, could be guilty of adultery unless he was having sex with another man's wife; the offense was therefore specifically located around married women. While this was consistent with the polygynous dimensions of customary marriage, there was in fact a further double standard: under the Natives Adultery Punishment Ordinance of 1916, a married African woman was only permitted to have sex with her husband, and a married African man could have sex with his wife or any other unmarried African woman, but a European man could have sex with any African woman, married or unmarried, without being guilty of adultery.

This highly differentiated hierarchy (in terms of gender first and then race) arose out of men's varied responses to adultery. Colonial authorities argued that, consistent with English law, a wife's adultery should not be criminalized but rather should be grounds for divorce. This suggestion was anathema to African elders who viewed that approach as tantamount to rewarding an adulterous woman with her freedom, when in fact what they wanted was for her to be forced back into line with her husband and for the cuckolding man to pay damages to the husband. In turn, colonial authorities worried that this would mean that a man could actually "benefit" from his wife's infidelity.[63] In attempting to allay African men's concerns, the resulting law served as a legal enshrinement of settler superiority. While it denied African women legal and sexual subjectivity, the prevailing context of rapid social and economic change was such that the law could never deliver to overanxious men the increased control over their wives that they were so determinedly seeking. More pertinently, the more the law regulated African marital relationships (prohibiting the pledging of young girls, ensuring the official registration of marriage, criminalizing adultery, permitting divorce, and so forth), the further control over reproductive and sexual matters shifted from the traditional domain of patriarchal, gerontocratic lineage to the newly formed, foreign apparatus of the state.[64]

The redefinition of sex and reproduction as invested with morality, sin, and labels of individual identity is one manifestation of "modernity" and western European philosophy in postcolonial African cultures. This has inevitably altered the significance ascribed to sexual conduct and led to an increasingly individualistic representation of the body. Both Christianity and medical science played their roles, on the one hand through the notion of individual sin and on the other through the practicalities of contraception, each in conjunction with a newly codified law that brought with it a new discourse on morality.[65] For women, this increased the differentiation between sexuality and reproduction. With kinship ties traditionally based so firmly on a notion of reproduction indivisible from sexuality and the subsequent development of contraceptive mechanisms undermining that indivisibility, the maintenance of traditional structures of power required the employment of new techniques to reassert men's control over women's sexuality. But how were men vested with "traditional" power to do this when the terrain was so quickly changing?

In writing about the politics of contraception in Zimbabwe, Amy Kaler outlines some of the relevant dynamics:

> Women's fertility in Africa has always been linked to the psychopolitical and spiritual well-being of communities. Fears of infertility act as metaphors for political instability and economic hard times, and dropping birth-rates are symbolically linked to declining temporal power. . . . Morality is also indexed by reproduction as women's failure to conceive or give birth are ascribed to their or their neighbour's sexual misdeeds. Conversely, reproductive sins, such as aborting or having sex during pregnancy, are thought to bring sickness and catastrophe to entire communities. Colonial regimes in Africa, as well as their successors, struggled to control reproductive practices, which they deemed not just undesirable, but actually dangerous to the health of the body politic. Throughout African history, sex and reproduction have been invested with power and symbolism above and beyond the mere biological mechanics of the acts.[66]

This has specific significance in that the use of contraception interfered dramatically with the traditional practices and beliefs that many Zimbabwean men relied on to be sure of their wives' fidelity and of their daughters' chastity. If other men's bodily fluids entered a man's wife, this could cause any breastfeeding child or fetus in the womb to become sick and die. Clearly, her ready access to contraception worked against his ability to ensure that she was either pregnant or breastfeeding and that these customary methods of ensuring chastity and fidelity were not being bypassed. What's more, the white settler state's provision of contraception meant that the African man was losing this control to an alien and frequently antagonistic force.[67] The state was again usurping instruments of control traditionally exercised through lineage structures, particularly by older men.

As is implicit in Kaler's statement, another fundamental distinction between Western medical philosophy and traditional Zimbabwean beliefs regarding the body was the idea of causality. Traditionally, the notion of *Ubuntu* (or *hunhu* in Shona) recognizes the inherent humanity of each person as deriving from his or her social relations; rather than our individual autonomy, it is belonging to society that gives us our humanity and, by implication, our human rights.[68] In much the same way, bodily functions are taken to reflect social problems. If sickness or death occurs, it might be attributed to a social event: someone has acted in such a way as to cause that sickness or death. Thus drought, famine, or other misfortunes could be attributed to sexual deviance.

In contrast, Western medicine generally looks to the body as the source of the problem. Rather than regulating the body through social action, Western power regulates social action through the body, as explained by Michel Foucault's concept of "bio-power."[69] And indeed, colonial authority was based not only on Darwinian concepts of race and evolution but also on an "anatomo-politics" of the human body (health, hygiene, efficiency, production)—a clear belief in the body as machine. Similarly, the ability to establish a modern industrial and bureaucratic state involved the monitoring and regulation of the population as a body. This was done through the construction of mining compounds, the development of missions and schools built around European concepts of discipline, and demographic monitoring carried out through mechanisms such as family planning, the Land Apportionment Act of 1930, the Pass Laws, curfews, and the removal of "squatters" from urban areas. To an extent, this administrative surveillance of the body as a necessary part of running a bureaucratic state continues to apply the "normalizing judgement"[70] required to produce an "obedient subject."[71] What defines this obedient subject are "habits, rules, orders, an authority that is exercised continually around him and upon him and which he must allow to function automatically in him."[72] Thus, we can trace the development of an individuated subject (with the rights and accountabilities of legal personhood and the individual subjectivity that accompanies the promise of sexual autonomy) through the growing structures of the state, moving further from the collective sociality of traditional lineage. This provides us with a clearer understanding of why those men investing most heavily in "traditional" African values would characterize a woman's expression of an independent sexuality as a "lack of self-discipline": she should know "automatically" not to wear a miniskirt or dress in such a way that men may consider her to be a "prostitute."[73] No questions are asked about the assumptions that men make concerning a woman's dress or behavior—it is enough that she should choose for herself how and when to be sexual for that to be taken as "prostitution" and "undisciplined." A discourse of "true tradition" therefore acts to promote the self-discipline integral to an "obedient subject," relying on perceptions of historical identity to create disciplined subjects of a modern nation-state that can be allied to lineage. This, of course, is bound to conflict with the notions of equality and human rights to which the state is formally committed through international treaty and convention, as well as its constitution. However, it is equally true that this representation of "traditional values" is rarely lived out so purely in reality.

Under colonial rule, the introduction of a capitalist economy commodified sex and the body on an unprecedented scale. A migrant labor system strictly regulated in terms of sexual division gave the labor power of male and female bodies radically different values. This differing labor power manifests in the reliance of urban women on operating within the informal sector of the economy.[74] It is this sector that offends the image of the city as a well-ordered symbol of modernity. Prostitution, for example, became one of the few avenues of survival available to independent women in areas of capitalist expansion. To this day, the government and the media comment on the amount of prostitution found at economic "growth points." And in the numerous sweeping arrests of women to "clean up" Harare between 1985 and 2013, suspected prostitutes and street-food vendors (predominantly women) were proclaimed specific targets.[75] Significantly, women on the streets who were not accompanied by a man or carrying a marriage certificate or proof of employment were arrested.[76] Inevitably, the variety of women arrested (for who does carry such certificates?) would suggest that the police had no difficulty viewing most women on the streets as sex workers.

A common Shona word for a prostitute is pfambi, which can be literally translated to mean "one who walks about," alluding directly to a long-standing anxiety about the independent mobility of women. To this day, Zimbabwean men espousing "traditional" values will characterize women with independent resources, particularly their own professional income, as mahure, or prostitutes. If a woman is earning money for herself and not beholden to a husband, then (by definition as much as by implication) she "must" be a prostitute; similarly, as she is single and a prostitute, she "must" be available and is therefore likely to get propositions from countless men each day. The then minister of home affairs made this clear in the early 1980s when he stated that the abolition of lobola (bridewealth) would "legalize prostitution," as "a woman for whom lobola was not paid could easily move to another man." (When a woman divorces, her parents are expected to return the lobola they were paid.) It was at this stage that the government argued that lobola was part of the "national heritage" and "western feminism . . . [was] a new form of cultural imperialism."[77]

Implicit in these statements is the suggestion that those women married under civil rather than customary law, for whom no lobola was paid, are censured as "legalized prostitutes" because of their potential freedom from the direct control of a man, a legally conferred freedom that is further censured as "cultural imperialism." Simultaneously, those women who are married through customary law, for whom lobola is paid and who are perpetual minors under the guardianship of their husbands, are championed as defenders of the "national heritage." Thus, not only are ideas of national allegiance and identity used to censure the independence of women, but an idealized notion of the virtuous subservience of traditional womanhood is used to promote the righteousness of a conservative national identity deeply rooted in "traditional" hierarchies.

Before independence, social issues arose within the framework of a repressive political regime, allowing "tradition" to act as a unifying force of resistance around which consensus was easily created. With the removal of the most repressive elements of government, social and economic development accelerated. However, the subsequent return of more despotic politics and the economic crisis precipitated by economic mismanagement, rampant hyperinflation, and violent land seizures delivered times of such insecurity and rapid social change that revisionist conceptions of tradition became increasingly relied on but less easily agreed on.[78]

In this way, calls to tradition serve as an anchor for conservative positions under threat from the consequences of change implicit in their own agenda of progress. On the one hand, access to the technology of Western modernity can increase political and economic development and can draw on greater resources of economic and political power. On the other hand, the selective production and promotion of notions of traditional culture facilitates the censure of those concomitant social developments that undermine established relationships of power. Thus, the empowerment of women (for example, through the 1982 Legal Age of Majority Act, which gave women full legal personhood) takes place as a necessary part of the development of political and economic resources, but it is tempered in such a way as to attempt to diffuse the threat that this poses to the authority that men exercise over women in the name of tradition. Thus, the Legal Age of Majority Act's significant legal empowerment of women is tempered by the fact that those women who still choose to marry under customary law automatically have their husbands as their guardians and, by implication, do not (cannot) have legal personhood. Many marriages in Zimbabwe are still entered into under customary law, and "the prerogative to choose what type of marriage one wants to enter into lies predominantly with the male partner."[79] The hegemonic power of men (both traditional and more egalitarian) is thereby maintained through the sustainment of a consensual ascendancy that pleases them both. Yet it is founded on a compromise that inevitably punctures the promise of equality, and there are constantly calls for reform of the legislation relating to marriage.

But Who Are These Men Claiming "Tradition"?

The male students encircling the women on the UZ campus in 1992 did not represent all men on campus or even most of them, but they were motivated enough to be there by the hundreds and assured enough to be actively aggressive. The initial assault on the first woman (who was stripped) was an explicit and violent attempt to censure her behavior, but it occurred as part of a far bigger conflict that involved gendered markers of students' identities as "traditional" or "modern." In 1992 on the UZ campus, these tended to be characterized as "rural" and "urban," respectively. This particular encounter was one dramatic moment in a continuous campaign of harassment of women (particularly "non-traditional" women) on campus that was becoming increasingly prominent. This campaign was institutionalized through the formation of the notorious University Bachelors' Association.[80] The attack was directed at one woman whose miniskirt identified that she was not "traditional," but it also served as a warning to all women that they were in danger of suffering similar sanctions if they did not behave according to the expectations of "conservative" SRB men (SRB meaning "from a strong or solid rural background") who made up the University Bachelors' Association.[81] The idea that other women (and a few men) would rally to support the woman who had been attacked and to demand even more vociferously respect of women's rights and independence was seen as a threat meriting a response of increased ferocity.[82] For women to assert a collective demand for control over the production of their own sexualities was far more threatening than a single miniskirt, as it represented a direct challenge to "traditional" gender relations and the "traditional" structures that the SRB students so clearly and forcibly espoused. And because this happened within the relatively contained space of a university campus, there was an opportunity to do what they believed had "become necessary": to intimidate, harass, and threaten so that the women would "listen."

Now, twenty-five years later, UZ students tend still to be identified (including by themselves) as belonging to either one of two groups. First, SRBs tend to be the children of rural farmers and working-class families from urban townships; the former are often regarded as more "unpolished, unsophisticated and lacking in social graces,"[83] but both tend to identify as "traditional" and espouse allegiance to the gerontocratic patriarchal structures of lineage (for example, tribal elders and chiefs). In contrast, *MaNozi*, or the "nose-brigaders," are distinctly middle-class urban men and women from professional, cosmopolitan families. They are visible followers of global popular culture who prefer to use English as their first language, but their fluent articulation leads them to be accused of speaking in the same "nasal" accent that black Zimbabweans commonly identify with white Zimbabweans. There are clear class differences between these two groups, with working-class urban students ("born location students") tending to fall somewhere in between, "for they aspire to the material symbols of wealth possessed by the 'nose brigade,' but are not comfortable with the cultural pollution which they perceive to have afflicted them."[84] But what really distinguishes the SRBs most clearly from the *MaNozi* is the tenacity with which SRBs defend what they consider to be "traditional" culture, while the *MaNozi* reject this culture and assert a more global black identity, along with a greater commitment to gender equality.

Although this categorization is a rather crude mechanism for unraveling complex social dynamics, this division reflects some key tensions in the definition of national identities, often manifested most obviously in gender relations and conflicting expectations of appropriate sexual demeanor. For example, *MaNozi* women have been characterized by SRBs and the University Bachelors' Association as "not ideal for a wife but good for pastime."[85] This characterization employs precisely the same reasoning as that used by the minister of home affairs in his comment that women free from the constraints of *lobola* were legalized prostitutes. It reflects the centrality of sexual autonomy to gender propriety, as it emphasizes not only that women's propriety is founded in her dependence on men but also that a man's ability to control his wife is central to his masculinity and the reproduction (both biological and social) of his patriarchal status. Thus, *MaNozi* women will expect to pursue their own careers, keep their own incomes, be entitled to refuse their husbands' wishes, and enjoy a power independently garnered rather than benevolently loaned, and this is what makes them "not ideal for a wife." On the other hand, *MaNozi* women are less concerned about their "reputations" and so are able to befriend men, express their own opinions, enjoy themselves less guardedly, and potentially consider sex outside marriage, and this is what makes them "good for pastime." This expresses succinctly the contradictory reaction of certain Zimbabwean men to "modern" women—and makes clear men's understanding of the threat posed by women's sexual autonomy to their "traditional" institutions.

The seriousness with which men viewed this threat in 1992 is illustrated by their widespread and violent reactions to miniskirts, which swiftly exceeded the constraints of campus. These attacks were targeted at specific women but with the express object of censuring the sexual independence of all women. In a longer historical process of shifting sexual boundaries, these were moments of crisis that gained momentum through men's panic about the gradual gains in women's power. The perception that the threat went to the heart of national culture and involved institutions fundamental to the production of women as "obedient subjects," combined with women's collective refusal to repent, spurred men to use both structural power and physical force to assert their authority. And by manipulating fantasy and reinventing tradition, they sought to reconstitute the discourse producing the hegemonic order. It was the parameters of consensus that appeared to have shifted by 2014, as they had opened up enough to allow some women access to those devices that defined how the issue was framed and, thus, how consensus achieved the hegemonic ascendancy that emerged afresh. By 2014, the men were clearly recognized to be the offenders, and the women were absolved or at least protected by the machinery of the state.

Conclusion

While this essay focuses on the miniskirt in Zimbabwe and details the historical factors that give it particular symbolic resonance, many postcolonial African states share enough of these historical dynamics for the same key signifiers of gender, race, culture, and sexuality to be similarly threaded through the fabric of their own miniskirts. This analysis of the Zimbabwean context has offered some avenues for understanding how miniskirts galvanize such strong reactions and campaigns, both locally and throughout other states in the region that have experienced similar incidents. This is because while all clothes inevitably offer a means of representing one's self to society, the miniskirt does this in a specifically gendered way, uniquely invoking conflicting responses of agency and desire, vulnerability and subversion, empowerment and oppression, each also then charged with sex. It is also ubiquitous because these labels and signifiers are then invested anew by the postcolonial context. This disturbs and disrupts traditional subjectivities, disinvesting the center of power and reinvigorating the subordinated marginal in a reversal that expands and compounds the multiple dimensions of the skirt's symbolic power, attributing to it yet more meaning, while rendering it no less conflictual.

In a context in which structural hierarchies have been dramatically impacted by colonization and in which subsequent postcolonial assertions of authenticity, "traditional" values, and gendered identity are all attributions of power on which they rely, a miniskirt remains something women cannot throw on with quotidian abandon, for the semiotics of dress and fashion are the swift prerogative of all, including those men who identify patriarchal privilege as fundamental to their socioeconomic capital. And yet none of these structures, hierarchies, and relationships is static; there are perceptible shifts in the designation and wielding of power, including access to those instruments that constitute and secure (or might reconstitute and challenge) gendered inequalities.

This can be detected in comparing the events of 1992 and those of 2014. In 1992 the women protesters on campus were massively outnumbered by the men attacking them, and their voices and the message they carried were significantly overwhelmed both by the tenor of the remarks of the male students as they rationalized their attacks on women students and by the mass support they quickly garnered in the national press from other men objecting to the sexual autonomy of women wearing miniskirts. This is significantly different from the events of 2014, when the women's campaign for action quickly resulted in the conviction of two men for sexual assault when they physically harassed a woman, tearing at her miniskirt and trying to grope her. The treatment by the press and the official response (including the conviction and sentencing of the offending men) served to highlight the extent to which women's formal empowerment, their access to authority, and their participation in defining public issues have all grown to produce a demonstrably greater impact, owing to their engagement of state institutions. And despite some significant qualifications (specifically, women continue to be assaulted, and authorities do not yet react appropriately on all occasions), the response of mainstream and social media appears to have evolved, becoming more conscious of equality (at least in the public realm).

The stripping of women wearing miniskirts in the late twentieth and early twenty-first centuries has been shown to reflect the extent to which the surveillance of African women's bodies has been continuously implicated in the disciplining of racial difference and the sexualization of race. But these miniskirt scenarios also remind us that African women cannot simply be represented as victims with "poor suffering bodies in need of protection" (a characterization that Alice M. Miller has critiqued as severely restricting their potential to be viewed as bearers of equality).[86] For women's protests after attacks or threats invariably involve the wearing of miniskirts as an implicit assertion of sexual agency and an explicit embodiment of political advocacy, and in 2014 it became clear that achieving these goals is significantly more likely when they have the support of women in public office, reflecting the importance of equality in the public realm. And their achievement was also rendered irresistible by the irrefutable and striking evidence filmed on a smartphone and uploaded for wide and effective dissemination through social media.

The reach of the miniskirt is therefore of particular interest not just because it provokes men's violent anxiety across numerous African states but also because it offers clear evidence of women's agency in asserting their right to define the cultural limits of sexual propriety. Zethu Matebeni's commentary on South African Zanele Muholi's queer African photography seems quite apposite here: "Without undermining the manner in which the black female body has been positioned and viewed as a site of numerous struggles in post-colonial African discourse, there exist other ways in which the black body can be seen beyond its colonial constraints and constructs."[87] As the site onto which so many social and existential anxieties have been projected and around which so many later battles have been fought, African women's bodies find themselves subject to censure and control while also remaining key instruments of self-empowerment and liberation. This controversy over miniskirts and sexual demeanor has therefore invited an analysis of gender relations and sexual agency in much of postcolonial Africa, with a view toward offering some explanation for the recurrence of these dynamics across regions and decades.

As pointed out earlier, it is striking in these scenarios how consistently each of the different protagonists makes a claim to law: the women involved assert their rights through law, while the men opposing them demand that women's dress be regulated through prohibition and criminalization. Does this overarching belief in legal remedies, born of such contradictory expectations, suggest that the law really is an even playing field of equal appeal to both contestants? Clearly, it is not magically imbued with the unique capacity to deliver all things to all people. So perhaps it is the legitimacy that legal enactment would lend to a campaign that makes the law such an attractive ally. The symbolic significance of legal measures is great, as dressing claims up in law does promise some reassurance of state support. The law has been complicit in producing new ways of being and new concepts of personhood for many Zimbabweans. These contradictory appeals to criminal law and human rights as instruments of resolution have specific resonance in postcolonial southern Africa, where the historical role of criminal law might primarily be characterized as that of an instrument of social control, while human rights might be more readily associated with historical claims to liberty and equality in the successful struggles against colonialism.

Either way, the development of a codified law and its accompanying discourse has established specific relations between individual subjects, including women, and the state. It brings with it both individual accountability for one's actions through criminal law (rather than the collective liability that devolves from the reparative payment of damages through kinship structures) and an investment in human rights as a mechanism for building new identities within and outside lineage that, along with Christian notions of sin and the impact of waged labor, give new value to individual subjectivities.[88] The claims to law as an instrument of resolution both by conservative men defending their notions of "tradition" and by protesting women demanding their rights to independence and equality reflect law's legitimating power; its capacity to engage the repressive apparatus of the state; its promise of protection, liberation, and rights; and all the contradictions that bedevil these intersecting roles. It reflects the dynamism of law as a platform through which identities are both produced and patrolled, but it also illustrates the greater strength and promise of equality in the public sphere, which can deliver structural change where the tolerance that accompanies the right to privacy can only deliver a temporary protection.

Perhaps just as radical or wholesale transformation is rather a lot to expect from claims to rights that are ordinarily remedial, these same rights do offer far more when they are simply one strategy in a panoply of strategic interventions. For the constitutions and conventions that promise human rights present us with platforms from which to build these promises into real options, but this can only be done if law is wielded with the authority of public office and the relevant tools to motivate mass media. And even with all those strategies in place, this may still be too much to expect from the law. Criminal laws already regulate the way we dress (for example, laws against public indecency and laws against cross-dressing), and international instruments guaranteeing women's rights to equality have been ratified by many of the states where these miniskirt attacks take place. And yet the mere existence of these laws does not and cannot bring into reality the conditions that they promise, for law is simply one tactic in these struggles.[89] In demanding the (patriarchal) state's intervention, the women in these miniskirt scenarios might be said to be in danger of positioning themselves as in need of "protection" rather than autonomy. For law to be effective, it has to be embedded in and supported by social education and policy; without the political will to develop that policy and then implement it effectively, law will have little impact and will be ineffective in helping to change social relations. This is particularly the case in countries where the reception of international human rights is complicated by postcolonial memory and the populist power of an anti-imperialist rhetoric that is regularly deployed to great effect by opportunistic politicians.

And it seems that that has often been the story of campaigns around miniskirts in southern Africa: Some men assault a woman whose skirt is alleged to be "too short," and they demand that the law should prohibit women from dressing in this way. Meanwhile, women start to protest these actions, and they call for the state to protect their rights to assembly, mobility, and freedom of expression, as well as the recognition of their rights to equality and justice. It seems trite to state that any law's efficacy is dependent on a developed understanding of the sociohistorical context in which it operates, but it bears repeating. Context matters. Recourse to the language of human rights and criminal law is bound up in the cultural and political dynamics of place and time. Understanding the specificities of these miniskirt attacks can nonetheless help us identify commonalities elsewhere and lay bare the underlying struggles surrounding gender, sexuality, reproduction, and the role of law.

CHAPTER 8

Abortion as Treason: Sexuality and Nationalism in France

Mindy Jane Roseman

History, it is said, has no straight lines—and the lines connecting the various regulatory histories of sex, gender, and reproduction are no exception. Other contributions to this volume examine the genealogies of nationalism, colonialism, postcolonialism, and desire that produced and legitimized heteronormative, procreative sexuality while simultaneously producing and stigmatizing most other sexualities and differently gendered ways of being (see especially Long and Moumneh, this volume). These contributions make visible the ways states and regimes deploy and consolidate power through the use of criminal law and its apparatuses by vilifying certain kinds of sexualities and gendered practices.

Abortion does not figure prominently in those chapters for a number of reasons. Where it is criminal today, abortion is not generally understood as involving sexual manners;[1] our contemporary framings surrounding abortion often define it as a matter of choice, justice, or health, on one side, and life, on the other. The gender- and sex-linked norm-setting aspects of criminal abortion law, therefore, get somewhat obscured. Yet when some (or all) abortions are labeled criminal, gender heteronormativity becomes visible: the law and its application draw a bright line between good and bad women and girls in many settings.[2] What the law expresses is the norm that "good" women and girls carry their pregnancies to term; "bad" ones do not.[3] Sometimes exceptions (known as indications) are carved out in criminal abortion laws. These indications recognize that pregnancies resulting from heterosexual sex may be forced, unwanted, unintended, unhealthy, or ill advised; yet obtaining the "indicated" abortion is often an ordeal, if not impossible in many settings. Criminalizing abortion polices heterosexual intercourse and therefore makes abortion emphatically a crime of a sexual and gendered character. Criminalizing abortion compels women and girls who become pregnant to become either mothers or felons.

Compulsory motherhood, which is the aim of criminal sanctions for abortion, has been the hallmark of pronatalist nationalist state building.[4] France, during the nineteenth and twentieth centuries, was deeply concerned with the dwindling size of its population and, therefore, its place in the international order. Women's gender deviance, as this chapter will discuss, was felt to be a leading cause of population decline, and at one point in its history, the French government equated abortion with treason. The 1942 "300 law" made procuring or performing an abortion punishable by death—expressly labeling abortion a "betrayal of the nation."[5] It was the three hundredth decree issued by Vichy (hence its name). This association brings to mind George Fletcher's call to take treason, "this ancient crime[,] more seriously in thinking about both the theory of criminal law and the mainsprings of criminal conduct,"[6] particularly in light of Patrick Devlin's 1965 assertion that just as "there are no theoretical limits to the power of the State to legislate against treason and sedition[,] . . . there can be no theoretical limits to legislation against immorality."[7] Fletcher's intuition about the influence that treason has on the elaboration of criminal law doctrine and Devlin's point of view about the unlimited reach of the state's police power where "immorality" is concerned should give us pause. How might the notion of treason, as a challenge to the very existence of the body politic, as well as to political authority, dwell in our conceptualizations of "immorality," as well as more generally in the theory and definition of crime? Might this association with treason be what societies fear about gender disorder and unregulated sexuality and reproduction?[8] And might these embedded and anxious associations with treason threaten to be revived as the contingencies of politics find expedient? If abortion and homosexuality (another instance of heterodox gendered sexual expression) still warrant (in some places and at certain moments) severe criminal treatment in terms of rhetoric, scope, and penalties, are there useful insights to be gained from examining the potential of a lingering conceptual connection to treason?

The Case of Giraud

Marie Louise Giraud was arrested, indicted, and imprisoned in 1943 for having performed twenty-seven abortions over the course of a few preceding years. Found guilty after a short trial, she was one of the few individuals to feel the full weight of the 300 law.[9] A guillotine blade cleaved her head from her body in the courtyard of La Rocquette Prison in Paris; such was the punishment for violating the law. The trial record is scant on details. Giraud did carry abortions out more or less successfully: one of her clients died. That death may have contributed to the state's interest in prosecuting Giraud, for none of the women or their families independently complained about Giraud to the police. It was only after an anonymous denunciation (rumored to be by Giraud's husband) opened the investigation that corroborating denunciations from the so-called victims came forward.

What appeared to trigger Giraud's prosecution, according to Colonel Farge, the state prosecutor at her trial, was her "disconcerting cynicism." What was this cynicism that antagonized the Vichy state? It needs to be unpacked, with attention to larger historical, social, and cultural contexts, in order to understand how her prosecution came about. Not all those accused, arrested, tried, and punished for abortion met Giraud's fate.[10] Yet her extraordinary treatment is worth our attention, for I contend that it was not a product of one overzealous individual but rather an intentional act of prosecutorial discretion in service of the state.[11]

While it is beyond the scope of this commentary to discuss all the political aspirations and struggles attending the Vichy regime, suffice it to say that the paternal authority of the Vichy state, with its promise to restore law and order, was largely welcomed.[12] In late 1940, the French had capitulated to Nazi Germany, submitted to an occupation, and embraced the anti-Republican, counterrevolutionary government of Vichy France. In the autumn of 1941, Parliament was abolished, and the rule of law was transformed into rule by executive decree.[13] The "National Revolution" (Vichy's official ideology) was decidedly counterrevolutionary in the sense that its adherents opposed the historical legacy of the French Revolution; in a word, it was antimodern.[14] The establishment of law and order meant ridding France of all its perceived corrupting forces—Jews, socialists, and immigrant foreigners, most prominently— but also (as will be discussed shortly) the lax morality and decadence that, in the eyes of the Vichy authorities, had characterized France during the interwar period and led to its defeat. The words that Vichy chose to replace the motto of the French Revolution (*Liberté, égalite, fraternité*) were *Travaille, famille, patrie* (work, family, fatherland). This speaks volumes.[15]

The Vichy regime found evidence of moral lassitude toward family formation in many places, including in French juries, which were considered quite lenient toward the crime of abortion.[16] Observations of the kind reached as far back as the mid-nineteenth century. Legislators perennially bemoaned the unchanged social norms and proposed work-arounds to impunity. All throughout the twentieth century, they tried various legal and procedural reforms:

decreasing penalties, constraining discretion, reclassifying abortion as an administrative offense, increasing penalties. Therefore, there is more continuity than not leading up to the 1942 300 law, which imposed a draconian death penalty for performing an abortion. This law also allowed serious cases of abortion to be tried before a court established to expeditiously dispatch members of the Resistance, as well as perpetrators of other crimes "likely to harm national unity, the State or the French people": the Tribunal d'État.[17] The less serious abortion cases would be tried before the ordinary Tribunaux Correctionnels, which, for the most part, treated abortion as it had done for the few previous decades—rhetorically, as an abomination, but in actuality, as a commonplace occurrence.[18] In other words, the removal of select abortion cases to this state tribunal meant that Vichy understood this crime to be a direct attack on the regime and a crime against the French race.[19]

The Giraud case, which was tried before the Tribunal d'État, must, therefore, have represented quite a threat to the Vichy government. Giraud, by her own account, was rather unrepentant for her acts and did not evoke much sympathy from the prosecutor or judge. Prosecutors played an essential role in determining the docket.[20] Vichy's minister of justice, Joseph Barthélemy, had long engaged in a personal crusade against abortion and lenient verdicts, seeing them as moral weakness, incompatible with the "new era."[21] Although there is a paucity of archival material, we can take an educated guess that Giraud's lack of shame contributed to her demise.[22]

Giraud, we learn from her dossier, was from modest, working-class origins, her schooling only through primary school.[23] Married at twenty-five years of age, she worked as a maid and took in laundry. Three of her five children died in infancy. Her life was difficult and depressing in the cold, drizzly, North Atlantic town of Cherbourg. After the German invasion in 1940, Giraud's husband was sent to work in Germany, as per the armistice agreement. He would have been one of the tens of thousands of able-bodied men conscripted into forced labor, along with the tens of thousands of others being held as prisoners of war. Without the wages of these men, many women had to generate or augment their income.

Presumably, the women of Cherbourg lacked more than finances; they also sought out emotional attachments and sexual companionship. That the Nazi occupying army was circulating freely in Cherbourg merely added to the potentiality that a single or married woman, whose husband or boyfriend was absent due to the war, might have found herself "illegitimately" pregnant. There would have been a market for the services Giraud was providing even without the occupying forces, especially since contraception (save condoms) was contraband under a 1920 law. Giraud may have seen an opportunity or had it foisted on her;

she easily might have learned to perform abortions from other women in her neighborhood.[24] Once she found her calling and word of her services spread, her abortion business thoroughly improved her standard of living, raising it to that of a white-collar worker. She rented comparatively opulent quarters, which, when she sublet some rooms to women selling sex, generated even more revenue.[25] Such activity may have been louche, but it was legal.[26] More likely, her willingness to use her home to generate income transgressed French social ideas about respectability.[27] Her association with prostitution (and with money) tainted her reputation, which was further magnified by her abortion business.[28]

Living above her station did not endear her to the authorities, especially when juxtaposed to the daily lives, as depicted in testimony before the tribunal, of people living in trying circumstances in the garrison town of Cherbourg.[29] The case was built on the interviews of 196 people who had knowledge about Giraud's business as clients, neighbors, or, in the case of three women, accomplices.[30] By this number alone we can assume that she and her operations were notorious in all connotations of the word. Yet, in the confessions of the women who frequented Giraud, the fear of losing a job or a reputation makes resort to abortion the stuff of everyday. "Afraid of losing my job at the Banque de France, I decide to get an abortion," recounted one woman who had kept company with a German soldier. "I have never been pregnant, despite the gossip," insisted another, who admitted that she had a liaison with a German soldier. Her husband, she confirmed, was a prisoner of war.[31] Other interviewees told stories of the struggles of families: one, a railway worker who could not support another mouth to feed, trying to make ends meet; another, embarrassed and angry at an unmarried daughter's pregnancy by someone of whom they disapproved.[32] These stories portray a working-class world upended by the war—families no longer intact, economies nominally functioning. Overlain with social and sexual manners of respectability (emulating the emergent bourgeois norm, even), Giraud's clients were motivated by financial necessity, as well as social shame. What those who sought Giraud's services really thought of abortion, or of Giraud herself, for that matter, is difficult to surmise: was she a compassionate woman providing a service or an unsavory peddler preying on the unfortunate? After the fact, many denounced her when questioned by the investigators and prosecutors, claiming a lack of consent or resistance to the abortion.[33] That was the expedient position to take.

That the Vichy government imposed a veneer of national betrayal on abortion was not a widely internalized sentiment. In none of the testimony was there an inkling of patriotic disloyalty. No one accused of performing abortions confessed to having betrayed the nation: the most the officials could extract was a barely contrite acknowledgment: "I knew it was wrong."[34] Thirty-eight individuals were criminally charged in relation to Giraud's activities; three women's cases were sent to the tribunal, where they were charged as accessories. Their sentences were lenient compared to Giraud's (that is, prison terms of ten or fewer years, some at hard labor and with fines). In terms of the prosecutor's insistence on, and the judge's compliance in, imposing the death penalty, I would argue that the "disconcerting cynicism" Giraud represented to the Vichy grandees was her moral nonchalance, the embodiment of decadence. She was neither shamed nor stigmatized. She did not appear, therefore, susceptible to any moral, interior repentance or rejuvenation. Certainly this, and the transgressive class gradient of the accused (that is, her social climbing), may have played a role in Giraud's sentencing, as well as in other abortion trials.[35] Vichy, in service of its program of national renewal, chose to excise Giraud from the body politic, presumably to assert ultimate authority over the population, if not to reassure itself of its power.

Recent scholarship on the attitude of the Vichy regime toward abortion stresses its continuity with the policies of the democratic republican governments that preceded and followed it.[36] Without knowing the "dark number" of how many abortions actually took place during the Vichy period, it is difficult to know with precision whether the Vichy officials amped their prosecutions up as much as their rhetoric.[37] Research suggests that fewer than 1 percent of all abortions were ever prosecuted by ordinary courts, and in the exceptional Tribunal d'État, abortion barely figured and was to some extent resisted by the judicial docket.[38] Abortion proved particularly impervious to criminal convictions—a stubborn fact that vexed the Vichy government, as it did the Third Republic's governments that preceded it and those of the Fourth Republic that followed.[39] Yet this continuity reveals a deeper layer that enriches our understanding of how the case of Giraud connects treason to the betrayal of the nation. It links the larger stakes of population policies and the longer history of France's fear that it was depopulating with the social norm of respectability, of a gendered and social order that reflected and reproduced the self-image of France throughout the Third Republic and Vichy France, if not beyond.

Criminalization of Abortion, Population Politics, and Respectability

Abortion had not always been a criminal affair, let alone one of national betrayal in France, Europe, and elsewhere. The national histories of abortion regulation are too varied to be summarized in a pithy sentence or two, but generally the criminalization of abortion is a modernization story—a narrative of industrialization and the transformation of economies from subsistent and agrarian to capitalized and industrial; these changes disrupted cultural, social, and political arrangements, including those related to sexuality, gender expression, and childbearing.[40] Relationships between government and the population became mediated in different ways, with medical and scientific discourses and institutions supplanting religious and traditional ones.[41]

What seems to have been the general turning point in industrializing countries in Europe and the Americas is the emergence of physicians' professionalizing aspirations. Many physicians were able to influence legislators and legislation to recognize their exclusive rights to dispense and oversee medical and related health care; they were also able to channel concerns over a range of social ills attributed to modernity—urban poverty, overcrowding, disease, malnutrition, unemployment—into discussions about national health and well-being.[42] By the mid- to late 1800s, a nation's population size, health indications, and composition increasingly became measures of strength. As nationalism reached a fevered pitch in the years leading up to World War I, criminal abortion laws (and the laconic enforcement thereof) rose more prominently on legislative agendas. The conceptual links made between the birthrate and patriotism imbued reproduction with political potency, rendering those who engaged in nonreproductive sexual practices putative criminals.[43] Yet the particular logic behind these pronatal criminalization policies focused more on the gender-inappropriate behavior of women who aborted potential "citizens," as well as those who assisted them.

We see this demographic imperative in the case of Giraud, the logic of which punctuated law and policy making in France certainly from 1920 onward, if not since its defeat by Prussia fifty years before. Population size, particularly in comparison to a unified Germany, an expansive Russia, and an exuberant United States, gave France (or certain French elites) a deep sense of inadequacy. The very facade of bourgeois civility and respectability, buttressed by all sorts of race, class, and gender divisions, was thought to be crumbling. Men, the argument went, were becoming more like women, women more like men: the proof was to be had in the falling birthrate, the increasing rates of infant abandonment and neglect, the depopulating villages, the overcrowding cities, and so on.[44]

In essence, the government was manufacturing and amplifying stigma and shame in the service of population size. Heterosexual marriage and the fruits of heterosexual sex were thought of as "normalizing"; these institutions corrected and socialized masturbators and homosexuals, whose sexual practices were con-

sidered impotent and thought to contribute to depopulation.[45] At the heart of
nationalism was (and is) a demographic demand and duty to reproduce. Insofar as the "national defense" alarm was raised, there was a presumptive suspicion that all kinds of sexual practices that were nonreproductive, such as
masturbation, homosexual sex, contraceptive use, and abortion, denied the nation its future population.[46] Abortion and contraception were viewed as a "refusal of maternity"—that is to say, evidence that a woman was shunning her
"natural" role as a mother and thereby defying the nation. Given the right conditions, sexual, gender, and reproductive nonconformity could be profound
enough to create plausible, not merely pretextual, anxieties about national survival.

Pronatalism—population policies designed to increase the birthrate—
became France's nonpartisan agenda.[47] Legislators, medical and legal professionals, educators, and social reformers all agreed that it was necessary to
increase the number of births and improve the health of, as well as the environment into which children were born.[48] How to achieve this, however, was a question that engendered much disagreement.[49] It took the pyrrhic victory of France
in World War I to motivate legislative action. France had won the Great War of
1914–18 but had lost millions of people—nearly six million missing or wounded
(even more if one includes victims of the Spanish flu). In 1919, from the Senate
floor, Georges Clemenceau, prime minister and one of the architects of the
Treaty of Versailles that ended the war, put a rather fine point on French national
survival: "The Treaty of Versailles does not mention that France pledges to have
more children. But it is the first thing that should have been written."[50] Shortly
thereafter, Parliament took up a bill to ban the advertisement and sale of contraception, as well as to increase the criminal penalties for abortion. The bill
had been languishing since 1914, having first been introduced in 1891.[51] This
bill, which became known as the *loi scélérate* (heinous law) of July 31, 1920, prohibited abortion absolutely (except in rare cases in which it was necessary to
save the life of the woman), subjecting practitioners, advertisers, and women
who induced their own abortions to steep fines and ten years in jail.[52] The same
law also criminalized the promotion, advertisement, distribution, and sale of
contraceptives. The law was passed with great urgency (under emergency parliamentary procedures) and without much opposition.[53]

Whether or not the French legislature believed that reforming the penal code
would reform social manners, juries continued to mete out lenient verdicts. In
1923, an amendment to the 1920 law was passed to permit certain abortion cases
to be tried before a judge as an administrative transgression (akin to a misdemeanor) and no longer a felony.[54] What was lost by this procedural circumvention

was the "moral gravitas"—the stigma and shame—that those wanting to end abortion demanded. However, legislators hoped that avoiding the jury would lead to more convictions and be a deterrent.

There is contradictory evidence on the effect of these reforms, and abortion continued to be feature in public discourse during the interwar period.[55] In the late 1930s Fernand Boverat, president of the largest and most influential prona-talist association—the Alliance nationale contre la depopulation—and member of the French government's Conseil supérieur de la natalité, drafted the abor-tion provision of a bill that became part of the 1939 Family Code.[56] The 1939 law, among other things, targeted judicial practices that led to acquittals, and raised penalties for those who were considered repeat offenders—a mandatory sentence of five to ten years and a fine of between 1,000 and 10,000 francs.[57] The strictest revisions, however, were made to the criminal code. Article 317, con-cerning abortion, made self-induction a crime, in the name of protecting the fetus (*l'enfant prénatal*), on the theory that it would be left sickly and deformed; any attempted abortion—whether or not the woman was in fact pregnant—would also be criminalized.[58] The rise in abortion conviction rates—that is to say, the decline in acquittals in ordinary courts—is ascribed to these provisions.[59]

The Family Code became the template for many of the decree-laws passed by the Vichy regime concerning reproduction, marriage, and divorce.[60] Many of the conservative pronatalist legislators and administrators of the Third Re-public hardly missed a beat as they carried on in their capacities as part of Vi-chy regime.[61] With the 300 law, issued February 15, 1942, they got what they had long sought. Abortion was made a capital offense "synonymous with trea-son,"[62] and shortly thereafter, cases of those suspected of routinely profiting from abortion were brought under the jurisdiction of the Tribunal d'État—Vichy's Star Chamber.

Conclusion

What was the (or an) objective in equating abortion with treason? Here, the dis-tinction between the symbolic or expressive work that criminal law accom-plishes, on the one hand, and its instrumental or utilitarian aims, on the other, is instructive.[63] As I have pointed out, deterring abortion had been a long-standing interest of France (as it is of many differentially modernizing states today).[64] The state had frequently used criminal law to accomplish its goals: weighing the cost and benefits of securing criminal convictions (a more instrumental objective) against those of threatening the imposition of harsh penalties (a more symbolic one). The 1923 law was meant to have struck a balance, but French politics turned more conservative, especially as related to gender and family formation. Under Vichy, the technical fix (prosecuting abortion as a misdemeanor) was no longer symbolically sufficient. Administrative penalties and sentences did not generate widespread social abhorrence or stigma. Arguably, more expressive force was required to condemn women who defied the Vichy state by exercising sexual autonomy and renouncing, as it were, the traditional gendered role of "mother" (never mind that the woman seeking an abortion might have had other children already).[65] Giraud, her accomplices, and the comparative handful of others prosecuted for abortion represented a conceptual threat to Vichy's idea of itself, if one can speak of a state's self-conceptualization. This was, and still is, the essence of treason. With family, work, and nation at Vichy's core, Giraud and others were its antithesis. Their activities undermined the heteronormative notions of the family, of work (*femme au foyer*— "housewife"—rather than *faiseuses d'ange*—"abortionist"), and of the *patrie*—the fatherland—where everyone submitted to the authority and strong will of the state, preferably out of love but, if need be, out of fear. Through this criminal prosecution, the symbolic (if not actual) state order was meant to be restored.[66]

Considering this exceptional prosecution of abortion as treason, what is illuminated? How does this unearth some connection initially gestured to by Lord Devlin and George Fletcher at the beginning of this chapter? First, the prosecution and execution of Giraud expose yet again that the power of the state has no rational limit when it comes to securing its existence or propounding its morality. Second, it highlights the connections among gender, national identity, belonging, and criminal law. An important purpose and objective of criminal sanction is to secure, stabilize, produce, and reproduce requisite behavior (in this case, gendered behavior) by threatening to harm the life, liberty, and property of those who do not conform. During the Vichy period in France, abortion symbolized the rejection of motherhood, an act thought to be so transgressive of Vichy's social and national order that the regime's criminal law classified it as a crime against the state and punished it as such.

Although no country equates abortion with treason, the complete criminalization of abortion (without an exception for the life of the woman) in states such as El Salvador, Nicaragua, and Malta comes close.[67] The national histories that brought these governments to absolutist prohibitions are multidetermined, but they all share common Catholic or authoritarian traditions. A similar message comes out of the mouths of state prosecutors who chastise women, regardless of their circumstances, for having spurned their natural duties as mothers by aborting (or miscarrying) and disturbing the moral, social order.[68] Promotion of a stereotypical idea that women's value and virtue are derived through motherhood and their sexuality is only acceptable if in a heterosexual marriage that results in pregnancy is imagined to be inextricably connected to the absolute criminalization of abortion. Whether concerned with deterrence or retribution, the severity of the criminal sanctions promotes a stereotype of women that spans religious and cultural traditions alike where patriarchal attitudes predominate.

Douglas Husak writes that the very purpose of criminal law is to exclude and to stigmatize.[69] His insight is echoed in Fletcher's aperçu that treason is the mainspring of our criminal theory of conduct (or bad act). Criminal law determines who is a loyal, valuable member of the polity and who is a worthless outlaw. Stigma inscribes the workings of criminal law on the body of the person so criminalized—driving him or her away from and out of society.[70] Shame—an internalization of this stigma—was precisely what was missing from Giraud's demeanor, what made her cynicism so disconcerting and dangerous, and what led to her death. Perhaps had she felt guiltier, she would have saved her life.

Much public health and human rights research and advocacy has been devoted to addressing and reducing stigma—first for HIV[71] and more recently for abortion.[72] Yet decades of work to decriminalize sex work, injection drug use, sexual orientation, and gender identity and expression, as well as to depoliticize abortion work, may come to naught in many countries in the thrall of moral panic and political opportunism.[73] Across the board, the perceptible turn to criminal law portends ill for the dignity and equality of people whose sense and expression of self is marked with stigma by society. Which brings me to a thread that runs throughout this book: is criminal law, particularly when used to enforce gender stereotypes, compatible with human rights?

For the last twenty years or so, scholarly literature and advocacy campaigns have elaborated human rights interpretations to include abortion.[74] Increasingly, stigma generation surrounding abortion has been viewed as a human rights violation.[75] Modern human rights law is predicated on the notion that all are equal in dignity and worth. Stigmatizing identities, including gender nonconforming practices, through the application of criminal law and concomitantly promulgating stereotypes diminishes dignity and worth and is precisely the sort of state action that human rights doctrine opposes.[76] Seeing how vital the criminalization of abortion can be to the conceptualization of a state's identity and survival, and how redolent of treason nonconforming gender practices may be during populist moments, it is even more urgent to construct potent human rights counterweights. For all the historical, cultural, and political differences that separate the contemporary moment from Giraud's time, there are continuities. Giraud behaved as if she had a right to abort pregnancies. Abortion, national self-definition, gendered expectations, and criminal law hang together in fairly predictable ways. At one end of the spectrum, they converge as treason; at the other, they permit sexual self-determination. Contemporary human rights doctrine and practice favor the latter.[77] But the future, like the past, has no straight lines.

PART III

Contemporary National Concerns

CHAPTER 9

Wanja Muguongo in Conversation with
Alice M. Miller: Interview

Wanja Muguongo describes herself as a queer African feminist and a firm believer in human rights and social justice. Her organization, UHAI EASHRI (East African Sexual Health and Rights Initiative), is an indigenous activist fund that provides "flexible and accessible resources to support civil society activism around issues of sexuality, health and human rights" in the East African region (Kenya, Uganda, Tanzania, Rwanda, and Burundi), with a specific focus on the rights of sexual minorities.[1] UHAI EASHRI seeks to build a strong, diverse, and organized movement for change through grant making, capacity support, conferences, and programming.

This interview with Ms. Muguongo was conducted by Alice M. Miller, over email and telephone, during the summer of 2014 and finalized in 2016. It relies on a number of UHAI's reports, which are cited as relevant.

ALICE MILLER [AM]. Wanja, your work on sexuality, rights, and health as an advocate and funder in East Africa puts you squarely in the current headlines on the politics of diversity, especially around the politics of homosexuality. In the swirl of incendiary speech and debate that has gone global, or perhaps been pushed into the global geopolitics of sex, you have established a clear voice that calls for paying attention to the local: local politics and local actors and the way their interests and practices engage, manipulate, and are instrumentalized in the global debates. As these debates on sexuality, rights, and health transit between global and local, what should we be paying attention to in "the local"?

WANJA MUGUONGO [WM]. I would like to start our discussion by laying the premise that the greatest impact of the criminal laws on sexual and gender nonconforming people in East Africa is effected through vagrancy and public order laws. These laws provide for extensive surveillance, abuse, and repression on grounds of sexual or gender deviance without mentioning sex. Thus, they do not attract condemnation, monitoring, and campaigns to end their abusive use as compared to the attention being garnered by "sodomy" and antihomosexuality laws.

Vagrancy laws, public order laws, and other administrative ordinances share a common denominator: they allow the power of the state to be used with impunity in the name of social order and of the material well-being of the dominant groups in society. Those at risk are at risk because of their vulnerability in public spaces, either through their poverty, their habitation of low-income neighborhoods, their visible nonconformity to gender norms or norms dictating sexual expression, or their lack of other social supports.

My work with UHAI calls attention to the fact that, although the high-decibel fights over same-sex sexual acts (so-called sodomy statutes) and the equally volatile fights over prostitution laws do matter for rights, so many of the laws that suppress nonconforming sexuality and gender never mention the word *sex*. These laws and practices should also be at the center of sexual rights advocacy.

AM. I remember you giving a talk at Yale at which you started not with the standard call to address "African homophobia" and "the export of U.S. homophobia by U.S. right-wingers"[2] but with a complex history of actors, national politics, and transnational players in which the East African struggles—for equitable responses to health and housing needs, for access to resources, for gender equality, and for national accountability—were woven into your story of how political headlining with calls to legal repression of "homosexuality" had become so central to local political success. You set out how transnational stories and local forces combined to manipulate public debates in the mode of populist politics. You also set out the way that local resistances were often undermined and occasionally strengthened by transborder actions of so-called allies.

WM. UHAI is interested in how to build from the ground up, to first strengthen local organizing and activist voices and then to take our voices and experiences and knowledge and frameworks into local politics, across the region and globally. UHAI works in a variety of interrelated ways: funding, strengthening capacity, facilitating advocacy, and doing research, such as producing the reports we talk about later in our discussions.

The new laws and legal environment of 2014 have changed some of our work, but other work remains the same. The year 2014 saw Uganda pass an antihomosexuality bill that would broaden the criminalization of same-sex relations and penalize individuals and groups that support LGBTI rights.[3] The Constitutional Court of Uganda struck down the law later that year. Uganda also passed a broad Anti-pornography Act that bans "the representation of the sexual parts of a person for primarily sexual excitement."[4] The act's signing immediately led to public attacks on women in miniskirts, with perpetrators claiming that they were helping to enforce the law.[5] Kenya and Tanzania have both seen lobbying to tighten sodomy laws, with a Kenyan legislator introducing a bill to make homosexual acts punishable by death or life in prison.[6] Tanzania has also deregistered nongovernmental civil society organizations for promoting gay rights.[7] UHAI and its partner organizations have been heavily involved in litigation challenging recent antigay laws.[8]

At UHAI, we have also been working to build up the space for and the capacity of people in sex work and people with nonconforming gender and sexual identities to advocate on their own behalf by using the language of rights, as well as broad ideas of social justice, citizenship, and political belonging. In 2010 UHAI released a report surveying the social, political, and legal space for sexually and gender diverse folks called *A People Condemned: The Human Rights Status of Lesbians, Gays, Bisexual, Transgender and Intersex Persons in East Africa, 2009–2010.*[9] We included a section on sodomy laws, but we also included research on other laws, as well as on the absence of antidiscrimination laws and laws to ensure protection from violence and abuse, such as rape of men, trans folks, or folks in sex work. We also included the social practices, government propaganda, and media and religious messages about gender stereotypes that affect everyone, including women who identify as lesbians and trans people—two groups that often drop out of traditional "gay-focused" work.

AM. I also think you have the perfect love-hate relationship with law going here. On the one hand, UHAI has said that "there is need for a considered and targeted use of the regional and international legal forums and systems to agitate for LGBTI rights. Some of the forums include The African Commission on Human and Peoples' Rights, the East African Court of Justice and committees under international human rights covenant such as the Human Rights Committee and the Committee on Economic, Social and Cultural Rights."[10] On the other hand, your comments here stress that you want us to notice that criminal law is a problem not only because it gives power but also because it is part of a bigger system of misunderstanding, stereotype, and inequality. Your work and UHAI's reports consistently engage with the need for public education and for the full participation of the people whose lives and dignity are at stake.

You also stress that "fixing" the law (the way lawyers fix it) can never be done by legal work alone. I noted that your 2013 report has been scathingly critical of the cowardice of many local lawyers who are afraid to take certain cases and of the limited vision of many national courts. Your report extensively cites a judgment from the Kenyan Constitutional Court responding to a petitioner seeking protection from discrimination on the grounds of intersex status. In that case, the court said,

We [the court] can issue orders and make declarations, but this will be of little effect considering that the stigma is connected with the public perception which is based on the public's limited knowledge of intersex status. Few seem to appreciate the fact that the issue of gender definition for an intersex person unlike a transsexual or a homosexual, is a matter of necessity and not choice. . . . The Kenyan society is predominantly a traditional African society in terms of social, moral and religious values . . . we have not reached the stage where such values involving matters of sexuality can be rationalised or compromised through science.[11]

Your report goes on to say, "Societal prejudice against LGBTI persons is deeply rooted even in what would be expected to be progressive quarters, including the courts. . . . This decision is the very embodiment of societal prejudice by a Constitutional court, which is rather expected to be the custodian of the fundamental rights of minorities and the oppressed."[12] UHAI seems to take a complicated position—one that simultaneously accepts that law will always embody some prejudices and that challenges it again and again to move past its biases and limits.

Moreover, in my opinion, your work here is powerful because it engages with but is not limited by the law. Most uniquely, it is powerful because of what I see as your manifestation of the idea that there should be solidarity and a common critique of the full range of laws regulating same-sex relationships, sex outside of marriage, and sex for money and body autonomy.

This kind of solidarity has not been a common approach anywhere in the world—UHAI is pioneering this move in East Africa and working with other Global South NGOs to engage others in this approach. What has been the reaction of other sex worker and LGBTI groups to this approach—on the continent and globally?

WM. This approach is not unique to UHAI. There is definitely a global recognition that oppression is interconnected and that a narrow, linear approach, which, for instance, elevates "gay rights" separate from other human rights, fails to appreciate the complexities of the use of the law as a tool of oppression.

AM. I'm interested in hearing more about the mechanics of how you started UHAI on a solidarity model that focuses on the full range of laws regulating same-sex relationships, sex outside of marriage, sex for money, and laws regulating one's bodily autonomy. There's a lot of scholarly support for this view, but I'm interested in the perspective that your organization can add as an activist fund. What were the challenges in starting UHAI that were particular to starting it with a solidarity approach rather than focusing on a narrower issue (e.g., only gay rights or only sex work)? Were you always certain that you would found UHAI on a solidarity approach? Did you consider if addressing a narrower range of issues would be easier? Did you encounter any resistance to thinking this way? Did other local organizations understand the benefits of the solidarity approach right away, or did some object to being grouped with others? What would you tell other local activists trying to build the first solidarity-based organization in their region?

WM. As an LGBTI and sex worker fund, the UHAI model is actually not about solidarity. It is about a recognition that a patriarchal, heteronormative society creates oppression, discrimination, and marginalization for us all: sex workers, intersex people, lesbians, gay men, trans people, and so forth. These oppressions stem from the fact that transgressing societal norms around sexuality and sexual expression, as well as any transgression of gender binaries, challenges the control and power of the patriarchy. It comes from a recognition that we share both enemies and allies; that the policeman who will rape a sex worker in lockup will also arrest a trans person for impersonation. The lawyer who will represent a gay man in court will likely be the same one that sex workers go to for legal aid.

When you also think about who LGBTI people are and who sex workers are, sometimes the differentiation can be an exercise in splitting hairs. A number of UHAI grantee partner organizations are made up of male sex workers who identify as gay. There are also trans sex workers and sex workers who identify as lesbian. A lot of the labeling we use does not adequately define the wholeness of our sexual and gender expressions.

Right from its inception, it was obvious for UHAI that being a fund for both LGBTI and sex worker organizing was the only way to go in order to comprehensively support the diversity of movements.

Once we explain our theory of problem (patriarchy) and our theory of change (organized voice), it becomes easier for people to understand why we are an LGBTI *and* sex worker fund.

AM. Given headlines popping up all over Africa—and globally—on how repression of "homosexuality" is un-African, how have you built your analysis about the laws and police practices that affect LGBTI people's daily lives?[13]

WM. The common rhetoric from politicians, clerics, the police, and those in state authority in various countries in Africa emphasizes the need to control and regulate sexuality and sexual expression in order to protect our societies from deviant, nonnormative sexual practice. A variety of legislation exists to criminalize behavior that is considered likely to "corrupt African morals." We have already described Uganda's infamous antihomosexuality propaganda from 2014, but here I want to call attention to the penal codes of Kenya, Tanzania, and Uganda, which criminalize carnal knowledge of any person against the order of nature, punishing contravention with imprisonment for fourteen years to life. In 2009 Burundi amended its penal code to criminalize same-sex intimacy for the first time. In the same year, Rwanda attempted to amend its penal law to criminalize "engaging in and inciting homosexual acts."[14] The proposal was tabled before the Rwandese Parliament but withdrawn: nevertheless, same-sex sexual conduct is deemed already criminal under Rwanda's "offences against public morals and sensitivities," which carries a maximum penalty of five years.[15]

AM. But you have been concerned that even as these laws and the new hyperattention to public propaganda laws make trouble for your constituency, the daily repression of LGTBI people goes on undercover—well, not so much undercover but in plain view, as your report describes. Furthermore, because it is low-level police abuse of "miscreants," the advocacy community doesn't respond. From our conversations, I know you have a clear critique of the way that sexual rights advocacy has avoided the tough work on the streets, where so much of the repression of diversity arises. Do you think that police and local government authorities (and their allies in the media and religion) understand that harassing and abusing folks under the cover of vagrancy and public order laws spares them from the criticism that they are enforcing sexual repression? It seems to me in the West that tolerance for "public order" policing is part of a certain desire for personal security in a very disordered world, and that gay rights and women's groups often buy into this kind of desire for "security in my backyard." For example, some of the most popular anti–sex work ordinances in the U.S. are the "prostitution-free zone" ordinances.[16]

WM. I am concerned that the majority of Africans prosecuted, detained, or harassed by the authorities for sexual "offenses" suffer under laws that have very little to say explicitly about sexuality itself. While there is so much global advocacy on sodomy legislation and its impact on criminalizing a section of society due to sexuality and on the decriminalization or legalization of sex work, a more commonly used entry point to persecution and regulation are public order laws.

In 2013 a study was done by UHAI on the human rights status of LGBTI people in East Africa between 2010 and 2013. The report revealed that while the arbitrary arrest of LGBTI persons is widespread throughout East Africa, in the end, they are charged only with misdemeanors or detained for days without trial in the hope of extorting money from colleagues or relatives. Local authority bylaws against loitering and vagrancy are used to persecute LGBTI individuals.[17]

This flagged for us that we need to pay a lot more attention to these kinds of things. Of course, the criminalization of same-sex behavior is wrong, but so is the blackmail that follows. Moreover, the incredible power of the police to arrest and then abuse folks with impunity—while never charging them—shows us that it is power without accountability, power aided by social prejudice, and power that is given a free pass by the criminal law.

AM. How does this work? Aren't the laws criminalizing sex, such as sex for money or transactional sex, used as the basis for prosecutions?

WM. Criminal law targeting sex work is often accompanied by the use of administrative law and municipal bylaws to achieve prohibitionist or other goals. In some jurisdictions, arrests of sex workers under these noncriminal statutes are more frequent than criminal arrests. These laws include loitering, vagrancy, impeding the flow of traffic, congregating for the purposes of prostitution, public indecency, and disorderly behavior.[18]

At UHAI, we think that it is so difficult to actually *prove* the crime of exchanging sex for money, or in the case of the sodomy laws, same-sex sexual activity, that the police use these laws as a pretext for harassment. Harassment and extortion as law enforcement![19]

For instance, in Kenya specifically, examining how rarely the law against prostitution is used (compared to other charges) easily illustrates how challenging proving the offense really is. For the offense of "living off the earnings of a prostitute," the court has to get evidence that a "[male] person knowingly lives with, or is habitually in the company of, a prostitute or is proved to have exercised control, direction, or influence over the movements of a prostitute in such a manner as to show that he is aiding, abetting, or compelling her prostitution with any other person. Generally, he shall, unless he satisfies the court to the contrary, be deemed to be knowingly living on the earnings of prostitution."[20]

Proving that the woman is a prostitute presents great difficulty. The prostitution offense is hardly investigated, and more often than not, no evidence is gathered. Rather, police sweeps are conducted indiscriminately in the streets at night and a lorry load of those found on the streets are locked overnight and charged the next day en masse. While in custody, other inmates advise those who fall prey to this charge to avoid pleading not guilty, as they risk repetitive fourteen-day remands until the case is next mentioned, ensuring a long, drawn-out process for one who may not be in a position to post bail or seek counsel.

Moreover, groups working on the ground have noted the range of laws used to punish the exchange of sex for money: public order laws employed in Uganda against sex workers and clients include laws against "being rogue and vagabond" (a kind of vagrancy law) and "frequenting a place used for smoking opium." Research carried out in Uganda by UHAI's grantee partner Human Rights Awareness and Promotion Forum (HRAPF) in the context of providing legal aid to LGBTI people and sex workers who find themselves afoul of the law reveals the haphazard and yet abusive ways that cases are dealt with, as well as an apparent arbitrary preference for using vagrancy laws rather than prostitution law.

For example, in 2011 and 2012 HRAPF found six cases (one in 2011, five in 2012) in which clients were charged not under the prostitution statute but under Section 168 of the penal code for being "rogue and vagabond." In the same two-year period, there were only two charges under the prostitution law (living on the earnings of prostitution). In 2013 twelve vagrancy cases were registered against people in the sex trade. Ten of these were "rogue and vagabond cases," while the remaining two were cases about frequenting a place used for smoking opium. In 2014 fourteen cases were registered under vagrancy laws and none were registered under the prostitution law. HRAPF considers that there is a visible and deliberate shift by law enforcement agencies toward bringing charges under blanket vagrancy offenses instead of under offenses against sex work.[21]

UHAI also notes that on the few occasions when sodomy laws were actually used to bring charges, the prosecution failed for lack of evidence. Two recent 2014 Ugandan cases come to mind: *Uganda v. Mukisa Kim* and *Uganda v. Ganafa Sam*. In both instances, the defendants were charged under Penal Code Act (Cap. 120) Section 145, offenses related to "carnal knowledge against the order of nature." Both cases attracted a lot of interest both in Uganda and globally, especially because they were prosecuted against the backdrop of the infamous Anti-homosexuality Act, which was signed into law in February 2014. Both cases were dismissed for the government's failure to take the necessary steps to prosecute ("want of prosecution"), after the continued failure of the state to produce witnesses and required evidence.[22]

In East Africa, we found that a reliance on vagrancy laws also provided a rich environment for extortion and blackmail. The UHAI EASHRI report quoted earlier, *Why Must I Cry?*, also revealed that out of the over six hundred respondents to the survey, of those who had encountered police harassment, 26 percent were blackmailed, while 33 percent were extorted, compared to only 4 percent who had been arrested and detained.[23]

A 2011 report by the International Gay and Lesbian Human Rights Commission about men who have sex with men in Malawi, Namibia, and Botswana found that blackmail was one of the most prevalent human rights abuses they faced, with 18 percent of those in Malawi, 21.3 percent of those in Namibia, and 26.5 percent of those in Botswana reporting incidents of blackmail.[24]

Among those surveyed across all three countries, the 21.2 percent of people who had been blackmailed because of their sexuality were a larger proportion than those who, on the same basis, were afraid to walk in their community (19 percent), were afraid to seek health services (18.5 percent), had been beaten up by a government or police official (12.2 percent), were denied housing (6.9 percent), or were denied health care (5.1 percent).[25]

Blackmail and extortion thrive within this environment of widespread disapproval of same-sex relationships and transactional sex.

Indeed, second to the use of vagrancy and public order laws, extortion and blackmail are the most commonly used tools of controlling sexuality.

AM. Is it fair to say, then, that the police are not capable of actually doing the police work required to prove criminality under the law? If East Africa is like the U.S., it often turns out that despite the fact that the law provides for certain penalties, the actual costs of policing these crimes is too high for local police or policing these crimes doesn't fit their priorities, for whatever reason. Yet promoting these laws is win-win for politicians and police, who trumpet the laws and claim public morality as their guide, while getting to control and extort money from vulnerable folks and doing little actual policing work.[26]

WM. The police forces in all East African states are rife with harmful and discriminative attitudes. States have responded to this violence with ambivalence at best, and encouraging prejudice at worse. However, our work is only scratching the surface of the abuse that occurs under the pretext of policing more serious crimes. It is clear that we must fight the regulation and criminalization of adult consensual sex and sexual expression with all possible tools, including advocacy for the repeal of criminal laws. However, there is a great need to invest in finding ways of dealing head on with administrative laws and ordinances on public order, vagrancy, and so forth, as well as to look into how these laws affect our populations.

AM. Your work with UHAI really begs for support for more in-depth research and documentation on these practices, mainly for the classic human rights work of documenting police abuse and torture. Yet this work doesn't get a lot of attention or great funding streams or transnational advocacy campaigns (like the Human Dignity Trust's campaign in the UK, which focuses high levels of attention on the repeal of so-called sodomy laws in former British colonies). Why do you think this work not only remains underappreciated in East Africa but also hasn't attracted the high-level attention of the big "repeal sodomy" campaigns?

WM. Of course, UHAI is on record as being opposed to the colonial-legacy sodomy laws, as well as to the new, more stringent antihomosexuality laws being legislated—both because of the stigma these laws condone as well as because of the harm they do through arrests and prosecutions. But they cannot be the only focus of change. There is growing evidence that antihomosexuality and antiprostitution laws are linked. Yet I am concerned that "the good gays" don't want to link themselves to people arrested under prostitution laws.

Moreover, the win-win situation thriving on hypocrisy that you describe for your local U.S. politicians and police is also happening here. But in our case, because of the high-profile, global attention to sodomy and antipropaganda laws, our so-called global allies are helping our local politicians dig in with these laws—and giving the police a free pass on abuse.

The difference between UHAI's analysis and that of international organizations or organizations based in the West is that, as an East African activist fund, our work is based on the lived realities of our communities here. A focus on antihomosexuality laws or on repealing sodomy legislation, while laudable, must be done in tandem with homegrown efforts that have a wider, more comprehensive understanding of oppression, as experienced.

I think the way forward is a more comprehensive understanding of criminalized sexualities within a context wider than just sexual laws. Homosexuals and sex workers in East Africa, for example, exist within a context of poverty, bad governance, impunity, a corrupt police force, and inaccessible judicial systems. Gay rights campaigns that are centered on sodomy laws can easily miss the point of a broader rights claim. Activists who live the daily life of criminality must be the genesis of any attack on criminal law. In my experience, their strategies speak of a contextual understanding and therefore lead to more effective efforts. One of UHAI's grantee partners is a national coalition that has developed what they call the multitiered approach to decriminalization of homosexuality. This approach includes work on vagrancy laws, work with health providers and policy makers, trainings with the judiciary and the police, work with the media and opinion makers, and so forth. This is the kind of work that I believe will move the dial forward for sexual rights in the region.

Epilogue

After the conclusion of this interview, UHAI supported a successful legal challenge to the enforcement of Kenya's sodomy laws. A five-judge bench of the Kenyan Court of Appeal handed down a ruling on March 22, 2018, regarding the State's cruel and degrading treatment of two Kenyan men arrested in Kwale county on suspicion that they were gay. The men were subjected to forced anal examinations and HIV testing under a magistrate's order to determine if they had engaged in consensual sexual acts in private. The Court held that the forced medical examinations violated the constitutional rights of the appellants and awarded costs against the director of public prosecutions.

UHAI also supported the 2016 constitutional challenge to Sections 162 (a) and (c) and 165 of the penal code that criminalizes same-sex sexuality. The case is currently pending in the High Court. (The High Court is the federal court of first instance, and the Court of Appeals is the court of intermediate appeals; the highest court is the Supreme Court.)[27]

Criminal Law, Activism, and Sexual and Reproductive Justice: What We Can Learn from the Sex Selection Campaign in India

Geetanjali Misra and Vrinda Marwah

The Decembers of 2012 and 2013 mark two watershed moments in sexual rights advocacy in India. On December 16, 2012, a twenty-three-year-old woman was brutally beaten and gang-raped on a bus in New Delhi. In the weeks that followed, waves of protests took place across India, putting the issue of sexual violence against women on the national agenda in unprecedented ways and leading to changes in the country's sexual assault laws through the passage of the Criminal Law (Amendment) Act, 2013. Almost exactly a year later, on December 11, 2013, the Supreme Court in *Suresh Kumar Kaushal v. Naz Foundation* overturned the historic Delhi High Court judgment of 2009, which decriminalized homosexuality in India, and instead, upheld the constitutionality of India's colonial antisodomy law, Section 377 of the Indian Penal Code. While all legal options to get the highest court of the land to self-correct its course are being pursued, this has been a huge setback for the LGBT and the human rights movements in India.[1]

These are not moments that stand apart from the movements and mobilizations that have preceded them or from the many struggles they continue to engender. Indeed, the women's and queer rights movements, in India and elsewhere, offer critiques of existing economic, sociocultural, and politico-legal systems and occupy a productive space within a larger fight for social justice. Yet these two Decembers straddle a special zone: both represent significant points in the fight for sexual autonomy, in law's engagement with our intimate lives, and in the criminalization and decriminalization of certain kinds of sexual misconduct. And while the conversation on how activism turns to the law—hoping that the gains will outweigh the risks—is not a new one, this may be an opportune moment to reflect more deeply on this theme.

Criminal law is a site where activists have sought to inscribe or challenge the limits of sexual relations—saying no to coercive sexual conduct and yes to same-sex sexual conduct, for instance. And although we are often acutely aware of the limits of the law as a force for social and systemic change, law also becomes a ready focus of a lot of our activism. When we engage with criminal law to further a human rights agenda, there are a range of issues, possibilities, and challenges that merit consideration.

The contemporary moment in India is one in which there is a heightened engagement with criminal law for gender and sexual rights activism. In this context, we want to examine and analyze more closely some common strategies around criminal law, activism, and sexual and reproductive justice. As we are gender justice advocates, whose work is focused on the area of sexual and reproductive health and rights, this is a conversation that is particularly relevant to our work. For the purposes of this chapter, we will focus on the campaign against sex selection in India, one that generated broad consensus on the use of criminal law as a tool for advancing women's rights and gender justice and gave us the Pre-conception and Pre-natal Diagnostic Techniques (Prohibition of Sex Selection) Act, 1994, amended in 2003. If we dig a bit deeper into the material conditions and rhetorical devices of anti-sex-selection advocacy, what can we learn?

We begin by exploring the complexity of determining evidence of and causes for a skewed female-to-male sex ratio. Then, we consider some of the messaging and advocacy intended to combat sex selection and ask whether these have inadvertently been counterproductive to a more transformative women's rights agenda. How and why might these messages fail to capture the nuances of the problem? Ultimately, we want to examine the question of what a principled use of criminal law may look like on the question of sex selection and abortion and, by extension, on the broader spectrum of sexual and reproductive health and rights issues.

Sex Ratio, Sex Selection, and Gender Equality: Where Exactly Does the Problem Lie?

In India, the debate over gender equality is often linked to India's skewed child sex ratio (CSR). The CSR is defined as the number of females per thousand males in the age group of zero to six years in the human population. While a CSR skewed in favor of boys is not a new phenomenon in India, the continuous—even growing—decline of the ratio of females to males in the past few censuses has become a matter of deep concern. Even though the declining CSR has been the focus of several governmental and nongovernmental interventions in recent years, it remains a stubborn blot on our development landscape. This ratio reached an all-time low in 2011, with the census recording a national average of 914 girls per 1,000 boys, a fall from the 2001 census figure of 927 girls per 1,000 boys. Census data also indicate that the imbalance is not only increasing, but also reaching new areas and populations. Much of this decline has occurred in places such as Punjab, Haryana, Delhi, Gujarat, and Maharashtra—places that enjoy relative economic prosperity—and among sections of the population that have seen a rise in literacy levels and a narrowing of the gap between male and female literacy. This makes India's CSR problem something of a development conundrum.[2]

The decline in the CSR has been interpreted, in India and globally, as the direct result of more sex-selective abortions of female fetuses, following prenatal diagnostic testing that has been made possible in recent times. However, in India, unlike in most countries of the world, more girls than boys have also been dying during childhood due to factors such as poor nutrition and health care and even willful neglect, and this contributes to the decline in the CSR. The higher the gender gap in mortalities among children under six, the more adverse the CSR will become for girls. Therefore, a more relevant indicator for examining the magnitude of sex selection is the sex ratio at birth (SRB), which is the ratio of female live births per one thousand male live births.[3] The SRB cannot be considered a foolproof indicator of sex selection, but it certainly comes much closer than the CSR.[4]

India undoubtedly has a skewed SRB, and sex selection plays some role yet limitations in data have precluded a national systematic analysis of how much of a role and a comprehensive sense of the contributory role of other mechanisms.[5] On the one hand, some research suggests that only 14 percent of women use prenatal diagnostic techniques, suggesting that the overall magnitude of sex selection may be less than initially assumed. Another study concluded that no more than 3 percent of pregnancies end in sex-selective abortion.[6] However, some studies at the micro level suggest a more substantial role for sex selection consistent with introduction of the ultrasound machines. For example, a 2008 study analyzed the delivery records at one hospital over multiple decades, during which the sex ratio decreased significantly after 1980.[7]

Moreover, this discussion is made more fraught by the fact that new, sophisticated, and noninvasive techniques of determining fetal genetics and sex are constantly being developed; a new, high-priced blood test can detect the sex of the fetus by the seventh week of pregnancy. The Union Health Ministry in India is considering expanding the scope of the Pre-conception and Pre-natal Diagnostic Techniques Act to include these tests.[8] This raises the important question of how we can keep up with rapid technological developments, if at all.

Part of our inquiry therefore considers that although sex-selective abortion seems to have played some role in skewing the SRB and CSR, a comprehensive understanding of its impact and its interaction with other factors, such as sex discrimination, is lacking. Yet in India, "sex-selective abortion" has become a prominent signifier of the "status of women," as well as of related questions of medical malpractice, technology, and so forth. This discourse has gone on to repose much faith in criminal law. While sex selection is indeed tied to gender inequality, making it both structurally generated and also politically and personally sensitive, the links between sex selection and sex ratios, abortion, regulation, and so forth are not as linear and self-evident as commonly imagined. In the next section, we consider the history of the activism against sex selection, its interaction with abortion rights, and its engagement with the law.

Advocacy and Policy: Anti-sex-selection Campaigning and the Law

Abortion has been legal in India since the Medical Termination of Pregnancy Act of 1971.[9] Unlike in many countries in the Global North, feminists in India have not had to organize into a "pro-choice" lobby to counter any consistent and organized antiabortion or "pro-life" opinions. On the contrary, a history of coercive population control policies and fierce campaigning against these has meant that Indian feminists have often viewed technology, especially technomedical interventions in reproduction, with suspicion.[10]

However, despite the Medical Termination of Pregnancy Act, access to safe abortion is hindered by the lack of adequate public health infrastructure and trained personnel. The rate of unsafe abortions remains high and contributes to a significant percentage of India's maternal mortality, which is one of the highest in the world. Further, abortion in India is also used to ensure birth spacing by married women. This, together with the fact that female sterilization continues to be the main method of fertility control in India, points to a bigger problem: there is a lack of real contraceptive choices for Indian women.[11]

These interrelated issues of contraception and abortion, along with other issues of maternal mortality and morbidity, highlight the fact that reproductive choice—women's right to determine whether, when, and how to reproduce—is a central issue for women's health in India. Access to safe and legal abortion must be considered within this spectrum, beyond its formal status as a legal (though restricted) right. A big question for Indian feminists has been, what are the real conditions surrounding access to abortion? In other words, who can access this right, and how? Who cannot, and why not?

In the 1980s Indian feminists found themselves confronted with reported instances of the selective abortion of female fetuses. Women's, civil rights, and public health groups launched a campaign against the practice of prenatal sex determination. This coalition achieved its first breakthrough in 1988, when the state of Maharashtra brought into force a law regulating the use of prenatal diagnostic techniques. The focus of the campaign then shifted to securing similar central or national legislation. In 1994, the Indian Parliament passed the Prenatal Diagnostic Techniques (Regulation and Prevention of Misuse) Act, under which the use of prenatal diagnostic techniques, including ultrasonography, to detect fetal sex for nonmedical reasons was made a criminal offense. In 2003, the act was amended to improve regulation by bringing preconception technology used in sex selection (for example, in vitro fertilization) within its ambit and was renamed the Pre-conception and Pre-natal Diagnostic Techniques (Prohibition of Sex Selection) Act.[12]

However, the law was drafted to ensure that the ban on sex selection does not hinder access to abortion as it exists in the law. Hence, this act focused only on the regulation and control of techniques of prenatal sex determination, not on the abortion that may follow such determination. For violating the act, doctors, medical persons, and persons connected with advertising sex-selection services, as well as persons seeking to know the sex of the fetus, can be punished, but the pregnant woman herself is protected from prosecution, as she is presumed to have been compelled to undergo sex-determination tests by her husband and relatives. In this way, the activism of the women's movement turned to criminal law to curb sex selection, but it simultaneously strove to put in place measures to ensure that the legality of abortion was not threatened for women.

The Contemporary Backdrop: Dangerous Politicking, Decoy Issues

In this section, we look at what some civil society and government responses to this focus on sex selection actually attend to. More importantly, we examine what these responses do not attend to and how they work. Are these interventions able to "walk the tightrope"—that is, to facilitate the implementation of criminal law to regulate sex selection while also advancing women's access to safe and legal abortion?

Let us examine some of the more recent responses. India's previous minister for women and child development, Renuka Chowdhury, made it mandatory to register all pregnancies and monitor abortions; a pilot project implemented in ten blocks[13] with a high malnutrition rate and a skewed sex ratio permitted abortions only for "valid and acceptable" reasons.[14] In 2010, the government of Maharashtra introduced the Silent Observer in Kolhapur District. The Silent Observer is a centrally located device, equipped with a satellite-based tracking mechanism that can monitor all sonographies being done across all ultrasonography centers in a given radius. All relevant data of the pregnant women who come in for ultrasonographies—legal and illegal—can be centrally stored on a government database.

In 2012, the Maharashtra state government decided to add to these existing measures and proposed to provide incentives to women who give birth to a third female child. It also proposed that digital photos of all aborted fetuses be stored in a central database. In addition, it was suggested that the legal twenty-week period in which a woman can have her pregnancy medically terminated be brought down to a ten-week one, a period within which the sex of the fetus is not discernible.[15] State health minister Suresh Shetty also sought an amendment to the Pre-conception and Pre-natal Diagnostic Techniques Act to make it possible to invoke murder charges against persons (including pregnant women) involved in sex-selective abortion.[16] Indian feminists protested strongly against this move and issued a letter to the Speaker of the assembly with a hundred signatories.

These proposals to store digital photos of fetuses, shorten the period for legal abortions, and make possible murder charges for those seeking sex-selective abortions may be indicative of politicking or small trends and not representative of actual laws that will be passed, but we need to take them seriously because they have the potential to severely and adversely impact women's rights. As advocates, it is important to monitor and respond to regressive shifts in public and policy discourses because something that seemed previously unlikely can become imminent very quickly when conditions become conducive, as with a change in political leadership.

India saw the ascent of a Hindu nationalist, right-wing government during the elections of 2014; this is a climate that calls for greater civil society vigilance and monitoring.[17] Confidentiality about women's identities will be severely compromised if all details about women seeking abortions are documented and accessed by state officials. Reducing the legal period for abortion is a curtailment that will most impact women who are poor and undernourished and, through malnutrition, have irregular menstrual cycles that make it difficult to track pregnancy, leaving them with no option but unsafe abortion. Incentivizing a third female child is a contradictory proposal;[18] some states in India still follow the two-child norm for population policy, and a couple cannot know if their third child is a girl without a sex-determination test, which is illegal. Further, all efforts to criminalize the woman seeking a sex-selective abortion, rather than recognizing her behavior as a response to patriarchal pressure, have been and must continue to be kept at bay.

Today, pregnant women are being monitored and tracked over the full duration of their pregnancy by doctors and public health workers. While this is prevalent in districts with particularly low CSRs, it is also gaining legitimacy as a governmental strategy to reduce maternal mortality by increasing institution-based over home-based deliveries. As a policy, this kind of surveillance can be in tension with basic principles of women's rights, especially their rights to autonomy, mobility, privacy, and freedom. States need to know what is happening in reproductive health, but this is at a population level and should not translate to the individual level in ways that violate rights. It is obvious that this kind of monitoring can and does curtail abortion decisions that bear no connection to sex selection.[19] Through such "pro-women" advocacy, women are counterintuitively being cast as stock to be replenished and protected as a means to achieve desired developmental goals, rather than as free and equal actors in development for whom an enabling and capacitating future must be envisaged.[20]

Exploring the Interactions among Advocacy, Messaging, and Rights

While there is no way to prove a simple, singular causal pathway from civil society campaigns to policy change, it seems reasonable to assume some relationship between (real and suggested) policy changes and the fact and content of civil society campaigning that precedes or accompanies it. As feminists interested in the interaction of policy and societal change, we think it is important to recognize this political and ethical engagement, indeed complicity, even as we are acutely aware that we do not exert control over policy processes in quite the way that we would like. A certain discourse on sex selection has crystallized over time, giving a concerted push to policies meant to be seen as "tough action" on the issue; many feminists have been reflecting on this dynamic, and we want to extend those conversations in this section.

How do we understand some of the strategies that are used in women's rights campaigns against sex selection in the context of India's complicated background—of legal access to abortion without a history of feminist struggle, of feminist efforts to criminalize ultrasound use linked to sex selection, and of increasing government surveillance of pregnant women more generally (in the name of curbing maternal mortality and sex selection)—and in light of the two Decembers that mark ongoing social and legal struggles for sexual rights?

Let us consider some of the words and visuals that are commonly used in advocacy campaigns.

- Example 1
  Slogans such as "India's missing daughters," "Disappearing daughters," "Hands soaked with a daughter's blood," "Beti nahin hogi toh bahu kahan se aayegi" (No daughter means no daughter-in-law)

- Example 2
  Posters with slogans such as "Save the girl child" (with images of a cartoon girl sporting two pigtails), variations of which include "Save the girl child. Your mother wasn't a boy either."

- Example 3
  Posters with images of a fetus being crushed by a hand or a noose or of an injection going through a fetus-bearing womb, with splattered blood and a speech bubble that says, "Don't kill me, Mommy" or "I want to live, Mommy."

- Example 4
  The first season of the *Oprah Winfrey Show*–like Indian television show *Satyamev Jayate* (loosely translated as "Truth alone triumphs"), hosted by one of Bollywood's leading actors, Aamir Khan, aired in 2012 and took up the issue of sex selection in its pilot episode. While the show made some pertinent points (such as clarifying that sex selection was common among the educated middle classes), its overall tone was highly emotive. Testimonies of three women, who had been forced to undergo sex-determination procedures and abortion of their fetuses, were shared. Scenarios that can result if sex selection is allowed to continue unabated were discussed; these included men remaining unmarried because of a shortage of women, the possible creation of a

marriage market where women are bought and sold like commodities, and an increase in harassment and violence against women.[21]

Such emotive messaging around sex selection and abortion has been quite commonplace in India in recent years, as the question of an adverse and declining female-to-male CSR comes to stand in for gender justice. Many of these messages are troubling in a variety of ways, and many feminist and progressive public heath activists, including those involved in anti-sex-selection advocacy, have pointed out these problems.

For example, let us consider examples 1 and 2. Messages that are meant to stop one (more tangible) harm can cause another (more intangible one): when we attribute the value of women to their roles as mothers, sisters, daughters, and daughters-in-law, we stress their worth in relation to men and not independently and inherently as human beings in their own right. Further, focusing on women in family and marriage—who are the picture of domesticity—by implication undervalues women who are outside this framework.

Other messages, such as images of a dying or speaking fetus ("Don't kill me, Mommy"), focus on the act of abortion itself. They aim to highlight the criminality and immorality of sex selection by casting it as murderous and genocidal. Significantly, they have the effect of promoting a bias against all abortions because they conflate sex selection and abortion. By representing the female fetus as an unborn child, such messages produce and promote the idea that a human life with human rights is "murdered" when it is aborted. This personification of the fetus has negative implications for women's rights, their bodily autonomy, and particularly their access to safe and legal abortion. It also individualizes what is an acutely systemic problem, that of gender injustice and women's devaluation. Such a discussion on sex selection is a reductive one and does not locate sex selection within the continuum of discrimination that women and girls have to face throughout their lives. These are critical connections, and to speak of sex-selective abortions as the sole problem without speaking of gender justice is to miss the forest for the trees.

Some might argue that the words and visuals used in campaign messaging need to be kept simple and that addressing the key nuances and complications of an issue either is not possible in a poster or radio jingle, or is possible only by making the whole thing so unwieldy as to be ineffective. Within such reasoning, feminist concerns about faulty sex-selection messaging's chipping away at abortion rights may seem too abstract or farfetched. However, we think these are real concerns with real consequences, and we must learn to think about them as formative and fundamental to the advocacy for women's autonomy and rights, rather than as a dilution of a hallowed, efficiency-driven communications strategy. After all, the efficacy of a campaign lies not just in changing behavior. Such an instrumentalist approach can be, and has been, counterproductive. Instead, campaigns must account for the politics of an issue and its interconnectedness with other issues and the structures that keep things unjust. Ultimately, campaigns must affirm, rather than violate, rights.

A Way Out? What Pro–Women's Rights Messaging and Advocacy Could Look Like

Firstly, we need to advocate *against* sex selection and *for* abortion rights together.

The Population Council undertook a study in a district in Rajasthan to analyze the content of information materials on abortion and sex determination, as well as people's perception of these materials. Posters and pamphlets produced by the government were found to use vague words and fear-inducing visuals that equated all abortion with murder and that created confusion about the legal status of abortion. The study found that this confusion was compounded by a lack of informational material about safe abortion in both the public and private sectors. The study recommended that future informational material address the issues of abortion and sex determination simultaneously, including the legal status of abortion, the conditions under which a woman can and cannot seek abortion, the availability of abortion services and providers, and the social norms that shape decision-making on abortion.[22]

More recently, a BBC World Service Trust study critically evaluated a mixed sample of anti-sex-selection messaging, produced by both governments and nongovernmental organizations using different formats on different mass media platforms.[23] The BBC study similarly concluded that messaging needs to simultaneously address laws related to women's right to abortion and the prohibition of sex-determination tests, in order to avoid the impression that all abortions are illegal. In addition, the study concluded that messaging must also "unrave[l] and challeng[e] social and cultural attitudes that fuel sex selection."[24] These could include a host of positive images of women that (a) challenge the notion that daughters are burdens, (b) blur the distinction between "good, traditional" and "bad, modern" women, and (c) encourage women to make their own decisions, including decisions about their bodies. While messages, visuals, and slogans need to be sharp, they should not be oversimplified. The problem of skewed sex ratios is a complex and challenging one, and oversimplification has not brought us, and likely will not bring us, closer to the solution.

Secondly, we must remember that messaging is never sufficient for changing behavior: conditions must also change.

As a strategy, messaging through campaigns may be necessary, but it is far from sufficient. Messaging by itself cannot transform a practice that has been consolidated over generations and under layers of economic, sociocultural, and political disempowerment, and we should not expect it to. Women's undervaluation is the reason families wish to eliminate female children both before and after birth. Therefore, good human rights and advocacy work must extend beyond messaging to support and advance structural change. Overall, we need structural change in order to ensure that life chances for girls are equal to those for boys, and that gender roles and expectations become more fluid.

Even when we consider messaging to combat sex selection, we must question the singular focus on saving the female child by stopping sex-selective abortions. As previously discussed, sex-selective abortions are not the only contributor to a skewed CSR. Along with sex selection, the deliberate neglect of female children is also a factor in low CSRs. An unwanted fetus can be eliminated through voluntary or induced miscarriage, or later through infanticide, neglect, and discrimination in nutrition and health. Indeed, there appears to be some continuity between the past and the present, with historical practices of the elimination of female children through infanticide and neglect having been transmuted into technologically facilitated prebirth elimination. It is important that we acknowledge this and consider the SRB, if we must, rather than the CSR.

Moreover, as gender rights advocates, we must ask ourselves, what happens after we "save the girl child"? What of her life cycle? She could face a denial of education and health care, as well as other kinds of discrimination. Later in life, she may confront various forms of state, communal, domestic, sexual, and other violences. She will probably lack contraceptive choice, and she may one day need and seek an abortion. Is our advocacy promoting her right to a fuller life?

In the report *Planning Families, Planning Gender*, which examines the adverse CSR in select districts of five states in India, the authors recommend interventions in the medium and long term, beyond the current focus on culpable medical facilities and practitioners.[25] They stress the need for interventions that can strengthen public health and public education; recognize the value of women's work and guarantee women paid employment; question marriage norms (particularly that of parents residing with the son); and create provisions for old-age care by taking the responsibility beyond the family and to the state.[26]

Such an approach, in which advocacy aims to create conditions that make another world possible, is perhaps more transformative. It focuses not only on the *acts* of sex selection, but also on the *culture* of sex selection. It recognizes sex selection as a symptom and as a means through which a socio-structurally induced daughter aversion is realized. Daughter aversion, rooted firmly in patriarchy and structural oppression, creates a culture in which acts of sex selection for abortion become desirable and possible. Studies have repeatedly shown that daughter aversion interacts with many variables, some old, some new, and some in flux, that make it very difficult to understand the problem in general terms.[27] A more honest solution to combating the symbolic and material harms of sex selection has to be gender justice, including reproductive and sexual autonomy—of which the right to choose whether, when, and how to reproduce is a big part. Today, campaigns that target the criminality or immorality of sex selection to the point of sacrificing women's reproductive autonomy may be guilty of misdiagnosing the problem and of potentially contributing to women's vulnerability.

A more gender expansive analysis is necessary to frame our advocacy beyond women's needs to consider also issues of women's interests.[28] How do we understand the issue on which we are focusing as linked to other issues in its immediate vicinity—in this case, sexual and reproductive health and rights—and to larger issues of gender justice and social justice? And how do we feed a more expansive analysis back into our work? Do we change our advocacy strategy, or do we continue in the same vein with the awareness that there are critical silences, maybe even contradictions? Perhaps there is no one answer to this, but reflecting on past and present advocacy and its effects could bring us closer to the right questions.

Criminal Law and Sexual and Reproductive Health and Rights: Reframing the Questions and Moving Forward

Against the backdrop of this interplay among sex selection, abortion, criminal law, and gender justice, two questions beg our consideration: Can feminist politics be proabortion and anti–sex selection? And can it be anti–sex selection for both its symbolic and possibly material effects without recourse to criminal law?

In her writing, leading feminist author Nivedita Menon warns that both the legal and social approval for abortion in India cannot be taken for granted.[29] By "legal approval," Menon means the framing and politics of the Medical Termination of Pregnancy Act, which does not confer abortion as an unqualified right that women can claim. She refers to a few legal cases regarding abortion that have come to the court, where the court has focused not on women's right to autonomy but on the centrality of their reproductive role in maintaining social order. That the social sanction for abortion is precarious is equally easy to imagine. Following the recent death of an Indian doctor in Ireland after she was denied an abortion, some debates in the mainstream media in India focused not on the provision of abortion services, the need to keep abortion safe and legal, or the relationship between inadequate abortion services and maternal deaths and morbidity, but instead on the moral and religious positions on abortion.[30]

Menon also points out that all decisions to abort, not just the decision to abort a female fetus, are mediated by social and cultural pressures in a patriarchal society. Moreover, recognizing that women are already constrained subjects, she also looks at the futures faced by pregnant women. She writes, "The painful question is this: As feminists, can we insist that individual women should have to deal with the consequences of giving birth to every kind of foetus, and that abortion should be permitted only if you know nothing about the foetus you are aborting? Can we hold the lives of existing women to ransom in order that the rights of abstract categories—'women,' 'the disabled'—can be protected?"[31]

Menon's questions get to the heart of the dilemma in anti-sex-selection interventions from a feminist perspective in the context of India, with relevance globally. The challenge with sex selection is to find a way to diminish its attractiveness for women and their families, outside criminal law and within the frame of gender justice. This reframes the question by asking what makes it more acceptable for a woman to give birth to a daughter than to a son, rather than merely telling her not to abort a female fetus. There is a mutually reinforcing link between the lack of autonomy women have in a patriarchal society and their undervaluation as human beings, between structural inequality and violations in individual lives. A rights-based intervention cannot restrict one in the interest of another without violating the essence of both. To us, that essence is autonomy. And it cuts across the sexual and reproductive health rights agenda.

One stream of the history of sexual and reproductive health and rights in India has been the struggle to secure women's autonomy over their sexual and reproductive lives—be it against coercive population control policies or sexual violence or for the right to choose their sexual partners irrespective of caste, religion, gender, and so forth. To limit the scope of abortion on any grounds sits uncomfortably with this vision and sets us off on a slippery slope where a woman's autonomy is subordinated to a higher principle. Conceptually or practically, can we, as feminists, demand anything but women's unqualified right to abort? From a human rights perspective, the practical consequences of denying an abortion to a woman who needs it here and now cannot be justified. Restricting access to a service that only women need is gender-based discrimination.

Additionally, in a context such as India, the effects of such a restriction are bound to disproportionately affect women who are already constrained, who are already economically and socially marginalized, and who do not have the resources to subvert the law and find ways to abort despite the law.

As we grapple with the effects of the Decembers of 2012 and 2013, both refracted through criminal law, we must work to keep sexual autonomy at the center of the conversation and to refer to the law as one of the means to this end. Criminal law is not an empty, neutral mechanism; rather, it operates within a judicial system that has some serious flaws, and when we bring it into our activism, it takes on a life and logic that can quickly slip from our grasp. And while the law will remain a site of struggle, as we advance human rights, we must be mindful of these dynamics when setting the terms on which we engage with the law. And the law, as well as its effects, must be used to increase autonomy, not to decrease it.

CHAPTER 11

Poisoned Gifts: Old Moralities under New Clothes?

Esteban Restrepo Saldarriaga

Since the end of World War II, judicial review has expanded spectacularly all around the world. This is a consequence of the enactment of new constitutions.[1] From Eastern Europe to Latin America to South Africa, supreme and constitutional courts have taken their transitional moments seriously through the forceful enforcement of a new constitutional order. Because of the rights guaranteed by newly enacted constitutions, judicial activism grounded in fundamental rights has been on the rise. One of the most salient characteristics of the new constitutional orders and the ensuing periods of judicial activism has been what some have described as the "constitutionalization of law."[2] The constitution and its rights "irradiate" (to use the German constitutional court's expression) or permeate the rest of the legal order, so that every aspect of private, criminal, and administrative law (the so-called ordinary law) reflects the constitution. An important task of new supreme and constitutional courts has thus been interpreting important questions of ordinary law in light of constitutional values, principles, and rights, revealing how the former are a reflection of the latter.

The intellectual and legal construction of criminal law has been closely tied to the guarantee of basic principles of autonomy and equality in the modern liberal nation-state. In both continental and common-law legal systems, liberal political philosophers and criminal law theorists have tried to find a "grand theory" that would systematically justify the use of criminal law to punish bad acts committed by free rational agents. Although such a theory is still lacking,[3] other principles have been discussed as the most appropriate candidates to limit the use of criminal law as an instrument (of last resort) in the achievement of social order and peace. For example, in the Anglo-American context, this discussion has revolved around using John Stuart Mill's harm principle and its modern elaborations to justify and set limits for criminal punishment.[4] In continental law systems, where German criminal law theory has exercised a deep influence, the "legal good" theory (*Rechtsgutstheorie*) has been the centerpiece of the debate on the limits of criminal law.[5] In both systems, however, each of these preeminent theories has proved to lack enough power to explain comprehensively the many ways in which criminal law is used in modern plural and democratic societies.

Given the difficulty of finding a satisfactory general theory of criminal law, the idea of the "constitutionalization of criminal law" has come to fill this theoretical and practical gap in many continental law jurisdictions. The principle of human dignity and the fundamental rights generally guaranteed by a constitution provide both a justification for and the limits of criminal punishment.[6] Some German criminal law theorists have thus linked the "legal good" theory to the notion that constitutional norms permeate the whole of criminal law. According to this idea, the constitution is the receptacle of those legal goods necessary to preserve peaceful common social coexistence and the development of personal freedom.[7] While it is the task of state legislature to devise the best means to protect legal goods (such as life, personal integrity, sexual autonomy, property, state security, and so forth), constitutional norms impose a limit on the legislative use of criminal law as an instrument for the guarantee of these goods. Insofar as criminal punishment impinges on personal freedom, and is therefore the most extreme response to behaviors that affect constitutionally protected legal goods, it only plays the "subsidiary role" of protection and should only be used in the complete absence of less intrusive means of protecting legal goods.[8]

The idea that human dignity and constitutional fundamental rights limit the use of criminal law has a number of key consequences. First, "mere immoralities" are not susceptible to criminalization.[9] Constitutional values and rights may well contradict individual moral views, even if a majority of citizens hold them. This is why, as Ronald Dworkin famously observed, rights are individual "trump cards" against the majority.[10] Alternatively, as Claus Roxin has submitted, "in our times, human beings live in multicultural societies based on the tolerance of conducts that may contradict our own value representations."[11] A second consequence of the constitutionalization of criminal law is that, as a general rule, feelings should not be protected by criminal norms. Finally, human dignity and constitutional fundamental rights rule out the criminalization of social taboos, such as nonconforming sexual practices.[12]

When criminal law has been constitutionalized and the constitution limits the legislative use of criminal law to achieve social order and peace, constitutional courts have the power to implement such limits.[13] It is generally believed that in a constitutional democracy, legislatures have broad power to establish what conduct should be criminalized; however, these legislative decisions could be overturned by constitutional judges when such laws infringe the limits set by the constitution and excessively impinge on personal freedom.[14] In modern times, the constitutional and supreme courts of many countries have produced important constitutional doctrines, such as proportionality methodology, to establish when the criminalization of conduct is within the constitutional limits of criminal law. A constitutional court may strike down a piece of criminal legislation if (1) it is not aimed at fulfilling some constitutional value or right, (2) it is not necessary and adequate to attain the constitutional goal for which it was passed, or (3) the costs of the restriction of personal freedom entailed by the criminalization of the conduct at hand are higher than the benefits brought about by the restriction.[15] A great deal of the constitutionalization of ordinary law by constitutional judges has thus consisted of bringing criminal law into the realm of the constitution through the use of proportionality tests. These tests, in essence, are intended to verify whether criminal law regulations achieve a balance among the duty of the state to guarantee social order and peace, the rights of those accused of criminal conduct, and the rights of crime victims.

As important criminal law commentators have argued, crimes involving sexual activity (designated in this essay as "sex crimes") generally serve as the litmus test for the idea that the constitution limits the power of legislatures to criminalize human behavior.[16] The specific way in which criminal law approaches sexuality is important evidence of the true democratic, libertarian, and egalitarian stance of a polity. It is generally understood that sex crimes have evolved from a view of sexuality that protected procreation and strict gender roles and privilege, to one in which individual self-determination, grounded in a strong notion of human autonomy (constitutionally guaranteed by a fundamental right to the "free development of personality"), and equality between the sexes is at issue. The evolution of sex crimes in liberal political communities with constitutions that protect human dignity and a generous set of fundamental rights thus seems to exemplify the idea that modern criminal law does not punish mere immoralities, feelings, or social taboos.

However, a closer look at the judicial dynamics of particular sexual criminal regulations in some jurisdictions may reveal a different and disturbing picture. When called to rule on the constitutionality of certain sex crimes deemed
problematic from a strict libertarian and egalitarian point of view, courts may
nevertheless affirm their constitutionality through sophisticated forms of reasoning that legitimize the moral worldviews and social taboos underlying such
crimes. This essay argues that the evolution in the modern law of sex crimes
toward the protection of neutral moral values is a promise yet to be fulfilled.

This peculiar dynamic particularly appears when sex crimes that, in direct
or indirect fashion, reflect moral views and taboos are brought before a constitutional court to dispute their constitutional validity. More often than not, the
resulting judicial decision will be a "poisoned gift." The ruling will apparently
affirm substantive constitutional values and rights by construing the crime as a
necessary means for their guarantee. In this sense, the decision is a "gift" of autonomy, equality, or some other constitutional value. Beneath this positive surface, however, lies the "poison" of a constitutionally incompatible cultural taboo
or moral worldview repackaged in the modern and progressive language of the
constitution. Disturbingly, the constitutional system has used its progressive values to validate some of the very dynamics that modern constitutional democracies sought to eradicate in the first place.

The "poisoned gift" dynamic therefore illustrates the main argument of this
essay—that the evolution of the modern law of sex crimes with regard to the
protection of neutral moral values is, at best, a work in progress. To substantiate this claim, the essay is divided into two sections. The first section briefly describes the evolution of sex crimes into their modern, supposedly morally
neutral, shape and relates that evolution to the "poisoned gift" dynamic. With
the help of recent criminal law theory, this section shows that this dynamic is
the constitutional manifestation of a regime that, in spite of much liberal legal
reform, is still quite sexually repressive. The second section illustrates the "poisoned gift" dynamic through the examples of same-sex sexual activity in the
military and prostitution.[17] These examples are based on constitutional court
jurisprudence from Colombia. Each case illustrates different forms of constitutional interpretation that are used to legitimize the moral views that underlie
certain sex crimes. One caveat: I do not call for the abandonment of constitutional rights and adjudication as a strategy to dismantle regimes of structural
inequality. Sometimes, if the rights at stake and the judges interpreting them
are in proper alignment, the outcome can be emancipatory. This is not, however, always the case, and the results may only partially eradicate the subordi-

nation or even work to immunize the oppression of the sexually nonconforming. My essay, therefore, is offered as a cautionary tale.

Sex Crimes and "Poisoned Gift" Dynamics

Continental modern criminal law theory describes the evolution of the legal regulation of sex crimes toward opposing "theological moral scholastic" or "medieval canonic law" models.[18] These models were aimed at protecting procreative sex, based on the view that men—through procreation—collaborated with God in continuing his work of creation. Any form of sex that deviated from the procreative goal was susceptible to being criminalized. These crimes included, in increasing order of gravity, "simple fornication," sexual intercourse through deception of the victim, adultery, incest, sacrilege (intercourse with a priest or a nun, particularly the latter), and "crimes against nature."[19] This last sex crime was considered to be the gravest, for it—in contrast to other acts, in which the procreative potential was preserved in some measure—had the utmost theological significance. Indeed, crimes such as "perfect" sodomy (anal or oral sex between men), "imperfect" sodomy (nonvaginal sex or, more generally, nonprocreative heterosexual sex), masturbation, and bestiality all implied the loss of sperm, the sterility of the sexual act, and the utter disruption of the "economy of creation."[20]

Criminal law reform during the Enlightenment severed sex crimes from their theological foundations, grounding them in supposedly morally neutral and taboo-free notions of sexual autonomy.[21] It has taken some time to dispel completely the moralistic views on "sexual normality" (that is, the criminalization of homosexuality), sexual propriety (that is, the criminalization of adultery), and men's and women's sexuality (that is, the notion that only females could be victims of rape or the way that sex crimes in some countries claim to protect "sexual honor"). Perhaps only now has it become commonplace to assert that the "legal good" that is protected through sex crimes is autonomy, understood as the possibility of any agent to freely decide when, where, and with whom to engage in sexual activity.[22] This story, however, has an alternative version.

In one of the most provocative and astute analyses of the modern law of sex crimes, Chilean criminal law theorist Antonio Bascuñán Rodríguez has identified an anomaly in the modern legal regulation of sex crimes with regard to the protection of personal autonomy. Although personal autonomy demands "moral neutrality with respect to material acts," the modern law of sex crimes is defined by "a radical asymmetry in how it values sexual autonomy."[23] The asymmetry lies in the exclusive criminalization of actions of sexual coercion and the impunity of the actions that prevent free agents from entering into sexual interaction. For Bascuñán, "that is the radical asymmetry: when confronted with an opposing will, the will of those who wish to abstain from sex is of an incomparably higher worth before the law than the will of those who wish to practice sex."[24]

Although Bascuñán tries to find several possible explanations for the asymmetrical configuration of modern sexual criminal law, he concludes that the only possible answer is that the medieval theological model of the law of sex crimes has never truly subsided, so that "the primary meaning of [modern sex crimes] is not the protection of autonomy, but the restriction of sexuality."[25] In his view, it is impossible to assert that modern sexual criminal law "is a consistent configuration of the distinction between legality and morality," so that "even in [its] revolutionary core, the conceptualization of sex crimes never liberated itself from a cultural imperative that represses sexuality."[26] In a rich and complex historical argument, Bascuñán shows how the history of sex crimes is not the history of "the transition between a repressive and a non-repressive sexual culture" but rather the history of the "variation of the rules that define the socially recognized modalities of lifting the exclusion [of sexual contact]."[27] For Bascuñán, the medieval model of sex crimes, with its restrictive view of sexuality, has contemporary manifestations not only in several forms of judicial practice but also in a worrisome tendency to overcriminalize sexuality.[28]

Taking Bascuñán's argument as a provocative starting point, I suggest that the "poisoned gift" dynamic in the judicial constitutionalization of sex crimes is one such instance of the persistence of medieval sexual criminal law. Indeed, when constitutional judges—wittingly or not—validate the criminalization of certain sexual acts, they are enforcing a view of sexuality that is at odds with the generous notion of personal autonomy (and sometimes other constitutional values) on which modern constitutions are based. What this chapter adds to Bascuñán's ideas is an analysis of some of the mechanisms through which constitutional judges legitimize the restrictive view of sexuality that operates as the foundation of certain modern sex crimes. The legitimization of this foundation is not an intellectual operation in which judges simply compare the restrictive view of sexuality to the constitutional values and rights they are supposed to defend and arrive at the clear conclusion that the latter is compatible with the former. Quite the contrary, if that was how the process operated, then the only possible conclusion would be that the restrictive view of sexuality clearly infringes on a number of the values and rights that characterize modern constitutions. The "poisoned gift" dynamic demonstrates how judges resort to respectable forms of constitutional interpretation—aimed at achieving judicial neutrality—through which they reconstruct the illegitimate foundations of certain sex crimes as true reflections of modern constitutional values and rights.

This form of analysis is not new. The "poisoned gift" approach to the constitutional litigation of sex crimes is inspired by what Reva Siegel has termed "preservation-through-transformation."[29] In a series of important articles,[30] Siegel has shown how when certain unjust status regimes are politically and legally contested, change occurs, "but not always the kind of change advocates seek."[31] While the contested regime changes by "gradually relinquishing [its] original rules and justificatory rhetoric," its status privileges are preserved through the establishment of "new rules and reasons" that justify these privileges in the language of more modern and acceptable constitutional values.[32] Rights reform, through a process Siegel calls "deformalization" or "modernization,"[33] thus "breathe[s] new life into a body of status law, by pressuring legal elites to translate it into a more contemporary, and less controversial, social idiom."[34] Mobilization attempting to dismantle a status regime may be successful at discrediting its legitimizing rhetoric; however, the ensuing reforms may preserve some of the same privileges of those elites who benefited from the previous regime.[35] As Siegel explains, the "preservation-through-transformation" dynamic is about both "continuity *and* change," for "a status regime is modernized (or deformalized) when, despite changes in its rules and rhetoric, it continues to distribute material and dignitary privileges . . . in such a way as to maintain the distinctions that comprise the regime . . . in relatively continuous terms."[36] Even though the modernization of the regime brings about some positive and visible transformations, the members of the subordinated groups are still worse off "in their capacity to achieve further, welfare-enhancing reform of the status regime in which they were subordinated."[37]

Insofar as the rules and reasons supporting the old regime have been translated into the rhetoric of modern constitutionalism, and the new regime can therefore be distinguished from its predecessor, it is now much more difficult to contest and dismantle the unjust distributions that were preserved in the transformation process.[38] For example, Siegel has shown how feminist activism during the nineteenth century in England and the United States led to the suppression of the law that allowed husbands to beat their wives. In spite of this reform and the insistence of courts in denying husbands this right, some forms of marital violence were immunized through the more modern and respectable discourses of "family privacy" and "domestic harmony."[39] Similarly, Siegel has examined how the discourse of "colorblindness" in the United States (usually vindicated by the federal judiciary as the form of racial justice stemming from the Equal Protection Clause) has validated certain practices that are formally racially neutral but have a disparate impact on racial minorities.[40]

Akin to "preservation-through-transformation," the "poisoned gift" mode of analysis concentrates on gauging the rhetorical transformations of status regimes. Some aspects of sexual criminal law may be said to contribute powerfully to the reproduction of structural inequality. Certain "identities" and sexual activities have historically been criminalized, reflecting strong societal moral condemnation. These "identities," or those who practice these activities, are considered to be so debased as to deserve criminal punishment. It is in this sense that sex crimes are part of what Siegel calls a "status regime." Although the "poisoned gift" analysis is not genealogical, it shows the mutability of the rules and reasons that support certain sex crimes. From its medieval roots, the sex-restrictive concept of sexuality that still authorizes these crimes has been dressed in new rhetorical clothes by the interventions of constitutional judges who have rationalized this through interpretive strategies. These judges are not malevolent or outright moralists or bigots. Quite the contrary, their resort to rights-balancing or proportionality methodologies clearly reveals a genuine intent to remain neutral and faithful to the postulates of the rule of law. In sum, the "poisoned gift" analysis is another way to show that the law—as Siegel has noted—is an instrument that may spark social change but, at the same time, has the potential to thwart the very progress it proposes to achieve.

"Poisoned Gifts" at Work: Two Examples

To illustrate this process, I have chosen two examples—homosexuality, specifically in the military, and prostitution—for the following reasons. First, they are sex crimes that involve "identities" or behaviors that have traditionally been morally condemned. Second, they are part of a regime of structural inequality. These crimes thus represent good cases to test the idea that their sex-restrictive foundation (expressed as social moral condemnation) has been "modernized" through constitutional litigation. Homosexuality and prostitution are useful cases to show how criminal law may work to reinforce and legitimize the reasons and rules that, for a long time, have operated to subordinate certain social groups.

Most Western, liberal political communities have decriminalized homosexuality and prostitution. In fact, the official history of the evolution of modern criminal law sees the decriminalization of such conduct as the most conspicuous example of the triumph of equality and autonomy.[41] However, as this section will demonstrate, even if prostitution and homosexuality are now usually beyond the province of criminal punishment, criminal law may none-theless wend its way to reasserting the social moral condemnation that still sur-rounds these practices. This dynamic is achieved in such a manner as to hide the spurious moral rationale of these crimes. Legislatures can create categories of criminal conduct that, without directly labeling prostitution or homosexuality criminal, will criminalize certain aspects (pimping or "sexual tourism," for ex-ample) or circumscribed circumstances (usually same-sex sexual activity in special social settings, such as the military or prisons). Some will perceive this circumvention strategy to be highly illegitimate, since it reasserts the sex-restrictive foundation that has historically supported the moral condemnation of homosexuality and prostitution. Should the illegitimacy of this form of crim-inalization be challenged in court as violating constitutional principles of per-sonal autonomy and equality, constitutional judges, then, might respond with a "poisoned gift." Judges may use sophisticated forms of constitutional judicial rea-soning (mainly rights balancing and proportionality methodologies) to "mod-ernize" the sex-restrictive foundation of these crimes, rationalizing them as a legitimate development of modern constitutional rights and values. We are then back to where we were.

The next two subsections illustrate such "poisoned gifts." These examples have been chosen from the jurisprudence of the Constitutional Court of Colom-bia. In 1991 Colombia underwent a political transition and enacted a new rights-rich constitution that guarantees dignity, freedom, and equality. The ju-risprudence of the Colombian Constitutional Court is widely recognized as hav-ing progressively enforced these values. For the Court, dignity is an overarching constitutional mandate against human vilification and instrumentalization, free-dom guarantees a strong principle of human autonomy, and equality is under-stood as a dictate to eradicate all forms of social subordination. The Constitutional Court of Colombia thus represents a good example of a court that, in spite of the general progressive tone of its doctrine, has nevertheless legitimized, through "poisoned gifts," some sexual crimes whose moral foundations become suspi-cious when viewed in terms of constitutional values such as dignity, autonomy, and equality.

Same-Sex Sexual Activity in the Military

As previously pointed out, most Western countries have decriminalized homo-sexuality as a status, as well as same-sex sexual activity. However, a measure of moral condemnation still appears in criminal and (more frequently) administrative regulations toward discrete forms of same-sex sexual activity. One common type of regulation is establishing what modern continental administrative law has termed "special subjection relationships."[42] Many democracies constitutionally allow administrative authorities to delimit the rights of certain categories of citizens who have a special relationship with the administration (for example, members of military forces, prison inmates, students of public schools and universities, and public officials).

In most states, members of military and police forces are subject to strict disciplinary regimes that impose a host of duties, rights restrictions, and sanctions. Although these prohibitions are not part of criminal law, they entail harsh administrative sanctions (discharge from military duty, among others) and could therefore be considered a manifestation of the punitive power of the state. One of the ambits in which these regimes have traditionally imposed restrictions on the rights of their subjects has been that of sexuality. More specifically, they have usually established that homosexuality (the mere status) and homosexual sexual activity affect military honor and discipline and are thus causes for discharge from service. While most democratic states have rejected the general criminalization of homosexuality in the name of equality and personal autonomy, many have uncritically accepted that members of military or police forces could be subject to administrative sanctions for being homosexual or engaging in homosexual sex. Military discipline and honor have usually been found to be acceptable purposes (or, in the language of means-ends rationality judicial tests, they are important or compelling state interests) for restricting the freedom and equality rights of members of military and police forces. These sorts of administrative provisions have recently been challenged for violating basic guarantees of equality, freedom, and privacy. Constitutional judges, however, have usually responded with "poisoned gifts."

In 1999 the Constitutional Court of Colombia considered a facial challenge[43] to the validity of some provisions of the 1989 disciplinary regime of Colombian armed forces.[44] These provisions established that members of the military committed faults against "military honor" if, on the one hand, they "associated" or had "notorious relationships" with such "antisocials" as "drug addicts, homosexuals, prostitutes, and pimps" and, on the other hand, if they "engaged in acts of homosexualism" (note the choice of words to designate the conduct) or if they "engaged in or encouraged prostitution." The Court found that the challenged provisions did not violate constitutional rights to freedom, equality, and privacy.

However, the decision forcefully asserted the rights to personal autonomy, equality, and privacy, apparently challenging this regime of social exclusion. In effect, the Colombian Constitutional Court had no trouble finding that the exclusion of gay people from the military for the sole fact of their *status* as homosexuals or for engaging in *homosexual conduct in private* was unconstitutional. For the Court, the administrative punishment of "acts of homosexualism" *is* "a stigma on the homosexual option" *and* "a violation of certain aspects that belong to the intimate sphere of the individual that, if performed in private, would not have to interfere with his condition as a member of the military."[45] The Court added that the "stigmatization of the homosexual" was a "clear form of discrimination, for only homosexuals were the subject of administrative punishment, as if any form of sexual option could be a criterion for establishing administrative sanctions."[46] With regard to the violation of privacy, the Court concluded that the prohibition of engaging in "acts of homosexualism"— given the "breadth and inaccuracy" of the verb "to engage" and the fact that the prohibition extended to acts performed while not on duty—included "all the manifestations of the homosexual option, even the most discreet and reserved, that the member of the military could perform in the space of his or her privacy."[47] The Colombian Constitutional Court starkly concluded that "what the impugned provision (engaging in acts of homosexualism) really seeks to punish is not the potential fault in which the subject may incur, but the human condition of being a homosexual and the legitimate exercise of this orientation, all of which seriously affects the right of the individual to freely exercise something as personal as his or her sexuality."[48] From a regime of *acts*, the Constitutional Court thus deduces discrimination based on homosexual *status*.

This strong characterization of the provision and its effects on the fundamental rights to autonomy, equality, and privacy did not, however, lead the Court to strike it down. Quite the contrary, the Constitutional Court decided to uphold it as part of the disciplinary regime of the Colombian military forces, provided that it was interpreted as prohibiting members of the military from engaging in *any* sort of sexual act (homosexual or heterosexual) in public, on duty, or on military premises. The only reasoning the Court offered for this decision was that *any form* of sexual activity performed in public, on duty, or on military premises is outside the ambit of protection of the rights to privacy and autonomy because "it affects the rights of third parties and is therefore incompatible with the principles that govern military life."[49] Strikingly, the Constitutional Court concluded that such principles "should operate within a framework characterized by institutional courage, integrity, and decorum, which are essential conditions for the existence of any military force."[50]

On its face, this decision seems to be a true "gift" to autonomy, substantive equality, and privacy, and a progressive evolution of the law. However, a closer

reading of its holding suggests that despite the seeming acceptance of homosexuality, it is rather just another occasion to reassert heterosexual privilege.

In this opinion, the Colombian Constitutional Court seemed to generously
extend the principles of human autonomy and substantive equality to the point
of ruling that military forces are constitutionally prohibited from discriminating on grounds of homosexual status. Openly gay men and lesbians could thus
freely become members of the military. Recall that the Court concluded that although the impugned provision only referred to "acts of homosexualism," what
it *truly* discriminated against was homosexual status. Given that homosexual
acts generally function metonymically to designate homosexual status[51] and
that discrimination based on the latter is constitutionally prohibited, striking
down the provision would have been the most appropriate and logical remedy
for the violation of autonomy and equality detected by the Court. Instead, the
majority of justices decided to "equalize" the provision by making *both* homosexual and heterosexual sexual acts "in public, on duty, or within military
premises" incompatible with the performance of military duties. This equalization strategy seems to lead to the most illogical consequence: if homosexual acts are prohibited and they *are* homosexual status, then it seems logical to
conclude that homosexual status is therefore prohibited. By means of its strange
equalizing remedy, the decision seems to end up reaffirming the original discriminatory prohibition of "homosexualism" it sought to eradicate in the first
place.

If, however, one goes beyond the mere lack of logic in the decision and seeks
to understand what could be at stake in the equation of heterosexual and homosexual sexual acts, one could reach the conclusion that the Court's decision
is grounded in a restrictive notion of sexuality that has traditionally condemned
both homosexuals and their sexual activities—but perhaps, this time, with a ven-
geance. Note that the practical consequence of this confusing decision (it seems
to simultaneously say yes and no to the presence of gays and lesbians in the Colombian military) may well be to catch gay and lesbian officers and soldiers in
an impossible double bind:[52] although the Court protected them from being discriminated against for their mere status as gays and lesbians, the prohibition
against the sexual acts they may perform *is* a prohibition of their own status,
given the fact that their acts *are* their status, which is not the case with heterosexuals, whose sexual status has not faced prosecution. If this opinion seemed
to break with a sort of Colombian inversion of "don't ask, don't tell" by allowing gay and lesbian officers and soldiers to freely express their orientation with
no punitive consequence, its practical effect is the reinstatement of the secrecy
of the closet in the name of efficient military performance—once individuals

assert that they are gay, they are "as if" asserting publicly that they practice homosexual sex, and they are therefore at risk of prosecution.

If Kendall Thomas is right, the military is "the most visibly contested site" of "the epistemic structure that has come to be known as the closet."[53] The "shower scene"—where the showering straight soldier knows that an unknown, closeted gay comrade might be watching him, does not want to be watched, and does not want the gay viewer to know that he knows that the gay man is watching him—operates as a site that exemplifies with peculiar force the epistemic dynamics warranting heterosexual supremacy.[54] For Thomas, the shower scene is equivalent to the closet because both provide heterosexuals with strategies for denying the presence of homosexuals in society (that is, based on the fact that the presence of gays in the military "is both something that 'we all know' and that 'no one knows'")[55] that allow the sustainment of a "presumption of heterosexuality."[56] The privilege of not knowing thus has the epistemic function of guaranteeing heterosexual privilege in modern Western culture.[57] Allowing openly gay men and lesbians in the military would immediately disrupt that privilege.[58]

The fear of producing a disruption of this sort may be the driving force behind the Court's strange equalization rationale. An apparently progressive gesture (that is, that now the military is constitutionally prohibited from discriminating on grounds of homosexual status) is immediately erased by the prohibition of any form of sexual activity in the military (that is, given that homosexual acts metonymically work to designate homosexual status, the latter becomes prohibited by means of the prohibition of the former). If the restrictive view of sexuality that morally condemns homosexuality is in fact operating as a background condition in the Court's opinion, the equation of homosexual sexual acts with heterosexual sexual acts only works to reinforce that very moral condemnation. To be sure, in light of the restrictive view of sexuality, heterosexual sex and homosexual sex have never been similarly situated in terms of their moral and social appreciation, and therefore the rules of repression work differently for differently situated acts and people.

The "poisoned gift" in this decision operates in the way the Constitutional Court of Colombia shuttles back and forth between homosexual acts and homosexual status to end up establishing a metonymical relationship between the two. Janet Halley has shown how this rhetorical strategy has been used by legislators and judges in diverse ways that are functional to heterosexual supremacy by catching homosexuals up in double binds that allow their exclusion—by either their status or their conduct—from myriad social spaces.[59] As Halley points out, while "the master of a double bind always has somewhere to go," those caught up in it can never win.[60] The peculiarity of the decision of the Colombian Constitutional Court rests on the way the metonymy between homosexual acts and status was rhetorically established, asymmetrically from how heterosexuality, and then faux egalitarianism, was established, by prohibiting both sets of acts. Here, the Court invoked and deployed all its doctrine on sexual orientation as a crucial manifestation of human autonomy and the correlative egalitarian doctrine on the prohibition to discriminate on grounds of sexual orientation as the justification to read homosexual status into statutory references to homosexual acts. In other words, the Court felt it *had* to read homosexual acts as the metonymy for homosexual status *because of* its powerful previous doctrine on the constitutional relevance of sexual orientation. Alas, the rhetorical meanderings of this good-faith "gift" to autonomy and equality allow bad-faith homophobes the possibility of a "poisonous," discriminatory reading.

Pimping, Prostitution, and Human Trafficking

In most countries in Latin America, the individual act of exchanging sex for money is beyond the reach of criminal law. What remains in the criminal codes and legislations are some forms of organized prostitution, pimping, enforced or coerced prostitution, and prostitution involving children and adolescents. More recently, however, there seems to be a trend toward surrounding the free exercise of prostitution with a number of new criminal conducts that have broadened the scope of pimping and similar activities. While the basic conduct of exchanging sex for money remains legal at both sides of the transaction, the criminalization of certain connected activities has made the exercise of prostitution itself more difficult. Interestingly, the expansion of the international law of human trafficking has played a key role in sparking these domestic dynamics. For example, until late 2012, the Criminal Code of Argentina only criminalized pimping when it involved children or adolescents or, in the case of adults, when deception, coercion, or violence was employed. This regulation dramatically changed with the December 2012 enactment of a statute aimed at the prevention and punishment of human trafficking, which now makes criminal any form of pimping involving both adults (even with their consent) and children and adolescents.[61] In Colombia, a 2008 statute added the crime of "inducement into prostitution" to the criminal code. Although the Colombian Congress did not justify the adoption of this crime as a means to prevent or punish human trafficking, the Constitutional Court later established this link as a conceptual precondition to uphold the constitutional validity of the crime.

These circumvention strategies are performed in the name of international human rights standards seeking to prevent and punish human trafficking. Yet, as a matter of international law, the relationships among human trafficking, pimping, and prostitution are not logically compelled. People could indeed be trafficked for purposes of prostitution, but also to be enslaved (in other sectors) or forcibly married, for example. At the domestic level, however, as the analysis of the Constitutional Court of Colombia's decision on "inducement into prostitution" makes clear, the common mistake is made of interpreting the international obligations of states to prevent and punish human trafficking as requiring the criminalization of pimping and similar conduct or, even worse, of equating prostitution and human trafficking. If, as previously noted, there is not a logical and necessary relationship between these two acts, one is left to wonder why states are establishing this link (sometimes to the point of synonymy).

One answer might be that international human trafficking law provides a safe and respectable argument to criminalize conduct without explicitly touching the freedom to exchange sex for money. Nevertheless, the link between prostitution and human trafficking stigmatizes many of the noncoercive and nonviolent activities that enable this exchange. While the symbolic commitment to a strong notion of human autonomy in the free decision to exchange sex for money (and become a prostitute) seems to be preserved, at the more practical level, the criminalization of activities surrounding prostitution significantly constrains such autonomy. If one accepts the idea that the restrictive notion of sexuality has not really waned in modern criminal law, one could argue that contemporary international human trafficking law is in fact providing cover for the moral condemnation of prostitution. In other words, the connection between human trafficking and prostitution must be constructed *legally* to make a case for the link's logical necessity. Courts and legislators have mobilized a number of arguments to establish this. The Argentine example demonstrates how convoluted the path establishing the relationship between human trafficking and the new forms of criminalizing pimping can be. Litigation on the constitutional validity of the crime of "inducement into prostitution" in Colombia illustrates some of the argumentative steps that may be taken to relate human trafficking and prostitution.

In 2009 the Constitutional Court of Colombia upheld the constitutional validity of the crime of "inducement into prostitution."[62] This Colombian Criminal Code offense carries a prison term of two to four years and a fine for whoever "induces another person to carnal commerce or prostitution with the purpose of obtaining economic profits or satisfying the desires of a third party."[63] Note that inducing another person to become a prostitute does not imply any requirement of force, violence, or coercion in the text of the statute; moreover, for the decision to become a prostitute entirely depends on the free will of the person who responds to the inducement. The Court validated the crime of inducement into prostitution on two grounds: a constitutional elaboration on human dignity and consent and personal autonomy.

The Constitutional Court noted that although prostitution is a social reality—the complete eradication of which is impossible—it is not a constitutionally neutral phenomenon. Quite the contrary, even though prostitution is not prohibited by the Constitution and its exercise cannot be criminally punished, the Court reasoned that it is a kind of "social reality" that violates human dignity and therefore imposes on state authorities the obligation to reduce its harmful effects.[64] For the Court, under the principle of human dignity, prostitution "is degrading for the human person."[65] Here, the Court mobilizes dignity in its purest and strongest Kantian version to construct a constitutional, overarching mandate against human instrumentalization and humiliation. The power of this form of expansive constitutional reasoning immediately operates to label all state action against prostitution as an indisputably humane cause. Reva Siegel has shown how the meaning of human dignity is highly contested in struggles over sexuality issues, such as abortion and same-sex marriage. Depending on which activists and judges use dignity, its substantive meaning varies dramatically.[66] Similarly, Matthias Mahlmann has noted that "under the cover of lofty 'dignity,' all kinds of subjective, relative, and heterogeneous ideas could infiltrate human rights regimes."[67]

This dignitarian argument functions as the entry point for the Constitutional Court to deploy its proportionality reasoning based on human autonomy. When proportionality methodology is used to establish the constitutional validity of criminal legislation, judges usually start with the premise that legislatures have broad leeway to criminalize human conduct and are only limited in this task by "fundamental rights and the liberal composition of the constitutional state."[68] More specifically, this latter assertion means that the criminalization of conduct ought to be a measure of last resort to maintain social order; it should only be used when every other possible means has proved insufficient.[69] Proportionality tests are thus used to determine whether criminal legislation has respected this limit. Any proportionality test begins by gauging the constitutional legitimacy of the ends pursued by the criminalization of conduct. In light of the dignitarian premises of the opinion, the Constitutional Court of Colombia observed that safeguarding human dignity was a legitimate constitutional purpose to be pursued because "commercially trading with one's own body is contrary to human dignity" and hence any act "aimed at promoting that another person becomes a prostitute is an incentive for the defilement of his or her own dignity."[70]

The key step in the proportionality test is the analysis of the necessity of criminalizing inducement into prostitution as a means of protecting human dignity. On the one hand, the Court established—with the help of international human rights law—that even if prostitution results from the free decisions of rational agents, its promotion affects a set of collective interests that warrant its criminalization. On the other hand, the Court rejected—again by resorting to international human rights law arguments—the claim that inducement into prostitution is not socially damaging conduct because it is based on the free decisions of those who respond to the inducement.

In the first part of its reasoning, the Constitutional Court ascertained the socially damaging nature of inducement into prostitution and the consequential need to criminalize it by showing that it is intrinsically related to organized crime. The decision to become a prostitute or to induce (without violence or coercion) another person to become a prostitute is never really an *individual* act but is always part of wider networks of organized criminality. The Court draws the authority to construct this surprising argument from a number of international human rights law documents (the 1949 Convention for the Suppression of the Traffic in Persons and of the Exploitation of the Prostitution of Others and the 2000 Convention against Transnational Organized Crime, and its Protocol to Prevent, Suppress and Punish Trafficking in Persons, Especially Women and Children). In the Court's view, these conventions clearly reveal a link not only between inducement into prostitution and human trafficking but also between inducement into prostitution and other forms of organized crime. Because international human rights law mandates states to criminalize human trafficking and other forms of transnational crime, the Court on its own deduces that international human rights law also imposes the obligation to criminalize inducement into prostitution, given the fact that the relationship between this latter conduct and other forms of transnational criminality is one of deep imbrication, not to say one of synonymy.[71]

The Court's argument to dismiss the consent of the person who, upon being induced by another, *freely* decides to become a prostitute is even more interesting, surprising, and disturbing. Just as before, the Constitutional Court uses its own interpretation of international law to construct a causal relationship that is not always empirically valid. Briefly, the argument here is that it would be a fallacy to believe that, given the current factual circumstances in which exchanges of sex for money tend to happen, a person could fully exercise his or her autonomy. For the Court, poverty and lack of opportunity mean that such persons who "choose" prostitution have no other choice; they allow themselves to be exploited by individuals who take advantage of their poverty. The Constitutional Court draws this conclusion from international human trafficking law. Citing experts on international migrations and UN soft law documents (the Tenth UN Congress on the Prevention of Crime and Treatment of Offenders, for example), the Court finds that they were "alerted" to the "evident fact" that, in current times, human trafficking had increased in areas of "high unemployment and financial crisis," where women and girls in particular are at great risk of becoming trafficked. The stark constitutional conclusion drawn from this observation is that "at the risk of offending personal dignity, as well as sexual self-determination and personal freedom, the victim's consent is not a sufficient safeguard."[72] Next, invoking the 2000 Convention against Transnational Organized Crime and its Protocol to Prevent, Suppress and Punish Trafficking in Persons, Especially Women and Children, the Constitutional Court extended its idea of the "fallacy of consent." In its view, those people in dire economic need (the only ones for whom prostitution could be a vital option) may initially consent to exchange sex for money by positively responding to an inducement into prostitution. This initial and apparently free consent is, however, highly obscured, for the decision to become a prostitute is, *in reality*, the entryway to the world of human trafficking and sexual slavery, where free will and human autonomy do not exist. The Court noted that it is "striking that, according to international documents and reports, the initial consent of the victim becomes an entry door to slavery and human trafficking networks, to true 'circles of violence' from which it is impossible to escape," and added that "an initial consent, vitiated by need or ignorance, is highly susceptible of becoming coercive subjection."[73] The "poisoned gift" has thus come full circle. Let's see how.

In this decision, the Constitutional Court of Colombia never formally abandoned the ideal of human autonomy in its purest libertarian sense. For the Court, the human actions implicated in the crime of inducement into prostitution (both of the perpetrator and of the victim) did not fall within the ambit of protection usually accorded by the constitutional principle of human autonomy and could therefore be legitimately restricted by criminal law. According to this principle, the acts of free agents may only and exceptionally be restricted by state authorities through criminal law if, and only if, they impinge on the rights of others or produce a social harm or if the agent is not truly autonomous. In *On Liberty*, John Stuart Mill set a notion of human autonomy that, to a great extent, has been understood by constitutional courts as foundational to the range of freedom rights guaranteed by modern constitutions. Proportionality tests have been used by constitutional judges as the most appropriate device to transform the philosophical Millian notion of autonomy into a set of workable steps aimed at assessing the reasonability of criminal legislation as the means to achieve social order and peace. In the doctrine of many modern constitutional courts, Mill's principle that "the only purpose for which power can be rightfully exercised over any member of a civilized community, against his will, is to prevent harm to others" takes the form of a proportionality test.[74] Under this device of constitutional interpretation, a social harm caused by a free agent warrants using criminal law to restrict the agent's freedom if the restriction pursues a valid constitutional purpose and is a necessary means to achieve this purpose. The proportionality methodology has achieved such widespread popularity among judges around the world because it offers a formal and (presumptively) objective template for reasoning that supposedly shields against personal biases, motivations, moralities, and worldviews.[75]

The Constitutional Court of Colombia's opinion on the constitutional legitimacy of inducement into prostitution is a textbook example of the use of a proportionality test in the decision of a morally contested issue. On its face, the ruling obediently follows every step of the proportionality test and seems to rely on a pure notion of human autonomy. The Court carefully constructs the free agents' acts as clear exceptions to the principle of respect for human autonomy. In effect, the acts of the agent whose conduct was criminalized (the person who induces another to become a prostitute) caused a social harm of such magnitude that they should be criminally curtailed (exception 1); the person who responds to the inducement is never a free agent, so his or her consent does not work to dissolve or lessen the social harm caused by the acts of the first agent (exception 2). The decision of the Constitutional Court thus never abandons the logic of the libertarian notion of human autonomy. In this sense, it is a "gift" to one of the foundational values of the Colombian Constitution.

Yet the "poison" that contaminates this opinion comes from the construction of the principle's two exceptions. According to the Colombian Constitutional Court, the principal agent's criminal acts produce both individual and collective harms. The individual harm consists of encouraging another person to "defile his or her own dignity" by becoming a prostitute. This harm is normatively constructed through the workings of the principle of human dignity. Exchanging sex for money is an instrumentalization of one's sexuality and therefore intrinsically corrupts human dignity. If, on its face, this conclusion may seem an unproblematic implementation of the principle of human dignity in its strongest Kantian dimension, a closer analysis of the argument shows that concluding that prostitution is a violation of human dignity is only possible if we assume a restrictive view of sexuality as a background condition. Only if sexuality is invested with an aura of sacredness or altruism and is thought to fulfill only a procreative function does its commercial trade become problematic from a human dignity point of view.

On the other hand, the collective dimension of the harm caused by inducement into prostitution comes from the Constitutional Court's reading of the international law of human trafficking. For the Court, extant international law warrants the conclusion that inducing another to become a prostitute is never an individual act, an exchange of minds between two free agents, but rather is part of a collective endeavor of organized crime networks. The harm is thus *collectivized* by means of a descriptive argument (that, by the way, lacks any sort of serious empirical support), showing that modern pimps *always* operate within criminal human trafficking organizations. This morally contentious domestic judicial reasoning gets its authority from a sui generis interpretation of international human rights law (and particularly from the spurious synonymy the Court draws between prostitution and human trafficking). Any problem of legitimacy that may arise from resorting to a restrictive view of sexuality (expressed through the characterization of inducement into prostitution as a serious harm to human dignity) is dispelled by transforming the argument into one of compliance with international law. The decision is thus presented not as the result of a specific set of moral worldviews that condemn prostitution but rather as an expression of the Colombian Constitution's commitment to international human rights law.

The second exception to the principle of human autonomy is also constructed through a peculiar interpretation of the international law of human trafficking. The agent who positively responds to an inducement into prostitution *never* freely consents because the contexts in which prostitution happens in the world today obscure the autonomy of those who decide to become prostitutes. The Court, drawing again on a supposed international law synonymy between prostitution and human trafficking, reaches three descriptive, but empirically unsupported, conclusions: first, all modern prostitutes are poor or needy people who decide to become prostitutes because no other option is available to fulfill their material needs; second, the decision to become a prostitute is the "entryway" to the world of human trafficking, from which it is impossible to escape; and third, all those who induce other people to become prostitutes use fraudulent and deceptive means because they are part of global human trafficking networks. This threefold argument works to portray the prostitute as a subject devoid of autonomy. It could be argued that someone who, in our times, "decides" to become a prostitute has made such a decision out of some sort of "circumstantial insanity," warranting paternalistic protection from his or her own self-injurious actions.

By reading international law in this way and using it to invest its decision with legitimacy, the Court produced a decision perfectly compatible with the dictates of the Millian notion of human autonomy. Mill not only thought that autonomy could be limited by the state when the acts of a free agent cause harm to others but also legitimized paternalistic state action when the agent was not "in the maturity of [his or her] faculties" and therefore had to "be protected against [his or her] own actions as well as against external injury."[76] Based on this second Millian exception, the Colombian Constitutional Court, deducing a number of factual assumptions from the international law of human trafficking, construed the crime of inducement into prostitution as a legitimate paternalistic measure that cancels the autonomy of the agent whose free decision could have worked to counteract the characterization of prostitution as a harm to human dignity. Again, the combination of a reading of international human rights law that equates prostitution and human trafficking and the logic of human autonomy invests an argument against prostitution with constitutional legitimacy.

*   *   *

This essay has sought to uncover a peculiar way of judicial reasoning in the constitutional review of sex crimes. This area of criminal law is the source of heated debates that reflect the social and cultural anxieties surrounding the legal regulation of sexuality. Should constitutional law trump morality? Are there forms of valid morality that may sustain constitutional norms? If so, could this morality be "discovered"? How is this morality compatible with the right of individuals to lead a healthy and enjoyable sexual life? Is there a way to completely disentangle criminal law from morality (even in its "thinner" conceptions)? Even though this essay does not directly answer these questions, it tries to show that the "poisoned gift" dynamic may arise from the many anxieties they spark. Not every judicial review of sex crimes will be a "poisoned gift." However, individuals and groups interested in keeping at bay the colonization of sexuality by criminal law should be alert to these dynamics when using constitutional courts to challenge the constitutionality of sex crimes.

CHAPTER 12

The Filth They Bring: Sex Panics and Racial Others in Lebanon

Rasha Moumneh

A Tale of Two Cities

On July 28, 2012, Lebanese Internal Security Forces raided a cinema known to screen pornographic films in the ethnically and nationally diverse working-class suburb of Burj Hammoud, northeast of Beirut in the Metn district, one of many such cinemas in and around the city. They arrested all thirty-six men who were there for "violating public decency" and engaging in "unnatural sex" with each other. At the police station, the men were humiliated and subjected to anal examinations on orders of the public prosecutor to determine whether they had engaged in receptive anal sex. The public outcry against these examinations was unprecedented. Mainstream media decried what they called "the republic of shame," describing the government's behavior as scandalous, uncivilized, and barbaric and drawing parallels with other demonstrations of the government's corruption and incompetence.[1] The lobbying efforts launched by gay and civil rights groups to end the practice of anal examinations marked the most successful gay-related policy-level campaign in Lebanon to date.

On April 21, 2013, the mayor of Dekwaneh, a suburb north of Beirut also in the Metn district, ordered the raid of Ghost, a well-known gay bar in the area, and arrested five Syrians—four men and one transgender woman. The municipal police humiliated them and subjected them to a litany of abuses, including forcing the transgender woman to strip, taking pictures of her nude, and circulating them through their mobile phones. All five were released the next day without charges, after which police hung a copy of the police report with the full names of the five individuals on the closed doors of the now-shut-down gay bar. The mayor appeared on the local television station LBCI, unapologetically describing his actions and justifying them as necessary to preserve the moral character of Dekwaneh.[2] Rights groups immediately took action and decided to take Mayor Antoine Shakhtoura to court for his flagrant abuse of power and for violating no fewer than eleven Lebanese laws through his actions.

These two events have received significant attention in both the national and international media, presented as evidence of an ongoing battle for gay rights in the country. However, in this essay, I argue that the framing in these cases is reductive and the focus on the gay rights claim serves to obfuscate a larger narrative of gendered and racialized sexual regulation in Lebanon that is not picked up in the same way by the international press. Rather than conceiving of sexual politics in terms of sexual orientation or identity, I follow Paul Amar's reconceptualization of the term as indicative of "security-sector struggles to discipline dangers and desires" that demarcate the boundaries of citizenship.[3] Reading these stories together reveals how sexuality is deployed to highlight "certain race, class, and gendered bodies as sources of danger and desire, while rendering invisible the political nature of hierarchy and the identity of powerful agents."[4]

A state's regulation of bodies it deems unruly—such as those of homosexuals, darker-skinned migrants and refugees, or wayward heterosexual women— is part of a deeply interconnected matrix of control whose purpose is the reproduction of the "proper" citizen of modern Lebanon. Paradoxically, public protests about some of these events played a key role in perpetuating such regulation, as advocates in contemporary Lebanon trade on notions of its exceptionalism, its modernity, and its fragility together in ways that reproduce its undergirding logic. In all these debates, criminal law plays a key role in contestation.

In this essay I analyze how these public reactions and state violations come together to produce a narrative of social control by exploring several cases of racial and ethnic purges, sex panics involving migrants, and legislative battles around the exclusion of a marital rape clause in the contested domestic violence bill. Rather than reading each of these events separately as distinct instances of gay or women's rights violations, I argue that they have a common instrumental role in shaping ideas of national belonging and gendered citizenship.

To do so, I first explore the discursive and socio-legal context within which these events take place. Second, I analyze the sexualized race panics that precipitated the arrests in both Burj Hammoud and Dekwaneh. Third, I contrast the campaign against anal examinations with the domestic violence campaign and the debates around its marital rape clause, illustrating the gendered legal regime regulating heteronormative reproduction, of which the criminalization of "unnatural sex" used to prosecute gay men is a part. I conclude by drawing attention to the ways in which the discourses of modernity and offended masculinity serve to further entrench the state's heteronormative imperatives.

Diversity, Tolerance, and Lebanese Exceptionalism

While Lebanon is often described as exceptional in the region for being more "secular" and "liberal" than its Arab neighbors, Lebanese secularism is consolidated through a practice of sectarianism in which sects such as Maronite Christian, Sunni Muslim, Shia Muslim, and Druze (among others) function as legal and political categories within a system of consociational power sharing. As Mahmood Mamdani has argued, state formation plays a critical role in producing and reifying political and sectarian identities.[5] Lebanon's unwritten National Pact of 1943 grounded the state's ideology as a country of minorities based on a purported compromise between different sectarian communities that allocated specific positions within the Lebanese government according to sect. The presidency is allotted to Maronite Christians, the premiership to Sunnis, the Speaker of Parliament to Shias, and parliamentary seats and ministerial positions are also divided among sects. On the level of the family, each sect is governed by its own personal status laws that adjudicate matters pertaining to marriage, divorce, custody, and inheritance. Tolerance of difference and diversity thus become qualities to be embodied by citizens in order to lend the nation its coherence, although Lebanon's sizable Palestinian and, more recently, Iraqi, Syrian, African, and South Asian populations of refugees and migrants are excluded from this formulation. As Maya Mikdashi has argued, political sectarianism is a political technology, an ideology, and a system that "posits the modern state as an arbiter between sectarian communities that precede it."[6] For secular activists, an end to political sectarianism was tied to ending the power of the religious elite within the state, which was regarded as the main obstacle to achieving legally protected personal freedoms in general, and sexual rights in particular.

Despite the fact that most laws constraining various freedoms, sexual or otherwise, are civil rather than religious, and religion had nothing to do with the porn theater and nightclub arrests, a discourse had already solidified that conflated the persecution of homosexuality with religious intolerance and, in particular, Muslim intolerance. The Lebanese state's ambiguous and ambivalent stance on homosexuality has allowed a patently Islamophobic logic to take hold: Lebanon is remarkable because it is an *Arab* country that is tolerant, a fact that is treated as if it can only be explained by the presence of Christians with "Western" values who in turn are able to influence their Muslim compatriots. In a short report for the Australian news station SBS, for example, a journalist tellingly declared, "In fact, its [Lebanon's] reputation for being relatively open and progressive extends to matters sexual as well as political, despite its 70% Muslim population."[7]

This discourse has also been uncritically reproduced by Helem, an LGBT rights organization based in Beirut, of which I was a member from 2004 to 2012. Helem's former coordinator has stated that "Lebanon, with its mixed population of Muslims and Christians, has a history of religious pluralism and exposure to the West. But elsewhere, homosexuals are on their own."[8]

On the one hand, Helem consciously deploys Lebanon's self-image as a country of religious minorities as a discursive strategy to carve out space for a sexual minority in the name of the Lebanese "tradition" of respecting diversity. On the other, it reproduces the idea that attitudes toward sexuality are to be understood primarily in terms of religion or sectarian community. In an interview with Canadian television channel TV5, a Helem board member stated that "Lebanon is ruled by religious leaders," and *because of that* homosexuality is generally rejected.[9] She went on to highlight the "differences" between religious communities by positing Christians as "generally more open about sex" than Muslims. These perceptions are disrupted by examining how the policing of homosexuality actually manifests on the ground: both the events described earlier, for example, took place in Christian areas. Moreover, such narratives misattribute the causal role of religion. Morality policing, such as in the cases mentioned earlier, needs to be understood as distinct from "religion" and as one method for the production and regulation of proper citizenship, rather than the maintenance of religious norms. In this sense, morality policing and the criminal laws that allow it serve explicitly nationalist goals.

Nonetheless, the advocacy efforts that followed the anal examinations of the men arrested in the Burj Hammoud porn theater rode the wave of the nascent civil and citizen rights movements, as well as the movement for secularism that had been gaining traction over the last few years. Most of these movements hinged on calling for an end to—or at least critiquing—the political and institutional sectarianism in the country, while identifying the main impediment to human rights as the lack of separation between religion and state.

In contemporary Lebanon, accusations of barbarism and backwardness that fold into the Islamophobic logic of the war on terror are bandied about increasingly in reference to how Lebanon treats its gays, matters of sexual freedom, and religious—specifically Muslim—influence more generally. This shift in attention is bolstered by campaigns by Global North governments to "enforce" the rights of LGBT people across the world, as evidenced by former U.S. secretary of state Hillary Clinton's speech on December 7, 2013, to the UN Human Rights Council, in which she outlined the U.S. government's commitment to global LGBT rights as an integral part of American foreign policy. These campaigns are useful precisely because they produce a new template of judgment that makes homosexuality the line of demarcation between "modern" and "traditional" states.

The Dekwaneh arrests happened around the same that France, Lebanon's former colonial power, legalized gay marriage, a coincidence that did not escape either local or international media. Comparisons were made that evoked the now familiar civilizational discourse of progress and backwardness. An article by Agence France-Presse on Lebanon's gay community, for example, stated that "at a time when gay marriage is winning approval in France, Lebanon's gay community feels 'light years' behind."[10] In this climate of international Global North "concern" for LGBT rights in the Global South, the "gay question" now runs alongside the "woman question" as a civilizational signpost. As such, it has a precarious but attractive status in public debate.

As noted earlier, the conflation of the persecution of homosexuality with religious or specifically Muslim intolerance allowed for the framing of sexualized violence by the state against male bodies, even those openly marked as gay, as a marker of civilizational regression. This posture contains echoes of the massive extent to which "Islam-identified regression" features within the now familiar discourse of the war on terror. As Jasbir Puar has argued, "The use of 'acceptance' and 'tolerance' for gay and lesbian subjects [has become] the barometer by which the legitimacy of, and capacity for national sovereignty is evaluated."[11]

Homosexuality and the State

The Lebanese state has cultivated an ambivalent relationship with the issue of homosexuality since it was pushed into the public sphere with the creation of Helem in 2004, the first aboveground LGBT rights organization in the Arab region, and the proliferation of gay bars and clubs from the late 1990s onward. State postures have ranged from open acknowledgment and acceptance in certain cases to disregard, outright hostility, and direct persecution in others.

Arrests of men for homosexual sex are not very common in Lebanon, despite legal sanction under Penal Code Article 534, which states that "sexual intercourse against the order of nature is punishable by up to one year in prison."[12]

Large-scale or high-profile arrests of individuals suspected of homosexuality are even rarer, though they have been known to happen. One might argue, as David Bell has, that gay men are able to claim sexual citizenship only insofar as it is relegated to specific spaces of consumption, such as the "marginal pleasure zones of clubbing and cruising," as well as "sites of campaigning and volunteerism."[13] The scandals of Dekwaneh and Buri Hammoud illustrate the precariousness of this partial citizenship and the specific contexts that make it vulnerable. After all, gay clubs and porn theaters have been around for decades with scant attention paid by the authorities.

Moving from private to public, while "unnatural sex" continues to be criminalized, the Lebanese government has established an uneasy relationship with Helem. It has refused to legally recognize the organization, despite the fact that the law of association automatically grants nongovernmental organizations legal recognition without requiring governmental permission once they inform the Ministry of Interior of their establishment. While this does not render Helem illegal, it can hinder the organization's work by making certain functions, such as establishing a bank account in the organization's name, more difficult. Such a position allows the state to oscillate between recognition and repudiation of this LGBT rights nongovernmental organization. Stipulations of international funding for HIV/AIDS prevention work, for example, have forced the government into an uneasy partnership with Helem through the Ministry of Health on various prevention and awareness-raising projects, though Helem was not listed as such on the ministry's website, unlike other organizations in the same project.

Sex Panics and the Specter of the "Foreigner"

The arrests that took place in Burj Hammoud and Dekwaneh occurred within the context of an economic crisis and a security situation that was unraveling along sectarian and political lines. In the following sections, I show how the arrests that occurred in working-class areas rife with racial and ethnic tensions were mapped onto anxieties concerning sexual propriety and sexual danger. As Lisa Marie Cacho has argued, "Race and racialized spaces are the signifiers that make an unsanctioned action legible as illicit and recognizable as a crime."[14] Anxieties over racial, ethnic, and national purity were thus displaced onto queer bodies made available for persecution.

In the summer of 2012, workers of the national electricity company had been on strike for three months to demand better wages and a stable contract, leading the authorities to revert to collective punishment by, quite literally, turning off the lights on the entire country. Civil violence continued unabated in the north of Lebanon in the wake of the militarization of the Syrian uprising against President Bashar al-Assad's regime. Forms of protest such as the construction of roadblocks and tire burning resurfaced as a commonplace feature of Lebanon's landscape. The all-too-familiar effects of strife became felt by a growing majority—from the families of eleven Lebanese citizens who had been kidnapped in Syria, to people angry about government negligence and corruption, and to those who were hot, sweaty, and sick from lack of electricity in the stifling heat of summer.

The influx of Syrian refugees fleeing the violence triggered Lebanese xenophobia and anxieties around sovereignty and of course offered a convenient scapegoat for many of the ills befalling the country due to the corruption and inefficiency of the ruling class. "Foreigners," mainly Asian domestic workers and laborers and Syrian refugees, became increasingly demonized.

Internal Debauchery: The Case of Burj Hammoud

Burj Hammoud is one of the most densely populated areas in Lebanon. While the majority of its population is Armenian, it is also home to Lebanese Shia Muslims and Christians, as well as laborers from Asia and Africa and refugees of various religious denominations from Iraq and Syria. In October 2011 the neighborhood was the target of an incendiary news report titled "Burj Hammoud: A Neighborhood in Danger," broadcast by the local television station MurrTV, a channel well known for its racist diatribes against migrant workers.[15] Activists reported a palpable increase in the security presence in the area where migrant workers live and congregate. Crime rates were attributed to the presence of foreigners, who were cast as sexually licentious and morally corrupt. Female migrant workers were accused of engaging in sex work, corrupting young Lebanese men and attracting foreign men who were then held responsible for "pickpocketing and other deviant behavior." Burj Hammoud was cast as a "problem spot" due to its multiethnic and multiracial character.

Soon afterward, the municipality embarked on a purging of the area, which entailed mass evictions of foreign workers under the dubious pretext of their not having rental agreements, despite this being a fairly common occurrence in Lebanon. The daily *Al-Akhbar* newspaper reported that the Lebanese army and

Internal Security Forces engaged in a wide campaign of arrests, at one point detaining an estimated one thousand migrants in one night for allegedly not having legal residency papers.[16] The mayor justified this by attributing a series of crimes, real and imagined, to migrants, ranging from assault of women to sexual harassment and public intoxication.[17] The foreign body was unequivocally cast as a dangerous, deviant, and sexually predatory one. Xenophobia was couched in the language of protection and borders, invoking the need to protect the neighborhood's "character" from an invasion of foreigners, fostering a moral panic around sexual deviance and racial otherness.

In May and June 2012, a MurrTV show called *Enta Horr* (You are free) broadcast a series of reports exposing the "social ills" threatening the fabric of Lebanese society and its youths. Two separate episodes featured investigative reports on two porn cinemas in Lebanon, where hidden cameras were sent to film men as they spoke about the sex they would engage in with each other there. The host, Joe Maalouf, urged the authorities to take swift action to stop "the debauchery." Not too long after, police shut down the two cinemas without detaining anybody, but, as previously mentioned, the Burj Hammoud cinema raid ended with the arrest of thirty-six men, Lebanese as well as migrants and refugees, on charges of public indecency and unnatural sexual relations.

Local gay rights activists made a direct link between Maalouf's exposé on porn cinemas and the Burj Hammoud cinema arrests, decrying them as a "gay crackdown." In her discussion on the importance of acknowledging the interlocking nature of systems of oppression, Sherene Razack reminds us that by "view[ing] . . . acts as evidence of the operation of one system that is merely complicated by another, we will end up missing something about the violence and its psychic origins."[18] Questions of class, race, and ethnic policing and persecution are effaced by such a singular focus on the arrests as violations of queer bodies. Given the securitization of Burj Hammoud along these lines, the cinema arrests may best be understood as a continuation of an *already* sexualized crackdown on "foreigners" rather than a bracketed manifestation of state homophobia.

Policing Borders, Policing Sex: The Case of Dekwaneh

The arrests in Dekwaneh also need to be considered in context. In the first months of 2013, several municipalities in the Christian-majority Mount Lebanon governorate, including Dekwaneh, instated illegal curfews for "foreigners," a decree that was aimed at controlling the movement of Syrian workers and refugees. Police and army harassment and abuse of Syrians was commonplace in many areas.

A salient trope in discourse concerning Syrian refugees has been the construction of Syrians as sexually licentious and predatory and hence as both a danger to local women and carriers of disease and moral degeneration. Such sex panics produce "reactive mechanisms of surveillance, regulation, discipline, and punishment."[19] This is of course not the first time racial and ethnic anxieties were mapped onto real or imagined crimes. Sexual crimes in particular invoke fears of emasculation and the erosion of female honor.

The reactions to sexual crimes committed by migrants and refugees tend to be particularly violent. In April 2010 residents of Ketermaya, a village in Mount Lebanon, stabbed to death an Egyptian man for allegedly murdering a family of four and raping a fifteen-year-old girl. The Egyptian national was already in police custody when the angry mob captured and killed him, dragging his naked body through the streets and then lynching him in the town square.[20]

In November 2011 twenty-eight-year-old Myriam Achkar from the Christian town of Sahel Alma, also in Mount Lebanon, was brutally raped and murdered by a Syrian migrant worker. The way this horrific event was framed reflected deep-seated xenophobic and sectarian fears. In its coverage of the attack, the local television station LBCI lambasted the authorities for allowing Lebanon to become "a stage for strangers to play in without any deterrence."[21] Making a point of highlighting her Christian faith and her sexual virtue, the report played on sectarian and nationalist animosity toward Syrians. In this context, what happened to Achkar was not just a crime but one committed by a Syrian against a Lebanese citizen, and specifically against a Lebanese Christian. A local priest went so far as to call her a "martyr of the church." "We will catch him. We have men here too!" yelled one of Achkar's relatives into the camera, adding that "Syrians are doing whatever they want in Lebanon without being brought to justice."[22] The ideal citizen—here marked as Christian, heteronormative, sexually virtuous, and honor bound—is juxtaposed to and constructed against the foreigner, who is marked as dangerous, godless, and sexually deviant.

In October 2012 members of the Lebanese army stormed into the rooms of around seventy-two male migrant workers in the Christian neighborhood of Geitawi in Beirut and beat them severely. Most were Syrian, while others were Egyptian and Sudanese. The men were not charged with any crime but were generally accused of "harassing women."[23] More recently, in December 2013, residents of a village in the Bekaa Valley burned down an informal camp housing around four hundred Syrian refugees after accusing four camp residents of sexually assaulting a mentally disabled man in what the *Al-Akhbar* newspaper claims to be a fabricated story to push refugees out of the campsite.[24] Whether or not this is true, it speaks to the potency of sexualized fears of the Other.

It is no coincidence, therefore, that all five individuals arrested at the gay club in Dekwaneh were Syrian. In fact, their nationality was brought up consistently during their interrogation at the police station. One of the arrested men said that the police officers asked him whether they "do this" in Syria and said bitterly that "this is what Syria brings us."[25] Sexual deviance was now completely grafted onto Syrian otherness. Banners quickly went up in Dekwaneh in support of Mayor Shakhtoura, placed by Christian political parties both allied with and opposed to Shakhtoura's own, invoking the nationalist tropes of masculinity, morality, and honor.

In an interview with a local television station, Shakhtoura defended his actions: "I refuse to have this in Dekwaneh. Dekwaneh is known for its vigor. It is a fortress of steadfastness. We fought to defend our land and our honor not to have people like this come in."[26] The language he chose is very telling in its almost verbatim reproduction of the right-wing Christian discourse against Palestinians (and later Syrians) during the fifteen-year civil war in Lebanon, which branded them as outsiders against whom the Christian "resistance" had to defend their land.

Regulating Reproduction: Keeping Lebanese Heterosexuality in Line

A key area of focus for gay activists mobilizing against the arrests in these two cases was the issue of anal examinations. In fact, the public outcry against the anal examinations was so damning that both the head of the syndicate of forensic doctors and the minister of justice issued statements describing the anal tests as a form of degrading and humiliating treatment—even torture—quoting language from the UN Convention against Torture and calling for an end to the practice. A spokesperson for the Internal Security Forces even went so far as to say that the police do not actually agree with Article 534 of the penal code but are forced to implement it as long as it is still law. Despite this admission, however, the practice has been reported to still happen.

I posit that this campaign and the ensuing reactions should be read alongside another, more long-standing lobbying effort to legislate for the protection of women from family violence, particularly as it pertains to the issue of marital rape, which remains unrecognized as rape in Lebanese law. Doing so illustrates the gendered logic underpinning the legal regulation of illicit sex in service of "protecting women" as the reproducers of the nation and maintaining heteronormative sexual reproduction within the bonds of marriage. It is through the traditional, patrilineal family, as both an "ideological construction and fundamental principle of social organization," that citizenship is reproduced.[27] Whatever may be allowed within the limited zones of "tolerance" of a certain space for modern Lebanese gayness, there must be no shifts on the other side of the controls, those patrolling marriage and reproduction.

One of the most contentious issues in the draft law was the explicit criminalization of marital rape, currently not a criminal offense. Article 503 of the Lebanese Penal Code states that "whoever coerces someone other than his wife through violence or threat into sexual intercourse, is punished with hard labor for no less than five years." In response to the backlash against the proposed criminalization of spousal rape, women's rights organizations launched media and lobbying campaigns to keep the draft law intact as is with the provision against marital rape. Despite these efforts, an extremely declawed version of the law without the provision was passed in 2013. In comparison to the public outrage elicited by the mediatized exposure of anal examinations, the response to the toleration of marital rape as a form of state-sanctioned sexual violence against women was minimal. The occasional sexual violation of male bodies (by the state) elicited a far more vicious public backlash than the habitual sexual violation of female bodies by their husbands.

This difference also points to how deeply invested the state is in the regulation of reproductive bodies (coded female, the primary site for the regulation of heterosexuality). Maya Mikdashi has argued that sex is the most legally salient category through which citizenship is constituted since "sex-based differentiation saturates most branches of Lebanese law,"[28] and Nizar Saghieh and Wahid Farchichi identified the principles of patriarchy, heteronormative reproduction, marriage, virginity, and public morality as undergirding laws governing sexual behavior, including the criminalization of "unnatural sex" under Article 534 in the Lebanese Penal Code.[29]

Laws against adultery, for example, make the protection of the marriage bond the business of the state. Article 487 of the penal code punishes the married parties in an adulterous relationship more harshly than the unmarried ones, and it also imposes harsher penalties on women. Article 503 punishes nonconsensual sex only if it happens outside the bond of marriage, and Article 522 allows rape charges to be dropped if the rapist marries his victim. The logic undergirding all of these laws is the "protection" of the marriage bond itself as the site of containment for heteronormative reproduction.

The protection of identifiable and legitimate paternity within the bond of marriage is also heavily inscribed in criminal law. For example, vaginal rape with a penis is considered far more grave than anal rape, whether between a man and a woman or two people of the same gender.

Although Article 503 defines rape as coerced "sexual intercourse," Saghieh and Farchichi point to a decision by the court of cassation in which anal rape of a woman by a man was punished according to Article 507, which states that "whoever coerces someone through violence or threat into violating public decency or fornication is punished with hard labor for no less than four years," one year less than the minimum sentence for rape as defined in Article 503.[30] It is only considered "real rape" if a penis comes into contact with a vagina, thus allowing for the possibility of illegitimate conception—all other illegitimate or nonconsensual sexual acts are considered "fornication." By the same logic, coercive sex that may lead to legitimate reproduction, as in the case between a husband and wife, is not considered a crime.

Lebanese nationality laws restrict women's rights even further, since they cannot give their foreign husbands or children born out of such a union their Lebanese nationality. Paradoxically, the only way a Lebanese mother can pass on her citizenship to her children is if she has a child out of wedlock and the father is unknown. The pressures for reproduction regardless of the interests of the woman are made even clearer in another policy set in the criminal law: abortion is illegal in all cases except to save the life of the mother.

Shaping Ideas of National Belonging and Gendered Citizenship

The persecution of homosexuality, like the persecution of wayward women, never happens in a void. State regulation of nonnormative bodies and the production and reproduction of the normative citizen always happens within an interconnected matrix of control. As Tamar Mayer writes, "The intersection of nation, gender and sexuality [and also race] is a discourse about moral code, which mobilizes men . . . to become its sole protectors and women its sole biological and symbolic reproducers."[31] As this essay explores, while women in Lebanon are held as the symbolic guardians of the nation, gay men occupy a contradictory position within this matrix. While the Ministry of Justice eventually acquiesced to the public's demand that the practice of anal examinations be stopped, this should not be taken as a sign of more openness toward homosexuality. State silence over the arrests and humiliation of the individuals in the

Dekwaneh gay club and the continuation of anal examinations (despite the directive to end them) should attest to this.

These differential reactions point to the need to uphold and retrench masculinity and to rescue it from feminizing penetration, but only insofar as this penetration has been exposed to the public. After all, activists framed the examinations as state rape of male anuses, and the state could not be seen as feminizing its own men, but it could be seen as ensuring the proper protection and penetration of its women as the reproducers of citizens. Furthermore, while the anal examinations are visual, relying on purportedly identifying habitual penetration by the shape of the anus and not on any type of penetrative test, gay rights activists have focused on the spectacle of illegitimate male anal penetration to garner support for the cause. The examination commonly became known as "the egg test," in reference to the supposed insertion of an egg into the examinee's anus—a patently false description, but one that nonetheless mobilizes patriarchal heterosexual anxieties over male anal penetration.

The rape of a woman by her husband, on the other hand, remains invisible—there is no metaphor that can make this harm legible as a state-enabled crime against either modernity or masculinity. In relying on this discourse of offended modernity and masculinity to generate outrage, gay activists not only miss how tightly heterosexuality and ethnic and racial others continue to be regulated, they help to contain the tight boundaries of appropriate "Lebaneseness," as they leave the structures of patriarchal heteronormativity intact.

These examples are some illustrations of how the legal regimes of the state, in particular the penal code, regulate and produce gendered and racialized insiders and outsiders and, through this, produce the state's social and political lexicon of proper citizenship. Though Lebanon struggles to signal itself as a modern state of exception in the Middle East, such a reliance on the "modern" is precarious. Gay sex is still despised, but it is primarily made despicable when it is shown to be "foreign." It is not surprising, then, that the vehement outrage of activists found public support when Lebanese men were subjected to anal examinations. While on the surface homosexual, racial, and gendered regulation appear to be separate, they are actually intimately connected through the state's juridical heteronormative imperatives.

CHAPTER 13

Objects in Political Mirrors May Not Be What They Appear

Scott Long

Editors' Note

Scott Long's wide-ranging reflections on sexual rights advocacy and legal recognition of same-sex marriage are perceptive and provocative in our consideration of criminal laws. The family—declared to be a natural and fundamental unit of human society in all the foundational human rights instruments—sits at the intersection of sexuality, reproduction, and gendered norms. What counts as a family, how families are formed, who is included, what legal protections are extended, and so on not only are dependent on legal institutions (formal and informal) but also are deeply imbricated in social and cultural institutions—and all their changing priorities as well. Most relevant to our conversations, which elsewhere focus on the pervasive use of criminal law to regulate sexual conduct, marriage is often seen as the foremost institution whereby state (and religious) authorities confer legitimacy on families and grant privacy to sexual conduct.[1] Sexual relations that are nonprocreative or outside wedlock have been deemed criminal, and penal codes have marked them as "incompatible with prevailing social norms . . . by incapacitating and punishing those who engage in such behavior."[2] The doctrines of family law and criminal law therefore create the architecture and armature for "legitimate" families. Notably, however, except at the moment that the crime of adultery or bigamy is committed, the two systems of law appear blind to each other. Few criminal law texts treat the regulation of marriage as the job of the penal state. Same-sex marriage, one of the sexual rights campaigns du jour, is generally not a crime.

What has never been raised during the drafting of any of the UN human rights covenants and conventions is a human right to marry an individual of the same sex. Its nonrecognition as a right was challenged before the UN Human Rights Committee in the 1999 case of *Joslin v. New Zealand*.[3] The Human Rights Committee affirmed the compromise that the UN initially made, to defer to state party practice absent some hugely egregious injustice.[4] Denial of the status "married" did not reach that standard, and it was, from the state's point of view, a nonissue. Same-sex marriage was not possible or recognized, simply null and void; such marriages, however, would not be considered criminal.[5]

What has been criminalized in many jurisdictions, however, are same-sex sexual practices. And with the rise of legal same-sex marriage, for the most part in the Global North,[6] there has been an energetic countermovement elsewhere to define marriage as between one man and one woman.[7] Moreover, homosexuality is vigorously denounced as a crime, as if to create a more defensible moat around heterosexual, normative marriage, a phenomenon discussed by Long.

Long first collected his insights on these subjects in a long-form, self-published essay on his blog, *Paper Bird*. We edited his essay for length and removed the hyperlinks and most visual material; some punctuation was changed, and citations have been added.

Tears

Of course, I cried. I cried because these nine antiquarian arbiters in funeral garb—five of them, anyway—each looking about as forward-thinking and progressive as a constipated grandparent, informed me at last that I am part of this Great Community they help to govern. I cried for the past, for all those years I never imagined this was possible, as if their words, rather than repealing that suffering, put it exactly in its place, just so, part of a long injustice necessary in some consoling theodicy so that justice could ultimately be done.

I cried because I remembered when *Bowers v. Hardwick* was handed down, twenty-nine years ago. Back then five of the nine said I should go to jail because "the Constitution does not confer a fundamental right upon homosexuals to engage in sodomy."[8] It was the last day of June. I spent that Fourth of July holiday holed up in a Cambridge apartment, crying with my queer friend Charlie Fulton. That was Liberty Weekend, the centenary of that old, welcoming statue, and there were fireworks in New York Harbor and endless blather about freedom and inclusion and Ronald Reagan intoning that "someday every people and every nation of the world will know the blessings of liberty."[9] Except us.

I cried because I remembered ten years later when they decided *Romer v. Evans*—"A State cannot so deem a class of persons a stranger to its laws."[10] I cried happy tears then, and I cried again eight years after that when the Supreme Court decided *Lawrence v. Texas* and told me I didn't need to go to jail after all.[11] Of course I cried this time. I cried because I was tired of crying. There had been too many tears.

Too many tears; yet tears are insufficient. Marriage ought to be an adult state. You can't just think about it from the tearful, bruised vantage of your youthful alienations. The gay movement in the United States makes a massive fetish of childhood: bullied kids, suicidal kids, kids in desperate need of role models. Why? Not just because of others' terrible stories but because, for lots of us, childhood is where *we* cried our hardest tears, suffered our deepest wounds.

The week after the Supreme Court decision, the big issue in Gay World wasn't what we'd fight next—job discrimination? Violence? It was a photo of a ten-year-old boy, crying (so the caption said) because, he said, "I'm homosexual, and I'm afraid about what my future will be and that people won't like me."[12] It went viral after Hillary Clinton herself stepped in to reassure him on Facebook, "Your future is going to be amazing."[13]

This said little about the kid, or Clinton, but lots about American gay men. Their torrent of identification, a flood that obliterated questions (was the photo real? Could a ten-year-old really consent to having it posted?), came because they saw *themselves* as that vulnerable child, under the cracked shell of adults whose movement had just won a historic triumph. Such infantilization not just of selves but of a whole social movement is strange. Why should Frank Bruni, resident gay at the sober *New York Times*, filter his whole hazy, sentimental reaction to the Supreme Court's ukase through "one 12-year-old boy" ("He has noticed that his heart beats faster not for girls but for other boys, and the sensation is as lonely and terrifying as it is intense")?[14]

This is memory politics, Marcel Proust mixed uneasily with Martin Luther King Jr. Our rights are about more than our unhappy childhoods. They speak to our maturity, our lives *now*. Marriage is not just a kiss the state bestows to make it better. We are not wounded children needing solace, but adults whose lives have already taken shape. It's in the frame of our grown-up decisions and defeats that we must measure what we've won, what marriage really means.

Recognition

So I turned to the decision itself. What did those nine constipated guardians say to us? When I downloaded *Obergefell v. Hodges*, the first thing that sprang out at me, honest to God, was this footnote: "People may choose to marry or not to marry. The decision to do so does not make one person more 'noble' than another. And the suggestion that Americans who choose not to marry are inferior to those who decide to enter such relationships is specious."[15] That's a good point, I thought, and wondered how it fit into Justice Anthony M. Kennedy's argument. Then I realized it was from Clarence Thomas's dissent—responding to Kennedy's suggestion that marriage confers "'nobility' on individuals."[16]

To agree with Thomas makes me want to scrub myself. Yet it points to a problem with Kennedy's writing, variously condemned, even by his supporters, as "gauzy," "vague," or "muddled."[17] His verbiage is a forest seemingly uncharted by any dictionary, where terms like "nobility," "dignity," and "liberty" roam without the taming governance of definitions. It's like being in Jurassic Park, with large words lumbering menacingly through the undergrowth; you can take their pictures, but you can't get close enough to find out what they mean. Non-lawyers, if they like the end result, enjoy the rousing rhetoric. Lawyers, even lefty ones, may secretly sympathize with Justice Antonin Scalia, whose scurrilous dissent said of one Kennedy sentence that "the Supreme Court of the United States has descended from the disciplined legal reasoning of John Marshall and Joseph Story to the mystical aphorisms of the fortune cookie."[18]

Kennedy's decisions on sexual orientation mostly avoid the set ways of determining whether unequal treatment is lawful, developed over the last hundred years or so in American law. These are the famous three levels of review: rational basis (for evaluating the intrusiveness of economic regulation, for instance), intermediate scrutiny (for discrimination claims based on gender), and strict scrutiny (for claims based on race). In rational-basis review, courts are very deferential to what the state is doing; in higher levels of scrutiny, states need to show they have an "important" or "compelling" interest in classifying people—and they often fail.

Instead of scrutiny, Kennedy introduces the idea of "animus": when laws treat people differently based on pure dislike. Any restriction based on animus is impermissible. The problem is, though, that legislators and—especially—lower courts need to fit Kennedy's precedents, and his language on "animus," back into the standards of scrutiny they still use to make decisions. *Obergefell* strongly suggests that sexual-orientation discrimination should receive strict scrutiny, but as Scott Lemieux writes, "Kennedy inexplicably refuses to say so."[19] He resembles a savant who refuses to use either long division or short division but solves math problems by staring at his knee. Maybe he's right, but students learn nothing from the way he got there.

Nonetheless, the word *animus*, which flowered in Kennedy's writing before marriage became an issue,[20] seems to capture something essential to the marriage struggles, and perhaps to some other contemporary forms of discrimination. If I pass an old-style law that makes it harder for black people to get jobs, it's clear what I want: for white people to get more jobs. With the rash of antimarriage amendments, it's different: no one ever believed that less marriage for the gays would mean more to go around for others. It's not discrimination that benefits anybody. The aim was solely to say to gays and lesbians, *You don't belong.*

In targeting "You don't belong" laws, Kennedy is constructing a jurisprudence about symbolic slights, where the intent of the legislation is crucial. This is a jurisprudence for a politics of *recognition*, in the terms that Nancy Fraser has made famous. Fraser drew a distinction between two visions of justice, dividing "the forces of progressive politics" into "two camps."[21] An older vision of "redistribution" draws on "traditions of egalitarian, labor and socialist organizing"; "political actors aligned with this orientation seek a more just allocation of resources and goods."[22] On the other side, the proponents of "recognition" talk about diversity and difference. Kennedy addresses people who want not resources and benefits but respect and solace. He largely imagines intangible rewards, hence the cloudy ungraspability of nouns like *liberty* and *dignity*, but his arguments are philosophically intelligible even if not always legally clear.

In the United States as in other countries, the whole campaign for marriage has revolved around recognition. The financial and material aspects of marriage might be crucial to actual people and were sometimes vital to litigation (inheritance-tax rights, for instance, were central to the 2013 *Windsor* decision).[23] However, they were downplayed by general agreement throughout the struggle, in favor of a greeting-card emphasis on "love" and its starved aspiration for due respect. Other LGBT needs that had clear material implications or implied redistributing goods or services (employment protections, or housing rights, or palpable and particular rights of citizenship like having your ID reflect who you are) were told to wait, while a goal constructed in symbolic and immaterial terms moved to the head of the line. . . .

I'm not so much criticizing this strategy as asking what happens next. People are already hawking their ideas for "new priorities" for the U.S. LGBT movement (though some precipitately want to shut it down completely); but there's little discussion about *how* you can wrench it back to a focus on material goals, when the whole movement has gone off in pursuit of the ghostly allurements of symbolic affirmation.

Kennedy's language may be frustrating, but it isn't accidental. The injustices he finds especially intolerable, the animus-driven laws he condemns, deny the desires of people to exercise their liberty and to be recognized in their dignity, with the identities and lives they've made. Liberty and dignity entail decision-making power for Kennedy. But an older, hierarchical implication keeps peeping through. The idea of "liberty" is historically prone to elevating certain uses of freedom above others. And when attached to marriage, both "liberty" and "equality" turn invidious, augmenting the dignity of some while leaving other choices, other relationships, rhetorically in the ditch.

Liberty

As Kennedy pulls out the stops, the word *liberty* swells to an anthropological attribute rather than a political value: every person's ability not just to do things but to decide who they are. He writes in *Obergefell*, "The Constitution promises liberty to all within its reach, a liberty that includes certain specific rights that allow persons, within a lawful realm, to define and express their identity."[24] (This is the sentence that drew Scalia's scorn earlier; but if I found that in my fortune cookie, I'd be happy.)

Perhaps Kennedy's most important lines are those where he draws an expansive picture of the ways that liberty is implicated in the intimate realm of life: "Like choices concerning contraception, family relationships, procreation, and childrearing, all of which are protected by the Constitution, decisions concerning marriage are among the most intimate that an individual can make."[25] Elevating autonomy and choice this way is powerful. It underpins what is, for lawyers, probably the most unsettling part of Kennedy's opinion: his preference for using a substantive due process argument, rather than an equal protection one. Substantive due process is one of the most controversial doctrines in American law. It is an interpretation of the Fourteenth Amendment that conservatives and liberals alike have used to identify rights—"liberties"—not specifically enumerated in the Constitution. For Kennedy, the liberty to marry is one of these. The framers didn't mention it; but surely it must be in our founding document, mute yet essential.

Whereas an equal protection argument contends the state should treat everyone equally—if some can marry, all should be able to—a substantive due process approach holds, with different emphasis, that marriage is so silently fundamental no one should be denied it. Equal protection would allow a government, in principle, to deny marriage equally to everybody across the board. But if marriage is a substantive due process right, it's inescapable: states *must* let people marry. Lots of lawyers mistrust this sleight of hand and the stealth freedoms it uncovers. But it's quite consistent with Kennedy's belief that what's at stake in same-sex marriage—and in LGBT rights in general—is less protecting equality than respecting every person's decision-making power.

It's this way of conceiving liberty that Clarence Thomas despises. He returns to old sources to assert a minimalist liberty as simple "freedom from physical restraint." In its narrowest sense—he's citing William Blackstone here—"liberty" most likely refers to "the power of loco-motion, of changing situation, or removing one's person to whatsoever place one's own inclination may direct; without imprisonment or restraint, unless by due course of law."[26]

"Or"—he's in the library again—"as one scholar put it in 1776, '[T]he common idea of liberty is merely negative.'"[27] In the marriage cases, nobody kept anybody from going anywhere. "Petitioners cannot claim, under the most plausible definition of 'liberty,' that they have been imprisoned or physically restrained."[28] Nothing to see here; move along.

This is, in fact, a very old dispute. Thomas's cantankerousness clarifies what Kennedy is talking about. Thomas defends negative liberty, as Isaiah Berlin classically defined it: "By being free in this sense I mean not being interfered with by others."[29] A long philosophical tradition distinguishes this from *positive liberty*, which conveys not only absence of restraint but also the capacity for action, the possession of personal power. Berlin wrote, "The 'positive' sense of the word 'liberty' derives from the wish on the part of the individual to be his own master. . . . I wish to be a doer—deciding, not being decided for, self-directed and not acted upon by external nature or by other men."[30] Kennedy is emphatically a partisan of positive liberty. His arguments draw strength from its strengths: its concern, for instance, for what governments and societies must do to enable independent and competent choices. His opinions are also endangered by its weaknesses. Berlin has traced better than any other thinker the paradoxes of positive liberty: the way its exaltation of human capacities can turn into a proscriptive mandate that those capacities be properly used.

Positive liberty tends to collapse into monism, as Berlin says, "the faith in a single criterion": the belief there is one overriding value people *ought* to be pursuing, one that redeems their power to choose by its syllogistic superiority as a choice. In this vision, "the rational ends of our 'true' natures must coincide, or be made to coincide, however, violently our poor, ignorant, desire-ridden, passionate, empirical selves may cry out against this process. . . . Liberty, so far from being incompatible with authority, becomes virtually identical with it."[31]

How much does Kennedy's idea of liberty remain neutral about the values people choose? How much does it regress into the faith that "all values can be graded on one scale, so that it is a mere matter of inspection to determine the highest"[32]—and that true liberty consists in choosing the highest?

If Kennedy's understanding of liberty risks sanctifying certain choices over others, it is a fortuity perhaps increased by his use of substantive due process. One reading of substantive due process doctrine is that if certain rights didn't actually get enumerated in the Constitution, it must be because they were so fundamental and obvious that the framers saw no need to mention them. Kennedy comes very close to saying this about marriage. If a right is that basic to being American, or human, then woe betide anyone who doesn't use it.

Dignity

For Kennedy, the greatest injustice lesbians and gays have suffered is a continuous insult to their human dignity, and nowhere does this play a grander role than in deciding whether the government will give gays "the basic dignity of recognizing" their marriages. Over generations, he writes, "many persons did not deem homosexuals to have dignity in their own distinct identity. A truthful declaration by same-sex couples of what was in their hearts had to remain unspoken. Even when a greater awareness of the humanity and integrity of homosexual persons came in the period after World War II, the argument that gays and lesbians had a just claim to dignity was in conflict with both law and widespread social conventions."[33]

However, Kennedy abjures defining the word *dignity*. Nor is it a clear term of art in U.S. jurisprudence. Although Kenji Yoshino finds that the Supreme Court has used it in more than nine hundred opinions,[34] as Leslie Meltzer Henry observes, for a word so often bandied about in constitutional law, "its importance, meaning, and function are commonly presupposed but rarely articulated."[35] Henry considers its legal uses diverse, flexible, "dynamic and context-driven."[36] This is a way of saying "vague."

This vagueness allows Clarence Thomas to claim that Kennedy sees dignity solely as something the government gives you. Maintaining to the contrary that dignity is innate, Thomas heads into an already notorious peroration: "Slaves did not lose their dignity (any more than they lost their humanity) because the government allowed them to be enslaved. . . . The government cannot bestow dignity, and it cannot take it away."[37]

In fact, Kennedy's own idea of dignity stands on firmer philosophical ground than Thomas's. He doesn't see it as a state endowment, but neither does he treat it as some mystic quiddity or *innere emigration* that even slavery can't strip away. Dignity is closely connected with his philosophy of liberty as choice. The question is whether it's threatened by the same dangers: whether his reliance on the word and concept risks undermining the legal framework of freedom he is trying to advance.

Some potted history here is useful. In Rome, Mette Lebech tells us, "*dignitas* [the Latin root for "dignity"] was the standing of the one who commanded respect, whether because of his political, military or administrative achievements."[38] The notion of dignity as a quality of all humans, detached from any particular class or role, only fully emerged in the Renaissance. Its most eloquent articulation was by the fifteenth-century philosopher Pico della Mirandola, in his oration *On the Dignity of Man*. Dignity lay in the universal human capacity to choose and change, to decide about yourself, to shift your very status on the Great Chain of Being: "The happiness of man! To man it is allowed to be whatever he chooses to be! . . . He fashions and transforms himself into any fleshly form and assumes the character of any creature whatsoever."[39]

Clearly this is ancestral to how Kennedy regards dignity; and it also suggests how he links dignity to liberty. For Kennedy, liberty includes being able to choose who we are or will become, shaping our identities rather than just taking what's given. Dignity comes when these choices can be acted on, witnessed, and recognized, but it also plays a peculiar role in Kennedy's marriage opinion. "The right to personal choice regarding marriage is inherent in the concept of individual autonomy," he writes.[40] But he doesn't stop there. The "choice regarding marriage" isn't neutral.[41] The "centrality of marriage to the human condition" makes it far more than just an option.[42] The dignity of marriage seems not to open possibilities but to dictate one above all.

The prose is full of fulsome praise for people who decide one way rather than the other: "No union is more profound than marriage, for it embodies the highest ideals of love, fidelity, devotion, sacrifice, and family. In forming a marital union, two people become something greater than once they were."[43] Indeed, marrying boosts your dignity: "The lifelong union of a man and a woman always has promised nobility and dignity to all persons, without regard to their station in life."[44] And, "from their beginning to their most recent page, the annals of human history reveal the transcendent importance of marriage. . . . Marriage is sacred to those who live by their religions and offers unique fulfillment to those who find meaning in the secular realm. Its dynamic allows two people to find a life that could not be found alone. . . . Rising from the most basic human needs, marriage is essential to our most profound hopes and aspirations."[45]

One can see in the contrast with reproductive rights how heavily weighted a choice marriage is to Kennedy. He calls decisions about contraception and procreation "among the most intimate that an individual can make"[46] and "protected by the Constitution."[47] These words posit procreating and not procreating as equivalent, neutral choices, veiled by their intimacy and importance from legal and moral valuation. Indeed, the right to contraception was only established in American law through long struggles asserting it was *not* less dignified, not less moral or proper, than becoming pregnant. But Kennedy offers no equivalent opposite to choosing marriage. He wastes no words praising the dignity of the single life. Not to elect marriage, he says, is "to be condemned to live in loneliness, excluded from one of civilization's oldest institutions."[48]

Kennedy and the concepts he uses are divided, torn. His idea of *liberty* as self-determination collapses back toward the belief that some decisions are better than others, because they show the self's mastery over what is irrational and wrong. His idea of *dignity* is the means for the implosion: it folds inadvertently into an older sense that some lifeways are superior in their rationality and rightfulness. Dignity-as-choice melts back into dignity-as-distinction. Kennedy obfuscates the difference while keeping them shoehorned in the same word.

The Wrong Side of History

Kennedy's libertarian language jars gratingly with a uncritical and coercive adulation of one particular life decision: marriage. His inflation of marriage into a "transcendent" choice is already echoing.[49] It gives rise to a sudden burst of judgmental Comstockery among gay people, as though a little government attention turned them all into Southern Baptist preachers (hypocrisy included). Take, for instance, this month's reactions to the word that the black sheep of the Palin clan was pregnant again "out of wedlock."[50] The gays were indignant; their first week *into* wedlock, and already they think anybody outside it must be a crack whore. I can't tell you how strange it feels to see this meme all over the Internet—stranger, too, when gay friends who I know have spent their nights on Grindr flaunt it on their Facebook pages.

This moralistic misogyny should be beneath the dignity of people who recently suffered from the same censorious opprobrium. I think Neil Patrick Harris is a nice person and Bristol Palin is not. I know, though, that neither their sex lives nor her single status has anything to do with how good they'll be as parents. And I'm as sure as I am of anything on earth that a human rights movement enlisted in the slut-shaming brigade has nothing, zero, to do with human rights anymore. If the gays are acting blind as any right-wing pundit, it's paradoxically the right-wingers who see clearly the multiple ways people define relationships now—even if they only invoke this variety as a drone target for their Jeremiads.

Consider this question: Are there legal means by which the state could, and should, recognize relationships with multiple partners? The gays (and many nice, liberal supporters) wax furious if anyone suggests this might be a logical extension of the liberties in marriage: as if, having gone two by two into the ark, they want to hoist the gangway and let the three-way perverts drown. What's astonishing is to see the liberals *categorically deny that such relationships exist in modern societies at all.* Justice Samuel A. Alito Jr. brought it up during the marriage hearing, trying to imagine polygamy in a contemporary context: for instance, "four people, two men and two women—it's not the sort of polygamous relationship, polygamous marriages that existed in other societies."[51] The *New Yorker* was flatly incredulous. Such a family, its reporter wrote, is "one that exists in Alitoland" alone.[52]

I didn't know I lived in Alitoland. But I do know many households like the ones Alito described: the lesbian who's bought a home (and is bringing up a child) with her current lover, her former lover, and her current lover's former lover; the trans man—prim as your favorite uncle—who's raised his kids with his two cis-female partners; the husband who lives with his wife and his wife's lesbian mate. You can perfectly well say these aren't common, but you won't know, because these arrangements tend not to turn up on census forms. It's a strange world when a George W. Bush–appointed Supreme Court justice may be more in touch than the *New Yorker* with the way people live now.

People today are choosing and living in many kinds of relationships of care—and building new ones. The law's challenge is to find how to recognize and protect these, because the law's job is to look after the ways people actually live. Hieratic talk about the primacy of two-person marriage may postpone this but can't avoid the need. In the last decade a few documents outlined vast gaps in what the law recognizes: a detailed Law Commission of Canada report, *Beyond Conjugality*, and a manifesto by U.S. activists, "Beyond Same-Sex Marriage."[53] The latter listed some of the "other kinds of kinship relationship, households, and families" that need protection. Among them were the following:

- Senior citizens living together, serving as each other's caregivers, partners, and/or constructed families;
- Care-giving and partnership relationships that have been developed to provide support systems to those living with HIV/AIDS;
- Close friends and siblings who live together in long-term, committed, non-conjugal relationships, serving as each other's primary support and caregivers;
- Extended families living under one roof, whose members care for one another;
- Queer couples who decide to jointly create and raise a child with another queer person or couple in two households;
- Single parent households; and
- Committed households in which there is more than one conjugal partner.[54]

Kennedy's opinion, in fact, doesn't even reflect the diversity of life choices *on the Supreme Court.* The pitiable, sad unmarried people whom he calls "condemned to loneliness" include two of the four justices who voted with him. A colleague of mine wonders what they really thought about this language. Probably they see it as what Scalia called "the price of a fifth vote."[55] I wonder rather more what Kennedy really thinks as he looks at them.

And this is what disappoints about Kennedy's words, and the exultation greeting them. They misunderstand radically what marriage actually means in the modern world, and what made its expansion possible. Marriage has not opened to lesbian and gay couples because it is "profound" or "transcendent." It expanded because it isn't that any more. The marriage decision is possible because marriage means less to us, because the last scraps of its exclusionary dignity are disappearing. Marriage is becoming simply one choice among others; the rhetoric trying to reclaim its sanctity is on the wrong side of history.

Worldwide, fewer and fewer are making that transcendent choice. In the United States, in particular, marriage rates have dropped from 8.2 per 1,000 people in 2000 to 6.9 in 2015.[56] The plunge among young American adults (aged twenty-five to thirty-four) has been particularly steady; the proportion of young adults who are married dropped by 10 percentage points from 2000 to 2009, and the number of Americans aged twenty-five to thirty-four who have never been married now exceeds the number who are married.[57] Statistics across Europe show the same trend.[58]

And it's not just the decaying West. What's striking is that in another country I know well, highly traditional Egypt, the rate has also fallen. The decline

Crude marriage rates

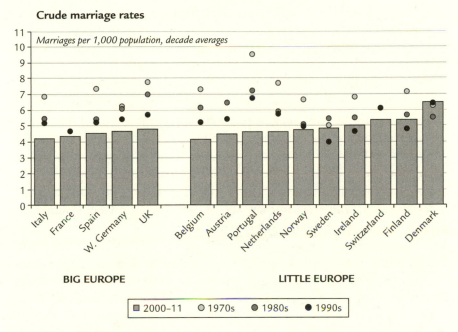

Figure 13.1. Phillip N. Cohen, "Marriage Is Declining Globally: Can You Say That?," *Family Inequality* (blog), June 12, 2013, https://www.familyinequality.wordpress.com /2013/06/12/marriage-is-declining/.

was less stark and steady, but the marriage rate dropped from 10.8 per 1,000 people in 1952 to 7.3 in 2006.[59] But the fall has been more dramatic in Egypt's two richest urban areas; in Alexandria, the figures sank to half the overall U.S. rate.[60] Evidently, people's economic and social independence plays a crucial role in marriage rates. The customary Egyptian explanation for the decline is that economic hardships make men reluctant to marry. For a century, in fact, Cairene intellectuals have been warning about a "marriage crisis" caused by men's ever-direr financial powerlessness.[61] Statistics suggest otherwise. Recent rises in Egypt's marriage rate—a 2.7 percent increase in 2012, for instance[62]—coincided with severe economic dislocation. It seems plausible that some want to postpone or avoid marriage as long as they can afford their independence, and turn to its strictures as a shelter only in hard times. When they can, they choose to be single.

There are as many explanations for all this as there are ideologies. Right now, it's the consequences I care about. Marriage is no longer an inescapable value. It's been demystified: an option, not an obligation. The sense that it is a choice is precisely what created the pressure to allow others to choose it. The gays were on the right side of this historical process, in demanding that marriage be expanded. The broadening of choice is something to rejoice in. But to continue treating marriage as a transcendent value rather than a contingent possibility is anachronistic.

Many today may want to raise their children in a community of shared responsibilities rather than a nuclear household. Many today may want decisions about their health or death made within a circle of friends, not by a single partner. Accommodating this in law is an imminent, not a transcendent, necessity.

When I call the loss of marriage's transcendence historically irreversible, I mean that in a democratic world, transcendence itself cannot be sustained. It's curious that the donnish, tweedy Isaiah Berlin should have expounded this postmodern insight with such urgency. The philosopher John Gray summarizes what Berlin saw: that ultimate values "are many, they often come into conflict with one another and are uncombinable in a single human being or a single society, and that in many of such conflicts there is no overarching standard whereby the competing claims of such ultimate values are rationally arbitral. Conflicts among such values are among incommensurables, and the choices we make among them are radical and tragic choices."[63] Gray writes that this "strikes a death-blow to the central, classical, Western tradition," with its belief that all positive values are rationally consistent—"and, it must be added, to the project of the Enlightenment."[64]

That may be too much. Yet to recognize the pluralism of values is to realize in the most rendingly personal way that we live in a disenchanted world. No one hands us final answers. There is no "most profound" or "highest" lifeway. Some people choose the *vita activa*, some the *vita contemplativa*. Some discover more purpose in public life than private life; to some, a tennis match matters more than a job promotion. Some people locate the highest value in a single uxorious relationship, some in the migratory ecstasies of sex; some will find the value of sex in mystical union, some in its market price. For some, love is the true meaning of marriage. For some, it's taxes. Berlin wrote,

> It may be that the idea of freedom to choose ends without claiming eternal validity for them, and the pluralism of values connected with this, is only the late fruit of our declining capitalist civilization: an idea which remote ages and primitive societies have not recognized, and one which posterity will regard with curiosity, even sympathy, but little comprehension. This may be so; but no skeptical conclusions seem to me to follow. . . . Indeed, our very desire for guarantees that our values are eternal and secured in some objective heaven is perhaps only a craving

for the certainties of childhood or the absolute values of our primitive past. . . . To demand [such guarantees] is perhaps a deep and incurable metaphysical need; but to allow such a need to determine one's practice is a symptom of an equally deep, and more dangerous, moral and political immaturity.[65]

That rebuke to our childishness may just be the truth we need.

CHAPTER 14

Harm Production: An Argument
for Decriminalization

Joanna N. Erdman

In 1999 Bernard Harcourt wrote a provocative article on the collapse of the harm principle.[1] This principle is famously cited in the Hart-Devlin debate on the criminalization of sexual conduct.[2] The debate followed the Wolfenden Committee's 1957 recommendation that homosexuality but not prostitution be decriminalized in Britain.[3] Criminal law, the committee reported, must protect the citizen from what is "offensive or injurious" but must not otherwise intervene in the private lives of citizens.[4] Lord Devlin disagreed. He argued that private immoral acts corrupted the social order. Criminal law must thus protect both citizens from harm and the social order from moral decline.[5] In defense of the committee's recommended restraint and in reply to Lord Devlin, H. L. A. Hart invoked the harm principle: sexual conduct may only be criminalized if it is harmful.[6]

In standard accounts, Hart won the debate, and the harm principle came to dominate liberal discourse on the criminalization of sex.[7] Progressive movements reclaimed conduct as neither harmful nor morally wrong in efforts to topple criminal sexual offenses. A transnational women's movement in the 1970s, for example, contested characterizations of abortion as harmful to women and to society and sought to publicly reclaim abortion as a civil right essential to women's equality and emancipation.[8] Advocates continue to argue the harm principle in criminalization debates today, reframing sexual conduct as respect worthy, not harmful, and warranting legal protection, not sanction.

Yet Harcourt provokes in his 1999 article by describing not the ascendance of the harm principle but rather its collapse. By this he means that the focus on harm has become so pervasive that proponents of criminalization are now converted and argue for the criminalization of sexual conduct by citing its harm rather than immorality. Harm has become the language of both criminal law and its limits, collapsing the structure of the debate.[9] Everyone now claims in harm. It is a harm free-for-all, a cacophony of competing harm claims. Hart's harm principle can no longer win the debate.

In this chapter, I explore the rise of a particular argument in this proliferation of harm discourse. Rather than deny the harmfulness of sexual conduct, advocates now argue for decriminalization based on the harms of criminalization itself. It is the criminalization of sex and reproduction that endangers lives and health, that creates its own order of harm more real and certain than any it seeks to prevent.[10] I call this argument *harm production*.

Harcourt gives an example of harm production in drug policy debates. Whereas marijuana use was once claimed a victimless or harmless crime, criminalization opponents today emphasize the harms of the "war on drugs."[11] They argue that many of the harms associated with illicit drug use result not from the drugs themselves but rather from their criminal prohibition. Drugs are criminalized not because they are unsafe; drugs are unsafe because they are criminalized. Matthew Weait carries the argument into the criminalization of sex using the phrase "unsafe law" in allusion to the discourse of "safe sex" in HIV prevention.[12] Weait explains that "law, like drug use, like sex, can be unsafe—but it need not be. It can and does result in harm—but it need not do so."[13]

Harm production is a prevalent form of argument in debates on the criminalization of sex and reproduction.[14] The UN special rapporteur on the right to health, for example, released a set of reports on the criminalization of abortion, conduct during pregnancy, contraception and family planning, education and information, same-sex conduct, sex work, and HIV transmission.[15] The reports' right-to-health arguments focus on the harms of criminalization—namely, how it undermines public health efforts, impedes access to health services, and adversely impacts health outcomes. In 2015 the *Lancet* published a series on HIV and sex work, documenting the significant effect that decriminalization would have on the course of HIV epidemics worldwide and thus calling on governments to decriminalize sex work as a humane and pragmatic public health intervention.[16]

Harm production arguments tend to treat sex and reproduction as a public health matter, challenging criminalization as a threat to life and health. In this respect, they stay true to a critical feature of the harm principle: its empiricism. Harm production relies on evidentiary claims of fact: demonstrable harm and causal attribution. Hart relied on these same elements to defeat legal moralism in his midcentury debate with Devlin.[17] He attacked legal moralism because it provided no evidence or causal account of how sexual immorality threatened the social order. The harm principle was thus aligned early with objective fact and set against normative verdicts of social corruption. Empirical, verifiable harm marked a bright line between law and morality. In the collapse of the harm principle, advocates again mobilize empiricism to rank competing claims of harm. In harm production arguments specifically, advocates use evidence to show what harm the law prevents, whom the law protects, and what the law costs in lives and health. The argument persuades by bracketing moral controversies in criminalization and compelling legal reform on the empirical fact of harm alone.

Or so the claim is made. This chapter asks whether harm production truly trades in empiricism alone. Is the fact that abortion laws harm, that prostitution laws endanger, that criminalization of HIV nondisclosure undermines public health persuasive enough? Does the mere evidence of harm alone provide a compelling rationale for decriminalization?

Harcourt saw the collapse of the harm principle as an opportunity to answer these questions. He argued that the repurposing of harm in criminalization debates allows us to see more clearly *judgment* in what constitutes harm and what causes harm, and to thus explain why some harm arguments succeed and others fail.[18] The collapse lets us see the normative judgment obscured in harm arguments. The simple fact of harm, after all, cannot explain why or how it matters to legal debate or provide the measure of balance among competing harms.[19] Harm becomes relevant to legal argument only through a normative framework. For Harcourt, "these hidden normative dimensions are what do the work . . . not the abstract, simple notion of harm."[20] The collapse of the harm principle invites us to surface that which gives harm meaning in criminalization debates.

Structured as a set of case studies, this chapter examines the normative dimensions of harm production arguments in a pair of Canadian Supreme Court judgments on the criminalization of sex work and HIV nondisclosure.[21] Both judgments canvass the argument that criminalization harms, an argument that persuades in one case and fails in the other. In *Canada v. Bedford* (2013), the Supreme Court struck down criminal prostitution laws as unconstitutional because they increased sex workers' risk of violence and other harms.[22] The argument and reasoning in the case resemble closely an older, touchstone Canadian judgment, *R. v. Morgentaler* (1988), which decriminalized abortion thirty years ago.[23] Set in contrast, in the companion cases of *R. v. Mabior* and *R. v. D.C.* (2012), the Supreme Court reaffirmed the criminalization of HIV nondisclosure in sexual relations, dismissing largely the claim of its adverse public health effects.[24] While there are undoubtedly many reasons why harm production arguments succeed or fail, this study focuses on differences in the Court's judgments about what constitutes harm, what causes harm, and ultimately the normative significance of harm in the decriminalization of sex and reproduction.[25]

The case study approach contextualizes the chapter, making its analysis particular to Canada—a country where in 1967, the year sodomy was decriminalized and lawful therapeutic abortion institutionalized, Prime Minister Pierre Trudeau declared, "There's no place for the state in the bedrooms of the nation."[26] The arguments studied in this chapter are legally grounded in the Canadian Criminal Code,[27] the Canadian constitutional bill of rights, the Canadian Charter of Rights and Freedoms,[28] and the judgments of the Supreme Court of Canada. Nonetheless, the chapter strives for broader relevance. While the normative values of harm production in Canadian law may not be universal, what may be shared across liberal legal systems is how harm production works as a legal argument—that is, its reliance on both the empirical and the normative, both fact and judgment.

The Harms of Criminalized Sex Work and Abortion

In December 2013 in *Canada v. Bedford*, a unanimous Supreme Court declared Canada's prostitution laws unconstitutional. While prostitution, the exchange of sex for money, was always legal in Canada, the keeping of a common bawdy house, living on the avails of prostitution, and public communication for the purposes of prostitution were not.[29] Neither was *Bedford* the first time that the Supreme Court reviewed the constitutionality of these laws. In the *Prostitution Reference* (1990), the Court upheld the prohibitions on bawdy houses and public communication, finding that the former violated no constitutional right and the latter was a justified infringement on the freedom of expression to prevent community nuisance.[30]

When sex workers challenged the prostitution laws before the Supreme Court in *Bedford*, the Court agreed to revisit its prior decision. Changed circumstances and evidence raised a new constitutional argument, which, the Court declared, "fundamentally shifts the parameters of debate."[31] In *Bedford*, the Supreme Court focused not on the wrongs or rights of sex work but rather on the harmful effects of the criminal prostitution laws. The Court held these laws unconstitutional because they prevent sex workers from taking safety measures against the risk of disease, violence, and death in violation of the right to security of the person. Because of the criminal law, sex workers cannot work in a regular indoor location, over which they may have greater control. They cannot hire managers, drivers, or security personnel for their protection. They cannot take time to screen clients on the street and to negotiate the terms of transactions. They are driven to work in isolated areas and in isolation from one another. The *Bedford* judgment is firmly anchored in a *harm production* argument.

Harm production carries special significance in Canada as a constitutional argument. In 1988 in *R. v. Morgentaler*, the Supreme Court struck down the country's criminal abortion law on a harm production rationale. The Court declared unconstitutional a criminal law that allowed therapeutic abortions only when authorized by a hospital committee. This requirement, a majority of the Court explained, created excessive delays and limited the availability of lawful therapeutic abortion, thereby endangering women's health, again in violation of the right to security of the person. Though separated by twenty-five years, *Morgentaler* and *Bedford* share much in common. Reading these judgments together reveals a repeating structure in harm production as a legal argument and allows us to see the normative framework through which the harms of criminal law are made constitutionally significant and the argument succeeds.

The first parallel in *Morgentaler* and *Bedford* is the way in which merely putting the facts of violence and physical harm at the forefront of the case reframes the larger debate: the nature of the social problem in criminalization, the facts that matter to its resolution, and the relevant arguments about these facts.[32] This reframing is early and explicit in the *Morgentaler* judgment. Its opening paragraphs declared the case as not about the "abortion question"—that is, the right of women to control their own bodies versus the right to life of the unborn child.[33] The Court would not enter this "loud and continuous," "vigorous and healthy" public debate.[34] Rather, the Court stripped abortion of its normative burden, treating criminalization as a technical issue of therapeutic risk and access to health care. Sheilah Martin observes that *Morgentaler* as a constitutional judgment that decriminalizes abortion thus "may appear disappointing: the arguments look technical and do not clearly capture and convey the rich and varied life experiences of the women they are intended to benefit."[35] Yet this was perhaps the point.

There is a shared historical view of those engaged in criminalized abortion and sex work as socially and morally disreputable. Third-party authorization in abortion law, such as hospital committees, is premised on this very mistrust. Women are unreliable narrators even of their own bodies and lives. The objectivity of empirical harm is thus called on to credit their claims with authority. It is hard to ignore harm as a verified fact, and medical evidence is the paragon of objective verification. The only harm argument with majority support in *Morgentaler* was that which relied on medical evidence. The judges accepted the argument that the hospital authorization regime delayed women's access to lawful health care, thereby increasing their risk of physical harm.[36] The argument, and its judicial endorsement, relied on the uncontroverted evidence that abortion techniques used later in pregnancy carry greater medical risk. Then-chief justice Robert George Brian Dickson wrote, "The increasing risks caused by delay are so clearly established that I have no difficulty concluding that the delay in obtaining therapeutic abortions . . . [infringes] the purely physical aspect of the individual's right to security of the person."[37] The Court assessed the constitutionality of the criminal abortion law by expert opinion on technical procedure and physical risk—a far cry from the loud and vigorous terms of public debate. In *Bedford*, the Supreme Court likewise distanced itself from the traditional terms of public debate on prostitution, stating early what the case was not about: whether prostitution should be legal.[38] The unassailable harms of disease, violence, and death were the facts of the legal dispute, making the constitutional problem in criminalization, a law that heightened these risks. Explicit about this fundamental reframing of the issue, Chief Justice Beverley McLachlin wrote, the "real gravamen of the complaint is not that *breaking* the law engages the applicants' liberty, but rather that *compliance* with the laws infringes the applicants' security of the person."[39]

The second parallel in *Morgentaler* and *Bedford* comes from the controversy over causation. It is one thing to identify harms associated with sex work and abortion. It is another to identify the criminal law as a cause of these harms. Causation was especially controversial in *Bedford*, as a consequence of a contested but ascendant argument in public and legal debate that the harms of sex work are inherent to the activity itself. In Canada and other countries, a radical feminist movement advocates for criminalization of the buyers and profiteers of commercialized sex on the view that sexual commodification is inherently violent and subordinating no matter how it is practiced or legally regulated.[40] Sex work is regarded as inherently degrading, exploitive, subordinating, parasitic, and propagating of gender, race, and other structural inequalities. Characterizing harm as inherent to prostitution collapses the question of causation. It simply does not make sense to ask of a connection between law and violence when structural violence is inherent to prostitution. A similar turn to inherent harm can be seen in the rise of abortion regret as a psychological phenomenon and a legal argument, with the parallel claim that no law can make abortion safe because a psychic harm inheres in the act itself.[41]

In *Bedford*, the Supreme Court sidestepped the issue of inherent harm by focusing on how criminalization makes sex work *more* dangerous—that is, by depriving those engaged in this *risky* but *lawful* activity the means to protect themselves.[42] The Court left the nature of the underlying risk unexamined, but its constant refrain that prostitution is lawful, and that these laws regulate but do not prohibit the activity, subtly challenged (or more artfully supported) the inherent harm argument. If prostitution is inherently harmful, why is it not criminalized directly?

Working with harm as physical violence, the Supreme Court relied on two main findings to attribute increased risk to the criminal law: first, that sex workers can reduce their risk by taking basic measures to change the location and conditions of their work, and second, that the criminal law prohibits sex workers from taking these measures.[43] The judgment is explicit, however, that causation is not a simple question of fact. Social science evidence is rarely definitive on causation, and with criminalization as a complex social phenomenon, conclusive or even convincing causal attribution can be difficult to show.[44] This is because the criminal law does not directly cause disease, violence, or death. It works through an intervening set of actors, those who sell, manage, and purchase sex and those who enforce the law, all moderated by a set of vulnerability factors: poverty, drug use, gender, race, and age. The *Bedford* Court, however, was not defeated by this complexity. Rather, the Supreme Court followed its practice in *Morgentaler*. Refusing to read causal effects from the mere words or intentions of the criminal law, the Court in both cases assessed how the law works in practice, incorporating the complexity of factual and social context into its analysis.

In *Morgentaler*, the majority relied on the "encyclopedic factual submissions" of a government commission tasked to investigate the workings of the abortion law.[45] These submissions incorporated data from Statistics Canada, interviews with officials of departments of health and justice, visits to hospitals across the country, and surveys of their staff and patients. The commission's report found the criminal regime dysfunctional, but more importantly, it attributed the dysfunction to the law itself.[46] The Supreme Court followed the report and rejected claims that limited budgets and a lack of personnel were the cause of delay. Budgets and personnel only became problems because the legal regime demanded them. The requirement that hospitals, for example, have three physicians to serve on the committee and another to perform the abortion disqualified a quarter of all Canadian hospitals from offering the service.[47] The law itself created the staffing problem, which decreased available services and increased delay.

The Court in *Bedford* similarly focused on the *real effects* of the criminal law as established by the social science evidence, the evidentiary record consisting of over twenty-five thousand pages of studies, expert reports, and parliamentary reviews.[48] Again the evidence showed the dysfunction of the legal regime. It prohibited the safest form of sex work (independently from a fixed location) and deprived sex workers of the means to make out-call and street work safer (hiring bodyguards and drivers, screening clients, and negotiating terms of service). Significantly, though, the *Bedford* Court did not rely strictly on expert studies but also heard from those with firsthand knowledge of the legal regime and its effects—namely, sex workers. The trial judge, and the Supreme Court on appeal, deferred to the lived experience of sex workers about how to negotiate and resist vulnerability to violence.[49] This marks a profound shift from *Morgentaler*. In *Bedford*, sex worker knowledge qualified as evidence, a standing earned through years of mobilization and collective action.[50]

Sex worker agency, however, is a double-edged sword in causation. In *Bedford*, the Supreme Court faced the argument that choice, not the law, was the real cause of harm. The attorneys general of Canada and Ontario argued that sex workers "can avoid the risk inherent in prostitution and any increased risk that the laws impose simply by choosing not to engage in this activity."[51] And if not the sex worker, they argued, then the source of the harm is third parties: "the johns who use and abuse prostitutes and the pimps who exploit them."[52] And if not a third party, then drugs, alcohol, and poverty were to blame. With judgment impaired by drugs and alcohol, or desperate for money and compelled to take the risk, they argued, a street sex worker could not avoid danger, even if she perceived it.[53]

The Supreme Court refused to play this blame-shifting game and reasoned that causation does not require that the law be the only or even the dominant cause of the harm suffered.[54] There is the choice to engage in sex work, but the law makes that choice riskier. A john may be the more immediate source of violence, but the law makes sex workers more vulnerable to it. Some street sex workers may take risks others would not, but if screening could have protected any one from violence or death, that is harm enough. The Court moreover named the hypocrisy of blaming destitution as the cause of harm, when the criminal law forces the destitute onto the street by preventing their resort to safe houses.[55] Government cannot lay blame on the very vulnerability that it creates.

Beyond the concepts and causes of harm, a third parallel in *Morgentaler* and *Bedford* is the significance of naming the criminal law as the cause of harm. This marks an express shift in the constitutional analysis from the empirical to the normative. Of course, the analysis of what constitutes and causes harm was also informed by normative considerations, but in the words of Harcourt, they remained hidden. On the question of what is the legal significance of criminalization's harms, the normative dimensions of harm production are made express.

Naming the criminal law as the cause of harm is about more than attribution. It turns misfortune into injustice and once again reframes the social problem of sex work and abortion. No longer do we focus on those who sell sex or terminate their pregnancies, the morality or harms of their conduct. Our gaze shifts to the state and its infliction of harm. We focus on its moral offense and ask for its redemption, or in the rhetoric of law, we ask for justification. As a state institution, even if repressive, criminal law aspires to legitimacy. Its power derives from and is constrained by principles of justice, reflected in the very expression *criminal justice*.[56] In *Morgentaler* and *Bedford*, the Supreme Court ultimately declared the criminal law unconstitutional not only because it threatened life and limb, depriving security of the person, but because it did so in a manner that failed to accord with the *principles of fundamental justice*.[57]

In *Morgentaler*, the Supreme Court declared the criminal law as manifestly unfair because its harms corresponded to no reasonable objective. It was an arbitrary law. There was no necessary connection between the requirement, for example, that all therapeutic abortions take place in hospitals and the objective of the law, allowing safe and lawful therapeutic abortion.[58] Rather, first-trimester abortions could be provided safely, even more safely, in specialized clinics. The harm resulting from this requirement was thus unnecessary, even arbitrary in creating rather than alleviating risk. The in-hospital requirement, if once justified, had become, in the Court's words, "exorbitant."[59] In *Bedford*, the Court declared the prohibition against living on the avails of prostitution offensive for the same reason. By failing to distinguish between exploitative and protective behavior, it prohibited both and thereby undermined its own safety rationale.[60] The prohibitions on bawdy houses and public communication offended in exorbitance, their harmful effects deemed grossly disproportionate to any reasonable objective of the law.[61] The homicide of street sex workers was too high a price to pay for a nuisance-free neighborhood. For the Supreme Court, "a law that prevents street prostitutes from resorting to a safe haven . . . while a suspected serial killer prowls the streets, is a law that has lost sight of its purpose."[62]

These principles of fundamental justice set limits on criminalization, precisely as the harm principle once did. Yet they are moral, not empirical, limits, a distinction reflected in the language of sacrifice and suffering rather than risk and harm.[63] Hart recognized this distinction. He opposed the criminalization of "homosexuality" not only because it was harmless conduct but also for the suffering and misery that its criminalization imposed.[64] Abhorrence for human suffering at the hand of the state is a normative limit on the reach of criminal law. The transgression of this limit may be revealed in violence, death, and injury, but the limit is grounded in morality.

This normative framework surfaces in the emotional tone of the Supreme Court's judgments. Different kinds of perceived moral transgressions produce different emotional reactions.[65] In *Bedford*, we have no disgust or revulsion, emotions traditionally associated with the criminalization of sex. On the contrary, the judgment is marked by emotions of compassion. By showing the harm that criminalization inflicts, its subjects become its victims. There is also anger and contempt for a society that would leave its members so vulnerable, a society that would care so little for their lives. In this, the *Bedford* judgment reflects a broader public discourse. It echoes medical journal editorials that call out the "hypocrisy" of criminal prostitution laws and that recognize "prostitutes are people too."[66] There are ways of treating others, such as requiring their sacrifice in death and violence, that cannot be tolerated no matter how laudable the goals of criminalization. The normative framework of harm production thus has a strong communal quality. It is not merely about individual rights of protection. It is equally, if not more so, about what the violation of these rights says about "us"— about Canadian society and its moral base. In *Bedford*, the Supreme Court affirmed this communal quality, describing the principles of fundamental justice as capturing the basic values of *our* constitutional order.[67] The criminal prostitution laws are unconstitutional because they endanger *others* in a way that runs afoul of *our* basic values.

The communal basis of this normative framework is worth noting, for it may suggest a broader shift in debates over the criminalization of sex and reproduction. In *R. v. Labaye* (2005), the Canadian Supreme Court quashed a conviction against proprietors of a sex club (a private club that organizes sex-related activities among its patrons) under the same bawdy house provision of the criminal code challenged in *Bedford*. This provision prohibits the use of a place for the purpose of prostitution and the practice of indecent acts.[68] *Labaye* did not involve a constitutional challenge to the criminal law but rather concerned the statutory interpretation of the word *indecent* in application of the law.

In Canada the legal test of indecency is no longer community tolerance but an objective measure of harm. This turn to objectivity, however, does not signal a rejection of morality in the tradition of the harm principle. On the contrary, in a case upholding criminal drug laws, *R. v. Malmo-Levine* (2003), the Supreme Court affirmed that the harm principle is not itself a principle of fundamental justice.[69] Rather, moral harm can justify criminalization, the Court in *Labaye* explained, if it is "objectively ascertainable."[70] What does this mean? The Court described an indecent and thus criminal act as one that causes harm to "a fundamental value reflected in our society's Constitution or similar fundamental laws."[71] The objectivity of the moral harm comes from its formal legal recognition, which "inspires confidence that the values upheld . . . are truly those of Canadian society. Autonomy, liberty, equality and human dignity are among these values."[72] Despite *Labaye*'s not being a constitutional case, its resolution on the reach of criminal law turns on constitutional values.

In a commentary on the case, Elaine Craig describes this constitutional grounding of *Labaye* as significant for the criminalization of sex in Canada.[73] For with this judgment, the Supreme Court substituted the normative foundations of criminal law: from a sexual morality to the political morality of Canadian constitutionalism. The values of the constitutional order—life, security of person, liberty, equality, and dignity—are the new morality of criminal law. The consequences of this switch are multiple. First, these constitutional values set limits on what sexual conduct may be criminalized. In the tradition of the harm principle, only the criminalization of sexual conduct that harms these fundamental values can be justified. Yet the rule of *Labaye* reaches further. By setting constitutional values as a normative limit on criminal law, they become more generally its measure of legitimacy, such that a criminal law that offends rather than protects these values—by causing death, injury, and suffering—will demand reform as a matter of constitutional justice. In other words, decriminalization becomes a protective imperative not only of individual rights but also of the communal constitutional order that harm at the hand of the state threatens.

In answer then to the questions, why does harm production succeed as a legal argument? and, what is the normative significance of harms that flow from criminalization? *Morgentaler*, *Bedford*, and *Labaye* all suggest that the harms of criminal law persuade where they implicate our collective morality, threaten our fundamental values, and weaken our constitutional foundations. Harm production works by turning the table and asking of the collective, How moral are we? Decriminalization becomes necessary for us to avoid living in a society that leaves its members defenseless, sacrifices them to violence, and cares not if they live or die. Harm production trades on the hard truth that it is not the empirical fact of suffering alone that compels reform but rather our moral discomfort of being named its cause.

To conclude the case study, I offer a brief comment on the consequences of the way in which harm production works as a decriminalization argument, and the normative framework through which it succeeds. Both *Bedford* and *Mor-*

gentaler largely read as sexless judgments. Their harms register in universals of bodily injury and death and compel legal reform by a collective constitutional morality. Yet a sexual morality has long animated criminal prostitution and abortion laws, whatever the official record of their purported ends. Moreover, it is a sexual morality that today inspires radical feminist calls for the criminalization of the sex trade, a sexual morality no less that draws on the very norms—security, equality, and dignity—of Canadian constitutional morality. It is therefore implausible for the Supreme Court to draw a line between sexual and political morality and pretend that it may entertain one without the other.

This very issue was manifest in *Morgentaler* in the division on the Court. A majority of justices found agreement in the criminal law's harms of delayed care, but Justice Bertha Wilson alone wrote of a more fundamental flaw: the criminal law took from women control over decisions affecting their own bodies.[74] What greater physical threat could there be, she asked, than to have one's body sacrificed to the state? For this reason, Justice Wilson defended a woman's right to terminate her pregnancy not merely as a right of personal security but as fundamental to political freedom.[75] To defend this right was to defend the very values of liberty, equality, and human dignity of our constitutional order.

In *Bedford*, the Supreme Court does not merely fail to acknowledge sexual liberty in sex work. The Court actively suppresses it to run the causation analysis. In admonishing the Attorneys General for arguing choice as the true cause of harm, the Court reasoned that while some may freely choose to engage in sex work, many have little choice because of "financial desperation, drug addictions, mental illness, or compulsion from pimps."[76] Diminished agency compels decriminalization as an act of mercy rather than as an entitlement of right. Interestingly, Lord Devlin would have excluded fornication and adultery from criminal prohibition not because they were less immoral than homosexuality but precisely because he saw them too as a "human weakness, and not suitably punished by imprisonment."[77] Disclaiming agency to make sexual conduct an improper subject of criminal law has a long history in liberal societies, most famously in the reclassification of homosexuality and other sexual deviances from crime to illness. In recounting debates over the 1969 repeal of the sodomy law in Canada, Stuart Chambers describes how the labeling of homosexuality as pathological allowed politicians to be more sympathetic to its decriminalization.[78]

With sexual morality off the table in *Bedford*, the Supreme Court never asked how sex work might be meaningful to the lives of those who engage in it. And so there is no exploration of how the criminalization of sex work, like the termination of pregnancy, engages liberty and equality as political freedoms. At most, the Court acknowledged that commercial sex is legal, and that as a moral society we cannot endanger the lives of those who engage in it. These are the minimal obligations of Canadian constitutional morality. Minimum obligations, however, do not preclude the state from doing more. Given a constitutional imperative to do no harm, legal reforms that seek to protect sex workers from harm are surely constitutionally sound, if not welcomed. These would include reforms such as labor and employment protections, increased social assistance, affordable housing and childcare, accessible mental health and substance abuse services, and immigration protections for migrant workers.[79] The government of Canada, however, opted for a new criminal prostitution law.

The Protection of Communities and Exploited Persons Act received royal assent in November 2014.[80] The stated objectives of the law are express in its title: to protect those who sell their sexual services from exploitation and to protect communities from the harms of prostitution. To achieve these ends, the law seeks to reduce the demand for sexual services by targeting the purchase of sex and various forms of profiteering from its sale. The preamble of the law claims its origins in "grave concerns about the exploitation that is inherent in prostitution and the risks of violence posed to those who engage in it . . . the social harm caused by the objectification of the human body and the commodification of sexual activity, . . . [and a commitment] to protect human dignity and the equality of all Canadians."[81] And therein lies its claimed constitutional validity: a reorientation in the criminal law toward prostitution as sexual exploitation and objectification in an asserted affront to human dignity and equality, ascertainable constitutional harms.

This is the conservative undertow of harm production as a legal argument. There is nothing in *Bedford* that formally precluded the criminal regulation of sex work. On the contrary, *Bedford* may have even invited it by concluding in the end, "The regulation of prostitution is a complex and delicate matter. It will be for Parliament, should it choose to do so, to devise a new approach."[82] Harm production locates the defects of criminal law in means and not ends, and so invites the state to try again.

The Harms of Criminalized HIV Nondisclosure

The sex work and abortion case studies suggest that harm production persuades by asking what the evidence of harm says about "us"—those who would criminalize, Canadian society—and our fundamental values. In HIV nondisclosure, these values work against rather than for arguments of decriminalization.

In October 2012, in the companion cases of *R. v. Mabior* and *R. v. D.C.*, a unanimous Supreme Court affirmed that failure to disclose one's HIV-positive status could constitute fraud and thereby turn consensual sexual activity into aggravated sexual assault.[83] Disclosure is required whenever there is a *significant risk of serious bodily harm*—a standard set by the Supreme Court in the earlier case of *R. v. Cuerrier* (1998).[84] Prosecutors routinely charged people living with HIV under this standard, which was widely criticized as uncertain and variably interpreted by the lower courts. In *Mabior*, the Supreme Court sought to bring clarity to the law. Criminal liability would only attach where there was a *realistic possibility* of HIV transmission.[85] In vaginal intercourse, this standard was met when the accused had a low viral load at the time of sexual relations *and* used condom protection.[86] Otherwise, nondisclosure was a criminal act.

In the early years of the AIDS epidemic in North America, plague and immorality aligned in biblical allusion to justify a scourge of legal sanctions against people living with HIV, including criminalization of nondisclosure in sexual relations.[87] The certainty of death at this time justified the criminality of sexual risk. Yet measures to reduce risk, especially antiretroviral therapy, shifted the debate. In *Mabior*, the harm-based claims that moved the Supreme Court were scientific risk assessments of exposure: the baseline risk for vaginal sexual intercourse when the male partner is HIV positive, and the reduction in this risk with condom use and antiretroviral therapy.[88] As the *Morgentaler* Court did in its therapeutic risk assessment, the *Mabior* Court assessed harm through the objectivity of expert testimony, systematic reviews, and wide-scale studies. *Mabior* may thus be read as a judgment motivated by the traditional harm principle: only *harmful* sexual conduct warrants criminalization. The Court occupied itself with the measure of harm in nondisclosure: the risk of contracting an incurable chronic infection that, if untreated, results in death, and the measures taken to reduce this risk.

Yet there were other harm-based claims in the case—namely, the argument that while antiretrovirals and condoms reduced risk, criminalization increased it. Thus, if the objective was to protect health and life, criminalization was a failed strategy. Criminalization of HIV nondisclosure, beyond deliberate and actual transmission, has long been resisted on a harm production rationale. Alana Klein describes how in Canada, "from the earliest days of the debate, critics have asserted that . . . recourse to the criminal law would interfere with and undermine the fight against the HIV/AIDS epidemic."[89] Arguments that frame HIV nondisclosure and prevention as a public health issue, inapt for resolution by criminal law, rebound in the international arena.[90] In 2012 the Global Commission on HIV and the Law documented the harmful effects of nondisclosure criminalization, based not only on expert reviews but also on lived experience.[91] Akin to the sex workers in *Bedford*, people living with HIV and those at risk of infection spoke not merely for themselves but as authorities on the legal regime and its effects.

When the Supreme Court first addressed the criminalization of HIV non-disclosure in *R. v. Cuerrier*, the majority named harm production as a discrete issue in the case: Would the application of the criminal code endanger public health?[92] The majority judgment of the Court canvassed the main arguments and rejected each in turn. The argument that criminalization deters HIV testing was deemed unreasonable. Who would forgo testing and treatment because they feared criminal prosecution for some future event?[93] Against the argument that criminalization undermines mutual responsibility for safer sex, Justice Peter deCarteret Cory challenged the premise. "In these circumstances it is, I trust, not too much to expect that the infected person would advise his partner of his infection."[94] Surely every member of society, no matter how marginalized, he reasoned, would be sufficiently responsible in this regard. "Responsibility cannot be lightly shifted to unknowing members of society who are wooed, pursued and encouraged by infected individuals to become their sexual partners."[95] However, ultimately, the Court criminalized both willful deceit and simple nondisclosure. In the end, two public health statistics proved persuasive to the Court: the alarmingly low percentage of persons using condoms, and the steadily rising rate of new infections.[96] Both were interpreted to signal a failure of public health and the need for criminal law.

The Supreme Court did not shut the door on harm production, but it offered that if criminalization really does harm public health efforts, legal reform is open to Parliament.[97] Research advocates accepted the challenge. Rather than turn away from harm production, they worked to build its evidence base. Researchers Eric Mykhalovskiy and Glenn Betteridge, for example, led a large, community-based project to create original empirical research on the impact of the criminal law.[98] In their words, they wanted to make the criminalization of HIV exposure "visible."[99] Paralleling *Morgentaler* and *Bedford*, they sought to reframe the debate on criminalization through evidence of its harms.

This generation of research focused on causation, challenging the Supreme Court's intuitive reasoning that criminalization of HIV nondisclosure would not affect HIV testing or otherwise undermine HIV prevention practices. Much as the Supreme Court did in *Bedford*, the researchers were not discouraged by the complexity of causation but set out to document the law in practice. They acknowledged that criminalization produces its effects through intervening actors and vulnerability factors, and they incorporated both into their causal account. Patrick O'Byrne and colleagues demonstrated how criminalization affects prevention in more diverse ways than simply HIV testing uptake.[100] Criminalization incentivizes the use of anonymous HIV testing, which, while informing an individual of his or her status, separates testing from HIV treatment and management and psychosocial support, all of which are critical to prevention. In a qualitative study, Mykhalovskiy focused on how criminalization adversely affects health providers in HIV counseling.[101] He described how criminal law distorts public health practice. While frontline counselors are familiar with public health concepts of risk, the uncertainty of the legal standard led many to advise blanket disclosure,[102] a requirement the Supreme Court would reject in *Mabior* as unfair and stigmatizing.[103] The preoccupation with legal risk also undermines the counseling relationship, discouraging members of already marginalized communities from speaking openly about their sexual activities, partners, and difficulties with disclosure, and thereby missing an opportunity to address real barriers in prevention.[104]

Cuerrier was read as a case of weak evidence, and so researchers turned to those with firsthand knowledge of how the criminal law works to substantiate claims of harm. Yet when the Supreme Court returned to the criminalization of HIV nondisclosure fourteen years later in *Mabior*, harm production arguments were equally unpersuasive. The risks of criminalization were no longer named an issue in the case and were swiftly dismissed when raised.[105] The Supreme Court emphasized the tentative, even contradictory, conclusions of studies, which at best suggested *probable* adverse effects. Overall, the evidence failed to justify the displacement of the criminal law. The contrast to *Bedford* is instructive. The Supreme Court in *Mabior* asked for more than probable cause, more than tentative conclusions. It demanded a degree of certainty social science could not provide.

Why was the Supreme Court so resolute that nondisclosure be criminalized? The answer is on the face of the judgment. Criminalization of HIV nondisclosure concerns the risk of disease and death as the consequences of a normative transgression—that is, as the empirical deprivations of a dishonest act. From *Cuerrier* onward, the Supreme Court has spoken in this blended empirical and normative register. The criminal law does not merely protect but in fact condemns.[106] The accused does not merely fail to disclose but rather "angrily" or "blithely" rejects advice to disclose, acting in ways not only dangerous but also "deplorable."[107] Nondisclosure endangers the body and "shocks the conscience."[108] The risk of infection is severe and "cruel," its fatal consequences grave and "invidious."[109] This emotive tone of the judgments is significant. The outrage and anger reveal the moral foundation of criminalized HIV nondisclosure, of which the *Mabior* Court was clear: "Morality infuses the criminal law."[110] HIV nondisclosure offends Canadian constitutional morality (that is, values of liberty, equality, security of person, and human dignity, expressed in the criminal law of sexual assault through the rule of consent).

In *Cuerrier*, the full Court agreed that without HIV disclosure there is no consent, and the sexual act amounts to aggravated sexual assault. It is Justice Claire L'Heureux-Dubé, writing a minority opinion, who most fully developed the line of argument.[111] What justifies criminal sanction in nondisclosure, she reasoned, is not the risk of bodily harm in disease or death. There is a more fundamental violation. The offense of nondisclosure lies in the inducement of consent through dishonesty. It deprives another of the free choice to engage in sex, and so violates both physical integrity and personal autonomy. For Justice L'Heureux-Dubé, but not the majority of the Court, the harm of the sexual act resides in the deprivation of sexual equality and freedom. This reasoning parallels Justice Wilson's in *Morgentaler*. She too identified a more fundamental harm in criminalization. Against the medical complications of delayed care was a woman's reproductive freedom, taken not by fraud but by coercion. The comparison is more significant still. By *Mabior*, the Supreme Court expressly defended the criminalization of nondisclosure on constitutional values of liberty, equality, and human dignity, precisely as Justice Wilson had defended the decriminalization of abortion.[112]

Although a case of criminal liability, *Mabior*, like *Bedford* and *Morgentaler*, ultimately turned on constitutional values, as did *Labaye*. While this political morality previously stayed the hand of criminal law, it compelled criminalization in HIV nondisclosure. In *Mabior*, the Supreme Court tied criminal liability to physical harm, the realistic possibility of HIV transmission, but did not abandon moral harm. Its gaze remained steadfast, in the words of the Court, on infected persons and their reckless, insensitive, cruel, and invidious conduct. Our moral commitments shape the way we see reality. For this reason, Martha Shaffer explains, the criminalization of HIV nondisclosure, like that of sex work, carries a particular resonance for some feminists.[113] It tests the limits of consent and thereby sexual freedom and equality in the ability, especially of women, to decide when, with whom, and under what conditions to engage in sex. It is precisely by these moral limits of consent, set by constitutional and thus communal values, that the Court defended criminalization in *Mabior*.[114] HIV nondisclosure deprives and degrades *others* in a way that runs afoul of *our* basic values, and in this respect, its harm resides in more than physical risk to an individual victim. In the sexual exploitation of another, HIV nondisclosure is said to offend Canadian constitutional values; its harms implicate our collective morality and thus warrant criminal sanction.

Richard Jochelson and Kirsten Kramar, writing on the political morality of *Labaye*, well predicted the judicial outcome in *Mabior* and the legislative response to *Bedford*.[115] In *Labaye*, the Court quashed the conviction because the activities of the sex club did not harm constitutional values. Yet Jochelson and Kramar asked, What are the consequences of setting the limit and reach of criminal law on harm to political values? The focus on harm to abstract political values cannot but diminish the relevance of evidenced-based harm. We no longer ask what harm the law really prevents, whom the law really protects, and what the law really costs in lives and health. We focus on "harm to constitutional values rather than people."[116] The analysis of harm becomes abstract, divorced from the reality of people's lives.

In *Cuerrier* and *Mabior*, the Supreme Court appeared lost in the reality of sexual relations, which made retrospective assessment of consent complex. Deceptions that today violated constitutional norms were yesterday the by-product of romance. Deceptions once left to the domains of song, verse, and social censure now warranted criminal sanction.[117] Should there be a relationship-based rule of consent? If so, who is owed more or less in disclosure: trusting wives, casual dates, or intoxicated young women?[118] We last had a relationship-based rule of consent in Victorian times, which denied wives and prostitutes for different reasons any claim to fraudulently induced consent. For the Supreme Court today, "such ideas strike the modern ear, attuned to equality, as offensive."[119] While an approach that accounts for the reasonable expectations of sexual partners would be fairer than a blanket rule, the Court rejected this too as simply unworkable, refusing to send a person to prison for a mistaken inference drawn in the heat and anticipation of the sexual moment.[120] In the end, the Supreme Court could not find its way through the varied social norms and expectations of sexual relations in the reality of people's lives and so abandoned the project. As a normative rationale for criminalization, the Supreme Court in *Mabior* offered only that "fraud is fraud" and that the criminal law punishes "wrongdoing qua wrongdoing."[121] The Supreme Court retreated into abstract tautology.

Yet this retreat offered the Supreme Court little respite. In the 2014 case *R. v. Hutchinson*, the Supreme Court convicted a man of sexual assault for having sabotaged condoms and impregnated his then partner against her express wishes.[122] A majority of the Court applied the standard of *Cuerrier* and *Mabior* to reason that although she had consented to the sexual activity, her consent was vitiated by fraud. His deception in the sabotaged condom exposed her to the harm of an increased risk of pregnancy. The case reopened the question of where to draw the line of criminality in dishonest sexual relations. Justice Rosalie Silberman Abella, writing in concurrence, resurrected the argument from *Cuerrier* that the physical injury of the sexual act, the risk of pregnancy, is irrelevant to the offense.[123] The harm of sexual assault resides in the denial of sexual freedom. The majority replied by emphasizing the limits on how completely criminal law can serve this value. "As the most serious interference by the state with peoples' lives and liberties, the criminal law should be used with *appropriate restraint*, to avoid over-criminalization."[124] The Court thus set the limit of the criminal law in physical harm. "Deceptions . . . will only vitiate consent if there is dishonesty which gives rise to a risk of physical harm, beyond the injury inherent in being lied to in order to induce consent."[125] Perhaps the best way to explain the outcome in *Hutchinson* is that the Supreme Court still sits uncomfortably in actualized sexual relations, the abstraction of political morality being as much an obstacle for the Court as its escape. Liberty, equality, and human dignity remain ensconced in formal legal recognition and apart from the factual context in which they are to govern.

The problem is that such moral absolutes betray, in fact, a point that Isabel Grant and Martha Shaffer raise as a reason for the different outcomes in *Mabior* and *D.C.*[126] In the Court's description, Clato Lual Mabior lived in Winnipeg, his house a party place where alcohol and drugs were freely dispensed and people came in and out, including a variety of young women with whom he had sex, sometimes with a condom, sometimes not.[127] D. C. is described as having learned she was HIV positive after the death of her husband. She had sex with the complainant, whom she met at a soccer match in which their sons were playing. In time, their relationship became intimate. They had sex on one occasion before D. C. disclosed her status. She explained her nondisclosure as fear that her son would bear the repercussions for it. The complainant broke off the relationship, but the couple reconciled a few weeks later. They moved in together and lived as a family for four years before the relationship ended in a violent encounter at the family home. The complainant assaulted D. C. and her son, and after charges were laid for the assault, filed a complaint against D. C. for nondisclosure.[128] In *D.C.*, the Supreme Court did not convict, reversing a finding of fact that the one sexual incident before disclosure was unprotected. Grant suggests several motivations for the Court's reversal: the substantiated fears of rejection and violence on disclosure, and the long-term intimacy of the family relationship, which challenged the normative framework of criminalization.[129] Which truly offends the political morality of Canadian constitutionalism: HIV nondisclosure or its criminalization?

D.C. suggests a way forward in the decriminalization of sex and reproduction in the yet further proliferation of harm-based claims, but this time in a moral register: harm production that abandons its empiricism, forgoes evidentiary authority in objective fact, and speaks to the *moral harms* of the criminal law. There is a cruelty in the broad criminalization of nondisclosure. People living with HIV are criminally suspect for conduct that millions of people engage in every day. Their sexual relations, or in the Supreme Court's own words, their acts of love, admiration, and respect, are suspect as criminal acts. Regardless of actual criminal sanction, its mere threat discredits this most intimate, most human of conduct—and so discredits the whole of the individual as a human being worthy of sexual intimacy and love. These are the facts that compel in *D.C.* and that return again to the collective morality of the Supreme Court in *Bedford*. There are simply certain ways of treating people that cannot be tolerated no matter how laudable the goals of criminalization. They are intolerable because they offend our most basic values. If HIV nondisclosure warrants criminal sanction because it deprives and degrades others, because it violates sexual liberty, equality, and human dignity, we risk hypocrisy as a society when we deny the same to people living with HIV. This argument does not challenge the criminalization of sex on constitutional values. Rather, it asks for something more than their formal declaration in law. It asks that we take real account of what these values mean in the lives of people before criminalization may be justified in their name.

Conclusion

This chapter investigates a prevalent argument in criminalization debates on abortion, sex work, and HIV nondisclosure across liberal societies. *Harm production* is an argument for decriminalization based on the evidenced harms of the criminal law—the injury, death, disease, and violence that it creates rather than protects against. Harm production, it is claimed, persuades in legal reasoning by drawing a bright line between the empirical and the normative. Yet a study of the argument in Canadian law challenges this claim and reveals not the abandonment of moral values in harm production but rather their reengagement on new terms. Harm becomes relevant to legal argument through a collective political, rather than sexual, morality. In the criminalization of sex and reproduction, it is this hidden morality that does the work, not the abstract, simple notion of harm.

NOTES

Introduction

1. Over the years, human rights has expanded its purview to include the uses and abuses of power by a wide range of other actors (corporations, religious institutions, armed groups, intergovernmental organizations, individuals, etc.). See, for example, Chris Jochnick, "Confronting the Impunity of Non-state Actors: New Fields for the Promotion of Human Rights," *Human Rights Quarterly* 21, no. 1 (1999): 56–79.

2. We take this term from the discussions following Christine Van den Wyngaert, as amplified in Francoise Tulkens, "The Paradoxical Relationship between Criminal Law and Human Rights," *Journal of International Criminal Justice* 9 (2011): 577–95.

3. Contradictions within movements for justice are not unique, perhaps, nor is the general difficulty of holding on to protection for the rights of the victim and the violator of rights. We are interested in how the questions that we ask, as engaged feminist and human rights scholars interested in matters of so-called individual liberty with a direct, more intimate role in the social construction of gender, also matter within these general contradictions within human rights' strong embrace of prosecution.

4. Markus Dubber, "A Political Theory of Criminal Law: Autonomy and the Legitimacy of State Punishment," *Social Science Research Network*, March 15, 2004. See also the discussion later in this introduction.

5. Michel Foucault, *Discipline and Punish: The Birth of the Prison* (New York: Vintage, 1977); Michael Ignatieff, *A Just Measure of Pain: The Penitentiary in the Industrial Revolution 1750–1850* (Prescott, AZ: Peregrine Books, 1989).

6. See James J. Silk, "International Criminal Justice and the Protection of Human Rights: The Rule of Law or the Hubris of Law?," *Yale Journal of International Law Online* 39 (2014) https://cpb-us-w2.wpmucdn.com/campuspress.yale.edu/dist/8/1581/files/2017/01/Silk-hubris-of-law-as-published-16ethn9.pdf. For the specific carceral aspects of feminist engagements with rights and law, see also Elizabeth Bernstein, "Militarized Humanitarianism Meets Carceral Feminism: The Politics of Sex, Rights, and Freedom in Contemporary Anti-trafficking Campaigns," *Signs* 40, no. 1 (2014): 45–72.

7. Uganda's 2014 Anti-homosexuality Act initially called for the death penalty for "aggravated" cases. Other countries where homosexuality is officially on the books as a capital crime include Iran, Mauritania, Saudi Arabia, Sudan, and Yemen. For more detail, see A. Carroll and L. R. Mendos, *State-Sponsored Homophobia 2017: A World Survey*

of Sexual Orientation Laws: Criminalisation, Protection and Recognition (Geneva: International Lesbian, Gay, Bisexual, Trans, and Intersex Association, 2017). Nigeria and Russia recently passed laws augmenting penalties for homosexual acts and "recruitment."

8. Chris Geidner, "Hate Crimes Act Makes Conference Report, Death Penalty Gone," *Law Dork* (blog), October 8, 2009, archived at http://www.eqfl.org/blog/766/766.

9. Nicaragua decriminalized homosexuality in its 2008 revised penal code (Article 36 [5]), and that same criminal code made abortion a crime under all circumstances (Articles 143 and 145). See Republic of Nicaragua, Penal Code, Law No. 64, 2008, http://www.poderjudicial.gob.ni/arc-pdf/CP_641.pdf.

10. AWARE-HIV/AIDS, "Regional Workshop to Adopt a Model Law for STI/HIV/AIDS for West and Central Africa—General Report," September 2004, annex 1, p. 7, cited in "UNAIDS Recommendations for Alternative Language to Some Problematic Articles in the N'Djamena Legislation on HIV (2004)," UNAIDS, 2008, 1, http://data.unaids.org/pub/Manual/2008/20080912_alternativelanguage_ndajema_legislation_en.pdf.

11. This model law was adopted by several West and Central African countries. See Richard Pearshouse, "Legislation Contagion: The Spread of Problematic New HIV Laws in Western Africa," *HIV/AIDS Policy and Law Review* 12, nos. 2–3 (2007): 5–11. For a global overview, see UNAIDS, "Criminalisation of HIV Non-disclosure, Exposure and Transmission: Background and Current Landscape," (background paper, Expert Meeting on the Science and Law of Criminalisation of HIV Non-disclosure, Exposure and Transmission, Geneva, Switzerland, August 31–September 2, 2011, revised February 2012), http://www.unaids.org/en/media/unaids/contentassets/documents/document/2012/BackgroundCurrentLandscapeCriminalisationHIV_Final.pdf.

12. See Aziza Ahmed, "HIV and Women: Incongruent Policies, Criminal Consequences," *Yale Journal of International Affairs* 6, no. 1 (Winter 2011): 32–42.

13. Regina v. Mabior, 2012 SCC 47, [2012] 2 S.C.R. 584 (Can.), http://scc-csc.lexum.com/scc-csc/scc-csc/en/item/10008/index.do; Uganda, HIV and AIDS Prevention and Control Act, 2014, http://www.hivlawandpolicy.org/sites/www.hivlawandpolicy.org/files/Ugandan-HIV%20Law.pdf. The law was overturned on a technicality. See William Helbling, "Uganda Constitutional Court Strikes Down Anti-gay Law," Jurist, August 1, 2014, http://jurist.org/paperchase/2014/08/uganda-constiutional-court-strikes-down-anti-gay-law.php.

14. UN General Assembly, *Protocol to Prevent, Suppress and Punish Trafficking in Persons, Especially Women and Children, Supplementing the United Nations Convention against Transnational Organized Crime*, A/RES/55/25, November 15, 2000, enforced starting December 25, 2003, http://www.refworld.org/docid/4720706c0.html. For more on the conflation of prostitution with sex trafficking, see Janie A. Chuang, "Rescuing Trafficking from Ideological Capture: Prostitution Reform and Anti-trafficking Law and Policy," *University of Pennsylvania Law Review* 158, no. 6 (2010): 1655–728.

15. See Protection of Communities and Exploited Persons Act, S.C. 2014, c. 25 (Can.), https://openparliament.ca/bills/41-2/C-36/.

16. See Amnesty International, "Global Movement Adopts Policy to Protect the Human Rights of Sex Workers," press release, August 11, 2015, https://www.amnesty

.org/en/latest/news/2015/08/global-movement-votes-to-adopt-policy-to-protect-human
-rights-of-sex-workers/; and Amnesty International, "Resolution on State Obligations to
Respect, Protect, and Fulfil the Human Rights of Sex Workers," accessed March 30, 2018,
https://www.amnesty.org/policy-on-state-obligations-to-respect-protect-and-fulfil-the
-human-rights-of-sex-workers/.

17. Alice M. Miller and Mindy J. Roseman, "Sexual and Reproductive Rights at the
United Nations: Frustration or Fulfillment?," *Reproductive Health Matters* 19, no. 38
(2011): 102–18.

18. Human Rights Watch and interACT, "'I Want to Be like Nature Made Me': Medically Unnecessary Surgeries on Intersex Children in the US," July 25, 2017, https://www
.hrw.org/report/2017/07/25/i-want-be-nature-made-me/medically-unnecessary
-surgeries-intersex-children-us.

19. Alice M. Miller, "Sexual but Not Reproductive: Exploring the Junction and Disjunction of Sexual and Reproductive Rights," *Health and Human Rights* 4, no. 2 (2000):
68–109.

20. Samuel Moyn, *The Last Utopia* (Cambridge, MA: Harvard University Press,
2010).

21. As we discuss in our conclusion, the indeterminacy of international human rights
and criminal law always means that there is play and no one "right" outcome. Absent the
certainty of a basis for law, this essay suggests that scholars and advocates must do what
critical legal studies scholars call a distributional analysis (to determine who benefits and
who is harmed). Such an analysis is best done through grounded experience and genuine
empathy for all of those who hold a stake—especially perpetrators. In other words, victims aren't the only ones who count, nor do they count more. Empathy and accountability for the pain (no matter how just) inflicted on others inhere in the concept of equality
of dignity and rights, as expressed in the Universal Declaration of Human Rights and
subsequent instruments. Recognition of prior existing structural inequality is also a
component of distributional analysis; it therefore should take into account power im-
balances and disparities that often cleave along gender, race, class, and other social
categories.

22. This idea borrows both from Dominick LaCapra's intellectual historical method-
ological writings and from Sally Engle Merry's ideas of a human rights vernacular. See
LaCapra, *Rethinking Intellectual History: Texts, Contexts, Language* (Ithaca, NY: Cornell
University Press, 1983); and Merry, "Legal Transplants and Cultural Translation: Making
Human Rights in the Vernacular," in *Human Rights: An Anthropological Reader*, ed.
Mark Goodale (Hoboken, NJ: Wiley-Blackwell, 2009), 265–302.

23. Miller and Roseman, "Sexual and Reproductive Rights."

24. When gender is expanded to encompass "gender identity" or transgender, it tran-
sits back in its associations to (gay) sexuality, as in the acronym SOGI (sexual orientation
and gender identity) or LGBT. See Ali Miller, "Fighting over the Figure of Gender," *Pace
Law Review* 31, no. 3 (June 2011): 837–72.

25. Kimberlé Crenshaw, "Mapping the Margins: Intersectionality, Identity Politics,
and Violence against Women of Color," *Stanford Law Review* 43, no. 6 (1991): 1241–99;

Sumi Cho, Kimberlé Williams Crenshaw, and Leslie McCall, "Toward a Field of Intersectionality Studies: Theory, Applications, and Praxis," *Signs* 38, no. 4 (2013): 785–810.

26. See Gayle Rubin, "Thinking Sex: Notes for a Radical Theory of the Politics of Sexuality" (1984), in *Social Perspectives in Lesbian and Gay Studies: A Reader*, ed. Peter M. Nardi and Beth E. Schneider (London: Routledge, 1998), 100–133.

27. U.S. foreign policy regarding overseas development assistance underscores the ways in which abortion is treated exceptionally. The Global Gag Rule (also known as the Mexico City Policy) prohibits any (non-U.S.) organization that receives U.S. global health assistance from advocating for, inter alia, the decriminalization of abortion, even with funds not sourced from the United States. This conditionality can make it difficult, if not impossible, to work in coalitions across decriminalization efforts; for example, an LGBT rights organization in Kenya supported through the United States Agency for International Development could not join forces with a women's rights organization working on improving access to abortions without risking its U.S. funding.

28. For one of the rare reports that does something like this, see Women's Refugee Commission, *Mean Streets: Identifying and Responding to Urban Refugees' Risks of Gender-Based Violence* (New York: Women's Refugee Commission, February 2016), http://www.refworld.org/docid/56d68f464.html.

29. For additional examples, see Janet Halley and Kerry Rittich, "Critical Directions in Comparative Family Law: Genealogies and Contemporary Studies of Family Law Exceptionalism," *American Journal of Comparative Law* 58, no. 4 (2010): 753–75.

30. See Rubin, "Thinking Sex"; and Stanley Cohen, *Folk Devils and Moral Panics: The Creation of Mods and Rockers* (New York: Psychology, 2002).

31. Michel Foucault, *The Birth of Biopolitics* (New York: Palgrave Macmillan, 2008); Michel Foucault, *The History of Sexuality*, vol. 1, *An Introduction* (New York: Vintage, 1978); Michel Foucault, *The History of Sexuality*, vol. 3, *The Care of the Self* (New York: Vintage, 1988).

32. Criminologists focus on the "risk" environment and the securitizing state, as do theorists of globalization and global power who work in the mode of sociology. See, for example, Saskia Sassen, "Territory and Territoriality in the Global Economy," *International Sociology* 15, no. 2 (2000): 372–93.

33. Mariana Valverde, *Law's Dream of a Common Knowledge* (Princeton, NJ: Princeton University Press, 2009).

34. See Samuel Moyn, *Christian Human Rights* (Cambridge, MA: Harvard University Press, 2015); and Costas Douzinas and Conor Gearty, eds., *The Meanings of Rights: The Philosophy and Social Theory of Human Rights* (Cambridge: Cambridge University Press, 2014).

35. See UN Office of the High Commissioner for Human Rights, *The Use of Criminal Law from a Human Rights, Women's Rights and Gender Equality Perspective*, meeting report, Geneva, Switzerland, March 29–31, 2017.

36. See for example, Principles, Siracusa. "Principles on the Limitation and Derogation of Provisions in the International Covenant on Civil and Political Rights, UN Doc. E/CN." (1984): 4.

37. Donald Braman, "Families and Incarceration," in *Invisible Punishment: The Collateral Consequences of Mass Imprisonment*, ed. Marc Mauer and Meda Chesney-Lind (New York: New Press, 2003), 117–35.

38. See, for instance, the World Health Organization's work on the underlying causes of unsafe abortion: David A. Grimes et al., "Unsafe Abortion: The Preventable Pandemic," *Lancet* 368, no. 9550 (2006): 1908–19; UNAIDS-OHCHR Expert Meeting Report, "Understanding and building synergies for addressing the misuse of the criminal law and its impact on women, sex workers, people who use drugs, people living with HIV and LGBT persons, (Unpublished, on file with authors, February 8–10, 2017, Bellagio, Italy).

39. For the beneficial posture and use of ambivalence, see Peter Rosenblum, "Teaching Human Rights: Ambivalent Activism, Multiple Discourses, and Lingering Dilemmas," *Harvard Human Rights Journal* 15 (2002): 301, http://heinonline.org/HOL/Page?handle= hein.journals/hhrj15&g_sent=1&id=305.

Chapter 1. Janet Halley in Conversation with Aziza Ahmed

1. Janet Halley, *Split Decisions: How and Why to Take a Break from Feminism* (Princeton, NJ: Princeton University Press, 2006).

2. For a non-neutral introduction to the US "sex wars," see Carole S. Vance, "Epilogue," in *Pleasure and Danger: Exploring Female Sexuality*, ed. Carole S. Vance (New York: Routledge and Kegan Paul, 1984), 431–39; and Carole S. Vance, "More Danger, More Pleasure: A Decade after the Barnard Sexuality Conference," *New York Law School Law Review* 38 (1993): 289–317.

3. Judith Butler, *Gender Trouble: Feminism and the Subversion of Identity* (London: Routledge, 1990).

4. Eve Kosofsky Sedgwick, *Epistemology of the Closet* (Berkeley: University of California Press, 1990).

5. For example, see Gayle Rubin, "Thinking Sex: Notes for a Radical Theory on the Politics of Sexuality," in Vance, *Pleasure and Danger*, 267–319.

6. Christopher Hill, *Milton and the English Revolution* (Oxford: Oxford University Press, 1978).

7. Janet Halley, "Rape in Berlin: Reconsidering the Criminalisation of Rape in the International Law of Armed Conflict," *Melbourne Journal of International Law* 9 (2008): 78–124. The article considers and reflects on an anonymous World War II-era text, *A Woman in Berlin* (German: *Eine Frau in Berlin*) (1959/2003), which describes a three-month period when the Soviet army (the Red Army) liberated and occupied Berlin. Halley reads the diary as a literary reflection on the idea that "rape is the fate worse than death."

8. For example, see Catharine A. MacKinnon, "Feminism, Marxism, Method, and the State: An Agenda for Theory," *Signs* 7 (1982): 515–544; Susan Brownmiller, *Against Our Will: Men, Women, and Rape* (London: Pelican Books, 1986); and Susan Estrich, *Real Rape* (Cambridge, MA: Harvard University Press, 1988).

9. Sharon Marcus, "Fighting Bodies, Fighting Words: A Theory and Politics of Rape Prevention," in *Feminists Theorize the Political*, ed. Judith Butler and Joan W. Scott (New York: Routledge, 1992), 385–403.

10. In the traditions of critical legal studies and of antiracist critique, critical race theory uses race and racism as a point of departure for legal analysis. For an excellent source, see Kimberlé Crenshaw et al., eds., *Critical Race Theory: The Key Writings That Formed the Movement* (New York: New Press, 1996).

11. Subaltern feminist work is a variant of critical theory and of postcolonial critique. For a classic example, see especially Gayatri Spivak, "Can the Subaltern Speak?," in *Marxism and the Interpretation of Culture*, ed. Cary Nelson and Lawrence Grossberg, (London: Macmillan, 1988), 271–313.

12. Spivak, "Can the Subaltern Speak?".

13. Angela P. Harris, "Race and Essentialism in Feminist Legal Theory," *Stanford Law Review* 42 (1990): 581–616; Regina Austin, "The 'Black Community,' Its Lawbreakers, and a Politics of Disidentification," *Southern California Law Review* 65 (1992): 1769–817.

14. Sedgwick, *Epistemology of the Closet*, 325.

15. Rubin, "Thinking Sex."

16. Since giving this interview, Halley has returned to feminism to engage in the American campus sexual assault debate. See Janet Halley, "Trading the Megaphone for the Gavel in Title IX Enforcement," *Harvard Law Review Forum* 128 (2015): 103–117.

17. For example, see Robin West, "Feminism, Postmodernism, and Law," in *Caring for Justice* (New York: New York University Press, 1997), 259–92; and Catharine A. MacKinnon, "Points against Postmodernism," *Chicago-Kent Law Review* 75 (2000): 687–712.

18. See *Griswold v. Connecticut*, 381 U.S. 479 (1965); *Eisenstadt v. Baird*, 405 U.S. 438 (1972); *Roe v. Wade*, 410 U.S. 113 (1973); *Planned Parenthood v. Casey*, 505 U.S. 833 (1992); *Gonzales v. Carhart*, 550 U.S. 124 (2007); *Whole Woman's Health v. Hellerstedt*, 136 S. Ct. 2292.

19. Since giving this interview, Halley has taught Reproductive Rights and Justice with Mindy Roseman. Roseman's syllabus (on file with author) exemplifies this queer turn in feminist work on reproduction.

20. Aziza Ahmed, "'Rugged Vaginas' and 'Vulnerable Rectums': The Sexual Identity, Epidemiology, and Law of the Global HIV Epidemic," *Columbia Journal of Gender and Law* 26, no. 1 (2013): 1–57.

21. For a more leisurely exposition, see Janet Halley, "Distribution and Decision: Assessing Governance Feminism," in Halley, et al, *Governance Feminism: An Introduction*, pp. 253–67.

22. Robert H. Mnookin and Lewis Kornhauser, "Bargaining in the Shadow of the Law: The Case of Divorce," *Yale Law Journal* 88 (1979): 950–97.

23. For example, see Karl N. Llewellyn, "Some Realism about Realism: Responding to Dean Pound," *Harvard Law Review* 44 (1931): 1222–64.

24. Janet Halley et al., "From the International to the Local in Feminist Legal Responses to Rape, Prostitution/Sex Work, and Sex Trafficking: Four Studies in Contemporary Governance Feminism," *Harvard Journal of Law and Gender* 29 (2006): 335–423. See also Janet Halley et al., *Governance Feminism: An Introduction* (Minneapolis: University of Minnesota Press, 2017).

25. Duncan Kennedy, "Sexual Abuse, Sexy Dressing, and the Eroticization of Domination," in *Sexy Dressing, Etc.* (Cambridge, MA: Harvard University Press, 1993), 136–38.

26. Elizabeth Bernstein, "The Sexual Politics of the 'New Abolitionism,'" *Differences: Journal of Feminist Cultural Studies* 18, no. 3 (2007): 128–51.

27. Halley et al., "From the International to the Local."

28. Janet Halley, "Where in the Legal Order Have Feminists Gained Inclusion?", in Halley et al., *Governance Feminism: An Introduction*, 3–21.

29. Bernstein, "Sexual Politics."

30. For example, see Hila Shamir, "The State of Care: Rethinking the Distributive Effects of Familial Care Policies in Liberal Welfare States," *American Journal of Comparative Law* 58 (2010): 953–86.

31. Allegra M. McLeod, "Exporting U.S. Criminal Justice: Crime, Development, and Empire after the Cold War" (PhD diss., Stanford University, 2008), https://pqdtopen .proquest.com/doc/304468806.html?FMT= ABS&pubnum=3343958.

32. See "Anti-Trafficking and the New Indenture," in Prabha Kotiswaran, ed., *Revisiting the Law and Governance of Trafficking, Forced Labor and Modern Slavery* (London: Cambridge University Press, 2017), 179–211.

33. For example, see International Agreement for the Suppression of the White Slave Traffic, May 18, 1904, 1 L.N.T.S. 83; International Convention for the Suppression of the White Slave Traffic, May 4, 1910, 8 L.N.T.S. 278; International Convention for the Suppression of the Traffic in Women and Children, Sept. 30, 1921, 9 L.N.T.S. 415; 1933 International Convention for the Suppression of the Traffic in Women of Full Age, Oct. 11, 1933, 150 L.N.T.S. 431; Protocol to Amend the 1921 Convention for the Suppression of the Traffic in Women and Children and the 1933 Convention for the Suppression of the Traffic in Women of Full Age, Nov. 12, 1947, 53 U.N.T.S. 770. See also G.A. Res. 317, Convention for the Suppression of the Traffic in Persons and of the Exploitation of the Prostitution of Others (Dec. 2, 1949).

34. See Janet Halley, "Rape at Rome: Feminist Interventions in the Criminalization of Sex-Related Violence in Positive International Criminal Law," *Michigan Journal of International Law* 30 (2008): 1–123.

35. Palermo Protocol Article 3(a) states, "Exploitation shall include, at a minimum, the exploitation of the prostitution of others or other forms of sexual exploitation, forced labor or services, slavery or practices similar to slavery, servitude or the removal of organs."

36. Victims of Trafficking and Violence Protection Act of 2000, H.R. 3244, 106th Cong. (2000).

37. Perhaps this carceral capacity in human rights is no mystery: as Karen Engle, Zinaida Miller, and Dennis Davis have shown in their new collection *Anti-Impunity and the Human Rights Agenda,* human rights has made its own carceral turn in the form of a strong stance that human rights violations must be criminally prosecuted. Karen Engle, Zinaida Miller, and D. M. Davis, eds., *Anti-Impunity and the Human Rights Agenda* (Cambridge: Cambridge University Press, 2016).

38. For an overview of the ad hoc and hybrid international criminal tribunals established in the 1990s and 2000s, see William A. Schabas, *An Introduction to the International Criminal Court* (Cambridge: Cambridge University Press, 2011).

39. Marcus, "Fighting Bodies, Fighting Words."

40. Center for Women's Global Leadership, *International Campaign for Women's Human Rights, 1992–93 Report* (New Brunswick, NJ: Rutgers University, 1993), 24.

41. See Karen Engle, "Feminism and Its (Dis)Contents: Criminalizing Wartime Rape in Bosnia and Herzegovina," *American Journal of International Law* 99 (2005): 778–816.

42. See Halley, "Rape at Rome."

Chapter 2. Seismic Shifts

Alice M. Miller thanks Rachel Wilkinson for her indispensable contributions to the analysis of child rights and criminal law.

1. Amnesty International, *Breaking the Silence: Human Rights Violations Based on Sexual Orientation* (London: Amnesty International, 1994); Human Rights Watch, *The Human Rights Watch Global Report on Women's Rights* (New York: Human Rights Watch, 1993); International Gay and Lesbian Human Rights Commission, *United Nations: Unspoken Rules—Sexual Orientation and Women's Human Rights* (San Francisco: Cassell, 1996); International Council on Human Rights Policy, *Sexuality and Human Rights: Discussion Paper* (Vernier, Switzerland: ATAR Roto, 2009); International Commission of Jurists, *Sexual Orientation, Gender Identity and Justice: A Comparative Law Casebook* (Geneva: International Commission of Jurists, 2011).

2. Toonen v. Australia, Communication No. 488/1332, U.N. Doc CCPR/C/50/D/488/1992 (1994); MC v. Bulgaria, App. No. 39272/98, ECtHR (2003). Also see UN Office of the High Commission for Human Rights (OHCHR), *Born Free and Equal: Sexual Orientation and Gender Identity in International Human Rights Law* (New York: OHCHR, 2012); OHCHR, *15 Years of the United Nations Special Rapporteur on Violence against Women, Its Causes and Consequences* (New York: OHCHR, 2009).

3. See Brief for Human Rights Watch as Amicus Curiae for Kaos v. Turkey, Application 4982/07 (2009); Lawyers Collective, Writ Petition for Naz Foundation (India) Trust v. Government of NCT of Delhi, Writ Petition (Civil) No. 4755 (2001).

4. Bernard E. Harcourt, "The Collapse of the Harm Principle," *Journal of Criminal Law and Criminology* 90, no. 1 (1999): 109–94; Meir Dan-Cohen, "Defending Dignity," in *Harmful Thoughts: Essays on Law, Self, and Morality*, ed. Meir Dan-Cohen (Princeton, NJ: Princeton University Press, 2002), 150–71.

5. Charlotte Bunch, "Women's Rights as Human Rights: Toward a Re-Vision of Human Rights," *Human Rights Quarterly* 12 (1990): 486–98.

6. Makau W. Matua, "Savages, Victims, and Saviors: The Metaphor of Human Rights," *Harvard International Law Journal* 42, no. 1 (2001): 201–45.

7. Kathryn Sikkink, *The Justice Cascade: How Human Rights Prosecutions Are Changing World Politics* (New York: W. W. Norton, 2011).

8. There is much debate about the contours of TJ. See Ruti Teitel, "Transitional Justice Genealogy," *Harvard Human Rights Journal* 16, no. 1 (2003): 69–94; Kara Apland, "The Power and Politics of Transitional Justice," *Justice in Conflict* (blog), January 16, 2012, https://justiceinconflict.org/2012/01/16/the-power-and-politics-of-transitional-justice/.

9. See Diane Orentlicher, "Settling Accounts: The Duty to Prosecute Human Rights Violations of a Previous Regime," *The Yale Law Journal* 100, no. 8 (1991): 2537–2615; see also Diane Orentlicher, "Judging Global Justice: Assessing the International Criminal Court," *Wisconsin International Law Journal* 21, no. 3 (2003): 495–512.

10. Hunjoon Kim and Kathryn Sikkink, "Explaining the Deterrence Effect of Human Rights Prosecutions for Transitional Countries," *International Studies Quarterly* 54, no. 4 (2010): 939–63.

11. The Nuremberg and Tokyo courts symbolically stand as early iterations of rights and prosecution in the post–World War II experience; later, ending dictatorships in Latin America, Europe, and Africa pushed criminal law to the sidelines to achieve peace: lustration, mob violence, or silence predominated, with the robust use of amnesties and immunity measures. See Lisa J. Laplante, "Outlawing Amnesty: The Return of Criminal Justice in Transitional Justice Schemes," *Virginia Journal of International Law* 49, no. 4 (2009): 915–84.

12. Alice Henken, *The Legacy of Abuse: Confronting the Past, Facing the Future* (Washington, DC: Aspen Institute, 2002). The European Court of Human Rights stated that "amnesty is generally incompatible with the states' duty to investigate acts of torture or barbarity." See *Ould Dah v. France*, App. No. 13113/03, ECtHR (2009).

13. Samuel Moyn, "Towards Instrumentalism at the International Criminal Court," *Yale International Law Journal Online* 39 (2014): 55–65.

14. Ibid.

15. Bronwyn Anne Leebaw, "The Irreconcilable Goals of Transitional Justice," *Human Rights Quarterly* 30, no. 1 (2008): 95–118.

16. Samuel Moyn, "Anti-Impunity as Deflection of Argument" in *Anti-Impunity and the Human Rights Agenda,* edited by Karen Engle, Zinaida Miller and D.M. Davis (Cambridge: Cambridge University Press, 2016), 68–94, at 76.

17. Amnesty International, *Oral Statement by Amnesty International before the United Nations Commission on Human Rights, Sub-committee on Prevention of Discrimination and Protection of Minorities* (Amnesty International, International Secretariat London, U.K., 1991), 1–4.

18. Criminal law can serve many purposes: punishment or retribution, rehabilitation, truth, memory, and deterrence or prevention. Human rights advocacy has also translated the "punishment" aspect into "therapy"—one of the promoted values of criminal tribunals is victim healing. See Mahmood Mamdani, *Saviors and Survivors: Darfur, Politics, and the War on Terror* (New York: Doubleday, 2009).

19. *The Prosecutor v. Mathieu Ngudjolo Chui*, ICC-01/04-02/12, Trial Chamber, December 18, 2012.

20. Tor Krever, "Dispensing Global Justice," *New Left Review* 85 (2014): 67–97, at 88.

21. James Silk, "International Criminal Justice and the Protection of Human Rights: The Rule of Law or the Hubris of Law?," *Yale Journal of International Law Online* 39 (2014): 94–114.

22. Karen Engle, "Anti-impunity and the Turn to Criminal Law in Human Rights," *Cornell Law Review* 100, no. 1069 (2015): 1070–27, at 1120.

23. This was understood and documented as harms only to cisgender women until recently.

24. We include in this (English-language-limited) canon the following: Rebecca Cook, *Human Rights of Women: National and International Perspectives* (Philadelphia: University of Pennsylvania Press, 1994); Julia Peters and Andrea Wolper, *Women's Rights, Human Rights: International Feminist Perspectives* (New York: Routledge, Psychology Press, 1995); and Marge Schuler, *From Basic Needs to Basic Rights* (Washington, DC: Women, Law and Development Institute, 1995), as well as early essays by Charlotte Bunch, Sunila Abeysekera, Florence Butegwa, Donna Sullivan, Sonia Corrêa, Rosalind Petchesky, and Roxanne Carrillo.

25. Alice M. Miller, "Sexuality, violence against women, and human rights: women make demands and ladies get protection," *Health and Human Rights* (2004): 16–47; Dianne Otto, "The Exile of Inclusion: Reflections on Gender Issues in International Law over the Last Decade," *Melbourne Journal of International Law* 10, no. 1 (2009): 11–26; Ratna Kapur, "Un-veiling Women's Rights in the 'War on Terrorism,'" *Duke Journal of Gender Law and Policy* 9 (2002): 211–25.

26. Petitions on file with author.

27. UN Committee on the Elimination of Discrimination against Women (CEDAW), *CEDAW General Recommendation No. 19 on Violence against Women* (1992).

28. Thomas Keenan, "Mobilizing Shame," *South Atlantic Quarterly* 103, no. 2 (2004): 435–49.

29. Ratna Kapur, "The Tragedy of Victimization Rhetoric: Resurrecting the 'Native' Subject in International/Post-colonial Feminist Legal Politics," *Harvard Human Rights Journal* 15, no. 1 (2002): 1–38.

30. Human Rights Watch, *Criminal Injustice: Violence against Women in Brazil* (New York: Human Rights Watch, 1993); Amnesty International, *Women in the Front Line: Human Rights Violations against Women* (New York: Amnesty International, 1991); Bunch, "Women's Rights as Human Rights"; Human Rights Watch, *A Modern Form of Slavery: Trafficking of Burmese Women and Girls into Brothels in Thailand* (New York: Human Rights Watch, 1994).

31. Amnesty International, *Respect, Protect, Fulfill—Women's Human Rights: State Responsibility for Abuses by "Non-state Actors"* (New York: Amnesty International, 2000).

32. United Nations, "Declaration on the Elimination of Violence against Women," A/RES/48/104, 1993; Amnesty International, *Making Rights a Reality: The Duty of States to Address Violence against Women* (New York: Amnesty International, 2004). See also Niamh Rielly, *Women's Human Rights: Seeking Gender Justice in a Globalizing Age* (London: Polity, 2009); and Francoise Tulkens, "The Paradoxical Relationship between Criminal Law and Human Rights," *Journal of International Criminal Justice* 9, no. 3 (2011): 577–95.

Tulkens characterizes rights law as moving its attention from vertical to horizontal obligations (i.e., from obligations to respect to those to protect) for the state, and notes that horizontal protection ("sword") is the central legal claim of women's rights.

33. See also Karen Engle, "Feminism and Its (Dis)Contents: Criminalizing Wartime Rape in Bosnia and Herzegovina," *American Journal of International Law* 99 (2005): 778–816.

34. Miller; Miriam Ticktin, "The Gendered Human of Humanitarianism: Medicalising and Politicising Sexual Violence," *Gender and History* 23, no. 2 (2011): 250–65; UN General Assembly, *Vienna Declaration and Programme of Action*, July 12, 1993, A/CONF .157/23, para. 38.

35. The realities of rape and other forms of sexual assault against men, boys, and trans* persons, including trans women, were not at this point regularly surfacing. Today, this myopia is being challenged by new documentation on rape of diversely gendered persons. See Chris Dolan, "Letting Go of the Gender Binary: Charting New Pathways for Humanitarian Interventions on Gender-Based Violence," *International Review of the Red Cross* 96, no. 894 (2014): 485–501.

36. Author Miller was a convening member of the caucus while at the International Human Rights Law Group in Washington, DC. See also Valerie Oosterveld, "The Definition of Gender in the Rome Statute of the International Criminal Court: A Step forward or back for International Criminal Justice?" *Harvard Human Rights Journal* 18 (2005): 55–84; Barbara Bedont and Katherine Hall-Martinez, "Ending Impunity for Gender Crimes under the International Criminal Court," *Brown Journal of World Affairs* 6, no. 1 (1999): 65–85.

37. For understanding the changing role of consent in sexuality, see Carole S. Vance, "Interrogating Consent," CREA, last modified February 2014, http://www.creaworld.org /sites/default/files/2.%20Interrogating%20Consent_0.pdf; International Planned Parenthood Federation, *Sexual Rights: An IPPF Declaration* (London: IPPF, 2008); International Panel of Experts in International Human Rights Law and on Sexual Orientation and Gender Identity, *The Yogyakarta Principles: Principles on the Application of International Human Rights Law in Relation to Sexual Orientation and Gender Identity* (n.p.: International Panel of Experts in International Human Rights Law and on Sexual Orientation and Gender Identity, 2007); Sonia Corrêa, Rosalind Petchesky, and Richard Parker, *Sexuality, Health and Human Rights* (New York: Routledge, 2008); Alice Miller, "Sexual but Not Reproductive: Exploring the Junction and Disjunction of Sexual and Reproductive Rights," *Health and Human Rights* 4, no. 2 (2000): 68–109; Joseph Fischel, *Sex and Harm in the Age of Consent* (Minneapolis: University of Minnesota Press, 2016).

38. Laina Y. Bay-Cheng and Rebecca K. Eliseo-Arras, "The Making of Unwanted Sex: Gendered and Neoliberal Norms in College Women's Unwanted Sexual Experiences," *Journal of Sex Research* 45, no. 4 (2008): 386–97.

39. Coalition against Trafficking in Women, "Open Letter to Amnesty International," July 22, 2015, http://catwinternational.org/Content/Images/Article/617/attachment.pdf.

40. See Mary E. Odem, *Our Delinquent Daughters: Protecting and Policing Adolescent Female Sexuality in the United States, 1885–1920* (Chapel Hill: University of North

Carolina Press, 2015); and Michele Godwin, "Law's Limits: Regulating Statutory Rape Law," *Wisconsin Law Review* (2013): 481–540.

41. R v. McNally, [2013] EWCA (Crim), 1051.

42. Vance has suggested that the idea of "informed consent" is creeping into criminal law from its origins in bioethics, resulting in obligations to disclose a growing range of status factors—HIV status, marital status, ethnic or religious identity, and gender identity—risking the charge of rape. Nondisclosure of HIV status is a (separate) assault crime in many jurisdictions. See Scott Burris and Edwin Cameron, "The Case against Criminalization of HIV Transmission," *Journal of the American Medical Association* 300, no. 5 (2008): 578–81.

43. Fischel, *Sex and Harm* (2016).

44. This focus on "young age" reminds us that older age needs much more attention in the fields of sexuality, gender, and reproduction. See Julia Twigg, "The Body, Gender, and Age: Feminist Insights in Social Gerontology," *Journal of Aging Studies* 18, no. 1 (2004): 59–73.

45. Committee on Economic, Social and Cultural Rights, *General Comment No. 22: on the Right to sexual and reproductive health (article 12 of the International Covenant on Economic, Social and Cultural Rights*, UN Doc. E/C.12/GC/22 (2016); Committee on the Rights of the Child, *General Comment 3: HIV/AIDS and the Rights of the Child*, UN Doc. CRC/GC/2003/3 (2003); Committee on the Rights of the Child, *General Comment 4: Adolescent Health and Development in the Context of the Convention on the Rights of the Child*, UN Doc. CRC/GC/2003/4 (2003).

46. OHCHR, "Threatening the Rights of LGBT Persons in Eastern Europe," August 14, 2013, http://www.ohchr.org/EN/NewsEvents/Pages/RightsOfLGBTPersonsInEastern Europe.aspx. See also OHCHR, "UN Rights Experts Advise Russian Duma to Scrap Bill on 'Homosexuality,'" February 1, 2013, https://www.ecoi.net/en/document/1131464.html.

47. See David Montgomery and Alan Bildner, "States Sue Obama Administration over Transgender Bathroom Policy," *New York Times*, May 25, 2016; Human Rights Campaign, "Anti-transgender Legislation Spreads Nationwide, Bills Targeting Transgender Children Surge," February 19, 2016, http://hrc-assets.s3-website-us-east-1 .amazonaws.com//files/assets/resources/HRC-Anti-Trans-Issue-Brief-FINAL-REV2.pdf; Sandra Battle and T. E. Wheeler II, "Dear Colleague Letter: Notice of Language Assistance," U.S. Department of Justice and U.S. Department of Education, February 22, 2017, http://i2.cdn.turner.com/cnn/2017/images/02/23/1atransletterpdf022317.pdf.

48. Amnesty International, *Violations of the Human Rights of Homosexuals—Extracts from Amnesty International Action Materials* (New York: Amnesty International, 1994).

49. Gerison Lansdown, *The Evolving Capacities of the Child* (Florence: UNICEF Innocenti Research Centre, 2005); Child Rights Information Network, *Measuring Maturity: Understanding Children's "Evolving Capacities,"* Review Number 23 (London: Child Rights Information Network, 2009).

50. On the Stop Killing Kids campaign in the United States, see American Civil Liberty Union (https://www.aclu.org/other/stop-killing-kids-why-its-time-end-indecent-practice -juvenile-death-penalty2015).

51. Margaret Greene and Timi Gerson, *What's Missing in the Fight against Early and Child Marriage: Insights from India* (New York: American Jewish World Service, 2015).

52. Carole S. Vance, "Innocence and Experience: Melodramatic Narratives of Sex Trafficking and Their Consequences for Law and Policy," *History of the Present* 2, no. 2 (2012): 200–218.

53. The US is slowly but incompletely stepping back from some of the most extreme aspects of this "de-childification" of racialized youth. Miller v. Alabama, 567 U.S. 460 (2012); 132 S. Ct. 2455 (2012).

54. Robyn Linde, "The Globalization of Childhood: The International Diffusion of Norms and Law against the Child Death Penalty," *European Journal of International Relations* 20, no. 2 (2013): 544–68.

55. Robyn Linde, *The International Diffusion of Norms and Law against the Child Death Penalty* (Oxford, 2016).

56. Linde (2016).

57. Linde (2016) reports that only two international legal standards before the CRC set eighteen as the determining age for the end of "childhood." The 1959 Declaration of the Rights of the Child set no age for childhood. See also Katarina Tomasevski, *Human Rights Obligations: Making Education Available, Accessible, Acceptable, and Adaptable* (Gothenburg, Sweden: Novum Grafiska, 2001); and Geraldine Van Bueren, *The International Law on the Rights of the Child* (London: Martinus Nijhoff, 1995).

58. Ibid Tomasevski. See also Rachel Hodgkin and Peter Newell, *Implementation Handbook for the Convention on the Rights of the Child*, rev. 3rd ed. (New York: UNICEF, 2007).

59. Alice M. Miller "Sexual but not reproductive: exploring the junction and disjunction of sexual and reproductive rights," *Health and Human Rights* (2000): 68–109.

60. Committee on the Rights of the Child, *General Comment 3*; Committee on the Rights of the Child, *General Comment 4* (2003)

61. "Age of Consent for Sexual Intercourse," Avert, last modified April 1, 2016, http://www.avert.org/sex-stis/age-of-consent; Sonja Shield, "The Doctor Won't See You Now: Rights of Transgender Adolescents to Sex Reassignment Treatment," *New York University Review of Law and Social Change* 31, no. 2 (2007): 361–433.

62. The Arab Charter on Human Rights and the Asian Human Rights Charter also followed the CRC.

63. See the subregional human rights court for the Economic Community of West African States decision in *Hadijatou Mani Koraou v. The Republic of Niger* (2008) (finding the state at fault for failing to prevent or punish the nine-year-long slavery and sexual exploitation of a girl [aged twelve to twenty-one] but declining to comment on the lawfulness of her marriage at twelve).

64. These issues arise regarding intersex children resisting medically unjustified surgeries and some trans* youths seeking access to medical bodily interventions. Sahar Sadjadi, "The Endocrinologist's Office—Puberty Suppression: Saving Children from a Natural Disaster?," *Journal of Medical Humanities* 34 (2013): 255–60.

65. Matthew Waites, "The Age of Consent and Sexual Citizenship in the United Kingdom: A History," In *Relating Intimacies*, edited by Paul Bagguley, 91–117 (London: Palgrave Macmillian, 1999).

66. Ryan Thoreson, "From Child Protection to Children's Rights: Rethinking Homosexual Propaganda Bans in Human Rights Law," *Yale Law Journal* 124, no. 4 (2015): 1327–44.

67. Fischel, *Sex and Harm* (2016), passim.

68. See Committee on Economic, Social and Cultural Rights, *General Comment No. 22*; Committee on the Rights of the Child, *General Comment 3*; Committee on the Rights of the Child, *General Comment 4*.

69. Human Rights Watch, *The Nail That Sticks Out Gets Hammered Down: LGBT Bullying and Exclusion in Japanese Schools* (New York: Human Rights Watch, 2016); Human Rights Watch, *Raised on the Registry: The Irreparable Harm of Placing Children on Sex Offender Registries in the US* (New York: Human Rights Watch, 2013); Human Rights Watch, *South Sudan: Terrifying Lives of Child Soldiers* (New York: Human Rights Watch, 2015).

70. Scott H. Decker, *International handbook of juvenile justice*. Edited by Nerea Marteache (Springer, 2016).

71. Interestingly, CEDAW does *not* comprehend women as criminals, defendants, or prisoners.

72. Samuel Moyn, "Human Rights in Heaven," in *Human Rights: Moral or Political?*, ed. Adam Etinson (Social Science Research Network), 2014, pp 1–35.

73. Sovereignty figures both as freedom from outside interference and thus a precondition for realizing rights and, more recently, as conditional to capacity, such that state incapacity to protect rights justifies intervention. See Anne Peters, "Humanity as the A and Ω of Sovereignty," *European Journal of International Law* 20, no. 3 (2009): 513–44; United Nations, *In Larger Freedom: Towards Development, Security, and Human Rights for All*, A/29/2005 (2005).

74. Amnesty International, *Stop Violence against Women: It's in Our Hands* (New York: Amnesty International, 2004); OHCHR, *A Framework to Underpin Action to Prevent Violence against Women* (n.p.: UN Women, 2011); United Nations, "Declaration on the Elimination of Violence against Women" (1993); Human Rights Campaign, *Addressing Anti-transgender Violence: Exploring Realities, Challenges, and Solutions* (New York: Human Rights Campaign, 2015).

75. Nigel Rodley and Matt Pollard, *The Treatment of Prisoners under International Law* (Oxford: Oxford University Press, 2009); OHCHR, *Human Rights and Prisons: Manual on Human Rights Training for Prison Officials* (New York: United Nations, 2005); Amnesty International, *Surviving Death: Police and Military Torture of Women in Mexico* (London: Amnesty International, 2016).

76. Katherine M. Franke, "Gendered Subjects of Transitional Justice," *Columbia Journal of Gender and Law* 15 (2006): 813–28; Boaventura de Sousa Santos, "Human Rights as an Emancipatory Script? Cultural and Political Conditions," in *Another Knowledge Is Possible: Beyond Northern Epistemologies,* ed. Boaventura de Sousa Santos (London: Verso, 2008), 3–40; Slavoj Zizek, "Against Human Rights," *New Left Review* 34 (2005): 115–31.

Chapter 3. The Harm Principle Meets Morality Offenses

1. Editors' note: "Morality" is a present concept—whether criminal law is used to repress or to liberate. It is a matter of identifying the kind of morality (or moralities) the criminal code is expressing. See our introduction to this volume.

2. John Stuart Mill, *On Liberty* (Harmondsworth, UK: Penguin, 1974).

3. Mill, 68.

4. Mill has also influenced regional and international human rights law. See *Toonen v. Australia*, Human Rights Committee, Comm. 488/1992, UN Doc. CCPR/C/50/D/488 /1992 (1994). More recent cases concerning freedom of assembly and expression have explicitly rejected "public morality" as grounds for limiting the rights of individuals. See *Alekseyev v. Russia*, App. Nos. 4916/07, 25924/08, and 14599/09, Eur. Ct. H.R. (2010), http://hudoc.echr.coe.int/eng?i=001-101257; and *Fedotova v. Russia*, Human Rights Committee, Comm. 1932/2010, UN Doc. CCPR/C/106/D/1932/2010 (2012).

5. Not limited to sexuality, morals offenses have at times included regulation of alcohol, gambling, and other "vices," such as cockfighting and lotteries. See Suzanne B. Goldberg, "Morals-Based Justifications for Lawmaking: Before and after *Lawrence v. Texas*," *Minnesota Law Review* 88 (2004): 1247–54. In a decision decriminalizing same-sex sexual conduct under the state constitutional right to privacy, the Supreme Court of Kentucky quoted at length a 1909 case called *Commonwealth v. Campbell*, in which the criminalization of possession of alcohol for private consumption was overturned on privacy grounds. "At the time *Campbell* was decided, the use of alcohol was as much an incendiary moral issue as deviate sexual behavior in private between consenting adults is today. Prohibition was the great moral issue of its time." Commonwealth v. Wasson, 842 S.W.2d 487, 495 (Ky. 1992).

6. Louis B. Schwartz, "Morals Offenses and the Model Penal Code," *Columbia Law Review* 63 (1963): 669–86, quote p. 669.

7. Schwartz, 670.

8. Chai R. Feldblum, "Gay Is Good: The Moral Case for Marriage Equality and More," *Yale Journal of Law and Feminism* 17 (2005): 147.

9. Even within "liberal" scholarship, there are efforts to reclaim what is substantively good in debates about equality and fairness. See Feldblum, "Gay Is Good"; and Carlos A. Ball, "Moral Foundations for a Discourse on Marriage for Same-Sex Couples: Looking beyond Political Liberalism," *Georgetown Law Journal* 85 (1997):1871–1944.

10. As quoted in Jean Hampton, "Retribution and the Liberal State," *Journal of Contemporary Legal Issues* 5 (1994): 137.

11. Joel Feinberg, "Autonomy, Sovereignty, and Privacy: Moral Ideals in the Constitution?," *Notre Dame Law Review* 58 (1983): 446.

12. The countries all use common law and are either partially or substantially influenced by Anglo-American legal discourse. Canadian jurisprudence regarding autonomy, privacy, and the harm principal diverges in interesting ways from these other common-law jurisdictions, in particular due to its Charter of Rights and Freedoms. For reasons of space, I've limited my analysis to the United States, South Africa, and India, although I do reference in passing a few Canadian cases and approaches.

13. Report of the Committee on Homosexual Offences and Prostitution (Wolfenden Committee), 1957, Cmnd. 247. Paragraphs 13 and 14.

14. Report of the Committee.

15. See Sexual Offences Act, 1967, c. 60 (Eng.). The Wolfenden Report recommendations were not adopted. See Cabinet Conclusions, November 28, 1957, http://filestore .nationalarchives.gov.uk/pdfs/large/cab-128-31.pdf.

16. Lord Patrick Devlin, "Morals and the Criminal Law," reprinted in Devlin, The Enforcement of Morals (Oxford: Oxford University Press, 1965), 1–25.

17. Devlin, 23.

18. *Model Penal Code and Commentaries (Official Draft and Revised Comments)*, Part II Sections 210–213.6 (Philadelphia: American Law Institute, 1980), footnote 39 on page 372. See also Charles Alan Wright, "A Modern Hamlet in the Judicial Pantheon," *Michigan Law Review* 93 (1955): 1849.

19. Presented to the Institute as Section 207.5 of Tentative Draft No. 4 and considered at the May 1955 meeting. Model Penal Code § 207.5 (Am. Law Inst., Tentative Draft No. 4, 1955).

20. Schwartz, "Morals Offenses," 676.

21. William N. Eskridge Jr., "Family Law Pluralism: The Guided-Choice Regime of Menus, Default Rules, and Override Rules," *Georgetown Law Journal* 100 (2012): 1899.

22. Schwartz, "Morals Offenses," 674.

23. *Model Penal Code and Commentaries*, 373.

24. William N. Eskridge, "Challenging the Apartheid of the Closet: Establishing Conditions for Lesbian and Gay Intimacy, Nomos and Citizenship," *Hofstra Law Review* 25 (1997): 842. Religious groups apparently acquiesced when the code's abortion provisions were narrowed. See Eskridge, 842n93.

25. William N. Eskridge, "Hardwick and Historiography," *University of Illinois Law Review* 2 (1999): 663–64.

26. Model Penal Code § 251.2 (Am. Law Inst., 1962).

27. Model Penal Code § 230.3 (2) (Am. Law Inst., 1962).

28. Schwartz, "Morals Offenses," 674. (citing Model Penal Code § 207.11 [Am. Law Inst., Tentative Draft No. 9, 1959]).

29. Corinna Barrett Lain, "Upside-Down Judicial Review," *Georgetown Law Journal* 101 (2012): 137.

30. Roe v. Wade, 410 U.S. 113, 140 n.37 (1973).

31. Eur. Conv. on H.R., art. 8, http://www.echr.coe.int/Documents/Convention _ENG.pdf.

32. Dudgeon v. United Kingdom, App. No. 7525/76, Eur. Ct. H.R. at para. 51 (1981), http://hudoc.echr.coe.int/eng?i=001-57473.

33. The Criminal Justice (Scotland) Act 1980 brought Scottish law into line with that of England and Wales.

34. *Dudgeon*, App. No. 7525/76, Eur. Ct. H.R. at para. 49.

35. Ibid. at para. 60.

36. Ibid. at paras. 60–61.

37. *Toonen v. Australia*, Human Rights Committee, Comm. 488/1992, UN Doc. CCPR/C/50/D/488/1992 (1994).

38. Ibid. at paras. 8.2, 8.6.

39. Laskey and Others v. United Kingdom, App. Nos. 21627/93, 21628/93, and 21974/93, 1997 Eur. Ct. of H.R. 4; Stübing v. Germany, App. No. 43547/08, Eur. Ct. H.R. (2012), http://hudoc.echr.coe.int/eng?i=001-110314.

40. At the European Commission of Human Rights level, however, Commissioner Loukis Loucaides, joined by six others, dissented on the grounds that the government had "not put forward any convincing justification for the prohibition under the criminal law of the applicants' consensual private behaviour which resulted in minor forms of bodily harm." By a vote of eleven to seven, the commission found no violation of Article 8; the Commission's report is annexed to the European Court of Human Rights decision. See Peter Duffy (editor) European Human Rights Report, Volume 24, 1–119 (1997), pp. 54–56.

41. Pretty v. United Kingdom, App. No. 2346/02, Eur. Ct. H.R. at paras. 61, 66, 74 (2002), http://hudoc.echr.coe.int/eng?i=001-60448.

42. K. A. et A. D. c. Belgique, App. Nos. 42758/98 and 45558/99, Eur. Ct. H.R. at para. 83 (2005), http://hudoc.echr.coe.int/fre?i=001-68354.

43. Ibid.

44. Ibid. at para. 84.

45. Ibid. at para. 85.

46. Note that the "victim," the spouse of one of the two men charged, did not allege that the acts were not consensual.

47. A, B, and C v. Ireland, App. No. 25579/05, Eur. Ct. H.R. at para. 213 (2010), http://hudoc.echr.coe.int/eng?i=001-102332. The Court has never held that Article 8 confers a right to abortion, but it has held that restrictions on abortion may sometimes interfere with private life to such an extent that there is an Article 8 violation.

48. Griswold v. Connecticut, 381 U.S. 479 (1965); Eisenstadt v. Baird, 405 U.S. 438 (1972); Roe v. Wade, 410 U.S. 113 (1973); Carey v. Population Services, 431 U.S. 678 (1977); Planned Parenthood of Southeastern Pennsylvania v. Casey, 505 U.S. 833 (1992) (reaffirming *Roe*).

49. *Roe* p. 153., 410 U.S. Earlier cases found the right to privacy in other constitutional provisions, including the First, Fourth, Fifth, and Ninth Amendments.

50. Compare *Carey*, 431 U.S. (constitutional protection of autonomy in matters of childbearing), with *Casey*, 505 U.S. 833, 851.(describing liberty as the "right to define one's own concept of existence, of meaning, of the universe, and of the mystery of human life").

51. Bowers v. Hardwick, 478 U.S. 186, 190 (1986). As has been much derided, Justice White conveniently ignored the fact that the Georgia statute criminalized anal and oral sex *regardless* of the sex of the partners.

52. Ibid. at 191.

53. Ibid. at 196.

54. Ibid. at 204.

55. Ibid. at 211–12.

56. Ibid. at 213.

57. Ibid. at 216.

58. Lawrence v. Texas, 539 U.S. 558, 562 (2003).

59. Ibid. at 565.

60. Ibid. at 565.

61. Ibid. at 572.

62. Ibid. at 572–73. Judge Frank H. Easterbrook, criticizing the use of the Wolfenden Report, wrote, "What *really* swayed the Justices in *Lawrence* was John Stuart Mill's *On Liberty* (1859): Government should not interfere with acts that do not harm third parties." Frank H. Easterbrook, "Foreign Sources and the American Constitution," *Harvard Journal of Law and Public Policy* 30 (2006): 225. He found the use of either "British moral philosophy" or European Court of Human Rights judgments inappropriate, referencing both as "arguments to the living (which is to say, the legislative and executive branches)." Easterbrook, 225.

63. *Lawrence*, 539 U.S. at 571.

64. Ibid. at 583.

65. Ibid. at 578.

66. Ibid. at 588.

67. Ibid. at 590. There are of course no laws banning masturbation.

68. Ibid. at 599.

69. For examples, see Cass R. Sunstein, "What Did Lawrence Hold? Of Autonomy, Desuetude, Sexuality and Marriage," *Supreme Court Review* 55 (2003): 27–74; and Nan D. Hunter, "Living with Lawrence," *Minnesota Law Review* 88 (2004): 1128–31.

70. Laura A. Rosenbury and Jennifer E. Rothman, "Sex in and out of Intimacy," *Emory Law Journal* 59 (2010): 809–68; Katherine M. Franke, "The Domesticated Liberty of *Lawrence v. Texas*," *Columbia Law Review* 104 (2004): 1399–426; Laurence H. Tribe, "*Lawrence v. Texas*: The 'Fundamental Right' That Dare Not Speak Its Name," *Harvard Law Review* 117 (2004): 1893–955 (observing that the Court focused on "the centrality of the relationship in which the intimate conduct occurs rather than the intimate conduct itself" and concluding, "It's not the sodomy. It's the relationship!").

71. Under rational basis review, legislation must serve a legitimate purpose and be rationally related to that purpose. In *Lawrence*, the Court stated, "The Texas statute furthers no legitimate state interest which can justify its intrusion into the personal and private life of the individual." *Lawrence*, 539 U.S. at 578. Cases cited by the *Lawrence* Court as precedent, such as *Griswold*, *Eisenstadt*, *Roe*, and *Casey*, concerned "fundamental rights" to which strict scrutiny is applied.

72. *Lawrence*, 539 U.S. at 599. For example, see Keith Burgess-Jackson, "Our Millian Constitution: The Supreme Court's Repudiation of Immorality as a Ground of Criminal Punishment," *Notre Dame Journal of Law, Ethics, and Public Policy* 18 (2004): 407–17; Goldberg, "Morals-Based Justifications for Lawmaking."

73. See John Lawrence Hill, "The Constitutional Status of Morals Legislation," *Kentucky Law Journal* 98 (2010): 5; J. Kelly Strader, "*Lawrence*'s Criminal Law," *Berkeley Journal of Criminal Law* 16 (2011): 42–43.

74. Strader, "*Lawrence*'s Criminal Law," appendix.

75. Ofer Raban, "Capitalism, Liberalism and the Right to Privacy," *Tulane Law Review* 86 (2012): 1243–1288, 1281.

76. See *Obergefell v. Hodges*, 135 S. Ct. 2584 (2015).

77. Martin v. Ziherl, 607 S.E.2d 367 (Va. 2005).

78. Ibid. at 370.

79. Ibid.

80. *Lawrence* was limited to "homosexual sodomy." It did not announce a "fundamental right, protected by the Constitution, for adults to engage in all manner of consensual sexual conduct." Muth v. Frank, 412 F.3d 808, 817 (7th Cir. 2005) (concerning adult consensual incest).

81. State v. Romano, 155 P.3d 1102, 1117 (Haw. 2007).

82. Ibid. at 1124.

83. Seven states had enacted laws prohibiting the sale or use of "obscene sexual devices," although three state supreme courts found the laws unconstitutional. See *Reliable Consultants v. Earle*, 517 F.3d 738, 741 nn.8–14 (5th Cir. 2008).

84. Williams v. Att'y Gen. of Ala., 378 F.3d 1232, 1235 (11th Cir. 2004).

85. Ibid. at 1240.

86. Ibid. at 1235.

87. Ibid. at 1235 n.8. The earlier Supreme Court cases dealt with public indecency, obscenity, and the death penalty.

88. *Reliable Consultants*, 517 F.3d.

89. Ibid. at 744.

90. Ibid. at 745.

91. Reliable Consultants v. Earle, 538 F.3d 355 (2008) (denying rehearing and rehearing en banc).

92. Franke, "Domesticated Liberty of *Lawrence v. Texas*," 1407.

93. Franke, 1409.

94. Sunstein, "What Did Lawrence Hold?"

95. Nan D. Hunter, "Reflections on Sexual Liberty and Equality: 'Through Seneca Falls and Selma and Stonewall,'" *University of California Los Angeles Law Review* 60 (2013): 172–73.

96. Lawrence v. Texas, 539 U.S. 558, 604–5 (2003) (citations omitted).

97. For a general comparison, see Laurel Grelewicz, "Equality and Abortion in Postapartheid South Africa: Inspiration for Choice Advocates in the United States," *Oregon Review of International Law* 13 (2011): 189–206.

98. *Christian Lawyers' Association v. National Minister of Health and Others* 2004 (10) BCLR 1086 (T) (S. Afr.); *Christian Lawyers' Association v. National Minister of Health* 1998 (11) BCLR 1 (T) (S. Afr.).

99. *Christian Lawyers' Association* 2004 (10) BCLR at *45.

100. *Bernstein v. Bester* 1996 (2) SA 751 (S. Afr.). In the case, concerning a search of corporate records, the Court referred to how the right to privacy "inheres in certain relationships" and cited *Griswold v. Connecticut*. Ibid. at n. 89.

101. *National Coalition for Gay and Lesbian Equality v. Minister of Justice*, 1999 (1) SA 6 at para. 32 (S. Afr.).

102. Ibid. at para. 37.

103. Ibid. at para. 119.

104. Ibid. at para. 118.

105. Ibid. at para. 136. Here, he is citing Judge Rosalie Silberman Abella in *R. v. C.M.*, 1995 CanLII 8924 (Can. O.N. C.A.).

106. South African Law Reform Commission, *Discussion Paper 1/2009—Sexual Offences: Adult Prostitution* (2009); South African Law Commission, *Issue Paper 19—Sexual Offences: Adult Prostitution* (2002); *Jordan v. State*, 2002 (4) SA 383 (CC) (S. Afr.); *Kylie v. Commission for Conciliation, Mediation and Arbitration*, 2010 (4) SA 383 (S. Afr. Lab. App. Ct. 2010); *Sex Worker Education and Advocacy Taskforce v. Minister of Safety and Security and Others* (6) SA 513 (S. Afr. Western Cape HC 2009). See also Rosaan Kruger, "Sex Work from a Feminist Perspective: A Visit to the *Jordan* Case," *South African Journal of Human Rights* 138 (2004): 138–50.

107. *Jordan*, 2002 (4) SA.

108. Ibid. at para. 27.

109. Ibid. at para. 83.

110. Ibid. at para. 82.

111. Ibid. at para. 83.

112. Ibid.

113. Ibid. at para. 86.

114. Ibid. at para. 92.

115. *Kylie* 2010 (4) SA at paras. 19–26.

116. *SWEAT v. Minister of Safety and Security and Others* 2009 (6) SA 513 (WC) at para. 57 (S. Afr.).

117. Ibid. at para. 60.

118. Nicole Fritz, "Crossing *Jordan*: Constitutional Space for (Un)Civil Sex?," *South African Journal on Human Rights* 20 (2004): 230–48.

119. Minister of Home Affairs and Another v Fourie and Another (CCT 60/04) [2005] ZACC 19; 2006 (3) BCLR 355 (CC); 2006 (1) SA 524 (CC) (December 2005), http://www .saflii.org.za/za/cases/ZACC/2005/19.html.

120. Naz Foundation v. Union of India, (2009) 160 DLT 277 (Del.). The case is currently on appeal before the Supreme Court of India. Section 377 criminalized "carnal intercourse against the order of nature."

121. Heather Timmons and Hari Kumar, "Indian Court Overturns Gay Sex Ban," *New York Times*, July 2, 2009, http://www.nytimes.com/2009/07/03/world/asia/03india.html.

122. Art. 12, Constitution of India.

123. See *Govind v. State of Madhya Pradesh*, (1978) 1 SCC 248 (India); *Kharak Singh v. State of Uttar Pradesh*, (1964) 1 SCR 332 (India) (minority opinion of Justice Subba Rao) (discussed in *Naz Foundation*, [2009] 160 DLT at paras. 35–37); and *District Registrar and Collector v. Canara Bank*, (2005) 1 SCC 496 (India) (discussed in *Naz Foundation*, [2009] 160 DLT at para. 39).

124. Saptarshi Mandal points out that the Andhra Pradesh High Court had held that a provision of the Hindu Marriage Act involving a decree of restitution of conjugal rights violated Article 21 "as the grant of such a decree offended the right to privacy of the woman against whom such a decree is sought." Sareetha v. Venkata Subbaiah, 1983 AIR 356 (Andhra Pradesh). However, this approach was not followed by other courts, including the Supreme Court. See Saptarshi Mandal, "'Right to Privacy' in *Naz Foundation*: A Counter-heteronormative Critique," *National University of Juridical Sciences Law Review* 2 (2009): 528–30.

125. Vikram Raghavan, "Navigating the Noteworthy and Nebulous in *Naz Foundation*," *National University of Juridical Sciences Law Review* 2 (2009): 397–418, p. 402.

126. *Naz Foundation*, (2009) 160 DLT at para. 75.

127. Ibid. at paras. 75–78.

128. Ibid. at para. 79. The Delhi High Court was clearly influenced by the South African Constitutional Court's use of constitutional morality to defend a vision of equality. In turn, this was apparently inspired by Judge Abella's language in the Ontario Court of Appeal case, *R. v. C.M.*, 1995 CanLII 8924 (Can. O.N. C.A.). Abella was appointed to the Supreme Court of Canada in 2004.

129. *Naz Foundation*, (2009) 160 DLT at para. 82.

130. See, for example, Rohit Sharma, "The Public and Constitutional Morality Conundrum: A Case-Note on the *Naz Foundation* Judgment," *National University of Juridical Sciences Law Review* 2 (2009): 445–54.

131. Raghavan, "Navigating the Noteworthy and Nebulous," 410.

132. Justice Verma's comments on the *Naz Foundation* judgment are available in "Justice J.S. Verma Comments on the Naz Foundation Judgment," *Law and Other Things* (blog), June 16, 2016, http://lawandotherthings.blogspot.ch/2009/07/justice-jsvermas-comment-on-naz.html.

133. A. P. Shah, "Decriminalization of Anti-sodomy Law in India—Tackling the Issues of Constitutional Morality, Public Health and Individual Rights" (Commonwealth HIV and Human Rights Lecture, London, November 2010).

134. Shah.

135. Suresh Kumar Koushal v. Naz Foundation, (2014) 1 SCC 1 (India).

136. Ibid. at para. 43.

137. Ibid. at para. 38.

138. Vishwajith Sadananda, "Naz and Reclaiming Counter-majoritarianism," Oxford Human Rights Hub, January 9, 2014, http://ohrh.law.ox.ac.uk/naz-and-reclaiming-counter-majoritarianism/; Siddarth Narrain, "Lost in Appeal: The Downward Spiral from Naz to Koushal," *National University of Juridical Sciences Law Review* 6 (2013): 575–84.

139. National Legal Services Authority v. Union of India, (2012) WP (Civil) No. 400 at para. 69 (India).

140. Right to Privacy Case, Writ Petition (Civil) No. 494 of 2012, August 24, 2017.

141. Ibid. at 262.

142. Ibid. at 109.

143. Ibid.

144. Ibid. at 123–24.

145. Ibid. at 125.

146. Writ Petition No. 76, 2016, Order Dated January 8, 2018 (Supreme Court of India); Krishnadas Rajagopal, "Áadhaar Pleas to be Heard from Jan. 17," *Hindu*, January 13, 2018.

147. Michal Buchhandler-Raphael, "Drugs, Dignity and Danger: Human Dignity as a Constitutional Constraint to Limit Overcriminalization," *Tennessee Law Review* 80 (2013): 291–345.

148. "In a wide array of contexts, the proponents of regulation and prohibition have turned away from arguments based on morality, and turned instead to harm arguments." Bernard E. Harcourt, "The Collapse of the Harm Principle," *Journal of Criminal Law and Criminology* 90 (1999): 110.

149. State v. Romano, 155 P.3d 1102, 1124 (Haw. 2007).

150. *Jordan v. State*, 2002 (4) SA 383 (CC) at paras. 86–94 (S. Afr.).

151. Dan M. Kahan, "Foreword: Neutral Principles, Motivated Cognition, and Some Problems for Constitutional Law," *Harvard Law Review* 125 (2011): 50.

152. See *R. v. Malmo-Levine; R. v. Caine* 2003 SCC 74, [2003] 3 S.C.R. 571 (Can.).

153. Harcourt, "Collapse of the Harm Principle."

154. David Kimmel and Daniel J. Robinson, "Sex, Crime, Pathology: Homosexuality and Criminal Code Reform in Canada, 1949–1969," *Canada Journal of Law and Society* 16 (2001): 160.

155. Dudgeon v. United Kingdom, App. No. 7525/76, Eur. Ct. H.R. at para. 61 (1981) ("'Decriminalisation' does not imply approval, and a fear that some sectors of the population might draw misguided conclusions in this respect from reform of the legislation does not afford a good ground for maintaining it in force with all its unjustifiable features.").

156. R. v. Butler, [1992] 1 S.C.R. 452 (Can.). See also *R. v. Labaye*, 2005 S.C.C. 80 at para. 33 (Can.).

157. Ronald Dworkin, "Lord Devlin and the Enforcement of Morals," *Yale Law Journal* 75 (1966): 1001.

158. Hunter, "Reflections on Sexual Liberty."

159. *Jordan v. State*, 2002 (4) SA 383 (CC) at para. 27 (S. Afr.).

160. Tara v. State, 2012 CRL 296/2012 at para. 12 (Delhi HC).

Chapter 4. Reflections of a Human Rights Activist

1. "Bad Dreams: Exploitation and Abuse of Migrant Workers in Saudi Arabia," Human Rights Watch, July 13, 2004, https://www.hrw.org/report/2004/07/13/bad-dreams /exploitation-and-abuse-migrant-workers-saudi-arabia.

2. Gita Sahgal, "A Statement by Gita Sahgal on Leaving Amnesty International," *New York Review of Books*, May 13, 2010, http://www.nybooks.com/articles/2010/05/13 /statement-gita-sahgal-leaving-amnesty-internationa/.

3. Ken Burns, David McMahon, and Sarah Burns, *The Central Park Five* (Public Broadcasting Service, 2013), DVD.

4. New York City settled for $40 million with those wrongfully convicted. See Benjamin Weiser, "5 Exonerated in Central Park Jogger Case Agree to Settle Suit for $40 Million," *New York Times*, June 14, 2014, http://www.nytimes.com/2014/06/20/nyregion/5 -exonerated-in-central-park-jogger-case-are-to-settle-suit-for-40-million.html?_r=0.

5. Sydney H. Schanberg, "A Journey through the Tangled Case of the Central Park Jogger," *Village Voice*, November 19, 2002, https://www.villagevoice.com/2002/11/19/a -journey-through-the-tangled-case-of-the-central-park-jogger/; Saul Kassin, "False Confession and the Jogger Case," *New York Times*, November 1, 2002, http://www.nytimes .com/2002/11/01/opinion/false-confessions-and-the-jogger-case.html.

6. *Wilding* was a colloquial slang term that was misinterpreted in media coverage around the case; its use by mainstream media carried embedded racial prejudices when describing large groups of kids of color spending time in what were described as "genteel" and "civilized" places like Central Park. For more on the role that language played in this case, see Stephen J. Mexal, "The Roots of 'Wilding': Black Literary Naturalism, the Language of Wilderness, and Hip Hop in the Central Park Jogger Rape," *African American Review* 46, no. 1 (2013): 101–15.

7. Joanna Walters, "Sara Reedy, the Rape Victim Accused of Lying and Jailed by US Police, Wins $1.5m Payout," *Guardian*, December, 15, 2012, https://www.theguardian .com/world/2012/dec/15/sara-reedy-rape-victim-wins-police-payout.

8. The Innocence Project works to overturn wrongful convictions. See http://www .innocenceproject.org/.

9. Editors' note: see the introduction for further discussion of "morality" in the justification of criminal law.

10. Amnesty International USA, *Maze of Injustice: The Failure to Protect Indigenous Women from Sexual Violence in the USA* (New York: Amnesty International USA, 2007).

11. Barbara Ann Sullivan, "Can a Prostitute Be Raped? Sex Workers, Women and the Politics of Rape Law Reform," *Refereed Papers from the 2003 APSA Conference* (Australasian Political Studies Association Conference, University of Tasmania, Hobart, September 29–October 1, 2003), pdf-1–pdf-22.

Chapter 5. Virtuous Rights

1. Gayle Rubin, "Thinking Sex: Notes for a Radical Theory of the Politics of Sexuality," in *Pleasure and Danger: Exploring Female Sexuality*, ed. Carole S. Vance (Boston: Routledge and Kegan Paul, 1984), 267.

2. "Anti-prostitution Law Constitutional, Says Court," *Korea Joongang Daily*, April 1, 2016. http://koreajoongangdaily.joins.com/news/article/Article.aspx?aid=3016972.

3. Park Hyun-chul and Choi Yu-bin, "Judge Seeks Constitutional Review of Law That Criminalizes Prostitution," *Hankyoreh*, January 11, 2013, http://english.hani.co.kr/arti /english_edition/ e_national/569290.html.

4. Lee Sun-Young, "Judge's Request Stirs Legal Debate on 'Voluntary Sex Work,'" *Korea Herald*, January 10, 2013, http://www.koreaherald.com/view.php?ud=20130110000725.

5. Globally, this right to sexual self-determination developed from the idea of reproductive health endorsed in the 1994 International Conference on Population and Devel-

opment, further affirmed in the 1995 Beijing Platform. See Susana T. Fried and Ilana Landsberg-Lewis, "Sexual Rights: From Concept to Strategy," in *Women and International Human Rights*, ed. Kelly D. Askin and Dorean M. Koenig (London: Transnational, 2001), 3:114–16.

6. Patriarchy in Korean feminism is generally understood as male domination of women across different spheres of life.

7. Fried and Landsberg-Lewis, "Sexual Rights."

8. Kyungja Jung, *Practicing Feminism in South Korea: The Women's Movement against Sexual Violence* (London: Routledge, 2014), 66.

9. Janet Halley defines *governance feminism* as "the incremental but by now quite noticeable installation of feminists and feminist ideas in actual legal-institutional power." Janet Halley et al., "From the International to the Local in Feminist Legal Responses to Rape, Prostitution/Sex Work, and Sex Trafficking: Four Studies in Contemporary Governance Feminism," *Harvard Journal of Law and Gender* 29 (2006): 335–423.

10. Sealing Cheng, "Embodying the Sexual Limits of Neoliberalism," *Scholar and Feminism* 11 (Fall 2012/Spring 2013), http://sfonline.barnard.edu/gender-justice-and -neoliberal-transformations/embodying-the-sexual-limits-of-neoliberalism/.

11. Jesook Song, *South Koreans in the Debt Crisis: The Creation of a Neoliberal Welfare Society* (Durham, NC: Duke University Press, 2009); Sealing Cheng and Eunjung Kim, "The Paradoxes of Neoliberalism: Migrant Korean Sex Workers in the United States and 'Sex Trafficking,'" *Social Politics* 21 (2014): 344–81.

12. Jesook Song, *South Koreans in the Debt Crisis*.

13. Nancy Abelmann, So Jin Park, and Hyunhee Kim, "College Rank and Neo-liberal Subjectivity in South Korea: The Burden of Self-Development," *Inter-Asia Cultural Studies* 10 (2009): 229.

14. Martina Deuchler, *The Confucian Transformation of Korea: A Study of Society and Ideology* (Cambridge, MA: Harvard University Press, 1995), 155.

15. Kyung Sook Bae, *Women and the Law in Korea* (Seoul: Korean League of Women Workers, 1973), 1.

16. Yang Hyunah, "Remembering the Korean Military Comfort Women," in *Dangerous Women: Gender and Korean Nationalism*, ed. Elaine H. Kim and Chungmoo Choi (London: Routledge, 1997), 118–35.

17. This term originated in one article in the colonial Japanese Criminal Code (Korea was a colony from 1910 to 1945): the crime of mediating debauchery penalized anyone who "makes a woman with no history of lewd acts commit adultery by soliciting lewd acts for profit." Park Jeong-Mi, "'Woman Free of Habitually Lewd Acts?': Criminal Law, Postcoloniality, and Women's Sexuality, 1953–1960," *Korean Social Sciences Review* 3 (2013): 223.

18. Criminal Code, art. 182 (S. Kor.).

19. Jeong-Mi Park found a tendency for courts to refer to "minors" (under eighteen or twenty-one) as "women with no habitual debauchery" so as to indicate victimhood. See Park, "'Woman Free of Habitually Lewd Acts?,'" 236.

20. Yeong-geun Oh, *Hyeong-beob Gak-roun* [Particulars of the criminal law] (Seoul: Park Myeon-sa, 2009), 800–802.

21. Criminal Code, art. 304 (S. Kor.).

22. Park Jeong-Mi, "'Woman Free of Habitually Lewd Acts?,'" 236–39. See also Park Jeong-Mi, 295.

23. Park Jeong-Mi, 241.

24. Park Jeong-Mi, 261.

25. Park Jeong-Mi, 244.

26. Park Jeong-Mi, "Han-kook seong-mae-mae-jeong-chaek-ae kwan-han yeon-gu [A study on prostitution policies in Korea]. Seoul National University doctoral dissertation (2011). 58–60.

27. Moon Seungsook highlights how militarized modernity under the Park dictatorship—through universal conscription and an industrializing economy—produced the ideal of Korean men as soldiers and breadwinners and of their female counterparts as dutiful mothers and rational household managers. See Moon Seungsook, *Militarized Modernity and Gendered Citizenship in South Korea* (Durham, NC: Duke University Press, 2005).

28. Until the 1990s, Korean laws and court decisions reflected the societal view that rape and other sexual assaults could only happen to women and that it violated a woman's chastity. Thus, the crime only occurs when "virtuous" women are raped.

29. Jung, *Practicing Feminism in South Korea*, 9.

30. Margaret E. Keck and Kathryn Sikkink, *Activists beyond Borders: Advocacy Networks in International Politics* (Ithaca, NY: Cornell University Press, 1998); Charlotte Bunch, "Women's Rights as Human Rights: Toward a Re-Vision of Human Rights," *Human Rights Quarterly* 12 (1990): 486–98.

31. Other groups addressing the issue of sexual violence were Korean Womenlink (1983–), Korean Women's Associations United (1987–), and the Sexual Violence Counseling Center (1991–).

32. Kuk Cho, "Korean Criminal Law under Controversy after Democratization," *Review of Korean Studies* 6 (2003): 50.

33. Cho.

34. Kyungja Min, "Seong-pog-nyeok yeo-seong-eun-dong-sa [A History of the Women's Movement against Sexual Violence," in *Hankuk yeoseonginkweon undongsa* [A history of the Korean women's rights movement], ed. Korean Women's Hotline (Seoul: Hanul Academy, 1999), 56.

35. Jung, *Practicing Feminism in South Korea*, 63.

36. The women's movement formed a Special Committee for Formulating and Promoting the Special Act on Sexual Violence in 1992; it defined sexual violence as a crime that violated a woman's right to sexual self-determination. See Younghee Shim, "Feminism and the Discourses of Sexuality in Korea: Continuities and Changes," *Human Studies* 24 (2001): 144.

37. Hyo-won Lee, "The Constitutional Decisions concerning the Right of Self Determination of Sexual Intercourse," *Seoul Law Journal* 53 (2012): 219–41.

38. Yoon Duk-kyung, "Hyeong-sa-bop-sang seong-jeok ja-gi-gyeol-jeong-kwon-ae bo-ho-ae gwan-han yeon-gu [Research on the Protection of a Right to Sexual Self-

Determination from Criminal Law Perspectives]" (2012). Doctoral Thesis, Law School, Ewha Women's University.

39. See Fried and Landsberg-Lewis, "Sexual Rights."

40. Shin Youngtae, "Self-Determination and Violence against Women in South Korea," *Asian Women* 11, no. 12 (2000): 27–48, 32.

41. Shin, 35–7.

42. Hye-Jin Park, "Hyeong-beop-sang Seong-jeok ja-gi-gyeol-jeong-kweon gyen-you-mae dae-han seong-chal" [A critical study on the concept of "sexual self-determination"], *Hyeongsa Jongjaek* [Criminal law policy] 22 (2010): 239–40.

43. Kuk Cho, "The Under-protection of Women under Korean Criminal Law," *Columbia Journal of Asian Law* 22 (2008): 119–41.

44. The law only addresses sexual violence against women: from our perspective, this means all persons are "underprotected," as the law does not address sexual harm to other groups (men, boys, trans*, and so on) in these terms.

45. Cho, "Under-protection of Women," 130.

46. Alice M. Miller, "Sexuality, Violence against Women, and Human Rights: Women Make Demands and Ladies Get Protection," *Health and Human Rights* 7 (2004): 25.

47. This view was challenged first by a local court in 2009 in the landmark conviction of a forty-two-year-old Korean man for raping his twenty-five-year-old Filipina wife at knifepoint. Limb Jae-un, "Busan Court Convicts 1st Korean Man of Spousal Rape," *Korea Joongang Daily*, January 17, 2009, http://koreajoongangdaily.joins.com/news/article/article.aspx?aid=2899971. The May 16, 2013, Supreme Court's judgment recognized marital rape. Supreme Court, 2012 Do14788 (S. Kor.).

48. Article 304, "Sexual Intercourse under Pretense of Marriage," stipulated that "individuals who have sexual relations with a woman with no habitual debauchery under the promise of marriage or by using other deceptive approaches will be given a maximum of two years' prison term or a penalty of up to 5 million won" (Constitutional Court, 2008Hun-Ba58, November 26, 2009 [S. Kor.]).

49. Park Jeong-Mi, "'Woman Free of Habitually Lewd Acts?'"

50. See Constitutional Court, 2008Hun-Ba58, November 26, 2009 (S. Kor)

51. "Adultery Law Upheld by Slimmest Margin," *Chosun Ilbo*, October 31, 2008, http://english.chosun.com/site/data/html_dir/2008/10/31/2008103161022.html; Song Sangho, "Court Rules Seduction Law Invalid," *Korea Herald*, March 30, 2010, http://www.koreaherald.com/view.php?ud=20091127000041.

52. Republic of Korea, "Eighth Periodic Report to the United Nations Convention on the Elimination of All Forms of Discrimination against Women," in *Convention on the Elimination of all Forms of Discrimination against Women* (Geneva, 2015), 4.

53. Constitutional challenges to the adultery law have been filed five times in the last two decades: in 1990, 1993, 2001, 2008, and 2011.

54. See Constitutional Court, 2007Hon-Ga17, October 30, 2008 (S. Kor).

55. Ibid.

56. See Constitutional Court, 2009Hun-Ba17, February 26, 2015 (S. Kor).

57. See Mark West, *Lovesick Japan: Sex * Marriage * Romance * Law* (Ithaca, NY: Cornell University Press, 2011).

58. Protocol to Prevent, Suppress and Punish Trafficking in Persons, Especially Women and Children, UN Doc. A/55/383, supplementing the Convention against Transnational Organized Crime, Nov. 15, 2000, 2237 U.N.T.S. 319, and the Victims of Trafficking and Violence Protection Act of 2000, Pub. L. No. 106-386, 1 Stat. 1464 (2002).

59. For example, see Wendy Chapkis, "Trafficking, Migration, and the Law: Protecting Innocents, Punishing Immigrants," *Gender and Society* 1796 (2003): 923–37; and Janie Chuang, "Rescuing Trafficking from Ideological Capture: Prostitution Reform and Anti-trafficking Law and Policy," *University of Pennsylvania Law Review* 158 (2010): 1655–728.

60. Grace Chang and Kathleen Kim, "Reconceptualizing Approaches to Human Trafficking: New Directions and Perspectives from the Field(s)," *Stanford Journal of Civil Rights and Civil Liberties* 3 (2007): 314.

61. Cheng, "Paradox of Vernacularization," 478.

62. The adultery law defenders introduced wives' material conditions as part of their argument for why the law was strategic, but this is different from an argument that the substance of the harm is dependent on material conditions.

63. Chapter 22 of the criminal code defines the crimes of "adultery" (Article 241), "arranging for prostitution" (Article 242), "distribution of obscene pictures" (Article 243), "manufacture of obscene pictures," (Article 244), and "public indecency" (Article 245).

64. Won Mihye, "A Life History Research of Women Who Sell Sex: The Temporal and Spatial Operationalization of Intersectional Sex Hierarchy." (Ph.D. Dissertation, Women's Studies, Ewha Women's University, 2010).

65. As the 2004 laws replaced "fallen women" with the gender-neutral term "victims of prostitution," men and transgender persons could theoretically be considered potential victims. Yet the state supports a network of women's NGOs to help only "prostituted women." See Dasi Hamkke, *Annual Report* (Seoul: Dasi Hamkke, 2008). Dasi Hamkke was the largest antiprostitution NGO in Seoul and offers no services to men or transgender persons.

66. Dasi Hamkke has taken on the majority of these class suits.

67. The Ministry of Gender Equality implemented pilot projects of rehabilitation programs in the cities of Busan and Incheon from December 2004 to February 2005. In total, 144 females received government rehabilitation aid for vocational training, living allowance, and medical treatment. The total number of individuals in the rehabilitation program was 1,500 in 2005.

68. On the Punishment of Sexual Traffic and Associated Acts (Punishment Act), Act No. 7196, 2004, art. 2(4) (S. Kor.).

69. Sealing Cheng, "The Paradox of Vernacularization: Women's Human Rights and the Gendering of Nationhood," *Anthropological Quarterly* 84, no. 2 (2011): 492.

70. On the Prevention of Sexual Traffic and Protection of Victims Thereof (Protection Act), Act No. 7212, 2004, art. 5(1) (S. Kor.).

71. Jesook Song, *South Koreans in the Debt Crisis*.

72. See Cho Youngsook, *The Role of Women's Organization for Gender Equality and Challenges Emerged* (Seoul: Korea Women's Associations United, 2004); Cho Youngsook, *The Prevention of the Sexual Exploitation of Women in Korea: From Impunity to Punishing Procuring Prostitution and the Purchase of Sexual Service* (Seoul: Korea Women's Associations United, 2005); and Sealing Cheng, "Paradox of Vernacularization." It has become a common understanding among Korean women activists and scholars that prostitution is a product of military aggression and capitalist patriarchy.

73. Cho Bae-sook quoted in Park Hyun-chul and Choi, "Judge Seeks Constitutional Review."

74. Park Hyun-chul and Choi.

75. Kim Hye-sook quoted in Claire Lee, "Court Reviews Anti-prostitution Laws," *Korea Herald*, April 9, 2015, http://www.koreaherald.com/view.php?ud=20150409001158.

76. See Elizabeth Bernstein. "Carceral Politics as Gender Justice? The 'Traffic in Women' and Neoliberal Circuits of Crime, Sex, and Rights," *Theory and Society* 41, no. 3 (2012), 33–259; and Sealing Cheng, "Paradox of Vernacularization."

77. See Cheng, "Paradox of Vernacularization"; and Cheng and Kim, "Paradoxes of Neoliberalism."

78. Kristin Bumiller, *In an Abusive State: How Neoliberalism Appropriated the Feminist Movement against Sexual Violence* (Durham, NC: Duke University Press, 2008), 5.

79. See Katharine Moon, "Resurrecting Prostitutes and Overturning Treaties: Gender Politics in the 'Anti-American' Movement in South Korea," *Journal of Asian Studies* 66, no. 1 (2007): 129–57.

80. See Minsook Heo, "Women's Movement and the Politics of Framing: The Construction of Anti-domestic Violence Legislation in South Korea," *Women's Studies International Forum* 33 (2010): 225–33.

81. Bumiller, *In an Abusive State.*

82. Jung, *Practicing Feminism in South Korea.*

83. Lauren Berlant, "The Subject of True Feeling: Pain, Privacy and Politics," in *Left Legalism/Left Critique*, ed. Wendy Brown and Janet Halley (Durham, NC: Duke University Press, 2002), 117.

84. Rubin, "Thinking Sex."

85. Rubin, 168.

86. Rubin's germinal idea of the sex hierarchy "grants virtue to the dominant groups, and relegates vice to the underprivileged." Rubin, 153. Sex work thereby becomes what she has called the "erotic DMZ": the barricade against sexual chaos, family ruins, national demise, and other unknown tragedies. Rubin, 152.

87. Other articles of the criminal code that have been changed similarly are Article 288, "Kidnapping"; Article 289, "Kidnapping and Trading for Transportation to Foreign Country," which was changed to "Human Trafficking," involving the buying and selling of "persons," as opposed to "women"; Article 303, "Sexual Intercourse by Abuse of Occupational Authority"; Article 305, "Sexual Intercourse or Indecent Act with Minor" (changed from "underage women" to "underage persons"); and Article 339, "Robbery and Rape."

88. Dong Keun Lee, "Country Report—Korea," in *Annual Report for 2006 and Resource Material Series* (Tokyo: United Nations Asia and Far East Institute for the Prevention of Crime and the Treatment of Offenders, 2007), 108.

89. Rubin, "Thinking Sex"; Alice M. Miller and Carole S. Vance, "Sexuality, Human Rights, and Health," *Health and Human Rights* 7 (2004): 5–15; Catherine Warrick Jordan, "The Vanishing Victim: Criminal Code and Gender," *Law and Society Review* 39 (2005): 315–48.

90. Michel Foucault, *The History of Sexuality*, vol. 1, *An Introduction*, trans. Robert Hurley (New York: Vintage, 1990); Victor Tadros, "Between Governance and Discipline: The Law and Michel Foucault," *Oxford Journal of Legal Studies* 18 (1998): 75–103.

91. Viviana Zelizer, *The Purchase of Intimacy* (New Jersey: Princeton University Press), 22.

92. Bumiller, *In an Abusive State*, xv.

93. Ki-young Shin, "The Politics of the Family Law Reform Movement in Contemporary Korea: A Contentious Space for Gender and the Nation," *Journal of Korean Studies* 11 (2006): 93. Shin found a changing discourse on the social functions of family law, with it being perceived as a carrier of tradition in the early postcolonial period, then a transmitter of economic development in the 1970s, and finally a catalyst for democracy in the late 1980s and afterward.

94. Abelmann, Park, and Kim, "College Rank and Neo-liberal Subjectivity." 229.

95. Tadros, "Between Governance and Discipline," 102.

96. Tadros, 103.

97. Zelizer, *Purchase of Intimacy*, 20–26.

98. Rubin, "Thinking Sex."

Chapter 6. Brazilian Sex Laws

1. Gilberto Freyre, *The Masters and the Slaves: A Study in the Development of Brazilian Civilization* (Berkeley: University of California Press, 1986); Paulo Prado, *Retrato do Brasil: Ensaio sobre a tristeza brasileira* (São Paulo: Companhia das Letras, 2001); Richard G. Parker, *Bodies, Pleasures, and Passions: Sexual Culture in Contemporary Brazil* (Nashville: Vanderbilt University Press, 2009).

2. Françoise Girard, "Negotiating Sexual Rights and Sexual Orientation at the UN," in *SexPolitics: Reports from the Front Line*, ed. Richard Parker, Rosalind Petchesky, and Robert Sember (Rio de Janeiro: Sexuality Policy Watch, 2007), 311–58, http://www.sxpolitics.org/frontlines/book/pdf/capitulo9_united_nations.pdf.

3. A major political shift has occurred in Brazil since 2016, reinforcing the tendencies toward hypercriminalization and conservative restoration. See Perry Anderson, "Crisis in Brazil," *London Review of Books*, April 21, 2016, http://www.lrb.co.uk/v38/n08/perry-anderson/crisis-in-brazil.

4. A study of the wills of freed slaves in Bahia from the nineteenth century found that in more than 70 percent of cases, urban dwellers bequeathed slaves to their descendants. Sandra Carvalho, *Direitos humanos no Brasil* (São Paulo: Justiça Global, 2002).

5. Emilia Viotti da Costa, *The Brazilian Empire: Myths and History* (Chapel Hill: University of North Carolina Press, 2000).

6. Sodomy, defined as sexual relations between persons of the same sex, was criminalized in Portuguese penal laws applied in Brazil before independence.

7. This terminology comes from the French. *Crimes de polícia* correspond to the currently named *contravenções penais*, which were essentially misdemeanors.

8. For example, police harassed and arrested *fanchonos* (gay men) and *travestis* accused of offending public morals in Rio de Janeiro in the second half of the nineteenth century. See Carlos Figari, "Violencia, repugnancia e indignación: Las travestis como lo otro abyecto," *Revista Gênero* (Universidade Federal Fluminense) 8, no. 2 (2008): 355–68.

9. The regime transition was the result of a seizure of power by a group of high-level military officers associated with sectors of the elites, with no popular mobilization or participation.

10. Richard Miskolci, *O Desejo da nação: Masculinidade e branquitude no Brasil de fins do XIX* (São Paulo: Annablume Editora, 2013), quoted in José Tadeu Arantes, "Masculinidade e branquitude na construção da República brasileira," *Agência FAPESP*, May 20, 2013, http://agencia.fapesp.br/masculinidade_e_branquitude_na_construcao_da_republica _brasileira/17292/.

11. Sérgio Carrara, *Tributo a Vênus: A luta contra a sífilis no Brasil, da passagem do século aos anos 40* (Rio de Janeiro: EditoraFiocruz, 1996).

12. Cristina Pereira, "Lavar, passar e receber visitas: Debates sobre a regulamentação da prostituição e experiências de trabalho sexual em Buenos Aires e no Rio de Janeiro, fim do século XIX," *CadernosPagu* 25 (2005): 25–54; Carolina Moraes Rabelo da Silva, "Fracisco José Viveiros de Castro: Sexualidade, cidadania e criminologia no fim século XIX" (PhD diss., Universidade Federal de Rio de Janeiro, 2012).

13. Marcos César Alvarez, Fernando Afonso Salla, and Luís Antônio de Souza, "A sociedade e a lei: O código penal de 1890 e as novas tendências penais na primeira república," *Revista Justiça e História* 3, no. 6 (2003).

Rabelo da Silva, "Viveiros de Castro: Sexualidade, cidadania e criminologia no Século 19" (dissertation project presented to the History Department of the Federal University of Rio de Janeiro), 2010.

14. In Portuguese, *mulheres de má vida* is best understood as "women with bad behavior," referring especially to prostitutes.

15. Carlos Steven Bakota, "Getúlio Vargas and the Estado Novo: An Inquiry into Ideology and Opportunism," *Latin American Research Review* 14 (1979): 205–10; Robert M. Levine, *The Vargas Regime: The Critical Years, 1934–1938* (New York: Columbia University Press, 1970); Thomas E. Skidmore, *Politics and Economic Policy Making in Authoritarian Brazil, 1937–71* (New Haven, CT: Yale University Press, 1973).

16. The most important regional rebellion was the 1932 Constitutionalist Revolution of São Paulo, which fundamentally expressed the not always progressive interests of the emerging industrial bourgeoisie, while at the same time criticizing delays in the adoption of a new constitution.

17. The 1937 Constitution, inspired by the charter of the dictatorial regime of Józef Pilsudski in Poland, was nicknamed "The Polish." This also evoked, in an overtly sexual tone, the moral degradation of the principles of the 1930 Revolution: Jewish prostitutes were also known as "Polish."

18. The 1937 "Polish" Constitution restored the death penalty for ordinary crimes (but never implemented it).

19. Conservative modernization is the conceptual frame crafted by Barrington Moore Jr. to analyze capitalist development and consolidation of modern nation-states in Germany and Japan in the nineteenth century. See Barrington Moore Jr., *Social Origins of Dictatorship and Democracy: Lord and Peasant in the Making of the Modern World* (New York: Penguin, 1966).

20. Carvalho, *Direitos humanos no Brasil*, 122.

21. *Laïcité* is a political principle grounded on the values of freedom of conscience and to manifest one's convictions within the limits of respect for public order, of separation between public institutions and religious organizations, and the equality of all before the law, whatever the individual's beliefs or convictions. *Laïcité* presupposes the separation of the State and religious organizations, and a political order is based solely on the sovereignty of the citizens' people. Within this frame, the state neither recognizes nor financially supports any form of cult, nor does it intervene in the internal functioning of religious organizations.

22. Carlos Vinícius Costa de Mendonça et al., "Luz, escuridão e penumbra: O Governo Vargas e a Igreja Católica," *Dimensões* 26 (2011): 277–91.

23. Andre Caetano, "Fertility Transition and the Diffusion of Female Sterilization in Northeastern Brazil: The Roles of Medicine and Politics," in *Book of Abstracts: XXIV General Population Conference* (Paris: International Union for the Scientific Study of Population [Union Internationale pour l'Etude Scientifique de la Population], 2001).

24. Nilo Batista, "O prazer e a lei penal," in *Temas de Direito Penal* (Rio de Janeiro: Editora Liber Juris, 1984), 304–12.

25. The guidelines concerning transnational trafficking of persons, as well as the Geneva Convention on Prisoners of War, are among the earliest examples of the use of international human rights laws as tools for "protecting" victims, dating from 1901 and restated in 1910, 1921, and 1933.

26. The provision criminalizing the distribution of information on contraceptive methods remained in force until 1979. Definitions concerning substances that induce abortion were revised in the 1990s and 2000s, and the advertisement and sale of misoprostol in Brazil was strictly prohibited. See Margareth Arilha, Thaís Lapa, and Tatiane Pisaneschi, *Aborto Medicamentoso no Brasil* (São Paulo: Comissão de Cidadania e Reprodução, 2001), http://www.ccr.org.br/livro-boletim-detalhe.asp?cod=44.

27. Skidmore, *Politics and Economic Policy Making*; Thomas E. Skidmore, *The Politics of Military Rule in Brazil, 1964–1985* (Oxford: Oxford University Press, 1990).

28. Lourdes Sola, "Limítes politicos ao choque heterodoxo no Brasil: Técnicos, políticos, democracia," *Revista Brasileira de Ciências Sociais* 3 (1989): 38–69.

29. During the period 1970–1974, there was a saying in Brazil: "Love it or leave it."

30. Elio Gaspari, *A ditadura envergonhada,* vols. 1–3 (São Paulo: Companhia das Letras, 2002–3).

31. Mala Htun, *Sex and the State: Abortion, Divorce and the Family under Latin American Dictatorships and Democracies* (New York: Cambridge University Press, 2003); Adriana R. B. Vianna and Sérgio Carrara, "Sexual Politics in Brazil: A Case Study," in Parker, Petchesky, and Sember, *SexPolitics,* 27–51, http://www.sxpolitics.org/frontlines /book/pdf/capitulo1_brazil.pdf.

32. Carvalho, *Direitos humanos no Brasil.*

33. Mario Pecheny and Rafael De la Dehesa, "Sexualidades y políticas en América Latina: Un esbozo para la discusión," *Diálogo Latinoamericano sobre Sexualidad y Geopolítica* (2009); Hannah Arendt, *The Human Condition* (Chicago: University of Chicago Press, 1958).

34. Leonardo Arvitzer, *Democracy and Public Space in Latin America* (Princeton, NJ: Princeton University Press, 2002).

35. Alessandro De Giorgi, *Il governo dell'eccedenza* (Verona: Ombre Corte, 2002); Alessandro De Giorgi, *Zero tolleranza: Strategie e pratiche della società di controllo* (Rome: Derive Approdi, 2000); Niklas Luhmann and Raffaele De Giorgi, *Teoría de la sociedad* (Guadalajara, Mexico: Universidad de Guadalajara, 1996); Loïc Wacquant, *Punishing the Poor: The Neoliberal Government of Social Insecurity* (Durham, NC: Duke University Press, 2009).

36. Barry Buzan, Ole Waever, and Jaap de Wilde, *Security: A New Framework for Analysis* (Boulder, CO: Lynne Rienner, 1998); Marco Antonio Vieira, "The Securitization of the HIV/AIDS Epidemic as a Norm: A Contribution to Constructivist Scholarship on the Emergence and Diffusion of International Norms," *Brazilian Political Science Review* 1 (2007): 137–81.

37. *Brazil: You Killed My Son: Homicides by the Military Police in the City of Rio de Janeiro* (London: Amnesty International, August 3, 2015), https://www.amnesty.org/en /documents/amr19/2068/2015/en/.

38. Maria Lucia Karam, "Drogas: Além da descriminalização do consumo," LEAP Brasil, September 2015, http://www.leapbrasil.com.br/site/wp-content/uploads/2017/04 /126_Drogas-Recife.pdf; Dan Werb et al., *Effect of Drug Law Enforcement on Drug-Related Violence: Evidence from a Scientific Review* (Vancouver, BC: International Center for Science in Drug Policy, 2010).

39. Maria Lucia Karam, "A Esquerda Punitiva," in *Discursos sediciosos: Crime, direito e sociedade* (Rio de Janeiro: Relume-Dumará, 1996), 1:79–92; Maria Lucia Karam, *Recuperar o desejo da liberdade e conter o poder punitivo* (Rio de Janeiro: Lumen Juris Editora, 2009).

40. The 1988 Constitution—which restored and reaffirmed fundamental rights of equality, freedom, and privacy—was already, paradoxically, moving in that direction. By admitting the possibility of exceptionally tough penal laws, it opened the door for hypercriminalizing infraconstitutional norms in subsequent years. For example, Law Number 8072 of 1990, known as the "Law of Heinous Crimes" (Lei dos crimes hediondos), in-

cluded rape and indecent assault in the list of crimes subject to especially punitive treatment. Before 1990, basic rape was punishable by three to eight years in prison and basic indecent assault was punishable by two to seven years of seclusion. However, Law Number 8072 increased the level of punishment to six to ten years for both crimes, when the minimum penalty (six years) is equivalent to the one applied to basic homicide.

41. See Sonia Corrêa et al., "Internet Regulation and Sexual Politics in Brazil," in *Erotics: Sex, Rights and the Internet*, ed. Jac sm Kee (Melville, SA: Association for Progressive Communications, 2011), 19–65. It is worth observing that while social panics have resulted in a call to raise the age of consent to eighteen, at the same time, there have been calls to lower the age of criminal responsibility to sixteen.

42. Law Number 10224, May 15, 2001 (Braz.), http://www.ilo.org/dyn/natlex /natlex4.detail?p_lang=&p_isn=59235&p_classification=01.04.

43. Article 234-A establishes that, if pregnancy results from any of the crimes under "Crimes against Sexual Dignity," the penalty is augmented 50 percent. The same article also aggravates the knowing transmission of an STD, making the sentence 16.6–50 percent longer. This has been interpreted as criminalization of HIV/AIDS transmission, even though this has not been the focus of the Brazilian AIDS movement.

44. This explains the 2005 suspension of the Brazil–United States Agency for International Development agreement for HIV/AIDS prevention. Both the government and civil society organizations refused to sign the prostitution oath of the U.S. President's Emergency Plan for AIDS Relief.

45. "Promover, intermediar ou facilitar, no território nacional, o recrutamento, o transporte, a transferência, o alojamento ou o acolhimento da pessoa que venha exercer a prostituição." Article 231-A.

46. "Submeter, induzir ou atrair à prostituição ou outra forma de exploração sexual alguém menor de 18 (dezoito) anos ou que, por enfermidade ou deficiência mental, não tem o necessário discernimento para a prática do ato, facilitá-la, impedir ou dificultar que a abandone." Article 218-B.

47. "Incorre nas mesmas penas: I—quem pratica conjunção carnal ou outro ato libidinoso com alguém menor de 18 (dezoito) e maior de 14 (catorze) anos na situação descrita no caput deste artigo; II—o proprietário, o gerente ou o responsável pelo local em que se verifiquem as práticas referidas no caput deste artigo." Article 218-B-I.

48. "Promover ou facilitar o deslocamento de alguém dentro do território nacional para o exercício da prostituição ou outra forma de exploração sexual; agenciar, aliciar, vender ou comprar a pessoa traficada, assim como, tendo conhecimento dessa condição, transportá-la, transferi-la ou alojá-la." Article 231-A.

49. The so-called Nordic model is also gaining a growing number of supporters. This model formally removes penalties from the sellers of sex and focuses on prosecuting buyers.

50. It is also worth noting that trafficking for sexual exploitation was the subject of a 2012 mainstream, primetime soap opera.

51. Law 13344 added Article 149-A to the Brazilian Penal Code, which criminalizes trafficking of persons for several purposes.

52. The provision was proposed by Jean Wyllys of the Party of Socialism and Freedom, an openly gay parliamentarian; the bill is named after Gabriela Leite, a well-known leader of Brazilian sex workers, who died in 2013.

53. Giuseppe Tomasi di Lampedusa, *The Leopard* (New York: Pantheon, 1960), p. 40

54. Luigi Ferrajoli, *Diritto e Ragione: Teoria del garantismo penale* (Rome: Editori Laterza, 2000).

55. Ferrajoli (2000), 446.

56. Ministério da Justiça, *Levantamento Nacional de Informações Penitenciárias INFOPEN—Atualização Junho 2016* (Departamento Penitenciário Nacional, 2017), http://www.justica.gov.br/noticias/ha-726-712-pessoas-presas-no-brasil/relatorio_2016_junho.pdf.

57. "World Prison Brief: Brazil," Institute for Criminal Policy Research, accessed July 26, 2016, http://www.prisonstudies.org/country/brazil.

58. "World Prison Brief."

59. "World Prison Brief."

Chapter 7. The Reach of a Skirt in Southern Africa

This chapter has taken shape over many years, during which time I have benefited enormously from comments and observations made by many of the students I have taught in the "Sexuality and Law" module of the LLM program at the Southern and Eastern African Regional Centre for Women and Law, University of Zimbabwe. The sage advice and intellectual rigor of my coconvener on this module, Sylvia Tamale, have also been key to the chapter's development.

1. Lynette A. Jackson, "Friday the 13th University of Zimbabwe Mini-skirt Saga," *Southern Africa Political and Economic Monthly*, December 1992/January 1993, 25–26.

2. Rudo Gaidzanwa, "The Politics of the Body and the Politics of Control: An Analysis of Class, Gender and Cultural Issues in Student Politics at the University of Zimbabwe," *Zambezia* 20 (1993): 29.

3. Rudo Gaidzanwa suggests twenty female students took part in the demonstration. Gaidzanwa, 30. My personal recollection and field notes put it nearer to forty. We both estimate the number of male students who threatened the women to be over five hundred. Describing the real fear that the women would be lynched or raped, Gaidzanwa agrees that "it is to the credit of the few male students protecting the women that the demonstration ended without a riot." Gaidzanwa, 30.

4. Gaidzanwa, 15.

5. "Who Said Educated People Were Corrupt?," *Daily Gazette*, (Harare, Zimbabwe) December 21, 1992, 6.

6. Shona is the language and culture of the largest ethnic group in Zimbabwe. "Mini Madness," *Herald* (Harare, Zimbabwe) December 21, 1992.

7. E. Hobsbawm and T. Ranger, eds., *The Invention of Tradition* (Cambridge: Cambridge University Press, 1983).

8. "Hwindi's Strip a Woman in Harare," last modified December 18, 2014 at https:// www.facebook.com/ZimHmetro/videos/993217404041633/ and also at https://www .youtube.com/watch?v= nmDCoFvynIo, both accessed on May 5, 2018.

9. "Zimbabwean Women Express Outrage at the Abuse and Stripping of a Woman at a Kombi Rank," posted December 19, 2014, video, 26:11, accessed May 4, 2018, https:// www.youtube.com/watch?v=X_tx4ezqNBY.

10. Msonza, Natasha "Reflections on the Zimbabwe Mini Skirt March: Interview with Winnet Shamuyarira," *Her Zimbabwe: Her Voice, Her Revolution*, December 23, 2014, http://herzimbabwe.co.zw/2014/12/reflections-on-the-zimbabwe-miniskirt-march/, accessed May 5, 2018.

11. "Net Closes in on 'Mini-skirt Touts,'" *Herald* (Harare, Zimbabwe), December 23, 2014, http://www.herald.co.zw/net-closes-in-on-mini-skirt-touts, accessed May 5, 2018.

12. "8 Months for 'Mini-skirt Touts,'" *Herald* (Harare, Zimbabwe), March 27, 2015, http://www.herald.co.zw/8-months-for-mini-skirt-touts, accessed May 5, 2018.

13. "Mini Skirt Touts Jailed Twelve Months Each," *NewsDay* (Harare, Zimbabwe), March 27, 2015, https://www.newsday.co.zw/2015/03/miniskirt-touts-jailed-12-months -each/, accessed May 5, 2018.

14. Uma Narayan, "Contesting Cultures: 'Westernization,' Respect for Cultures, and Third-World Feminists," in *Dislocating Cultures: Identities, Traditions, and Third World Feminists* (New York: Routledge, 1997), 3–39.

15. Majome made these comments outside the courtroom where the accused men were on trial, but they are repeated in Moshenburg, Dan, "In Zimbabwe, Women Say #DontMinimizeMyRights" January 6, 2015, in *Women in and Beyond the Global*, http:// www.womeninandbeyond.org/?p=18103, accessed May 5, 2018.

16. Malawi also patrolled men's clothing and public presentation through law during this period, with rules concerning hair length, earrings, and beards. "Hippies" were prohibited from entering the country.

17. "Malawi Lifts Miniskirt Ban," BBC News, June 14, 2000, https://www.bbc.co.uk /programmes/p03jsbb4; "Malawian Women Protest over 'Trouser Attacks,'" BBC News, January 20, 2012, http://www.bbc.co.uk/news/world-africa-16645594, both URLs accessed May 5, 2018.

18. "Mini-skirt 'Ban' Worries Kenyans," BBC News, March 1, 2004, http://news.bbc.co .uk/1/hi/world/africa/3522391.stm, accessed May 5, 2018.

19. "Anger at SA Woman Trouser 'Ban,'" BBC News, July 26, 2007, http://news.bbc.co .uk/1/hi/world/africa/6917332.stm; "South Africa Miniskirt March in Protest over Attacks," BBC News, February 17, 2012, http://www.bbc.co.uk/news/world-africa-17078304, both accessed May 5, 2018.

20. Sandile Lukhele, "Miniskirts, Tanktops Banned in Swaziland," IOL News, December 24, 2012, http://www.iol.co.za/news/africa/miniskirts-tanktops-banned-in -swaziland-1.1444732#.UvlnSvmTWSo, accessed May 5, 2018.

21. See Amy Fallon, "Will Uganda Really Ban the Miniskirt?," *Guardian*, February 3, 2014, http://www.theguardian.com/fashion/fashion-blog/2014/feb/03/will-uganda-ban -miniskirts, accessed May 5, 2018.

22. David Smith, "Uganda Proposes Ban on Miniskirts in Move against Women's Rights," *Guardian*, April 5, 2013, https://www.theguardian.com/world/2013/apr/05/uganda -ban-miniskirts-womens-right, accessed May 5, 2018.

23. These campaigns were featured on Facebook and Twitter under the hashtag #SaveMiniSkirt.

24. The bill defined pornography as "any cultural practice, radio or television programme, writing, publication, advertisement, broadcast, upload on internet, display, entertainment, music, dance, picture, audio or video recording, show, exhibition or any combination of the preceding that depicts sexual parts of a person such as breasts, thighs, buttocks and genitalia," among other meanings. Offenders could face a 10 million shilling (US$2,700) fine or a maximum of ten years in jail, or both. See Parliament of Uganda, *Official Report of the Proceedings of Parliament, Third Session, Seventh Sitting, Second Meeting*, December 19, 2013, http://klug.cfsites.org/files/hansard_for_the_passing_of _the_anti_pornography_bill_thirdsession7thsittingsecondmeetingdec19th.pdf, accessed May 5, 2018.

25. The Anti-pornography Act of 2014 received presidential assent on February 6, 2014. Section 2 defines pornography as "any representation through publication, exhibition, cinematography, indecent show, information technology or by whatever means, of a person engaged in real or simulated explicit sexual activities or any representation of the sexual parts of a person for primarily sexual excitement." Anti-pornography Act, February 6, 2014 (Uganda), https://www.ulii.org/ug/legislation/act/2014/1/Anti%20Pornography%20Act%20of%202014.pdf, accessed May 5, 2018.

26. "Wolokoso: Lokodo tries to arrest MP wearing miniskirts," *The Observer*, April 19, 2015, http://www.observer.ug/news-headlines/37413-wolokoso-lokodo-tries-to-arrest-mp-wearing-miniskirt, accessed March 7, 2018.

27. "Uganda Miniskirt Ban: Police Stop Protest March," BBC News, February 26, 2014, http://www.bbc.co.uk/news/world-africa-26351087, accessed May 5, 2018.

28. Raymond Mpubani, "Uganda's Anti-pornography Law Targets Media More Than Miniskirts," Wits Journalism, March 9, 2014, http://www.journalism.co.za/blog/ugandas -anti-pornography-law-targets-media-more-than-miniskirts/, accessed May 5, 2018.

29. See Pius Muteekani Katunzi, "Uganda: Why Are Ugandans Killing, Undressing Their Girls?" *Observer* (Kampala, Uganda), February 23, 2014, http://allafrica.com/stories /201402240124.html, accessed May 5, 2018. See also John Campbell, "Uganda: Miniskirt Ban," Nigeria Village Square, March 20, 2014, http://www.social.nigeriavillagesquare .com/articles/uganda-miniskirt-ban.html, accessed May 5, 2018.

30. Anneeth Kaur Hundle, "Of Militarization and Miniskirts: Sovereignty and Sexuality in Urban Uganda," *Los Angeles Review of Books*, December 14, 2015, https:// lareviewofbooks.org/essay/of-militarization-and-miniskirts-sovereignty-and-sexuality -in-urban-uganda, accessed May 5, 2018.

31. Amy Fallon, "Confusion over Uganda's 'Miniskirt Ban' Leads to Public Attacks on Women," *Guardian*, February 28, 2014, http://www.theguardian.com/fashion/fashion -blog/2014/feb/28/uganda-miniskirt-ban-attacks-women, accessed May 5, 2018.

32. Bibi Bakare-Yussuf, "Nudity and Morality: Legislating Women's Bodies and Dress in Nigeria," in *African Sexualities: A Reader*, ed. Sylvia Tamale (Oxford: Pambazuka, 2011), 118.

33. "Indecent Dressing," *Lawyer's Chronicle*, November 19, 2013 (no longer accessible on web but accessed on May 5, 2018), at Samuel Adesina blog "The menace of indecent dressing in our society," http://talebearers.blogspot.co.uk/2012/03/menace-of-indecent -dressing-in-our.html.

34. Ndahi Marama, "Nigeria: 20 Ladies in Mini-skirts Slaughtered in Maiduguri," *Vanguard* (Lagos), November 23, 2012, https://www.vanguardngr.com/2012/11/20-ladies -in-mini-skirts-slaughtered-in-maiduguri/ accessed May 5, 2018.

35. Hamza Idris, "Nigeria: JTF Says Murder of 20 Women in Maiduguri Not True," *Daily Trust* (Abuja, Nigeria), November 25, 2012, http://allafrica.com/stories/201211250277 .html, accessed May 5, 2018.

36. Isaac Pinielo, "Woman Stripped for Wearing Miniskirt," Palapye.com, July 27, 2010, http://palapye.wordpress.com/2010/07/27/woman-stripped-for-wearing-miniskirt/, accessed May 5, 2018.

37. Magreth Nunuhe, "Namibia: Mini-skirt Firestorm Scorches Ndeitunga," *New Era* (Windhoek, Namibia), February 21, 2013, http://allafrica.com/stories/201302210720 .html, accessed May 5, 2018.

38. For a detailed discussion of Zambia, see Karen Tranberg Hansen, "Dressing Dangerously: Miniskirts, Gender Relations and Sexuality in Zambia," in *Fashioning Africa: Power and the Politics of Dress*, ed. Jean Allman (Bloomington: Indiana University Press, 2004), 166–85.

39. Steve Inskeep, "Miniskirt Ban in Chile Cut Short after Protests," NPR, August 19, 2010, http://www.npr.org/templates/story/story.php?storyId=129295367, accessed May 5, 2018.

40. Jessica Misener, "Indonesia Declares Miniskirts 'Pornographic,' Seeks to Ban Them," *Huffington Post*, March 29, 2012, http://www.huffingtonpost.com/2012/03/29 /indonesia-miniskirts-ban_n_1388653.html, accessed May 5, 2018.

41. Brian Ashcraft, "Why Mini-skirts Could Become Illegal in South Korea," Kotaku, March 22, 2013, http://kotaku.com/5991862/why-mini-skirts-could-become -illegal-in-south-korea, accessed May 5, 2018.

42. "Italian Seaside Town Planning Miniskirt Ban," BBC News, October 20, 2010, http://www.bbc.co.uk/news/world-europe-11617091, accessed May 5, 2018.

43. Jay Diamond and Ellen Diamond, *The World of Fashion* (New York: Fairchild, 2006).

44. Hildi Hendrikson, *Clothing and Difference: Embodied Identities in Colonial and Post-colonial Africa* (Durham, NC: Duke University Press, 1996), 2.

45. See Stuart Hall and Tony Jefferson, *Resistance through Rituals: Youth Subcultures in Post-war Britain* (London: Routledge, 1993); and Dick Hebdige, *Subculture: The Meaning of Style* (London: Methuen, 1979).

46. Judith Butler, *Gender Trouble: Feminism and Subversion of Identity* (New York: Routledge, 1990).

47. For statistics reflecting the widespread violence faced by trans individuals, see "IDAHOT 2016—Trans Murder Monitoring Update," Trans Respect versus Transphobia

Worldwide, May 12, 2016, http://transrespect.org/en/idahot-2016-tmm-update/, accessed May 5, 2018.

48. Caroline Evans and Minna Thornton, *Women and Fashion: A New Look* (London: Quartet Books, 1989), 2.

49. Ratna Kapur, *Erotic Justice: Law and the New Politics of Postcolonialism* (London: Glasshouse, 2005), 51.

50. Butler, *Gender Trouble*, 164.

51. For a succinct analysis and articulation of the regional hegemonic structures of sexuality and gender, see Kapano Ratele, "Male Sexualities and Masculinities," in Tamale, *African Sexualities*, 399–420.

52. In 2005 in the United Kingdom, more than a quarter (26 percent) of those asked said that they thought a woman was partially or totally responsible for being raped if she was wearing sexy or revealing clothing. ICM Research, *Sexual Assault Research Summary Report* (Amnesty International United Kingdom, 2005). For a discussion of the United States, see Rebecca M. Hayes-Smith and Lora M. Levett, "Student Perceptions of Sexual Assault Resources and Prevalence of Rape Myth Attitudes," *Feminist Criminology* 5 (2010): 335–54.

53. Kevin Howells et al., "Perceptions of Rape in a British Sample: Effects of Relationship, Victim Status, Sex, and Attitudes to Women," *British Journal of Social Psychology* 23 (1984): 35–40. See also Louise Ellison and Vanessa E. Munroe, "Reacting to Rape: Exploring Mock Jurors' Assessments of Complainant Credibility," *British Journal of Criminology* 49 (2009): 202–19.

54. "Kenyan Women Protest at 'Trouser Police,'" BBC News, February 3, 2003, http://news.bbc.co.uk/1/hi/world/africa/2721249.stm, accessed May 5, 2018.

55. Quoted in "After Attacks, Malawi Prez Retracts Negative View of Women in Pants," *Key Newsjournal* (Lexington, KY), January 25, 2012, http://keyconversationsradio.com/after-attacks-malawi-prez-retracts-negative-view-of-women-in-pants/, accessed May 5, 2018.

56. "South Africa Mini-skirt March in Protest over Attacks," BBC News, February 17, 2012, http://www.bbc.co.uk/news/world-africa-17078304, accessed May 5, 2018.

57. I am indebted to Dean Spade for this phrase. Dean Spade, "Trans Politics on a Neo-liberal Landscape" (keynote address, Gender Futures Conference, Centre for Law Gender and Sexuality, Westminster University, London, April 3–4, 2009).

58. Tim Burke, *Lifebuoy Men, Lux Women: Commodification, Consumption and Cleanliness in Modern Zimbabwe* (Durham, NC: Duke University Press, 1996).

59. Rachel Holmes, *The Hottentot Venus* (London: Bloomsbury, 2007), 70, 184–86; Sander L. Gilman, *Difference and Pathology: Stereotypes of Sexuality, Race, and Madness* (Ithaca, NY: Cornell University Press, 1985).

60. Oliver Phillips, "(Dis)Continuities of Custom in Zimbabwe and South Africa: The Implications for Gendered and Sexual Rights," *Health and Human Rights* 7 (2004): 82–113.

61. Oliver Phillips, "The 'Perils' of Sex and the Panics of Race: The Dangers of Interracial Sex in Southern Rhodesia," in Tamale, *African Sexualities*, 101–15. See also Diana Jeater, *Marriage, Perversion and Power: The Construction of Moral Discourse in Southern*

Rhodesia, 1894–1930 (Oxford: Clarendon, 1993); Nancy Folbre, "Patriarchal Social Formations in Zimbabwe," in *Patriarchy and Class: African Women in the Home and the Workforce*, ed. Sharon B. Stichter and Jane L. Parpart (Boulder, CO: Westview, 1988), 68; and Elizabeth Schmidt, *Peasants, Traders, and Wives: Shona Women in the History of Zimbabwe, 1870–1939* (Portsmouth, NH: Heinemann Educational Books, 1992), 633–34. Under the Indecency Suppression Ordinance of 1916, any hint of sexual contact between black men and white women was strictly outlawed, mainly as a result of the panic existing around "black peril" (the rape of white women by black men) and also "white peril" (sexual advances by white women on black men or overfamiliarity between the two). There was never any legislation outlawing the more common sexual relations between black women and white men, despite the continuous protestations of both white women's organizations and black men. See also Dane Kennedy, *Islands of White: Settler Society and Culture in Kenya and Southern Rhodesia, 1890–1939* (Durham, NC: Duke University Press, 1987), 12–47; John Pape, "Black and White: The 'Perils of Sex' in Colonial Zimbabwe," *Journal of Southern African Studies* 16 (1990): 699–720; and Hansen, Karen T. (1989), *Distant Companions: Servants and Employers in Zambia 1900–1985* Cornell University Press: London, pp. 100–104.

62. Phillips, "(Dis)Continuities of Custom."

63. Jeater, *Marriage, Perversion and Power*, 119–40.

64. Jeater, 119–40.

65. Jeater, 119–40.

66. Amy Kaler, *Running after Pills: Politics, Gender, and Contraception in Colonial Zimbabwe* (Portsmouth, NH: Heinemann Educational Books, 2003), 2.

67. Kaler, 110.

68. This might help the reader understand why Robert Mugabe, in one of his earliest but most widely reported quotes relating to homosexuality, spoke (in Shona) of gay people as "worse than dogs and pigs." Phillips, "(Dis)Continuities of Custom." p. 96.

69. Michel Foucault, *The History of Sexuality: An Introduction* (London: Peregrine, 1978), 139–41.

70. Michel Foucault, *Discipline and Punish: The Birth of the Prison* (London: Peregrine, 1979), 184.

71. Foucault, *Discipline and Punish*, 128.

72. Foucault, *Discipline and Punish*, 128–129.

73. The similar "indiscipline" of women and their "neglect of traditional roles" have been used by some Nigerian men to explain the economic crisis that led to a coup d'état. Carolyne Dennis, "Women and the State in Nigeria: The Case of the Federal Military Government 1984–85," in *Women, State, and Ideology: Studies from Africa and Asia*, ed. Haleh Afshar (London: Macmillan, 1987), 13–27.

74. In a study of urban women, Olivia Muchena found that 50 percent of women were "housewives, unemployed"; 37 percent were involved in the informal sector; and 13 percent were in formal employment. Joyce L. Kazembe, "The Women Issue," in *Zimbabwe: The Political Economy of Transition, 1980–1986*, ed. Ibbo Mandaza (Harare, Zimbabwe: Jongwe, 1987), 397. However, since the economic crisis of 2005–8, 90 percent of men

and women are said to be unemployed. Dependence on the informal sector is estimated to have increased significantly, and it was measured to contribute over 50 percent of the GDP in 2000. Nelson Chenga, "Informal Sector: The Major Challenge," *Financial Gazette* (Harare, Zimbabwe), September 26, 2013, http://www.financialgazette.co.zw/informal-sector-the-major-challenge/, accessed May 5, 2018.

75. Susie M. Jacobs and Tracey Howard, "Women in Zimbabwe: Stated Policy and State Action," in Afshar, *Women, State, and Ideology*, 41.

76. Gay W. Seidman, "Women in Zimbabwe: Post-independence Struggles," *Feminist Studies* 10 (1984): 419.

77. Seidman, 432.

78. Leroy Vail, ed., *The Creation of Tribalism in Southern Africa* (Berkeley: University of California Press, 1989), 1–19.

79. Rumbidzai Dube, *Till Death Do Us Part? Marriage in Zimbabwe* (Harare, Zimbabwe: Research and Advocacy Unit, 2013), http://researchandadvocacyunit.org/system/files/Marriage%20In%20Zimbabwe.pdf, accessed May 5, 2018.

80. Jackson, "Friday the 13th," 26.

81. SRB may also refer to "severe rural background." Gaidzanwa, "Politics of the Body."

82. The women's protest was framed as civil rights: the right to dress as they choose, the right to walk where they choose, the right to control their own lives, etc. The women also questioned the men's definition of culture.

83. Gaidzanwa, "Politics of the Body," 23.

84. Gaidzanwa, 23.

85. P. M. Toriro, "Culture: The 'Nose Brigades' and 'Uncivilised' Gulf," *University of Zimbabwe Focus Student Magazine* 2 (1992): 9.

86. Alice M. Miller, "Sexuality, Violence Against Women, and Human Rights: Women Make Demands and Ladies Get Protection," *Health and Human Rights* 7 (2004): 23.

87. Zethu Matebeni, "Intimacy, Queerness, Race," *Cultural Studies* 27 (2013): 405.

88. John L. Comaroff, "The Discourse of Rights in Colonial South Africa: Subjectivity, Sovereignty, Modernity," in *Identities, Politics, and Rights*, ed. Austin Sarat and Thomas R. Kearns (Ann Arbor: University of Michigan Press, 1997), 193–236.

89. Dean Spade, "Law as Tactics," *Columbia Journal of Gender and Law* 21 (2011): 442.

Chapter 8. Abortion as Treason

1. By *manners* I mean practices, but I am also alluding to the process by which our practices are "civilized" by social expectations. See Norbert Elias, *The Civilizing Process: The History of Manners* (New York: Urizen Books, 1978).

2. See Reva Siegel and Linda Greenhouse, *Before Roe: Voices That Shaped the Abortion Debate* (New York: Kaplan, 2011).

3. See Melissa Murray, "Strange Bedfellows: Criminal Law, Family Law, and the Legal Construction of Intimate Life," *Iowa Law Review* 94 (2008): 1253–1313. For nineteenth- and twentieth-century literature, see Nathaniel Hawthorne's *The Scarlet Letter*, Leo Tolstoy's *Anna Karenina*, and E. M. Forster's *Howards End*.

4. States' interests in their populations are expressed in myriad ways—through, for example, tax codes, immigration laws, contraception subsidies, and family bonuses. At times, states restrict population size, using force when incentives fail to work, as in India in the mid-1970s and China in the late twentieth century.

5. Loi du 15 février 1942 relative à la répression de l'avortement, *Bulletin annoté des lois et décrets*, Journal Officiel de la République Française, Mar. 7, 1942, p. 53. This law technically was an executive decree issued by Marshal Philippe Petain without any legislative debate or deliberation.

6. George Fletcher, "The Case for Treason," *Maryland Law Review* 41 (1982): 194.

7. Patrick Devlin, *The Enforcement of Morals* (Oxford: Oxford University Press, 1965), 13–14.

8. Fatema Mernissi, "Femininity as Subversion: Reflection on the Muslim Concept of Nushuz," in *Speaking of Faith: Global Perspectives on Women, Religion, and Social Change*, ed. Diana L. Eck and Devaki Jain (Philadelphia: New Society, 1987), 464–476.

9. Giraud's is the most discussed case with respect to the 300 law. See Michèle Bordeaux, *La victoire de la famille dans la France défaite: Vichy 1940–1944* (Paris: Flammarion, 2002); Francine Muel-Dreyfus, *Vichy et l'éternel féminin* (Paris: Le Seuil, 1996). Her case was inspiration for the 1988 film *The Story of Women*, starring Isabelle Huppert. Only one other person, Mr. Désiré P., fared similarly: having been convicted of three instances of abortion, he too was beheaded in 1943. See Miranda Pollard, "Vichy and Abortion: Policing the Body and the New Moral Order in Everyday Life," in *France at War: Vichy and the Historians*, ed. Sarah Fishman et al. (Oxford: Berg, 2000), 192; and Marc Boninchi, *Vichy et l'ordre moral* (Paris: Presses Universitaires de France, 2005), 290.

10. The Tribunal d'État, a court of "exception" established in 1942 and abolished in 1944, heard thirty-nine abortion cases, sentencing fourteen to life imprisonment and the others to terms up to twenty years, many at hard labor and with steep fines. Most abortion cases—approximately eleven thousand in this time period—were still heard in the ordinary courts. Cyril Olivier, *Le vice ou la vertu: Vichy et les politiques de la sexualité* (Toulouse: Presses Universitaires du Mirail, 2005), 152–57.

11. Boninchi, *Vichy et l'ordre moral*, 286.

12. Robert O. Paxton, *Vichy France: Old Guard and New Order, 1940–1944* (New York: Columbia University Press, 2001); Miranda Pollard, *Reign of Virtue: Mobilizing Gender in Vichy France* (Chicago: University of Chicago Press, 1998).

13. Gladys M. Kammerer, "The Political Theory of Vichy," *Journal of Politics* 5 (1943): 418–19.

14. For example, see Simon Kitson, "From Enthusiasm to Disenchantment: The French Police and the Vichy Regime, 1940–1944," *Contemporary European History* 11 (2002): 371–90.

15. See Pollard, *Reign of Virtue*; Sarah Fishman, "Waiting for the Captive Sons of France: Prisoner of War Wives 1940–1945," in *Behind the Lines: Gender and the Two World Wars*, ed. Margaret R. Higonnet et al. (New Haven, CT: Yale University Press, 1987), 182–93; and Christine Bard et al., *Femmes et justice pénale, XIXe et XXe siècles* (Rennes, France: University of Rennes, 2002).

16. Fabrice Cahen, "De l'"efficacité' des politiques publiques: La lutte contre l'avortement 'criminel' en France, 1890–1950, " *Revue d'histoire moderne et contemporaine* 58 (2011): 90–117.

17. Alain Bancaud, "La magistrature et la répression politique de Vichy ou l'histoire d'un demi-échec," *Droit et société* 34 (1996): 557–74. This court was established by the law of September 7, 1941, to try members of the Resistance, those who conducted black-market activity, and those who participated in the disruption of war materiel and its resupply; it also had jurisdiction over ordinary common-law crimes, extended to cover abortion in March 7, 1942. Cyril Olivier, "Du 'crime contre la race': L'avortement dans la France de la Révolution Nationale," in Bard et al., *Femmes et justice*, 256. These tribunals operated in secret without jury or right of appeal. Pollard, *Reign of Virtue*, 178. The Tribunaux Correctionnels shared concurrent jurisdiction with the Tribunal d'État.

18. Boninchi, *Vichy et l'ordre moral*, 273; Olivier, "Du 'crime contre la race,'" 257.

19. See Boninchi, *Vichy et l'ordre moral*; Olivier, "Du 'crime contre la race'"; and Olivier, *Le vice ou la vertu*, 191–95. The Tribunal d'État had two jurisdictions: Paris covered crimes in the occupied zone, and Lyons in Vichy-administered France. Paris issued the two capital abortion sentences.

20. Boninchi, *Vichy et l'ordre moral*, 286. In its twenty-two months of existence, fewer than fifty cases came before the Tribunal d'État's sections, which amounts to 0.6 percent of all abortion cases tried before the Tribunaux Correctionnels. Boninchi stresses that fewer than 1 percent of all abortions were ever prosecuted: one out of seventeen thousand acts, which he calls "negligible." Boninchi, 287.

21. Boninchi, 282.

22. Boninchi, 286.

23. I rely on Pollard's "Vichy and Abortion" for these accounts (193–94).

24. Regarding female knowledge networks surrounding contraceptive use, see Elinor A. Accampo, "The Gendered Nature of Contraception in France: Neo-Malthusianism, 1900–1920," *Journal of Interdisciplinary History* 34 (2003): 235–62.

25. See Cheryl Koos, "'On les aura!': The Gendered Politics of Abortion and the Alliance Nationale Contre la Depopulation, 1938–1944," *Modern and Contemporary France* 7 (1999): 21–33. Giraud apparently rented out her children's bedrooms to prostitutes.

26. Cherbourg was a seaport and the home to a naval base, likely with a legally regulated sex trade, and during the war, such trade might have been one of the few expanding economic opportunities. There is no charge that Giraud ran a *maison tolèrée* without official registration, which would have been considered living off the avails of prostitution.

27. See George Mosse's work on respectability, "Nationalism and Respectability: Normal and Abnormal Sexuality in the Nineteenth Century," *Journal of Contemporary History* 17 (1982): 221–46.

28. There might be lingering anxiety about the sexual and gender "disorder" in renting rooms to single women unsupervised by family. See Rachel G. Fuchs and Leslie Page Moch, "Pregnant, Single, and Far from Home: Migrant Women in Nineteenth-Century Paris," *American Historical Review* (1990): 1007–31.

29. For a view of life in occupied Cherbourg, see Gustave Dumas, "Documents from Occupied France," *Thought* 16 (1941): 132–41.

30. Pollard, "Vichy and Abortion," 196n11.

31. Pollard, 196.

32. Pollard, 196.

33. From Pollard we learn of much post hoc regret—a father who disapproved of his daughter's fiancé (and pregnancy) but never imagined she would get an abortion, or an aunt who accompanied her niece to the abortion, only to state later that she should have stopped it. See Pollard, 196–98.

34. Pollard, 199.

35. Pollard, 201. See also Olivier, "Du 'crime contre la race,'" 256, noting that abortion prosecutions seemed more concerned with repressing *coquetterie* (flirtation or loose morals) than "feminism" (political posturing toward equality).

36. See Boninchi, *Vichy et l'ordre moral*; and Olivier, *Le vice ou la vertu*.

37. No one has modeled the number of live births that should have been expected during these four years against the number recorded, which would indicate the scale of abortion as a practice. Olivier, in "Du 'crime contre la race'" (256), mentions that many of the antiabortion commentators estimated that between five hundred thousand and one million abortions took place each year during the decade of the 1930s. There is good reason to discount these figures' accuracy.

38. See Boninchi, *Vichy et l'ordre moral*, 290. Also see Olivier, *Le vice ou la vertu*, 183, which addresses how the judiciary under Vichy negotiated the tension between exemplary justice (crimes prosecuted before the Tribunal d'État) and ordinary justice.

39. Olivier, "Du 'crime contre la race,'" 257.

40. For some classic literature on modernization in France, see Eugen Weber, *Peasants into Frenchmen: The Modernization of Rural France, 1870–1914* (Stanford, CA: Stanford University Press, 1976); and Joan W. Scott and Louise A. Tilly, "Women's Work and the Family in Nineteenth-Century Europe," *Comparative Studies in Society and History* 17 (1975): 36–64. In terms of European colonies (including those in Latin America), decolonization, and postcolonial thought, there is a vast literature critical of modernization theory and not easily summarized. For example, see Fernando Coronil, *Latin American Postcolonial Studies and Global Decolonization*, ed. Neil Lazarus (Cambridge: Cambridge University Press, 2004); and Frederick Cooper, *Colonialism in Question: Theory, Knowledge, History* (Berkeley: University of California Press, 2005).

41. For discussions of the criminalization of abortion and the professionalization of medicine, see Irving Loudon, *Death in Childbirth: An International Study of Maternal Care and Maternal Mortality, 1800–1950* (Oxford: Oxford University Press, 1992); and Mindy Jane Roseman, "Birthing the Republic: Midwives, Medicine, and Morality in France, 1890 to 1920" (PhD diss., Columbia University, 1999). For information about biomedicine and public health interventions in service of colonization and empire, see Megan Vaughan, *Curing Their Ills: Colonial Power and African Illness* (Stanford, CA: Stanford University Press, 1991).

42. Matthew Ramsey, "Public Health in France," in *The History of Public Health and the Modern State*, ed. Dorothy Porter (Amsterdam: Editions Rodopi, 1994), 45–118.

43. Alice M. Miller, "Sexual but not Reproductive: Exploring the Junction and Disjunction of Sexual and Reproductive Rights," *Health and Human Rights* (2000): 68–109; Lynn P. Freedman and Stephen L. Isaacs, "Human Rights and Reproductive Choice," *Studies in Family Planning* 24 (1993): 18–30.

44. Angus McLaren, *Sexuality and Social Order: The Debate over the Fertility of Women and Workers in France, 1770–1920* (Teaneck, NJ: Homes and Meier, 1983), 154. For the connection with nationalism, see Mosse, "Nationalism and Respectability"; Mary Russo, Doris Sommer, and Patricia Yaeger, eds., *Nationalisms and Sexualities* (New York: Routledge, 1992); and Nira Yuval-Davis, *Gender and Nation* (London: Sage, 1997).

45. Mosse, "Nationalism and Respectability," 222.

46. Thomas W. Laqueur, *Solitary Sex: A Cultural History of Masturbation* (New York: Zone Books, 2003).

47. Karen Offen, "Depopulation, Nationalism and Feminism in Fin-de-Siècle France," *American Historical Review* 89 (1984): 648–76.

48. Jack D. Ellis, *The Physician-Legislators of France: Medicine and Politics in the Early Third Republic, 1870–1914* (Cambridge: Cambridge University Press, 1990).

49. Marie-Monique Huss, "Pronatalism in the Inter-war Period in France," *Journal of Contemporary History* 25 (1990): 39–68. See also Roseman, "Birthing the Republic," 3–6; and Catherine Rollet-Echalier, *La politique à l'égard de la petite enface sous la IIIème République* (Paris: Presses Universitaires France, 1990).

50. Paul V. Dutton, *Origins of the French Welfare State: The Struggle for Social Reform in France, 1914–1947* (Cambridge: Cambridge University Press, 2002), 22.

51. Mary Louise Roberts, *Civilization without Sexes: Reconstructing Gender in Postwar France, 1917–1927*, (Chicago: University of Chicago Press, 1994), 94. Much of the dithering over the bill had to do with medical confidentiality, which eventually was settled.

52. Loi réprimant la provocation à l'avortement et la propagande anticonceptionnelle, Journal Officiel de la République Française, Aug. 1, 1920.

53. The opposition came from some socialist members who believed that the misery of working-class families was compounded by having too many children to support.

54. See Loi du 27 mars 1923, dite "loi BARTHOU," portant modification de l'article 317 du Code pénal.

55. Cahen, "De l'"efficacité' des politiques publiques," 99.

56. Décret-loi du 29 juillet 1939 relatif à la famille et à la natalité française, Journal Officiel de la République Française, July 30, 1939, p. 9607. See Laura Levine Frader, *Breadwinners and Citizens: Gender in the Making of the French Social Model* (Durham, NC: Duke University Press, 2008), 20–21.

57. Boninchi, *Vichy et l'ordre moral*, 275. Additional provisions included tighter regulation and supervision of abortifacients and devices used to induce miscarriages.

58. Boninchi, 277. Apparently, many criminal cases fell apart when medical experts could not establish that a woman had been pregnant when the abortion took place—she

might be in the process of miscarrying or have already miscarried; the judge would have to acquit, as the act would be a *délit impossible*.

59. Boninchi, 278. Acquittals dropped from about 15 percent to 10 percent. The Family Code was essentially in force from the time of its adoption through Vichy and into the Fourth Republic.

60. Olivier, "Du 'crime contre la race,'" 255. Olivier notes that in the fall of 1941, the Vichy government began to revise the Third Republic's laws.

61. Olivier, 255, mentioning the overlap and continuity of personnel.

62. Pollard, *Reign of Virtue*, 174 ("de nature à nuire au people Français").

63. Joel Feinberg, "The Expressive Function of Punishment," in *Why Punish? How Much? A Reader on Punishment*, ed. Michael Tonry (Oxford: Oxford University Press, 2011), 111–25. One might suppose that setting a harsh example was intended as deterrence, but news of Giraud's crime and execution barely circulated.

64. By this, I mean states with plural moral and religious tensions that may (or may not) track socioeconomically yet are channeled into political aims. In the United States, we see this in states such as Texas, Pennsylvania, Missouri, etc., where urban populations tend to vote for liberal, noncriminal abortion positions and rural, religious or conservative (antimodern) populations tend toward criminal restrictions. See Michele Dillon and Sarah Savage, *Values and Religion in Rural America: Attitudes toward Abortion and Same-Sex Relations* (Durham, NH: University of New Hampshire, 2006). Such generalizations might be ventured for Nicaragua, El Salvador, and parts of Mexico. See Bonnie Shepard, "The 'Double Discourse' on Sexual and Reproductive Rights in Latin America: The Chasm between Public Policy and Private Actions," *Health and Human Rights* (2000): 110–43.

65. See Cyril Olivier, "Les couples illégitimes dans la France de Vichy et la répression sexuée de l'infidélité (1940–1944)," *Crime, Histoire et Sociétés* 9 (2005): 99–123. It should be noted that in this period, adultery, fornication, sex work, and homosexuality were recriminalized. Marc Boninchi's *Vichy et l'ordre moral* covers this extensively.

66. For a similar argument, see Miranda Pollard, "A Story of Women? Vichy and the Politics of Abortion, 1942–44," in *Reign of Virtue*, 174–94. Conversely, by executing Giraud, Vichy's failure to instill its ideology in the population—as represented by Giraud—was also eliminated.

67. For a current list, see "2018 World's Abortion Laws," Center for Reproductive Rights, accessed April 26, 2018, http://worldabortionlaws.com.

68. See Jocelyn Viterna and Jose Santos Guardado Bautista, "Independent Analysis of Systemic Gender Discrimination in El Salvador Judicial Process against 17 Women Accused of Aggravated Homicide against Their Newborns," November 17, 2014, unpublished White Paper, available at https://scholar.harvard.edu/files/viterna/files/final_report_english_pdf.pdf.

69. Douglas Husak, *Overcriminalization* (Oxford: Oxford University Press, 2009).

70. Erving Goffman, *Stigma: Notes on the Management of Spoiled Identity* (New York: Simon and Schuster, 2009).

71. See especially J. Mann et al., "Health and Human Rights," *Journal of Health and Human Rights* 1 (1994): 6–23.

72. A. Norris et al., "Abortion Stigma: A Reconceptualization of Constituents, Causes, and Consequences," *Women's Health Issues* 21 (2011): 49–54.

73. Attention to the sexual practices and gender expressions of stigmatized populations distracts citizens from the mismanagement, corruption, and economic inequality that many face in the very countries developing antihomosexuality laws and criminalizing abortion.

74. See, for example, Christina Zampas and Jaime Todd-Gher, "Abortion as a Human Right—International and Regional Standards," *Human Rights Law Review* 8 (2008): 249–94; *Bringing Rights to Bear: Preventing Maternal Mortality and Ensuring Safe Pregnancy* (New York: Center for Reproductive Rights, October 2008). International human rights mechanisms, such as the UN Human Rights Committee, and nations, such as Chile and Ireland, are inclined to recognize that absolute criminal prohibitions of abortion violate human rights.

75. Simone Cusack and Rebecca Cook, "Stereotyping Women in the Health Sector: Lessons from CEDAW," *Journal of Civil Rights and Social Justice* 16 (2010): 47–78.

76. This is, of course, precisely the bone of contention.

77. See Rebecca Cook, "Stigmatized Meanings of Criminal Abortion Law" in Abortion Law in Transnational Perspective: Cases and Controversies, ed. Rebecca J. Cook, Joanna N. Erdman, and Bernard M. Dickens (University of Pennsylvania Press, 2014), 347–369.

Chapter 9. Wanja Muguongo in Conversation with Alice M. Miller

1. "Welcome," UHAI EASHRI, accessed June 27, 2016, http://www.uhai-eashri.org.

2. British colonialism first imported antihomosexual laws to Africa. Today, American evangelical groups support recent legislation, supplying money, missionaries, and language based on the notion that homosexuality poses a threat to family units. Daniel Englander, "Protecting the Human Rights of LGBT People in Uganda in the Wake of Uganda's 'Anti Homosexuality Bill, 2009,'" *Emory International Law Review* 25 (2011): 1270. For instance, in 2012, the Center for Constitutional Rights filed a lawsuit, under the Alien Tort Statute, against Scott Lively, the U.S.-based president of Abiding Truth Ministries, for his involvement in antihomosexual efforts in Uganda. On June 5, 2017, a U.S. federal court dismissed the lawsuit brought by Sexual Minorities Uganda (SMUG) on narrow technical (jurisdictional) grounds, ruling that although evidence supported SMUG's claims that Lively's actions were not only bigoted but sought to deprive them of fundamental rights, the court did not have the power to hear the claims, because of a 2013 Supreme Court ruling (*Kiobel v. Royal Dutch Shell*) that limited the extraterritorial reach of the Alien Tort Statute, under which SMUG brought its claim. Judge Michael Ponsor of the U.S. district court in Springfield, Massachusetts, wrote that no one should doubt that the "defendant's actions in aiding and abetting efforts to demonize, intimidate, and injure LGBTI people in Uganda constitute violations of international law. They do." At time of writing, the case is still possibly open, because, despite winning on the summary dismissal, Lively's lawyers filed on June 8, 2017, a notice of appeal to call for review of what they call "extraneous but prejudicial language." For more information on the timeline of the case, see "Sexual Minorities Uganda v. Scott Lively," Center for Constitutional Rights,

accessed June 28, 2016, http://ccrjustice.org/LGBTUganda/; and, for more on the recent appeal, see *Sexual Minorities Uganda v. Scott Lively*, No. 3:12-cv-30051-MAP (D.M.A. June 8, 2017). See also James D. Wilets, "From Divergence to Convergence? A Comparative and International Law Analysis of LGBTI Rights in the Context of Race and Post-colonialism," *Duke Journal of Comparative and International Law* 21 (2011): 631–85; "This Alien Legacy: The Origins of 'Sodomy' Laws in British Colonialism," Human Rights Watch, December 17, 2008, http://www.hrw.org/reports/2008/12/17/alien-legacy-0; and Tiffany M. Lebrón, "'Death to Gays!' Uganda's 'One Step Forward, One Step Back' Approach to Human Rights," *Buffalo Human Rights Law Review* 17 (2011): 173–206.

3. Anti-homosexuality Act, 2014 (Uganda).

4. Anti-pornography Act, 2014 (Uganda).

5. "Uganda Miniskirt Ban: Police Stop Protest March," BBC News, February 26, 2014, http://www.bbc.com/news/world-africa-26351087.

6. Emmanuel Muga, "Dar Plans to Introduce Tougher Gay Bill," *East African* (Nairobi, Kenya), March 29, 2014, http://www.theeastafrican.co.ke/news/Dar-plans-to-introduce-tougher-anti-gay-Bill--/-/2558/2262374/-/iq7xix/-/index.html; Oliver Mathenge, "New Kenya Bill Wants Gays Stoned in Public," *Star* (Nairobi, Kenya), August 12, 2014, http://www.the-star.co.ke/news/2014/08/12/new-kenya-bill-wants-gays-stoned-in-public_c986305.

7. Bernard Mwinzi, "Jittery as Tanzania Tightens Grip on Its Civil Society ahead of General Elections," *Daily Nation* (Nairobi, Kenya), November 13, 2014, http://www.nation.co.ke/lifestyle/DN2/Tanzania-civil-society-General-Elections/-/957860/2521646/-/beqlwkz/-/index.html.

8. Colin Stewart, "Challenge to Ugandan Anti-gay Law Seeks Regional Impact," *Erasing 76 Crimes* (blog), November 11, 2014, http://76crimes.com/2014/11/11/challenge-to-ugandan-anti-gay-law-seeks-regional-impact/.

9. Andiah Kisia and Milka Wahu, *A People Condemned: The Human Rights Status of Lesbians, Gays, Bisexual, Transgender and Intersex Persons in East Africa, 2009–2010* (Nairobi, Kenya: UHAI EASHRI, 2010), http://www.uhai-eashri.org/ENG/resources?4:uhai-a-people-condemned.

10. UHAI EASHRI, *Why Must I Cry? Sadness and Laughter of the LGBTI Community in East Africa* (Nairobi, Kenya: UHAI EASHRI, 2013), 29, http://www.uhai-eashri.org/ENG/resources?download=20:why-must-i-cry.

11. Quoted in UHAI EASHRI, 18.

12. UHAI EASHRI, 18.

13. See, for instance, Jacob Rukweza, "Is Homosexuality Really 'UnAfrican'?," *Pabazuka News*, March 23, 2006, http://www.pambazuka.org/governance/homosexuality-really-%E2%80%9Cunafrican%E2%80%9D.

14. "Rwanda: New Law Criminalizing Same-Sex Conduct Proposed," OutRight Action International, January 23, 2007, https://www.outrightinternational.org/content/rwanda-new-law-criminalizing-same-sex-conduct-proposed.

15. UHAI EASHRI, *Why Must I Cry?*, 11.

16. Alliance for a Safe and Diverse DC, *Move Along: Policing Sex Work in Washington, D.C.* (Washington, DC: Different Avenues, 2008), http://dctranscoalition.files .wordpress.com/2010/05/movealongreport.pdf.

17. UHAI EASHRI, *Why Must I Cry?*, 21.

18. Daughtie Ogutu, presentation at Changing Faces, Changing Spaces Conference, May 2013, Naivasha, Kenya.

19. Vagrancy laws have been used more often than sodomy statutes to criminalize perceived homosexual behavior. For instance, in the United States, "because of problems of proof, sodomy laws were less popular in policing homosexuals than solicitation, vagrancy, and disorderly conduct laws." William N. Eskridge Jr., "Privacy Jurisprudence and the Apartheid of the Closet, 1946–1961," *Florida State University Law Review* 24 (1997): 779. See also William N. Eskridge Jr., "Challenging the Apartheid of the Closet: Establishing Conditions for Lesbian and Gay Intimacy, Nomos, and Citizenship, 1961–1981," *Hofstra Law Review* 25 (1997): 817–970. In Africa, vagrancy laws were first used during the colonial period to "allow the state to arrest people on the presumption of sodomy, without proof of an actual act." Alok Gupta, "This Alien Legacy: The Origins of 'Sodomy' Laws in British Colonialism," Human Rights Watch, December 17, 2008, http://www.hrw .org/reports/2008/12/17/alien-legacy-0.

20. Penal Code art. 153, "Male person living on earnings of prostitution or soliciting" (2008) (Kenya), http://www.kenyalaw.org/kenyalaw/klr_app/frames.php.

21. Human Rights Awareness and Promotion Forum, "Summary on the Use of Vagrancy Offences Vis à Vis Other Offences between the Period January 2011–September 2014" (on file with authors).

22. Colin Stewart, "2 LGBTI Defendants Win Their Freedom in Uganda," *Erasing 76 Crimes* (blog), October 22, 2014, https://76crimes.com/2014/10/22/2-lgbti-defendants -win-their-freedom-in-uganda/; Colin Stewart, "Ugandan Court Dismisses Case against Activist Sam Ganafa," *Erasing 76 Crimes* (blog), October 28, 2014, https:// 76crimes.com/2014/10/28/ugandan-court-dismisses-case-against-activist-sam-ganafa/.

23. UHAI EASHRI, *Why Must I Cry?*, 29.

24. International Gay and Lesbian Human Rights Commission, *Nowhere to Turn: Blackmail and Extortion of LGBT People in Sub-Saharan Africa*, ed. Ryan Thoreson and Sam Cook (New York: International Gay and Lesbian Human Rights Commission, 2011), http://www.iglhrc.org/sites/default/files/484-1.pdf.

25. International Gay and Lesbian Human Rights Commission.

26. Studies of public order policing in the United States and globally suggest a similar dynamic. See Jonathan Simon, "Crime, Community, and Criminal Justice," *California Law Review* 90 (2002): 1415–22. The International Council on Human Rights Policy documented the same phenomenon in countries where, "as a result of rising crime, hardline law and order policies attract public support." *Crime, Public Order, and Human Rights* (Versoix, Switzerland: International Council on Human Rights Policy, 2003), http://www.ichrp.org /files/summaries/10/114_summary_en.pdf. See also Dorothy E. Roberts, "Foreword: Race, Vagueness, and the Social Meaning of Order-Maintenance Policing," *Journal of Criminal Law and Criminology* 89 (1999): 775–836; and Andrew J. Kozusko III, "Dashing Chicago's

Hopes: Favoring the 'Right' to Loiter 'Innocently' over the Fundamental Need for Safety in *City of Chicago v. Morales*," *University of Pittsburgh Law Review* 62 (2000): 409–27.

27. Nita Bhalla, Rare win for gay rights as Kenya court rules forced anal tests illegal, March 22, 2018, https://www.reuters.com/article/us-kenya-lgbt-anal-tests/rare-win-for-gay -rights-as-kenya-court-rules-forced-anal-tests-illegal-idUSKBN1GY2SI.

Chapter 10. Criminal Law, Activism, and Sexual and Reproductive Justice

We would like to acknowledge Sundari Ravindran, Suchitra Dalvie, and Rupsa Mallik for their helpful comments on this chapter.

1. Suresh Kumar Koushal and Another v. NAZ Foundation and Others, Civil Appeal No. 10972 of 2013, Supreme Court of India. The review petitions were dismissed by the Supreme Court on January 28, 2014. In February 2016 the Supreme Court announced that it would refer several curative petitions against Section 377 to a five-judge constitutional bench for an in-depth hearing. Krishnadas Rajagopal, "Five-Judge Constitution Bench to Take a Call on Section 377," *Hindu* (Chennai, India), February 2, 2016, http:// www.thehindu.com/news/national/Five-judge-Constitution-Bench-to-take-a-call-on -Section-377/article14056992.ece.

2. Mary E. John et al., *Planning Families, Planning Gender: The Adverse Child Sex Ratio in Selected Districts of Madhya Pradesh, Rajasthan, Himachal Pradesh, Haryana, and Punjab* (New Delhi: Action Aid, 2008), http://idl-bnc.idrc.ca/dspace/bitstream /10625/39996/1/128703.pdf.

3. John et al. See also "How Many Girls Are Missing in India? Trends in Sex Ration at Birth (2001–2012)," UNFPA [United Nations Population Fund] India, July 2015, http:// countryoffice.unfpa.org/india/drive/MissingGirlsBrochure_LowResPDF.pdf.

4. SRBs are not universal constants and may change without deliberate intervention or due to other causes, including underenumeration of female births. T. K. Sundari Ravindran, *Sex-Selective Abortion and India's Declining Female Sex Ratio* (Mumbai: CommonHealth, 2012), http://www.commonhealth.in/factsheet-malaria-and20sex-selective -abortion/2.20factsheet20Sex20selective20abortion20and20declining20female20sex20r atio.pdf.

5. Christophe Z. Guilmoto and Roger Depledge, "Economic, Social and Spatial Dimensions of India's Excess Child Masculinity," *Population* 63 (2008): 91–117.

6. P. N. Mari Bhat and A. J. Francis Zavier, "Factors Influencing the Use of Prenatal Diagnostic Techniques and the Sex Ratio at Birth in India," *Economic and Political Weekly* 42, no. 24 (2007): 2292–303.

7. Mohit Sahni et al., "Missing Girls in India: Infanticide, Feticide, and Made-to-Order Pregnancies? Insight from Hospital-Based Sex-Ratio-at-Birth over the Last Century," *PLoS One* 3, no. 5 (2008): e2224.

8. Umesh Isalkar, "Latest Blood Test in PCPNDT Act Purview," *Times of India* (Mumbai), November 21, 2013, http://timesofindia.indiatimes.com/city/pune/Latest-blood-test -in-PCPNDT-Act-purview/articleshow/26120384.cms.

9. The Medical Termination of Pregnancy Act does not technically give women an unqualified right to abortion on demand; the prerogative to abort rests with the doctor,

whom a woman must approach, citing grounds allowed under the act, such as contraceptive failure or risks to mental health. Thus, the Medical Termination of Pregnancy Act merely sets aside, under certain circumstances, the criminalization of abortion, which is still valid in the Indian Penal Code.

10. Rupsa Mallik, *"Negative Choice": Sex Determination and Sex Selective Abortion in India* (Mumbai: Centre for Enquiry into Health and Allied Themes, 2003), http://www.cehat.org/go/uploads/AapIndia/work6.pdf; Nivedita Menon, *Recovering Subversion: Feminist Politics beyond the Law* (Delhi: Permanent Black, 2004).

11. P. N. Mari Bhat et al., *National Family Health Survey (NFHS-3), 2005–06, India*, vol. 1 (Mumbai: International Institute for Population Sciences, 2007).

12. Isalkar, "Latest Blood Test."

13. A block is one of four district subdivisions made for planning and administrative purposes in India.

14. Chetan Chauhan, "Govt to Monitor Pregnancies and Abortions," *Hindustan Times* (New Delhi), July 13, 2007, http://www.hindustantimes.com/india/govt-to-monitor-pregnancies-and-abortions/story-kHk4KcRCIswkzHNZS6qqAJ.html.

15. Rakhi Ghoshal and Anup Dhar, "Child Sex Ratio and the Politics of 'Enemisation,'" *Economic and Political Weekly* 47, no. 49 (2012): 20–22.

16. "Women's Groups Oppose Murder Charge for Foeticide," *Times of India* (Mumbai), July 12, 2012, http://timesofindia.indiatimes.com/city/mumbai/Womens-groups-oppose-murder-charge-for-foeticide/articleshow/14832902.cms?referral= PM.

17. Indian feminists have suggested that in a climate of growing communalism and antiminority politics, it is not difficult to imagine that the Hindu right in India would follow aggressively pronatalist policies and seek to increase the population of their community vis-à-vis the Muslim minority. See Menon, *Recovering Subversion.*

18. Ghoshal and Dhar, "Child Sex Ratio."

19. This misdirected zeal flies in the face of the fact that unsafe abortions account for over 10 percent of maternal deaths in India, as discussed previously. Ghoshal and Dhar.

20. Ghoshal and Dhar.

21. *Satyamev Jayate*, "Female Foeticide," StarPlus, 2012, video, 1:04:29 http://www.satyamevjayate.in/watch-the-episodes/female-foeticide/watch-full-episode-hindi.aspx.

22. Vijaya Nidadavolu and Hillary Bracken, "Abortion and Sex Determination: Conflicting Messages in Information Materials in a District of Rajasthan, India," *Reproductive Health Matters* 14, no. 27 (2006): 160–71.

23. Farah Naqvi, *Images and Icons: Harnessing the Power of Mass Media to Promote Gender Equality and Reduce Practices of Sex Selection* (New Delhi: BBC World Service Trust, 2006), http://downloads.bbc.co.uk/worldservice/trust/pdf/india_sex_selection/India_sex_selection.pdf.

24. Naqvi, 8.

25. John et al., *Planning Families, Planning Gender.*

26. For example, the recent improvement in South Korea's sex ratio is attributed to the long-term effects of legislation that supports greater rights for women and less dependency on support from sons. Sneha Barot, "A Problem-and-Solution Mismatch: Son Pref-

erence and Sex-Selective Abortion Bans," *Guttmacher Policy Review* 15, no. 2 (Spring 2012): 18–22, https://www.guttmacher.org/sites/default/files/article_files/gpr150218.pdf.

27. Variables include socioeconomic status; caste; location (urban or rural); geographic region; family size, which may be kept small out of fear of land fragmentation in agricultural communities; age and education level at marriage, which can impact sex selection both negatively and positively; health indicators such as child mortality and fertility patterns; valuation of women's work; the state's policy on population, access to contraceptives, and spacing methods; maternal mortality and morbidity; access to money and technology; neglect and infanticide; patrilineal descent and inheritance; patrivirilocal marriage (wherein a woman, upon her marriage, becomes a member of another household, which is at a distance of a few miles from her own and which gains the right to her reproductive labor); marriage and dowry as social compulsions; rising costs of living, particularly education; anxiety about the sexuality of young, single women; and agrarian crisis, lack of livelihoods, and related migration.

28. Maxine Molyneux, "Mobilization without Emancipation? Women's Interests, the State, and Revolution in Nicaragua," *Feminist Studies* 11, no. 2 (1985): 227–54.

29. Nivedita Menon, *Seeing like a Feminist* (New Delhi: Zubaan and Penguin, 2012).

30. The NDTV debate featured a reverend and an Islamic scholar, alongside two medical doctors, a model, and a researcher. "Abortion Debate: Pro-life or Pro-choice?," NDTV, November 24, 2012, video, 46:39, http://www.ndtv.com/video/player/the-big -fight/abortion-debate-pro-life-or-pro-choice/255946.

31. Menon, *Seeing like a Feminist*, 210.

Chapter 11. Poisoned Gifts

All translations from Spanish into English are my own.

1. C. Neal Tate and Torbjörn Vallinder, "The Global Expansion of Judicial Power: The Judicialization of Politics," in *The Global Expansion of Judicial Power*, ed. C. Neal Tate and Torbjörn Vallinder (New York: New York University Press, 1995), 1–10; Bruce Ackerman, "The Rise of World Constitutionalism," *Virginia Law Review* 83 (1997): 771–97.

2. Ricardo Guastini, "La 'constitucionalización' del ordenamiento jurídico: El caso italiano," in *Neoconstitucionalismo(s)*, ed. Miguel Carbonell (Madrid: Trotta, 2003), 49–73.

3. Antony Duff, "Theorizing Criminal Law," *Oxford Journal of Legal Studies* 25 (2005): 353–67; Douglas Husak, *Overcriminalization* (Oxford: Oxford University Press, 2007); Andrew Hirsch, "El concepto de bien jurídico y el 'principio del daño,'" in *La teoría del bien jurídico*, ed. Roland Hefendehl (Madrid: Marcial Pons, 2007), 37–52; Antony Duff, "Theories of Criminal Law," in *Stanford Encyclopedia of Philosophy*, ed. Edward N. Zalta, article published October 14, 2002, last modified May 14, 2013, http://plato .stanford.edu/archives/sum2013/entries/criminal-law/.

4. John Stuart Mill, *On Liberty and Other Essays* (Oxford: Oxford University Press, 1998); Joel Feinberg, *Harm to Others* (Oxford: Oxford University Press, 1984).

5. Claus Roxin, *Derecho penal: Parte general* (Madrid: Civitas, 1997); Bernd Schünemann, "El principio de protección de bienes jurídicos como punto de fuga de los límites

constitucionales de los tipos penales y de su interpretación," in Hefendehl, *La teoría del bien jurídico*, 197–226.

6. Luigi Ferrajoli, *Derecho y razón: Teoría del garantismo penal* (Madrid: Trotta, 1995), 335–36; Detle Sternberg-Lieben, "Bien jurídico, proporcionalidad y libertad del legislador penal," in Hefendehl, *La teoría del bien jurídico*, 105–28; Otto Lagodny, "El derecho penal sustantivo como piedra de toque de la dogmática constitucional," in Hefendehl, 129–36.

7. Ferrajoli, *Derecho y razón*, 335–36; Sternberg-Lieben, "Bien jurídico, proporcionalidad y libertad," 107; Roxin, *Derecho penal*, 55–56; Claus Roxin, "¿Es la protección de bienes jurídicos una finalidad del derecho penal?," in Hefendehl, *La teoría del bien jurídico*, 448.

8. Ferrajoli, *Derecho y razón*, 335–36; Roxin, *Derecho penal*, 65–67; Roxin, "¿Es la protección?," 446–49.

9. Roxin, *Derecho penal*, 52; Tatjana Hörnle, "Penal Law and Sexuality: Recent Reforms in German Criminal Law," *Buffalo Criminal Law Review* 3 (2000): 639–85.

10. Ronald Dworkin, *Taking Rights Seriously* (Cambridge, MA: Harvard University Press, 1978), xi.

11. Roxin, "¿Es la protección?," 450; Hörnle, "Penal Law and Sexuality."

12. Roxin, "¿Es la protección?," 451; Hörnle, "Penal Law and Sexuality."

13. Schünemann, "El principio de protección de bienes jurídicos," 208.

14. Sternberg-Lieben, "Bien jurídico, proporcionalidad y libertad," 107.

15. Lagodny, "El derecho penal sustantivo," 130–31.

16. Roxin, "¿Es la protección?," 444–45. The definition of sex crimes in this essay is restricted to crimes where some form of sexual intercourse (violent or consensual, heterosexual or homosexual) is involved. Doctrinally, I follow the strict definition of sex crimes in continental law jurisdictions—Germany and Spain being particularly illustrative. These criminal codes articulate a legal good alternatively called "sexual freedom," "sexual autonomy," or "sexual self-determination." This good protects the possibility of every human agent to decide freely whether to have sexual contact with another free human agent. In general, these crimes punish violations of such autonomy rights (different forms of violence, coercion, or deception). See Hörnle, "Penal Law and Sexuality"; Manuel Cancio Meliá, "Una nueva reforma de los delitos contra la libertad sexual," *La ley penal* 80 (2011): 5–20. This notion of "sex crimes" does not therefore involve a broader notion of sexuality. Abortion and infanticide, for example, are not included in this notion.

17. Another obvious example is incest. Globally, a number of courts have validated the criminalization of consensual sexual intercourse between family members on different grounds that rationalize what has historically been considered a social taboo as producing a grave social harm (generally to the family as "the basic unit" of society) and warranting criminalization. This harm has been judicially ascertained using empirical evidence (medicine, genetics, anthropology, psychology, and psychoanalysis, most prominently). Two important decisions illustrate this. In 1998 and 2008 the Constitutional Court of Colombia and the Constitutional Court of Germany, respectively, upheld as constitutionally valid the criminalization of incest. Corte Constitucional [C.C.] [Constitu-

tional Court], agosto 10, 1998, Sentencia C-404/98 (Colom.), *Gaceta de la Corte Constitucional* 7(1998): 81–116; Incest Case, 120 BVerfG [Constitutional Court of the Federal Republic of Germany] 224, Feb. 26, 2008. For reasons of length, I omit a consideration of incest in this chapter. For further discussion, see George P. Fletcher, "The Relevance of Law to the Incest Taboo," in *Festschrift für Winfried Hassemer*, ed. Felix Herzog and Ulfrid Neumann (Munich: C. F. Müller, 2010), 321–30; and Markus D. Dubber, "Policing Morality: Constitutional Law and the Criminalization of Incest," *University of Toronto Law Journal* 61 (2011): 737–59.

18. Francisco Tomás y Valiente, "El crimen y pecado contra natura," in *Sexo barroco y otras transgresiones premodernas*, Francisco Tomás y Valiente et al. (Madrid: Alianza, 1990), 33–55; Antonio Bascuñán Rodríguez, "El derecho penal sexual moderno ¿afirma seriamente lo que dice?," in *Derecho y sexualidades*, ed. Marcelo Alegre et al. (Buenos Aires: 2010), 211–12.

19. Tomás y Valiente, "El crimen y pecado contra natura," 36–37.

20. Tomás y Valiente, 38; Federico Garza Carvajal, *Butterflies Will Burn: Prosecuting Sodomites in Early Modern Spain and Mexico* (Austin: University of Texas Press, 2003), 39–73.

21. Bascuñán Rodríguez, "El derecho penal sexual moderno," 211–12.

22. Bascuñán Rodríguez, 209–10.

23. Bascuñán Rodríguez, 209.

24. Bascuñán Rodríguez, 209.

25. Bascuñán Rodríguez, 210.

26. Bascuñán Rodríguez, 216.

27. Bascuñán Rodríguez, 216.

28. Bascuñán Rodríguez, 216–19.

29. Reva B. Siegel, "'The Rule of Love': Wife Beating as Prerogative and Privacy," *Yale Law Journal* 105 (1996): 2117–207. Siegel's "preservation-through-transformation" model is based on a number of important methodological assumptions that are worth keeping in mind. First, her methodology is historical or, better, proceeds by "genealogical excavation." Siegel, 2175. Second, "preservation-through-transformation" presupposes that the rules and reasons that support a status regime are highly mutable and adaptable. Siegel, 2175. They have "no 'essential' or transhistorical form," so they "will evolve over time, changing shape as [they are] contested." Siegel, 2179. Third, "preservation-through-transformation" is not a dynamic that obeys "the conspiratorial or malevolent motivations of the legal elites directing reform." Siegel, 2180. On the contrary, it may well be that these elites proceed out of "good faith." Siegel, 2180. Finally, "preservation-through-transformation" shows, in more general terms, that law is a "double-edged weapon of social change, repeatedly demonstrating the capacity to legitimate privileges it seems at first to challenge." Siegel, 2183. The "poisoned gift" dynamic does not strictly follow all of these assumptions. Most particularly, the analysis of some constitutional judicial decisions in the next section is not the sort of judicious genealogical exercise Siegel undertakes in her work on "preservation-through-transformation." The "poisoned gift" analysis focuses exclusively on the *forms of interpretation* that constitutional judges draw on when determining

whether the criminalization of conduct respects constitutional values and rights. This analysis shows that, in many cases, the sex-restrictive foundation of certain sex crimes gets modernized through constitutional judicial interpretation, becoming immune from further contestation. Yet the "poisoned gift" mode of analysis bears some important similarities to the "preservation-through-transformation" model.

30. Siegel, "'Rule of Love'"; Reva B. Siegel, "Why Equal Protection No Longer Protects: The Evolving Forms of Status-Enforcing State Action," *Stanford Law Review* 49 (1997): 1111–48; Reva B. Siegel, "Discrimination in the Eyes of the Law: How 'Color Blindness' Discourse Disrupts and Rationalizes Social Stratification," *California Law Review* 88 (2000): 77–118.

31. Siegel, "'Rule of Love,'" 2119.

32. Siegel, 2119.

33. Siegel, 2178.

34. Siegel, 2119.

35. Siegel, 2179.

36. Siegel, 2184.

37. Siegel, 2184.

38. Siegel, 2184.

39. Siegel, 2118, 2121–74.

40. Siegel, "Why Equal Protection"; Siegel, "Discrimination."

41. Roxin, *Derecho penal*, 444–46; Schünemann, "El principio de protección de bienes jurídicos," 211–12.

42. Ricardo García Macho, *Las relaciones de especial sujeción en la constitución española* (Madrid: Tecnos, 1992).

43. Editors' note: "Facial" challenges are challenges based on the text of the law alone, not requiring proof of harm in the application of the law.

44. Corte Constitucional [C.C.] [Constitutional Court], julio 14, 1999, Sentencia C-507/99 (Colom.), *Gaceta de la Corte Constitucional* 6(1999): 264–283].

45. Ibid. at ¶ 5.11.

46. Ibid.

47. Ibid.

48. Ibid.

49. Ibid. at ¶ 5.12.

50. Ibid.

51. Janet E. Halley, "Reasoning about Sodomy: Act and Identity in and after *Bowers v. Hardwick*," *Virginia Law Review* 79 (1993): 1721–80.

52. Halley, 1723, 1748.

53. Kendall Thomas, "Shower/Closet," *Assemblage* 20 (1993): 80.

54. Thomas, 81.

55. Thomas, 80.

56. Thomas, 81.

57. Thomas, 81.

58. Thomas, 80.

59. Halley, "Reasoning about Sodomy"; Janet E. Halley, "The Status/Conduct Distinction in the 1993 Revisions to Military Anti-gay Policy: A Legal Archaeology," *GLQ: A Journal of Lesbian and Gay Studies* 3 (1996): 159–252.

60. Halley, "Reasoning about Sodomy," 1748–49.

61. Law No. 26.842, December 26, 2012, Prevention and punishment of human trafficking and assistance to its victims, arts. 21, 22, and 23, amended arts. 125bis, 126, and 127 of the Criminal Code of Argentina. According to the amended version of Article 125bis, "Whoever promotes or facilitates the prostitution of a person will be sentenced to prison for four to six years, even with the consent of the victim." Similarly, Article 127 of the Argentine Criminal Code was amended and now sets forth that "whoever economically exploits the exercise of prostitution, even with the consent of the victim, will be sentenced to prison from four to six years." In its previous drafting, Article 125bis only punished the promotion or facilitation of prostitution when the victim was below the age of eighteen or when the victim was of any age but "deception, violence, threat, abuse of authority or any other means of intimidation or coercion" was used or the perpetrator was an ascendant relative, spouse, sibling, or guardian or a person with whom the victim lived or who was in charge of his or her education or guardianship. The economic exploitation of prostitution, as found in the previous wording of Article 127, was only punished when there was "deception, coercive or intimidating abuse, or a relationship of dependency or authority, violence, threat, or any other means of intimidation or coercion."

62. Corte Constitucional [C.C.] [Constitutional Court], Septiembre 16, 2009, Sentencia C-636/09 (Colom.), http://www.corteconstitucional.gov.co/relatoria/2009/C-636 -09.htm.

63. Ibid.

64. Ibid. at ¶ 5.2.

65. Ibid. at ¶ 5.4.

66. Reva B. Siegel, "Dignity and Sexuality: Claims on Dignity in Transnational Debates over Abortion and Same-Sex Marriage," *International Journal of Constitutional Law* 10 (2012): 355–79; Matthias Mahlmann, "Human Dignity and the Culture of Republicanism," *German Law Journal* 11 (2010): 9–31. This phenomenon may lead, in Christopher McCrudden's words, to "significant judicial manipulation." Christopher McCrudden, "Human Dignity and Judicial Interpretation of Human Rights," *European Journal of International Law* 19 (2008): 655. A leading interpretation of human dignity (initiated, to a great extent, by the German Constitutional Court) tends to liken it to Immanuel Kant's second formulation of the categorical imperative on the principle of humanity: "Act in such a way that you treat humanity, whether in your own person or in the person of any other, never simply as a means, but always at the same time as an end." Immanuel Kant, *The Moral Law: Groundwork of the Metaphysic of Morals*, trans. H. J. Paton (New York: Routledge, 1991), 106–7. Even if this version of human dignity might be criticized for several reasons (see Mahlmann, "Human Dignity," 20–21), it nevertheless offers an important ground for validating state action aimed at preserving a notion of humanity premised on specific notions of autonomy and rationality. In any case, it is important to bear in mind that judges can *choose* among different available options of human dignity, the Kantian being

just one example. As Siegel shows, in matters of sexuality, advocates and judges can select the notion of human dignity that better supports their specific claims and arguments. For further discussion, see Siegel, "Dignity and Sexuality." When dealing with prostitution (a case Siegel does not consider), the traditional moral (religious) condemnation against selling one's sexuality looks perfectly reasonable if clothed with the Kantian principle of humanity against any form of human instrumentalization. See Mahlmann, "Human Dignity," 19.

67. Mahlmann, 11.

68. Corte Constitucional, 2009, Sentencia C-636/09, ¶ 6.2.

69. Ibid. at ¶ 7.2.1. Note that the idea of criminal law as ultima ratio is inimical to the high degree of deference courts usually grant legislatures in matters of criminal legislation. If constitutional courts took seriously the idea that criminal law is subsidiary in the resolution of social conflicts, they would *always* be forced to exercise forms of strict scrutiny when examining the criminalization of human conduct.

70. Ibid. at ¶ 7.1.1.

71. Ibid. at ¶ 7.2.2.

72. Ibid. at ¶ 7.2.3.2.

73. Ibid. at ¶ 7.2.3.3.

74. Mill, *On Liberty and Other Essays*, 14.

75. David M. Beatty, *The Ultimate Rule of Law* (New York: Oxford University Press, 2005).

76. Mill, *On Liberty and Other Essays*, 14.

Chapter 12. The Filth They Bring

1. LBCI News, "LBCI NEWS 31-7-2012," posted July 31, 2012, video, 2:58, http://www.youtube.com/watch?v= iOqMhTfutjY.

2. LBCI News, "LBCI News—Closure of a Gay Bar in Dekwaneh," posted April 23, 2013, video, 2:14, http://www.youtube.com/watch?v= AVcTrkZ4W2Y.

3. Paul Amar, *The Security Archipelago: Human-Security States, Sexuality Politics, and the End of Neoliberalism* (Durham, NC: Duke University Press, 2013), 17. Kimberlé Crenshaw similarly theorizes privilege and oppression conferred through social categories such as sex, gender, race, and class as mutually constitutive and intersectional. See Kimberlé Crenshaw, "Mapping the Margins: Intersectionality, Identity Politics, and Violence against Women of Color," *Stanford Law Review* (1991): 1241–99.

4. Amar, p. 17.

5. Mahmood Mamdani, *Citizen and Subject: Contemporary Africa and the Legacy of Late Colonialism* (Princeton, NJ: Princeton University Press, 1996).

6. Maya Mikdashi, "What Is Political Sectarianism?," *Jadaliyya*, March 25, 2011, http://www.jadaliyya.com/pages/index/1008/what-is-political-sectarianism.

7. SBS, "Lebanon Out of the Closet," *Dateline*, March 14, 2005, video, 13:18, http://www.journeyman.tv/18345/short-films/out-of-the-closet.html.

8. Quoted in Jessy Chahine, "Helem Publishes Region's First Magazine for Gay Arabs," *Daily Star* (Beirut), October 10, 2005, http://www.dailystar.com.lb/News/Lebanon

-News/2005/Oct-10/5569-helem-publishes-regions-first-magazine-for-gay-arabs .ashx#axzz2uaa4vOzC.

9. *Le sexe autour du monde, Season 2, Episode 1: Liban,* aired 2011 on TV5, http://tv5 .ca/le-sexe-autour-du-monde.

10. Agence France-Presse, "Lebanon Considered 'Liberal' in Middle East but Still Arrests LGBT," Raw Story, May 8, 2013, http://www.rawstory.com/rs/2013/05/08/lebanon -considered-liberal-in-middle-east-but-still-arrests-lgbt/.

11. Jasbir Puar, "Homonationalism as Assemblage: Viral Travels, Affective Sexualities," *Jindal Global Law Review* 4, no. 2 (2013): 24.

12. Graeme Reid, "Lebanon Edges Closer to Decriminalizing Same-Sex Conduct," Human Rights Watch, February 2, 2017, https://www.hrw.org/news/2017/02/02/lebanon -edges-closer-decriminalizing-same-sex-conduct.

13. David Bell, "Pleasure and Danger: The Paradoxical Spaces of Sexual Citizenship," *Political Geography* 14, no. 2 (1995): 141.

14. Lisa Marie Cacho, *Social Death: Racialized Rightlessness and the Criminalization of the Unprotected* (New York: New York University Press, 2012), 38.

15. Annie Slemrod, "Racist Feelings High in Burj Hammoud," *Daily Star* (Beirut), November 1, 2011, http://www.dailystar.com.lb/News/Local-News/2011/Nov-01/152753 -racist-feelings-high-in-burj-hammoud.ashx#axzz2nZ5UjjR4.

16. Ahmad Mohsen, "Foreign Workers: The Scapegoats of Bourj Hammoud," *Al-Akhbar* (Beirut), November 3, 2011, http://english.al-akhbar.com/node/1213.

17. Mohsen.

18. Sherene Razack, *Casting Out: The Eviction of Muslims from Western Law and Politics* (Toronto: University of Toronto Press, 2008), 63.

19. Gilbert Herdt, "Introduction: Moral Panics, Sexual Rights, and Cultural Anger," in *Moral Panics, Sex Panics: Fear and the Fight over Sexual Rights,* ed. Gilbert Herdt (New York: New York University Press, 2001), 1.

20. Mail Foreign Service, "Angry Mob of Lebanese Villagers Lynch Murder Suspect in Town Centre in Gruesome Vigilante Attack," *Daily Mail* (London), April 29, 2010, http://www.dailymail.co.uk/news/article-1269814/Angry-mob-Lebanese-villagers -lynch-murder-suspect-Mohammed-Msallem.html.

21. LBC News (posted by bmcharbel), "Myriam Ackkar Will Never Forget You," posted November 24, 2011, video, 5:41, http://www.youtube.com/watch?v=_K-39NIcT6o &feature= youtu.be.

22. LBC News.

23. Human Rights Watch, *Lebanon: Investigate and Punish Army Attacks on Migrants* (New York: Human Rights Watch, 2012).

24. Agence France-Presse, "Lebanese Burn Down Syrian Refugee Camp," *Al-Akhbar* (Beirut), December 2, 2013, http://english.al-akhbar.com/node/17783.

25. LBCI News (posted by Raynbow Lebanon), "LBCI Reports Again on Dekwaneh Arrest, Closure of Gay Bar," posted April 25, 2013, video, 1:38, http://www.youtube .com/watch?feature= player_detailpage&v= UXfb40nRazA.

26. LBCI News, "LBCI News—Closure of a Gay Bar in Dekwaneh."

27. Patricia Hill Collins, "It's All in the Family: Intersections of Gender, Race, and Nation," *Hypatia* 13, no. 3 (1998): 63.

28. Maya Mikdashi, "A Legal Guide to Being a Lebanese Woman (Part 1)," *Jadaliyya*, December 3, 2010, http://www.jadaliyya.com/pages/index/376/a-legal-guide-to-being-a -lebanese-woman-(part-1).

29. Nizar Saghieh and Wahid Farchichi, *Homosexual Relations in the Penal Codes: General Study Regarding the Laws in the Arab Countries with a Report on Lebanon and Tunisia* (Beirut: Helem, 2009).

30. Saghieh and Farchichi.

31. Tamar Mayer, "Gender Ironies of Nationalism: Setting the Stage," in *Gender Ironies of Nationalism: Sexing the Nation*, ed. Tamar Mayer (London: Routledge, 2000), 6.

Chapter 13. Objects in Political Mirrors May Not Be What They Appear

Reprinted with permission from Scott Long, "The Dignity of Marriage: Gays on the Wrong Side of History," *Paper Bird* (blog), July 14, 2015, http://paper-bird.net/2015/07/14 /the-dignity-of-marriage/.

1. Melissa Murray, "Strange Bedfellows: Criminal Law, Family Law, and the Legal Construction of Intimate Life," *Iowa Law Review* 94 (2008): 1256.

2. Murray, 1259–60.

3. Juliet Joslin v. New Zealand, Communication, Human Rights Council, No. 902/1999, UN Doc. A/57/40, at 214 (2002).

4. Ibid. However, jurisprudential developments in the European Court of Human Rights and elsewhere point to a trend toward recognizing the denial of marital rights to same-sex consenting adults as discrimination.

5. In some states in the United States, such as Indiana, same-sex marriage was a crime; however, it is likely that the peculiarities of free speech jurisprudence would have protected individuals engaging in expressive acts that had no legal consequence (e.g., the parties really "weren't" married). We find no evidence of prosecution. After the 2014 U.S. Supreme Court case *Obergefell v. Hodges*, same-sex marriage is legal. See *Obergefell v. Hodges*, 135 S. Ct. 2584 (2015).

6. Argentina, some Mexican states, Uruguay, and South Africa are exceptions. See A. Carroll and L. P. Itaborahy, *State-Sponsored Homophobia 2015: A World Survey of Laws: Criminalisation, Protection and Recognition of Same-Sex Love* (Geneva: International Lesbian, Gay, Bisexual, Trans and Intersex Association, 2015), 41.

7. Carroll and Itaborahy, 41.

8. Bowers v. Hardwick, 478 U.S. 186, 190 (1986).

9. Ronald Reagan, "Address to the Nation on Independence Day," July 4, 1986, Ronald Reagan Library and Museum, U.S. National Archives and Records Administration, transcript, https://www.reaganlibrary.gov/sites/default/files/archives/speeches/1986/70486c.htm.

10. Romer v. Evans, 517 U.S. 620, 635 (1996).

11. Lawrence v. Texas, 539 U.S. 558 (2003).

12. Liam Stack, "Hillary Clinton Reassures Gay Youth in Viral Facebook Photo," *New York Times*, July 4, 2015, http://www.nytimes.com/2015/07/05/us/politics/hillary -clinton-reassures-gay-youth-in-viral-facebook-photo.html?smid= tw-nytimes&_r=0.

13. Stack.

14. Frank Bruni, "Our Weddings, Our Worth," *New York Times*, June 26, 2015, http:// www.nytimes.com/2015/06/28/opinion/sunday/frank-bruni-same-sex-marriage -supreme-court-our-weddings-our-worth.html.

15. Obergefell v. Hodges, 576 U.S. ___, 135 S. Ct. 2584, 2639 (2015).

16. Ibid., Thomas dissent, footnote 8, pg. 16, https://www.supremecourt.gov/opinions /14pdf/14-556_3204.pdf.

17. Mark Joseph Stern, "Supreme Court Breakfast Table: Kennedy's Marriage Equality Decision Is Gorgeous, Heartfelt, and a Little Mystifying," *Slate*, June 26, 2015, http://www.slate.com/articles/news_and_politics/the_breakfast_table/features /2015/scotus_roundup/supreme_court_2015_decoding_anthony_kennedy_s_gay _marriage_decision.html; Ilya Somin, "A Great Decision on Same-Sex Marriage—but Based on Dubious Reasoning," *Volokh Conspiracy* (blog), *Washington Post*, June 26, 2015, https://www.washingtonpost.com/news/volokh-conspiracy/wp/2015/06/26/a-great -decision-on-same-sex-marriage-but-based-on-dubious-reasoning/?noredirect= on&utm_term=.373c177311db; Brian Beutler, "Anthony Kennedy's Same-Sex Marriage Opinion Was a Logical Disaster," *New Republic*, July 1, 2015, https://newrepublic.com /article/122210/anthony-kennedys-same-sex-marriage-opinion-was-logical-disaster.

18. *Obergefell*, 135 S. Ct. at 2630.

19. Scott Lemieux, "Does the Same-Sex Marriage Ruling Mean Trouble for Other LGBT Rights Cases?," *Guardian*, June 26, 2015, https://www.theguardian.com/comment isfree/2015/jun/26/same-sex-marriage-court-cases-lgbt-rights.

20. For an in-depth analysis of "animus" in the United States, see Susannah William Pollvogt, "Unconstitutional Animus," *Fordham Law Review* 81 (2012): 887–938.

21. Nancy Fraser, "Recognition without Ethics?," *Theory, Culture, and Society* 18, no. 21 (2001): 21.

22. Fraser, 21.

23. See *United States v. Windsor*, 133 S. Ct. 2675 (2013).

24. *Obergefell*, 135 S. Ct. at 2593.

25. Ibid. at 2599.

26. Ibid. at 2632.

27. Ibid. at 2635.

28. Ibid.

29. Isaiah Berlin, "Two Concepts of Liberty," in *Four Essays on Liberty* (Oxford: Oxford University Press, 1969), 122–3.

30. Berlin, 131.

31. Berlin, 148.

32. Berlin, 171.

33. *Obergefell v. Hodges*, 135 S. Ct. 2584, 2596 (2015).

34. See Kenji Yoshino, "The Anti-humiliation Principle and Same-Sex Marriage," *Yale Law Journal* 123, no. 8 (2014): 3078. Predictably, in an age of recognition, "its [the Court's] use of the word has increased." Kennedy is "particularly drawn to it," Yoshino writes. "When Justice Kennedy ascribes dignity to an entity, that entity generally prevails." Yoshino, 3087–88.

35. Leslie Meltzer Henry, "The Jurisprudence of Dignity," *University of Pennsylvania Law Review* 160 (2011): 172.

36. Henry, 229.

37. *Obergefell*, 135 S. Ct. at 2639.

38. Mette Lebech, "What Is Human Dignity?," *Maynooth Philosophical Papers* 2 (2004): 61.

39. Pico della Mirandola, *On the Dignity of Man* (Adelaide: University of Adelaide eBooks, 2014), https://ebooks.adelaide.edu.au/p/pico_della_mirandola/giovanni/dignity/.

40. *Obergefell*, 135 S. Ct. at 2589.

41. Ibid.

42. Ibid. at 2594.

43. Ibid. at 2608.

44. Ibid. at 2594.

45. Ibid. at 2593.

46. Ibid. at 2599.

47. Ibid. at 2589.

48. Ibid. at 2608.

49. Ibid. at 2590.

50. "Report: Father of Bristol Palin's Baby Revealed!," *Extra*, June 26, 2015, http://extratv.com/2015/06/26/father-of-bristol-palin-s-baby-revealed/.

51. Transcript of Oral Argument at 18, *Obergefell v. Hodges*, 135 S. Ct. 2584 (2015) (No. 14-556).

52. Amy Davidson, "Justice Alito's Polygamy Perplex," *New Yorker*, April 30, 2015, http://www.newyorker.com/news/amy-davidson/justice-alitos-polygamy-perplex.

53. "Beyond Same-Sex Marriage: A New Strategic Vision for All Our Families and Relationships," Beyond Marriage, accessed March 2, 2016, http://www.beyondmarriage.org/full_statement.html; Law Commission of Canada, *Beyond Conjugality: Recognizing and Supporting Close Personal Adult Relationships* (Ottawa, ON: Law Commission of Canada, 2001).

54. "Beyond Same-Sex Marriage."

55. *Obergefell*, 135 S. Ct. at 2630.

56. National Center for Health Statistics, "National Marriage and Divorce Rate Trends," Centers for Disease Control and Prevention, accessed August 25, 2017, https://www.cdc.gov/nchs/nvss/marriage_divorce_tables.htm.

57. Mark Mather and Diana Lavery, "In U.S., Proportion Married at Lowest Record Levels," Population Reference Bureau, September 2010, http://www.prb.org/Publications/Articles/2010/usmarriagedecline.aspx.

58. Philip N. Cohen, "Marriage Is Declining Globally: Can You Say That?," *Family Inequality* (blog), June 12, 2013, https://familyinequality.wordpress.com/2013/06/12/marriage-is-declining/.

59. Magued Osman and Hanan Girgis, *Marriage Patterns in Egypt* (Cairo: Information and Decision Support Center, Egyptian Cabinet, 2009).

60. Osman and Girgis.

61. Hanan Kholoussy, *For Better, for Worse: The Marriage Crisis That Made Modern Egypt* (Stanford, CA: Stanford University Press, 2010).

62. "Egypt Marriages up by 2.7%, Divorces up by 2.2%," Ahram Online, May 19, 2013, http://english.ahram.org.eg/NewsContent/1/64/71797/Egypt/Politics-/Egypt-marriages-up-by-,-divorces-up-by-.aspx.

63. John Gray, *Post-liberalism: Studies in Political Thought* (London: Routledge, 1996). p. 65.

64. Gray, p. 65.

65. Berlin, 172.

Chapter 14. Harm Production

This chapter was researched and written in August 2014, with subsequent minor edits in May 2015 and May 2016.

1. Bernard E. Harcourt, "The Collapse of the Harm Principle," *Journal of Criminal Law and Criminology* 90 (1999): 109.

2. Peter Cane, "Taking Law Seriously: Starting Points of the Hart/Devlin Debate," *Journal of Ethics* 10 (2006): 21.

3. Report of the Committee on Homosexual Offences and Prostitution, 1957, Cmnd. 247.

4. Report of the Committee, 143.

5. Patrick Devlin, *The Enforcement of Morals* (Oxford: Oxford University Press, 1965).

6. H. L. A. Hart, *Law, Liberty and Morality* (Oxford: Oxford University Press, 1963).

7. See Joel Feinberg, *Harmless Wrongdoing* (New York: Oxford University Press, 1988).

8. Reva B. Siegel, "The Constitutionalization of Abortion," in *The Oxford Handbook of Comparative Constitutional Law*, ed. Michel Rosenfeld and András Sajó (Oxford: Oxford University Press, 2012), 1057.

9. Harcourt, "Collapse of the Harm Principle," 118–20.

10. See also, e.g., Carol Smart, *Feminism and the Power of Law* (New York: Routledge, 1989), 161: "It is commonplace that the 'legal' cure is frequently as bad as the initial harm. It is less well established that the very legal process itself creates its own harms; it creates its own order of damage. . . . It is glaringly obvious that the criminal law does not provide a remedy, it is increasingly obvious that it causes harm."

11. Harcourt, "Collapse of the Harm Principle," 175.

12. Matthew Weait, "Unsafe Law: Health, Rights and the Legal Response," *International Journal of Law in Context* 9 (2013): 535.

13. Weait, 536.

14. See M. Berer, "Criminalization, Sexual and Reproductive Rights, Public Health and Justice," *Reproductive Health Matters* 17 (2009): 4.

15. UN Special Rapporteur, *Report of the Special Rapporteur on the Right of Everyone to the Enjoyment of the Highest Attainable Standard of Physical and Mental Health*, UN Doc. A/HRC/14/20, April 27, 2010, https://documents-dds-ny.un.org/doc/UNDOC/GEN /G10/131/18/PDF/G1013118.pdf?OpenElement; UN Special Rapporteur, *Right of Everyone to the Highest Attainable Standard of Physical and Mental Health*, UN Doc. A/66/254, August 3, 2011, https://documents-dds-ny.un.org/doc/UNDOC/GEN/N11/443/58/PDF /N1144358.pdf?OpenElement.

16. See Pamela Das and Richard Horton, "Bringing Sex Workers to the Centre of the HIV Response," *Lancet* 385 (2015): 260–73; and Kate Shannon et al., "Global Epidemiology of HIV among Female Sex Workers: Influence of Structural Determinants," *Lancet* 385 (2015): 55.

17. Hart, *Law, Liberty and Morality*, 20.

18. Harcourt, "Collapse of the Harm Principle," 185–92.

19. See Carolyn Boyes-Watson and Kay Pranis, "Science Cannot Fix This: The Limitations of Evidence-Based Practice," *Contemporary Justice Review* 15 (2012): 265.

20. Harcourt, "Collapse of the Harm Principle," 185.

21. This chapter builds on scholarly work on Canadian law and the harm principle, including Bradley W. Miller, "Moral Laws in an Age of Rights: Hart and Devlin at the Supreme Court of Canada," *American Journal of Jurisprudence* 55 (2010): 79.

22. Canada (Attorney General) v. Bedford, [2013] 3 S.C.R. 1101 (Can.).

23. R. v. Morgentaler, [1988] 1 S.C.R. 30 (Can.).

24. R. v. Mabior, [2012] 2 S.C.R. 584 (Can.); R. v. D.C., [2012] 2 S.C.R. 626 (Can.).

25. For a broader discussion, see Katherine Swinton, "What Do the Courts Want from the Social Sciences?," in *Charter Litigation*, ed. Robert J. Sharpe (Toronto: Butterworths, 1987), 187; and John Hagan, "Can Social Science Save Us? The Problems and Prospects of Social Science Evidence in Constitutional Litigation," in Sharpe, 213.

26. Pierre Trudeau, "Canada Must Be a Just Society," CBC Television, December 21, 1967, video, 2:20, http://www.cbc.ca/archives/entry/pierre-trudeau-canada-must-be-a -just-society.

27. Criminal Code, R.S.C. 1985, c. C-46 (Can.).

28. Canadian Charter of Rights and Freedoms, Constitution Act, 1982, Schedule B to the Canada Act, 1982, c 11 (UK).

29. Criminal Code, §§ 197(1), 210, 212(1)(j), 213(1)(c).

30. Reference re ss. 193 & 195.1(1)(c) of Criminal Code (Can.) (the Prostitution Reference), [1990] 1 S.C.R. 1123.

31. Canada (Attorney General) v. Bedford, [2013] 3 S.C.R. 1101, para. 42 (Can.).

32. See Donald A. Schön and Martin Rein, *Frame Reflection: Towards the Resolution of Intractable Policy Controversies* (New York: Basic Books, 1994).

33. R. v. Morgentaler, [1988] 1 S.C.R. 30, 46 (Can.).

34. Ibid. at 45 (quoting Morgentaler v. R., [1976] 1 S.C.R. 616, 671 [Can.]).

35. Sheilah Martin, "Abortion Litigation," in *Women's Legal Strategies in Canada*, ed. Radha Jhappan (Toronto: University of Toronto Press, 2002), 335, 352.

36. *Morgentaler*, 1 S.C.R. at 57–60, 91–106, 173.

37. Ibid. at 59. A majority of the Court recognized that delay carried greater risk of physical and psychological harm, though the former alone was said to be sufficient to ground the claim.

38. Canada (Attorney General) v. Bedford, [2013] 3 S.C.R. 1101, para. 2 (Can.).

39. Ibid. at n.1.

40. See Factum of the Interveners, Intervening as the Women's Coalition for the Abolition of Prostitution, Canada (Attorney General) v. Bedford, [2013] 3 S.C.R. 1101, Court File No. 34788, http://www.rapereliefshelter.bc.ca/sites/default/files/imce/SCC%20Factum%20of%20Intervner%20Women%27s%20Coalition.pdf. As authority for the radical feminist theory of prostitution as inherent harm, the intervention cites Catharine A. MacKinnon, "Trafficking, Prostitution, and Inequality," *Harvard Civil Rights-Civil Liberties Law Review* 46 (2011): 272. See also Maddy Coy, *Prostitution, Harm and Gender Inequality: Theory, Research and Policy* (Burlington, VT: Ashgate, 2012); and Janine Benedet, *For the Sake of Equality: Arguments for Adapting the Nordic Model of Prostitution Law to Canada* (Vancouver, BC: Women's Coalition for the Abolition of Prostitution, 2014), http://www.rapereliefshelter.bc.ca/learn/resources/sake-equality-arguments-adapting-nordic-model-prostitution-law-canada.

41. See *Gonzales v. Carhart*, 550 U.S. 124 (2007); and Susan Frelich Appleton, "Reproduction and Regret," *Yale Journal of Law and Feminism* 23 (2011): 255.

42. *Bedford*, 3 S.C.R. at para. 60.

43. Ibid. at paras. 61–72.

44. See Ken Young et al., "Social Science and the Evidence-Based Policy Movement," *Social Policy and Society* 13 (2002): 215; and Ian Sanderson, "Complexity, Practical Rationality and Evidence-Based Policy Making," *Policy and Politics* 34 (2006): 115.

45. R. v. Morgentaler, [1988] 1 S.C.R. 30, 56 (Can.).

46. Ibid. at 65–69, 91–100.

47. Ibid. at 66–67, 93–98.

48. *Bedford*, 3 S.C.R. at para. 15.

49. See David M. Frost and Suzanne C. Ouellette, "A Search for Meaning: Recognizing the Potential of Narrative Research in Social Policy-Making Efforts," *Sexuality Research and Social Policy* 8 (2011): 151.

50. Emily van der Meulen, Elya M. Durisin, and Victoria Love, eds., *Selling Sex: Experience, Advocacy, and Research on Sex Work in Canada* (Vancouver: University of British Columbia Press, 2013).

51. *Bedford*, 3 S.C.R. at para. 79.

52. Ibid. at para. 84.

53. Ibid. at para. 157.

54. Ibid. at para. 76.

55. Ibid. at para. 64.

56. See Nicola Lacey, "Introduction: Making Sense of Criminal Justice," in *Criminal Justice*, ed. Nicola Lacey (Oxford: Oxford University Press, 1994), 1–35.

57. The Canadian Charter of Rights and Freedoms states, "Everyone has the right to life, liberty and security of the person and the right not to be deprived thereof except in accordance with the principles of fundamental justice." Canadian Charter of Rights and Freedoms, Constitution Act, 1982, Schedule B to the Canada Act, 1982, c 11, § 7 (UK).

58. R. v. Morgentaler, [1988] 1 S.C.R. 30, 114–19 (Can.).

59. Ibid. at 116.

60. *Bedford*, 3 S.C.R. at para. 142.

61. Ibid. at paras. 134, 159.

62. Ibid. at para. 136.

63. This is a version of Hart's critical morality, or the use of moral principles to critique social institutions, including criminal law. See Hart, *Law, Liberty and Morality*, 20.

64. Hart, 43, 57, 65, 69.

65. Bettina Lange, "The Emotional Dimension in Legal Regulation," *Journal of Law and Society* 29 (2002): 197. There is a large literature on the relationship between emotion and reason in criminal law. See, e.g., Arie Freiberg, "Affective versus Justice: Instrumentalism and Emotionalism in Criminal Justice," *Punishment and Society* 3 (2001): 265; and Susanne Karstedt, "Emotions and Criminal Justice," *Theoretical Criminology* 6 (2002): 299.

66. "Prostitutes Are People Too," editorial, *Lancet* 365 (2005): 1598; "Prostitution Laws: Health Risks and Hypocrisy," editorial, *Canadian Medical Association Journal* 171 (2004): 109.

67. *Bedford*, 3 S.C.R. at para. 96.

68. R. v. Labaye, [2005] 3 S.C.R. 728 (Can.).

69. R. v. Malmo-Levine, [2003] 3 S.C.R. 571 (Can.).

70. *Labaye*, 3 S.C.R. at para. 14.

71. Ibid. at para. 33.

72. Ibid.

73. Elaine Craig, "Laws of Desire: The Political Morality of Public Sex," *McGill Law Journal* 54 (2009): 355. See also Elaine Craig, "Interpreting the Criminal Regulation of Sex Work in Light of *R v. Labaye*," *Canadian Criminal Law Review* 12 (2008): 327.

74. R. v. Morgentaler, [1988] 1 S.C.R. 30, 161–72 (Can.).

75. Ibid. at 176–80.

76. Canada (Attorney General) v. Bedford, [2013] 3 S.C.R. 1101, para. 86 (Can.).

77. Devlin, *Enforcement of Morals*, 22.

78. Stuart Chambers, "Pierre Elliot Trudeau and Bill C-150: A Rational Approach to Homosexual Acts, 1968–69," *Journal of Homosexuality* 57 (2010): 249, 259–60.

79. Lisa M. Kelly and Katrina Pacey, "Why Anti-john Laws Don't Work," *Toronto Star*, October 19, 2011, http://www.thestar.com/opinion/editorialopinion/2011/10/19/why_antijohn_laws_dont_work.html.

80. Protection of Communities and Exploited Persons Act, S.C. 2014, c 25 (Can.).

81. Ibid. at Preamble.

82. *Bedford*, 3 S.C.R. at para. 165.

83. R. v. Mabior, [2012] 2 S.C.R. 584 (Can.); R. v. D.C., [2012] 2 S.C.R. 626 (Can.).

84. R. v. Cuerrier, [1998] 2 S.C.R. 371 (Can.).

85. *Mabior*, 2 S.C.R. at para. 84.

86. Ibid. at para. 94.

87. See Harcourt, "Collapse of the Harm Principle," 162–64.

88. *Mabior*, 2 S.C.R. at para. 96.

89. Alana Klein, "Criminal Law, Public Health and Governance of HIV Exposure and Transmission," *International Journal of Human Rights* 13 (2009): 251, 255.

90. Weait, "Unsafe Law," 551, citing the work of UNAIDS from the late 1990s. UN-AIDS, *International Guidelines on HIV/AIDS and Human Rights* (Geneva: UNAIDS, 1998; consolidated ed., 2006); UNAIDS, *The Criminalization of HIV Transmission: Policy Brief* (Geneva: UNAIDS, 2008). See also Sofia Gruskin and Laura Ferguson, "Government Regulation of Sex and Sexuality: In Their Own Words," *Reproductive Health Matters* 17 (2009): 108.

91. Global Commission on HIV and the Law, *Risks, Rights and Health* (New York: United Nations Development Programme, 2012), 20–25. See also Matthew Weait, *Criminalization of HIV Exposure and Transmission: A Global Review* (New York: Global Commission on HIV and the Law, 2011).

92. R. v. Cuerrier, [1998] 2 S.C.R. 371, para. 77 (Can.).

93. Ibid. at para. 143.

94. Ibid. at para. 144.

95. Ibid.

96. Ibid. at para. 146.

97. Ibid. at para. 147.

98. Eric Mykhalovskiy, Glenn Betteridge, and David McLay, *HIV Non-disclosure and the Criminal Law: Establishing Policy Options for Ontario* (Toronto: Ontario HIV Treatment Network, 2010).

99. Eric Mykhalovskiy and Glenn Betteridge, "Who? What? Where? When? And with What Consequences? An Analysis of Criminal Cases of HIV Non-disclosure in Canada," *Canadian Journal of Law and Society* 27 (2012): 51.

100. Patrick O'Byrne, Alyssa Bryan, and Marie Roy, "Sexual Practices and STI/HIV Testing among Gay, Bisexual, and Men Who Have Sex with Men in Ottawa, Canada: Examining Nondisclosure Prosecutions and HIV Prevention," *Critical Public Health* 23 (2013): 225.

101. Eric Mykhalovskiy, "The Problem of 'Significant Risk': Exploring the Public Health Impact of Criminalizing HIV Non-disclosure," *Social Science and Medicine* 73 (2011): 670.

102. Mykhalovskiy, 671.

103. R. v. Mabior, [2012] 2 S.C.R. 584, para. 67 (Can.).

104. Mykhalovskiy, "Problem of 'Significant Risk,'" 671–72.

105. *Mabior*, 2 S.C.R. at paras. 59–60.

106. R. v. Cuerrier, [1998] 2 S.C.R. 371, para. 22 (Can.).

107. Ibid. at paras. 78, 133, 141.

108. Ibid. at para. 74.

109. Ibid. at para. 142.

110. *Mabior*, 2 S.C.R. at para. 23.

111. *Cuerrier*, 2 S.C.R. at para. 147.

112. *Mabior*, 2 S.C.R. at paras. 44–48.

113. Martha Shaffer, "Sex, Lies, and HIV: *Mabior* and the Concept of Sexual Fraud," *University of Toronto Law Journal* 63 (2013): 466.

114. *Mabior*, 2 S.C.R. at para. 45.

115. Richard Jochelson and Kirsten Kramar, "Governing through Precaution to Protect Equality and Freedom: Obscenity and Indecency Law in Canada after *R v. Labaye* [2005]," *Canadian Journal of Sociology* 36 (2011): 283.

116. Jochelson and Kramar, 285.

117. *Cuerrier*, 2 S.C.R. at para. 47.

118. *Mabior*, 2 S.C.R. at paras. 65, 72.

119. Ibid. at para. 75.

120. Ibid. at para. 80.

121. Ibid. at paras. 23, 65.

122. R. v. Hutchinson, [2014] 1 S.C.R. 346 (Can.).

123. Ibid. at paras. 88, 91.

124. Ibid. at para. 18.

125. Ibid. at para. 42.

126. See Isabel Grant, "The Overcriminalization of Persons with HIV," *University of Toronto Law Journal* 63 (2013): 475; Shaffer, "Sex, Lies, and HIV," 466.

127. *Mabior*, 2 S.C.R. at paras. 5–6.

128. R. v. D.C., [2012] 2 S.C.R. 626, paras. 4–7 (Can.).

129. Grant, "Overcriminalization of Persons with HIV," 481.

CONTRIBUTORS

Aziza Ahmed, JD, MS, is professor at Northeastern University School of Law and an affiliate of the university's Bouvé College of Health Sciences.

Widney Brown, JD, is a managing director of policy at Drug Policy Alliance and previously was the director of programs at Physicians for Human Rights.

Sealing Cheng, DPhil, is associate professor in anthropology at the Chinese University of Hong Kong.

Sonia Corrêa, MA, is a founder of Instituto Feminista para Democracia and the Commission of Citizenship and Reproduction in Brazil, as well as cochair of the global organization Sexuality Policy Watch.

Joanna N. Erdman, JD, LLM, is an associate professor and the MacBain Chair in Health and Law Policy at the Schulich School of Law, Dalhousie University, Halifax, Nova Scotia.

Janet Halley, JD, PhD, is the Royall Professor of Law at Harvard Law School.

Alli Jernow, JD, is the program director at Wellspring Philanthropic Fund.

Hon. Maria Lucia Karam (ret.) served as a judge in Brazil from 1982 to 2000, presiding in both criminal and family court.

Ae-Ryung Kim, PhD, is a researcher at the Institute for the Humanities of Ewha Woman's University in Korea. She is also an affiliate of the Courageous Women Research Center.

Scott Long, PhD, is an independent scholar, most recently a visiting fellow of the Human Rights Program at Harvard Law School.

Alice M. Miller, JD, is the codirector of the Global Health Justice Partnership at Yale University, associate scholar for international human rights at Yale Law School, an assistant clinical professor at the Yale School of Public Health, and a lecturer at the university's Jackson Institute for Global Affairs.

Vrinda Marwah is a doctoral candidate and formerly program coordinator with Creating Resources for Empowerment and Action.

Geetanjali Misra, MA, is the executive director for Creating Resources for Empowerment and Action. She is also the treasurer of the Women's Initiative for Gender Justice and an affiliate of the Ford Foundation.

Rasha Moumneh, MA, is the program coordinator, Campaigns, Center for Women's Global Leadership, Rutgers University.

Wanja Muguongo is the executive director of UHAI EASHRI (East African Sexual Health and Rights Initiative).

Oliver Phillips, PhD, is a reader at the University of Westminster School of Law.

Zain Rizvi, JD, is a Gruber Post-Graduate Fellow in Global Justice and a 2017 graduate of the Yale Law School, as well as a member of the Global Health Justice Partnership at Yale University.

Mindy Jane Roseman, JD, PhD, is the director of the Gruber Program for Global Justice and Women's Rights and director of International Law Programs at the Yale Law School.

Esteban Restrepo Saldarriaga, JSD, LLM, is associate professor at the Universidad de los Andes School of Law in Colombia.

Tara Zivkovic, JD, is a 2017 graduate of the Yale Law School.

INDEX

Aadhaar, 71–72

abduction, in Brazilian law, 116, 119, 123, 128

able-bodiedness, social categorization based on, 8

abortion and abortion law: in Brazil, 117, 118, 123–24; calls for recriminalization of, 9; in Canada, 250–54, 256, 259; as civil right, 248; criminalization of, 3; criminalization of abortion, 159, 164–68, 249–60; criminal regulation of, 8; in El Salvador, 167; European Court of Human Rights on, 61; in France, 158–69; harm principle and, 59; harm production in criminalization of, 251–60; human rights arguments for decriminalization of, 4; in India, 187–97; inherent harm in, 253; in Lebanon, 231; in Malta, 167; in Nicaragua, 3, 167; South African courts on, 66–67; in the United States, 58, 61

accountability, 13, 14

Act on the Abolition of State-Sanctioned Prostitution Systems (South Korea), 106

Act to Prevent Immoral Behavior (South Korea), 97, 106

adolescents: Brazilian law on, 127, 131; sexual abuse of, in Brazil, 127

adultery and adultery law, 233: adultery as morals offense, 54, 57, 82; in Brazil, 117, 118, 122, 128; in Lebanon, 230; relative immorality of adultery, 259; in southern Africa, 145–46; in South Korea, 103–5; in the United States, 57, 64

Africa: age-sensitive legal regimes in, 49; conflict over miniskirts and trousers in, 134–57; conflict over women's clothing in South Africa, 139, 144; contestation over and discipline of women's bodies in, 145–50; intersections of race, gender, culture, and sexuality in, 145–50, 153; model legislation addressing HIV epidemic

in West Africa, 3; morals offenses in South Africa, 66–69; UHAI EASHRI work in East Africa, 173–84

the Americas: age-sensitive legal regimes in, 49; physicians' professionalizing aspirations in, 164. *See also* individual countries

anal rape, in Lebanese law, 231

anal sex, as morals offense, 54

animus-driven laws, 236–38

Anti-homosexuality Act (Uganda), 181

Anti-pornography Act (Uganda), 139, 140, 175

antipropaganda laws, in East Africa, 183

appeals processes, 87

Argentina, prostitution law in, 212, 213

armed conflict: consensual sex during, 37–38; rape committed in, 28–29, 36–38; sexual violence committed in, 28–29

assisted suicide, 60

Australia: incarceration of marginalized people in, 85; sentences in, 86; sodomy law in Tasmania, 60

autonomy: as Canadian constitutional value, 258; constitutionalization of criminal law and, 199, 201, 202, 214–19; harm principle and, 54; and homosexuality/same-sex sexual activity in Colombian military, 208–10; as human rights principle, 45; liberty and, 238; related to same-sex sexual conduct, 58–72. *See also* sexual autonomy; women's autonomy

autonomy feminists, 32

Baartman, Saartjie, 145

Barnard Sexuality Conference (1982), 17

Belém do Pará Convention for the Eradication of Violence against Women, 128

Berlin, Isaiah, 239, 246–47

Beyond Conjugality (Law Commission of Canada), 243

"Beyond Same-Sex Marriage," 243
bigamy, 233; as morals offense, 54, 64; United
    States law on, 64
blackmail based on sexuality, in East Africa,
    181–82
Blackstone, William, 239
bodily integrity rights, 42, 45, 66
Botswana, 140, 181
Bowers v. Hardwick, 62, 63, 234
Brazil: 1830 and 1890 penal codes in, 115–20;
    citizenship in, 115, 116, 122, 125; conserva-
    tive modernization in, 121–24; criminal
    codes in, 114–24, 132; current sexual
    regulation and rights in, 125–31; dictator-
    ship in, 124; 1940 penal code in, 120–24,
    127; reformist initiatives in, 120–21; sex
    laws in, 114–33; slavery in, 115–17; social
    conservatism in, 126–27; transition to
    democracy in, 124–25; urban criminality
    and violence in, 126
Burj Hammoud, Lebanon, 220, 225–27
Burundi, same-sex intimacy law in, 178
Butler, Judith, 18, 21–23, 136

Canada, 250–67; criminalization of
    intentional HIV transmission in, 3;
    criminalized sex work and abortion and,
    251–60; decriminalization of sodomy in,
    251; harm principle in, 73; harm produc-
    tion in, 251–67; HIV nondisclosure in, 251,
    260–67; laws on sale of sex in, 3–4;
    prostitution law in, 250, 251; sodomy laws
    in, 251, 259
Canada v. Bedford, 250–60
capital punishment/death penalty: for
    abortion in France, 166; in Brazil, 115;
    excluded in international rights regime, 3;
    for homosexuals, 3; for performing
    abortions in France, 159–60; states'
    monopoly over legitimate force and, 29
carceral feminism, 31
The Central Park Five (documentary), 79–80
chastity: and contraception in Zimbabwe, 147;
    refocusing of laws away from, 39, 45; South
    Korean law and, 96–98, 100–104, 111–12
child, "global," 49
children: assimilating women to, 46–47;
    guilty of crimes and horrific acts, 51–52;
    innocence of, 50–51; pimping of, 212; rape of,
    in Brazil, 131; sexual abuse of, in Brazil, 127;
    sexual exploitation of, in Brazil, 127, 129

children's rights: age as defining feature of,
    48–49; in Brazil, 126, 127; criminal law
    and, 46–52; gender, sexual, and reproduc-
    tive rights of, 47, 50–51
child sex trafficking, campaigns against, 48
Chile, proposal to ban miniskirts in, 141
Choice on Termination of Pregnancy Act
    (South Africa), 66–67
civilian oversight of law enforcement,
    88–89
civil rights: and abortion as women's issue,
    24–25; advocacy for, in Lebanon, 220–21
Clinton, Hillary, 224, 235
clothing/dress, 136; "indecent dressing" in
    Nigeria, 140; in postindustrial cultures,
    144; symbolic power of, 141–44, 153; and
    traditional values, 148; women's trousers or
    miniskirts in Africa, 134–57, 175
Coalition for the International Criminal
    Court (CICC), 43
Colombia: constitutional court jurisprudence
    in, 202; homosexuality and same-sex sexual
    activity in the military in, 207–12;
    prostitution, pimping, and human
    trafficking in, 212–19
commercial sex. *See* sex work/commercial
    sex
Committee on Homosexual Offenses and
    Prostitution, 56–57. *See also* Wolfenden
    Committee
Confucianism, 94–96, 98
consensual incest, adult: sexual autonomy
    and, 60; United States law on, 64
consensual sex: during armed conflict, 37–38;
    morals offenses and, 54–55
consensual sex work, decriminalization of, 4
constitutional morality, 70, 259, 260, 264n.,
    291
consent: age of, in Brazilian law, 119, 122;
    deceptions and, 265–66; fallacy of, 216;
    HIV disclosure and, 264; meaningful, 46;
    prosecution to "end" violence against
    women and diminishment of, 44–46; in
    prostitution, 110; relationship-based rule
    of, 265
constitutionalization of criminal law,
    199–219; for homosexuality, 206–12;
    "poisoned gift" dynamic in, 202–19; for
    prostitution, 206–7, 212–19; for sex crimes,
    201–6
Constitution of Brazil (1824), 115

Constitution of Brazil (1934), 121
Constitution of South Korea, 99
contraception: in African cultures, 146–47;
    criminalization of, 249; in India, 188–89;
    and population size in France, 165
contraceptives, 61, 165
Convention against Transnational Organized
    Crime, and its Protocol to Prevent,
    Suppress and Punish Trafficking in
    Persons, Especially Women and Children,
    215, 216
Convention for the Suppression of the Traffic
    in Persons and of the Exploitation of the
    Prostitution of Others, 215
Convention for the Suppression of the Traffic
    in Women and Children, 123
Convention for the Suppression of the Traffic
    in Women of Full Age, 123
Convention on the Rights of Children, 127
Convention on the Rights of the Child (CRC),
    48–52
corruption: abuses within criminal justice
    systems and, 79; among police, 86, 183;
    human rights advocates' distrust of
    nation-states for, 42; of Lebanese govern-
    ment, 220, 226; legal allowance of, 82; of
    minors, in Brazilian law, 119, 122; of
    morals, legislation to prevent, 178; social,
    248, 250
CRC (Convention on the Rights of the Child),
    48–52
criminality: activists living life of, 183;
    attributed to classes of people, 85; in Brazil,
    126; constructing/deconstructing, 76–78;
    of dishonest sexual relations, 261, 266;
    police work required to prove, 182; of sex
    selection, 193, 196; transnational, 215
criminalization: of abortion, 3, 9, 159, 164–68,
    249–60; of buyers/profiteers of sex work,
    253; of contraceptives, 165; defining crimes,
    82; of drugs, 249; feminism's turn toward,
    28–31; harms of, 249 (see also harm produc-
    tion); of HIV nondisclosure, 251, 260–67; of
    homosexuality, 256–57; hypercriminaliza-
    tion, 127, 133; of identities, 206; of
    intentional HIV transmission, 3; neoliber-
    alism and, 32–33; of prostitution, 3;
    rights-based calls for decriminalization, 2;
    of sex trade, 259; of sexual assault, 4; of
    sexual conduct, 57, 70, 248 (see also specific
    types of conduct); and undercriminaliza-

tion, 82–83. See also harm principle; specific
    criminalized practices
criminal justice: communal basis of, 257;
    harm production and, 256; selective
    administration of, 8
criminal justice systems: addressing failures
    of, 87–89; appeals process in, 87; as both
    source of and antidotes to human rights
    violations, 126; corruption in, 86;
    disparity in sentencing in, 86; equal
    protection of law under, 75–90; interna-
    tional, 29; judicial independence in,
    86–87; positionality of affected persons
    and, 76–78; profiling and, 83; and
    protection of fundamental rights, 133;
    rules of evidence and procedures in, 84,
    88; state, 29; states' role in, 78–81. See also
    individual countries
criminal law: activism and, 186; biases in, 82;
    as cause of harm, 253–56, 262–63 (see also
    harm production); children's rights and,
    46–52; civilian oversight of enforcement of,
    88–89; constitutionalization of, 199–219;
    constitutional limits on, vs. function of, 59;
    constitutional values as normative limit on,
    258; in defense of traditional values, 2–3;
    defined, 2; in enforcing gender stereotypes,
    168–69; family law and, 233; feminists'
    engagement with, 28–31; harm principle
    and, 39–40, 52, 55–58, 248–50, 261; human
    rights and, 1–4, 11–12, 42, 155–57; and
    increased reliance on prosecution to
    vindicate rights, 39–53; limiting scope of,
    87–88, 200–201; normative models
    produced by, 11; ordering of gender
    privilege and sexual and reproductive
    practices in, 9; in postcolonial southern
    Africa, 155; in promotion of modern
    human rights, 2–3; proportionality tests of,
    201, 214–15, 216–17; prostitution law in,
    3–4; purpose and objective of, 167, 168,
    199; in regulating sex, gender, and
    reproduction, 2, 3, 9–10; rights-based, 39,
    40; as sole tool to bring justice after regime
    changes, 42–43; theories of, 199; in
    transitional justice movement, 41–44. See
    also specific topics
critical legal studies (CLS), 25–31
critical race theorists (race crits), 21
culture, intersections of race, sexuality,
    gender and, 145–50, 153

death penalty. (*See* capital punishment/death penalty)

decriminalization, harm production (*See* harm production)

Devlin, Patrick, 57, 70, 74, 159, 248, 259

dignity: in Brazilian law, 118, 123, 128; as Canadian constitutional value, 258, 264, 266; choice of morality and, 132; in Colombian constitution, 207; in Colombian law, 214, 218; defining, 236, 237; in human rights regimes, 214; as justification for and limit of criminal punishment, 200–201; Kennedy on, 238, 240–42; liberty and, 241; in South African law, 67–69; in South Korean law, 99, 102; for those marked with stigma, 168

discrimination: based on sexual orientation, 236–37; in Brazilian law, 114, 133; connections of other topics to, 7; contemporary forms of, 237; in East African law, 175–77; against homosexuals, 209, 210; law reform efforts and, 13; profiling and, 85–86; same-sex marriage and, 69; sex-selection in India and, 195; against sexual minorities in India, 71, 72; sexual-orientation, 236; in South African law, 66, 68; against women, 44–45, 102, 108, 143, 144, 193, 197; workplace, 27, 108. *See also* equality and inequality

distributional analysis: for International Criminal Court, 36; of sexual violence framework, 37; shift from feminism neoformalism to, 31–38

diversity: in civilian oversight of criminal law enforcement, 88–89; gender, 110, 111, 175; of gender identities, 71; information rights and, 50; in junctures of human rights and criminal law, 4, 6; in Lebanon, 220, 222, 223; LGBTI as signifier of, 8–9; politics of, 173; in rights advocacy, 44, 178; sexual, 110, 175; in talk about recognition, 237

divorce: in France, 166; in southern Africa, 146, 149; in U.S. family law, 28

domestic violence (DV): in Lebanese law, 221–22; in South Korean law, 95

dominance feminism, 17, 24, 32–37

drug policy, 249

Dudgeon v. United Kingdom, 59–60, 70, 73

Dworkin, Ronald, 74, 200

East Africa: blackmail and extortion based on sexuality in, 181–82; LGBTI rights in, 175, 179; UHAI EASHRI work in, 173–84; vagrancy and public order laws in, 174

El Salvador, criminalization of abortion in, 167

empathy, 12–14

Engle, Karen, 37, 43

Epistemology of the Closet (Eve Kosofsky Sedgwick), 18, 22–23

equality and inequality: in Brazil, 114, 115, 120, 124, 125, 127; as Canadian constitutional value, 258, 264, 266; in Colombian constitution, 207; constitutionalization of criminal law and, 199, 201, 202; equality as political freedom, 259–60; gender equality, 186–87; and homosexuality/same-sex sexual activity in Colombian military, 208–10; as human rights principle, 45; India's child sex ratio and, 186–87; marriage equality, 66; racial equality, 127; sex equality, 9; sex work and, 253; South Korean law and, 102–4, 111, 112; structural inequality, 95, 206, 253; for those marked with stigma, 168

equal protection of the law: criminal justice system and, 75–90; same-sex marriage and, 238–39

ethnicity: persecution in Lebanon based on, 225, 227–28, 232; social categorization based on, 8

Europe: age-sensitive legal regimes in, 49; incarceration of marginalized people in, 85; marriage rates in, 244; physicians' professionalizing aspirations in, 164. *See also individual countries*

European Convention for the Protection of Human Rights and Fundamental Freedoms, 59

European Court of Human Rights, 59–61, 73

extortion based on sexuality, in East Africa, 181–82

families, 167, 233

Family Code (France), 166

feminism: distributional analysis and, 31–38; impact of *Split Decisions* on, 20–21; international criminal law and, 38; m>f concept in, 22; m/f distinction in, 18, 21–24; and other sources of work on sexuality, 23; radical, 17–18; taking a break from, 22, 23,

26. *See also specific types of feminism, e.g.:* dominance feminism

feminists: activism for suppression of law allowing wife beating, 205; Barnard Sexuality Conference of 1982 and, 17; creation of International Criminal Court and, 36; criminalization of HIV nondisclosure and, 264; in early women's rights advocacy, 44; engagement with criminal law by, 28–31; in India, abortion and, 188–90, 192; legal advocacy by, 19–21, 128; on limits of right to sexual self-determination, 99–100; trafficking and, 34–35; women's uncompensated labor in the home and, 27–28

fornication: in Lebanese law, 231; as morals offense, 54, 82; relative immorality of, 259; in United States law, 57, 64

Fourie v. Minister of Home Affairs, 69

Fourteenth Amendment, U.S. Constitution, 61–62, 65, 73, 238

France: abortion in, 158–69; population size in, 164–65; pronatalism in, 165–66; sexuality and nationalism in, 158–69; Vichy regime in, 159–63, 167

freedom(s): in Colombian constitution, 207; of expression, 78–79; political, 259–60; sexual, 65–66, 110, 133, 259–60; of women in Malawi, 144; zone of privacy for, 110. *See also* liberty

free will: in entering prostitution, 214; European court on consensual sex and, 61; in legal discussions of sex in South Korea, 103, 104, 110, 111; sexual slavery and human trafficking and, 216. *See also* autonomy

gay rights: centered on sodomy laws, 183; gay movement in the United States, 235; and harm as rights violation, 39; in Lebanon, 220–21, 224–25, 227; in the 1980s, 17–18; in Tanzania, 175. *See also* same-sex/gay marriage

gender: in Africa, intersections of race, culture, sexuality and, 145–50, 153; analyses of expressions of, 8; biases in Brazilian law regarding, 116; child sex ratio, 186–87; ideals of, in human rights advocacy, 7; and innocence of children, 51; normative models of, 11; regulation of, 2–4, 9–11; sex selection campaign in India and,

185–98; of sexual partner, meaningful consent and, 46; social categorization based on, 8; stereotypes for same-sex sexual conduct and, 9; use of criminal law to enforce stereotypes of, 168–69

gender-based violence: Brazilian movements against, 127; redressed through criminal justice systems, 133; victim precipitation of, 143

gendered citizenship, in Lebanon, 221, 231–32

gender equality: and India's child sex ratio, 186–87; South Korean law and, 102–4, 111, 112

gender hierarchy(-ies): in Africa, 143; in Brazilian law, 117, 132. *See also* sex hierarchy(-ies)

gender identities: bias-related violence based on, 76; Indian law on, 71

gender rights: for children and young people, 47, 50; sex selection campaign in India and, 186–98

Gender Trouble (Judith Butler), 18, 21–23

GF (governance feminism), 31–34, 95

Giraud, Marie Louise, 159–63, 167, 169

"global child," 49

Global Commission on HIV and the Law, 261–62

Global North: enforcement of LGBT rights and, 224; legalization of same-sex marriage in, 234; new anti-trafficking system and, 33; use of criminal law in service of women's rights in, 4

Global South: focus of prosecution on, 43; use of criminal law in service of women's rights in, 4

globalization, resistance to, 9

governance feminism (GF), 31–34, 95

Great Britain, Wolfenden Committee in, 56–58

Griswold v. Connecticut, 61, 63

Harare, Zimbabwe, 135, 136

Harcourt, Bernard, 73, 248–50

harm principle, 11; collapse of, 248–50; criminal law and, 39–40, 52, 55–58, 248–50, 261; morals offenses and, 54–74; related to same-sex sexual conduct, 58–74

harm production, 248–67; in criminalized HIV nondisclosure, 260–67; in criminalized sex work and abortion, 251–60; in debates on criminalization of sex and reproduction, 249; defined, 249; in drug policy debates, 249

harm(s): in advocacy to end violence against
    women, 44–46; competing, 250; of
    criminalization, 249; defining, 88; evidence
    of, 253, 255, 261–63; in inducement into
    prostitution, 217–18; inherent, 253, 254;
    judgment in what constitutes/causes, 250;
    to political values, 265; as rights violation,
    39; transitional justice movement and, 41;
    use and abuse of notion of, 73
Hart, H.L.A., 57, 70, 248–50, 256–57
health: as human rights principle, 45;
    meaningful consent and information
    about, 46; right to, 249; sexual, public
    health framing of, 25
heteronormativity: and abortions as criminal,
    158–59; definitions of gender and, 143;
    Lebanese law and, 230; marriage and, 97; in
    notions of family, 167; patriarchy and, 141,
    177, 232; reproduction and, 222, 230; in
    sexualizing female body, 142
HIV epidemic(s): decriminalization of sex
    work and, 249; in 1980s United States,
    17–18; West African nations' model
    legislation addressing, 3
HIV status: bias-related violence based on, 76;
    harm production in criminalized
    nondisclosure of, 251, 260–67; as reproduc-
    tive rights issue, 25
HIV transmission: criminalization of, 249;
    intentional, 3; risk of, 261
homosexuality: Brazilian law on, 118–19;
    constitutionalization of criminal law for,
    206–12; criminalization of, 256–57; East
    African antihomosexuality laws, 175, 178,
    182; in India, 184; in Lebanon, 220–25,
    231–32; male, Wolfenden Report on, 56;
    multitiered approach to decriminalization
    of, 183; and population size in France,
    164–65; populist politics repression of, 174;
    reclassified as illness, 259; reflections on
    same-sex marriage and, 233–47; Ugandan
    antihomosexuality bill, 175. See also
    same-sex sexual behavior
homosexuals/gays: "acceptance" and
    "tolerance" for, 224; death penalty for, 3;
    death penalty for killers of, 3; in East
    Africa, 183; insult to dignity of, 240;
    marriage for, 244 (see also same-sex/gay
    marriage); "you don't belong" laws and, 237.
    See also gay rights; lesbians
Hottentot Venus, 145

human body: beliefs and discourse about,
    147–48, 154, 155; bodily integrity rights,
    42, 45, 66; commodification of, in
    Zimbabwe, 149; morals offenses and, 54;
    states' regulation of, 221; women's rights to
    decisions affecting, 259
human rights, 1, 10; in Brazil, 125–31; and call
    to end impunity, 3; core principles within,
    40; creation of International Criminal
    Court and, 35–36; criminal law and, 1–4,
    11–12, 42, 155–57 (see also specific topics);
    dignity and, 214; as guide and limit to use
    of criminal law, 39; instrumentalization of
    claims for, by other actors, 41; as justifica-
    tion for and limit of criminal punishment,
    200–201; and legal enforcement of gender
    stereotypes, 168–69; for LGBTI people in
    East Africa, 179; in postcolonial southern
    Africa, 155; power and, 1; regulation of
    sexual, reproductive, and gender practices
    and expressions in, 2, 3; to same-sex
    marriage, 234; time/timing and salience of
    ideologies and practices for, 41; United
    States' violations of, 84–85; universalizing
    language of, 6–7; vision of "the good life"
    in, 52. See also international human rights;
    rights; specific topics
human rights advocacy: activists and
    criminal justice systems, 75–90; for
    children's rights, 46–52; distrust of states
    by advocates, 42, 52–53; to "end" violence
    against women, 44–46; "gender" in, 7; for
    the International Criminal Court, 41–44;
    prosecutions called on in, 40; "reproduc-
    tion" in, 7; "sexuality" in, 7; siloes in, 7;
    thematic categorization of, 8
human rights feminists, 34, 35
human rights law: public morals exception
    in, 88; rights-based legal systems as new-
    comers in sex, gender, and reproduction
    realms, 4
human trafficking/trafficking, 123; antitraf-
    ficking conventions and prostitution law, 3;
    in Argentina, 212–13; Brazilian anti-
    trafficking measures, 130; in Colombian
    law, 215–16, 218–19; conflation of
    prostitution with, 3, 32, 94, 104–11, 213,
    219; constitutionalization of criminal law
    for, 212–19; feminist advocacy and, 34;
    feminists and anti-trafficking system,
    32–35; global anti-trafficking campaigns,

104–5; inducement into prostitution and organized crime and, 215; internal, in Brazilian law, 129, 130; international, in Brazilian law, 123, 129; international criminal law on, 213, 216, 218, 219; in Latin America, 212; relationships among pimping, prostitution, and, 213; for sexual exploitation, 129, 130; social movements against, 127; South Korean anti-trafficking campaigns, 93, 104–11; in South Korean law, 105, 111, 112; women's rights group prosecuted for, 99

ICC (International Criminal Court), 35–36, 41–44
ICCPR (International Covenant on Civil and Political Rights), 57, 60
ICTs (International Criminal Tribunals), 36, 37
identities: criminalization of, 206; gender, bias-related violence based on, 76; gender, Indian law on, 71; law as platform for producing/patrolling, 156; national, tradition and, 136, 152–53; political and sectarian, 222; traditional vs. modern, in Zimbabwe, 136, 151–52
incarceration: alternatives to, 86, 89; in Brazil, 133; disproportionate, 85–86; for rape, 29; states' monopoly over legitimate force and, 29; transparency in prison system, 89; in the United States, 87
incest: adult consensual, 60, 64; criminalization of, 64, 203; as morals offense, 54; pregnancies resulting from, 58
indecent assault: in Brazilian law, 116, 118, 119, 123, 128; in Zimbabwe, 136–37
indecent exposure by fraud, in Brazilian law, 123, 128
India: incarceration of marginalized people in, 85; morals offenses in, 69–72; prosecution of rapists in, 3; reproductive choice in, 188–89; sex ratio in, 186–88; sex selection in (See sex selection campaign [India]); sexual violence against women in, 185
indigenous activist funding, from UHAI EASHRI, 173
Indonesia, proposal to ban miniskirts in, 141
innocence: of children, 50–51; presumption of, 85
International Covenant on Civil and Political Rights (ICCPR), 57, 60

International Criminal Court (ICC), 35–36, 41–44
international criminal law: child rights in, 46–52; feminist engagement with, 38; on human trafficking, 213, 215, 216, 218–19; major force behind rise of, 33; of rape, 35–36
international criminal system: monopoly over legitimate force and, 29; trafficking in, 33–34
International Criminal Tribunals (ICTs), 36, 37
international feminism, 37–38
International Gay and Lesbian Human Rights Commission, 181
international human rights, 10–11, 84–85; relationships among trafficking, pimping, and prostitution in, 213; standards for, 39; state role in implementing law of, 132–33; United States' violations of, 84–85. See also transnational theory and practice
international human rights organizations, siloes in, 7
intersectional analysis, of sexual violence framework, 37
intersectionality, 21, 22
intersex persons: discrimination against, 176; prosecution as a human rights advocacy tool for, 4; rights for younger people, 50
"is/ought" distinction, 28
Italy, proposal to ban miniskirts in, 141

Jordan v. State, 67–69, 73
Joslin v. New Zealand, 234
judicial activism, 199. See also constitutionalization of criminal law
judicial review, 199, 236. See also constitutionalization of criminal law
justice: "is/ought" distinction in, 28; juvenile, rehabilitation as rationale for, 51; "redistribution" and "recognition" visions of, 237; sex selection campaign in India and, 185–98; transitional justice movement, 41–44. See also criminal justice; criminal justice systems
justice cascade, 42–43
juvenile justice, rehabilitation as rationale for, 51

K. A. and A. D. v. Belgium, 60–61
Kenya: conflict over women's trousers or miniskirts in, 139; intersex discrimination in, 176; law on nonnormative sexual practice in, 178; prostitution law in, 180; sodomy laws in, 175, 183–84

Korean Criminal Code, 93, 97–100, 110–12
*Kylie v. Commission for Conciliation,
    Mediation and Arbitration,* 68, 69

labor feminists, 32
Laskey v. United Kingdom, 60
law: different protagonists' claims to, 155–56;
    morality and, 132, 250; ordinary, 199. *See
    also* criminal law
Lawrence v. Texas, 62–66, 70, 72–74, 235
League of Nations, 123
Lebanon, 220–32; anal examinations in, 220,
    223, 229–32; citizenship laws in, 231;
    diversity, tolerance, and exceptionalism in,
    222–24; homosexuality issue in, 220–25,
    231–32; marital rape in, 229–30, 232;
    national belonging and gendered citizen-
    ship in, 231–32; reproduction regulation in,
    229–31; sectarianism in, 222, 223, 228; sex
    panics in, 225–29; types of rape in, 231;
    xenophobia in, 226–28
"legal good" theory, 200
legal moralism, 57, 249–50
lesbians: "acceptance" and "tolerance" for,
    224; in the Colombian military, 210–11;
    harm as rights violation for, 39; insult to
    dignity of, 240; marriage for, 244 (*see also*
    same-sex/gay marriage); politics around
    sexuality for, 18; sex workers who identify
    as, 178; social subordination of, 65;
    traditional "gay-focused" work and, 175;
    "you don't belong" laws and, 237. *See also*
    LGBTI persons, women, and feminism
Levinson, Steve H., 64
LGBTI persons: as grouping to understand
    law, 8–9; in multiple-partner relationships,
    243; societal prejudice against, 176;
    solidarity among groups advocating for,
    176–77. *See also* homosexuals/gays; intersex
    persons; lesbians; transgender persons
LGBTI rights: Brazilian movements for, 127;
    East African forums for, 175; Global
    North's campaigns for, 224; UHAI activism
    for, 176–77; new priorities for LGBT
    movement, 237–38
liberal feminists, 32, 36–37
liberalism, 9, 116, 118
liberal selfhood, 95
liberty: as Canadian constitutional value, 258,
    264, 266; defining, 236, 237; deprivation of,
    2, 13, 61, 69, 167; dignity and, 241;

Fourteenth Amendment and, 61, 62; in
    Indian law, 71; Kennedy on, 63, 238–42;
    Mills on, 54–56; morality and, 70; negative,
    239; as political freedom, 259–60; positive,
    239; Reagan on, 235; for same-sex
    marriage, 66; zone of privacy for, 110. *See
    also* freedom(s)
local activism and politics, 174
Lokoto, Simon, 139–40
love: in legal discussions of sex in South
    Korea, 103, 104, 110, 111; marriage and, 237,
    241, 246
Loving v. Virginia, 62–63

m>f concept (men, maleness, masculinity
    advantage over f), 22, 24–25
Malawi: blackmail for male same-sex conduct
    in, 181; freedom of women in, 144; women's
    clothing conflicts in, 139
Malta, criminalization of abortion in, 167
Mamdani, Mahmood, 43, 222
marginalized individuals/groups: dispropor-
    tionate incarceration of, 85–86; state
    actions and, 79; violence toward, 78; in war
    on drugs, 84
marital rape: in Lebanon, 222, 229–30, 232; in
    South Korea, 100, 101, 103; women's rights
    advocacy against, 45
marital violence, 205
marriage (heterosexual): in Africa, 145;
    bigamy, 54, 63, 64, 233; early/forced,
    campaigns against, 48; in France, 164–65;
    institution of, 97, 103, 104, 108, 113, 123,
    164, 166- 168, 193, 195, 230, 244, 246;
    judgmentalism about, 242–43; Kennedy on,
    241–44; Lebanese law on, 229–31; proof,
    142, 145, ; to rape victims, in Brazilian law,
    117; relationships of care and, 243; sex
    outside of (*see also* prostitution law,
    homosexual conduct), 152, 176, 235; in
    southern Africa, 146; in South Korean law,
    104, 105; in Zimbabwe, 150. *See also*
    same-sex/gay marriage
Martin v. Ziherl, 64
Massachusetts, sex trafficking in, 35
Medical Termination of Pregnancy Act
    (India), 188, 196
medicine, idea of causality in, 147–48
men, as a category: innocent, conviction of,
    29–31; South Korean gender distinctions,
    96, 98, 99, 101, 104; as victims in Brazilian

law, 118–19; in violence over skirt length, 134–38, 140, 143, 151

m/f (men/women, masculinity/femininity male/female) distinction, 18, 21–24

migrant workers: in Lebanon, 226–29; sexual violence against, in Saudi Arabia, 76–77

military: administrative sanctions for, 208; homosexuality and same-sex sexual activity in, 206–12

Mill, John Stuart, 52, 54, 55, 57, 200, 216–17, 219

miniskirts, conflicts over, 134–57, 175

Ministry of Gender Equality (South Korea), 95, 102

minors, corruption of, 119, 122

Model Penal Code(MPC), 54–55, 57–58

Modinos v. Cyprus, 60

Moldova, children's rights in, 47–48

morality, 11; constitutionalization of criminal law and, 202 (*see also* "poisoned gift" dynamic); crimes based on, 82, 88, 259 (*see also* morals offenses); distinction between law and, 132; harm production and, 256–58; and immorality as treason, 159; line between law and, 250; related to same-sex sexual conduct, 58–72. *See also* political morality; constitutional morality

morality jurisprudence, 55

morals offenses, 54–74; in American courts, 61–66; application of harm, morality, and autonomy related to same-sex sexual conduct, 58–72; in Brazilian law, 123, 128; defined, 54–55; in European Court of Human Rights, 59–61; harm principle and the function of criminal law, 56–58; in India, 69–72; in South African courts, 66–69. *See also* specific types of offenses

Moyn, Samuel, 42–43, 52

multiple-partner relationships, 243–44

Namibia, 140, 181

national belonging, in Lebanon, 221, 231–32

National Coalition for Gay and Lesbian Equality (South Africa), 67

national historical perspectives: abortion as treason in France, 158–69; Brazilian sex laws, 114–33; prostitution exceptionalism in South Korea, 93–113; skirt length in Zimbabwe, 134–57

National Human Rights Commission (South Korea), 95

national identity, tradition and, 136, 152–53

nationalism: birthrates and, 164, 165; in Lebanon, 228, 229; sexuality and, in France, 158–69

National Legal Services Authority v. Union of India, 71

Naz Foundation v. Union of India, 69–70

negative liberty, 239

neoliberalism: in Brazil, 125–26; criminalization and, 32–33; neoliberal sex hierarchy, 93, 110; resistance to, 9; self-generation of life and, 104; sex work and, 108–11; in South Korea, 93, 95, 111–13

NGOs. (*See* nongovernmental organizations)

Nicaragua: criminalization of abortion in, 3, 167; decriminalization of same-sex sexual conduct in, 3

Nigeria: "indecent dressing" in, 140; miniskirt ban in, 143

nonconforming sexuality and gender: laws used to suppress, 174; UHAI advocacy for, 175

nongovernmental organizations (NGOs): in Coalition for the International Criminal Court, 43; feminist, at Rome Conference, 38; legal recognition of, 225; limited scope of, 7

nonprocreative sex: as morals offense, 54; "poisoned gift" dynamic and, 203

Norris v. Ireland, 60

Northern Ireland, sodomy law in, 59–60

Obergefell v. Hodges, 236–38

On Liberty (John Stuart Mill), 54, 55, 216–17

Optional Protocol to the Convention on the Rights of the Child on the Sale of Children, Child Prostitution and Child Pornography, 127, 129

oral sex, as morals offense, 54

ordinary law, 199

O'Regan, Justice (South Africa), 68, 73

Palermo Protocol to Prevent, Suppress and Punish Trafficking in Persons, Especially Women and Children, 34–35, 127, 129

patriarchal power structure: in Africa, 142–43, 152; in Brazil, 119; criminal justice systems and, 133; heteronormative structures undergirding, 141; in India, 197; in Lebanon, 230; in South Korea, 94–95; stereotype of women in, 168

A People Condemned (UHAI), 175
Pimping (crime defined as): in Brazilian law, 119, 123, 129; constitutionalization of criminal law for, 207, 212–19; Massachusetts law on, 35; in South Korean law, 106, 109; in United States law, 58
Planning Families report, 195
"Pleasure and Danger" feminists, 17, 32
"poisoned gift" dynamic, 202–19; for homosexuality, 206–7; for prostitution, 206–7, 212–19; for same-sex sexual activity in the military, 207–12; for sex crimes, 202–6
police abuse, 76; designing systems to stop, 79–80; in East African states, 182
police forces, administrative sanctions for, 208
police power: in Brazil, 120; in East Africa, 179, 182; where "immorality" is concerned, 159
political morality, 11, 258, 259, 264–266
politics: of accountability, 13, 14; of diversity, 173–84; of recognition, 237
polygamy, 243
population size, as measure of strength, 164–65
pornography law: in Brazil, 117, 127; child pornography, 127, 129; in Uganda, 139, 140, 175
positive liberty, 239
postcolonial feminists, 21, 32
poverty: abuses within criminal justice systems and, 79; meaningful consent negated by, 46; prostitution and, 105, 109, 216; risk of abuse or repression and, 174; women's right to self-determination and, 110
power differences: gendered, 142; in negotiating sex, 47
Pre-conception and Pre-natal Diagnostic Techniques (Prohibition of Sex Selection) Act (India), 186, 188–90
pregnancy: criminalization of conduct during, 249; criminal regulation of, 8; illegal, in Saudi Arabia, 76–77; monitoring of, in India, 190, 191; undisclosed risk of, as sexual assault, 265–66. *See also* abortion and abortion law
Pre-natal Diagnostic Techniques (Regulation and Prevention of Misuse) Act (India), 189
presumption of innocence, 85

Pretty v. United Kingdom, 60
Prevention of Sexual Traffic and Protection of Victims Thereof (South Korea), 105
prison population, in Brazil, 133
prison system, transparency in, 89
privacy, 55; and homosexuality/same-sex sexual activity in Colombian military, 208–10; morals offenses and, 54–73; sex work and, 110; in South African law, 67, 71; South Korean law and, 94, 96, 101–5, 110, 111
privilege. in Brazilian law, 117. working of criminal justice system and, 75–78. *See also* privileged vantage points
privileged vantage points, 6, 8, 9, 30, 36, 50, 75, 78
profiling, 83
prosecution: children's rights and, 46–52; to "end" violence against women, 44–46; harm principle and, 39–40, 52; increased reliance on, 39–53; of miniskirt assault perpetrators in Zimbabwe, 136–38; for rape committed during armed conflict, 36–38; states' monopoly over legitimate force and, 29; of those racially marginalized in the United States, 13; and transitional justice movement, 41–44
prosecutors, abuse of discretion by, 83–84, 89
prostitutes: evidence against, 180; South Korean legal classification of, 97–98
prostitution and prostitution law, 3–4; antiprostitution laws in South Korea, 93–95, 104–11; in Brazil, 117, 119, 123, 128, 129–31; in Canada, 250, 251; conflation of trafficking and prostitution, 3, 32, 94, 104–11, 213, 219; constitutionalization of criminal law for prostitution, 206–7, 212–19; dominance feminist stand on, 34; East African antiprostitution laws, 182; South African courts on, 67; South Korean antiprostitution laws, 93, 104–11; Wolfenden Report on, 56; in Zimbabwe, 149–50. *See also* sex work/commercial sex
prostitution exceptionalism: defined, 105. in South Korea, 93, 105–13
Prostitution Reference, 251
public morality, 55. *See also* morality
public order laws. in East Africa, 174, 179; in Uganda, 180; in the West, 179
"public outrage on decency," as crime in Brazil, 119
Punishment of Sexual Traffic and Associated Acts (South Korea), 105, 106, 107

queer rights movement, in India, 185
queer theory, 18, 20–21, 24

R. v. Butler, 73–74
R. v. Cuerrier, 261–65
R. v. D.C., 250–51, 261, 266–67
R. v. Hutchinson, 265–66
R. v. Labaye, 257–58, 264, 265
R. v. Mabior, 250–51, 261, 263–66
R. v. Malmo-Levine, 257–58
R. v. Morgentaler, 250, 252–56, 258–59, 264
"Race and Essentialism" (Angela Harris), 22
race and racism: in Africa, intersections of
    culture, sexuality, gender and, 145–50, 153,
    154; antiracist work and, 22; in Brazil and
    Brazilian law, 117, 126, 127, 131; colorblind-
    ness in the United States, 205–6; consent
    and, 46; disparate punishment based on,
    86; harm based on, 126; and innocence of
    children, 51; in Lebanon, 221, 225–28, 232;
    prosecutions in the United States and, 13;
    racism of imprisonment, 133; social
    categorization based on, 8
radical feminism, 17–18, 24, 253, 259
rape: in Brazilian law, 116–16, 119, 122, 123,
    128, 131; committed in armed conflict,
    28–29, 36, 37; international criminal law of,
    35–36; Lebanese law on, 229–31; marital,
    45, 100, 101, 103, 222, 229–30, 232; privilege
    in cases involving, 75–76; prosecution of
    rapists, 3; as *representation* as well as *event*,
    20; role of "consent" in defining, 45–46;
    South Korean law on, 100–101, 105; and
    tolerated residuum of abuse, 29–31; and
    transgression of convention of propriety,
    143
recognition: politics of, 237; of relationships
    of care, 243–44; of same-sex/gay marriage,
    236–38
refugees: Syrian, in Lebanon, 227–29; women,
    category-exclusionary analyses of, 8
relationships of care, 243–44
Reliable consultants v. Earle, 65
religious intolerance, in Lebanon, 222–24
religious laws, penal codes built around, 88
reproduction: in African cultures, 146;
    contraception and, 146–47; criminalization
    of, 249 (*see also* harm production); in
    human rights advocacy, 7; Lebanon's
    regulation of, 229–31; normative models of,
    11; public health framing of, 25; as public

health matter, 249; regulation of, 2–4, 9–11;
    reproductive conduct as a harm for the
    young, 47; and sex selection campaign in
    India, 185–98; reproductive justice, in
    India, 185–98
reproductive rights, 2; for children, 47; as
    cornerstone of equality projects, 25; South
    African courts on, 66; in southern Africa,
    145
rights: to bodily integrity, 42, 45, 66; of
    children, 46–52, 125, 127; civil rights,
    24–25, 220–21; to health, 249; not
    specifically enumerated in U.S. Constitu-
    tion, 238, 240. *See also* human rights;
    specific rights, e.g., women's rights
rights advocates
and harm as rights violation, 39
and human rights as guide and limit to use of
    criminal law, 39
in Lebanon, 220–21
as newcomers in sex, gender, and reproduc-
    tion realms, 4
use of state power invoked by, 11
Roe v. Wade, 61, 63, 66
Rome Conference, 36–38
Romer v. Evans, 235
Rome Statute, 36
Rousseff, Dilma, 130
Roxin, Claus, 200
Rubin, Gayle, 18, 23, 93, 110
rules of evidence and procedures, 84, 88
Rwanda, antihomosexuality law in, 178

sadomasochistic sex: autonomy and, 60–61;
    as morals offense, 54; South African courts
    on, 67
same-sex/gay marriage, 233–44; dignity and,
    240–42; in Lebanon, 224; liberty and,
    238–40; recognition of, 236–38; in the
    United States, 234–42
same-sex sexual behavior: Amnesty
    International policy on decriminalization
    of, 48; analyses of, 8; application of harm,
    morality, and autonomy to, 58–74;
    blackmail for, 181; in Brazilian law, 117;
    constitutionalization of criminal law for,
    206–12; criminalization of, 249; in East
    Africa, 184; gender stereotypes for, 9; in
    Nicaragua, 3; "special subjection relation-
    ships" and, 208. *See also* homosexuality;
    sodomy and sodomy laws

Saudi Arabia: incarceration of marginalized
    people in, 85; position of girls and women
    in, 76–77; use of torture in, 77, 82
secrecy laws, 85
security of the person, as Canadian constitu-
    tional value, 264
seduction: in Brazilian law, 116, 119, 122, 123,
    128; in South Korean law, 93, 97, 101–2, 105,
    108
sentencing practices, 86
sex crimes: constitutionalization of criminal
    law for, 201–6; as deviations from
    procreative sex, 203; distinction between
    sexual violence crimes and, 100; by
    migrants and refugees in Lebanon, 228;
    opposing models for regulation of, 203; as
    repression of sexuality, 204. See also
    specific countries; specific types of crimes
sex equality, 9
sex hierarchy(-ies): in Brazilian law, 132;
    neoliberal, 93, 110, 113; in patriarchal
    African culture, 142. See also gender
    hierarchy(-ies)
sex offender registries, 84
sex panics, in Lebanon, 225–29
sex ratio, in India, 186–88
sex selection campaign (India), 185–98;
    advocacy, messaging, and rights in, 194–96;
    civil society and government responses to,
    189–91; and India's sex ratios, 186–88;
    reframing questions in, 196–98; relation-
    ship between policy change and civil
    society campaigning in, 191–94; and
    reproductive choice in India, 188–89
sex toys/sexual devices, U.S. law on, 64–65
sex trafficking, 35, 48. See also human
    trafficking/trafficking
sexual abuse: of children and adolescents, in
    Brazil, 127; South Korean law on, 100–101;
    tolerated residuum of, 29–31. See also
    specific types of abuse, e.g.: marital rape
sexual activity/conduct: criminalization of,
    57, 70, 206, 248, 249 (see also harm
    principle; harm production); criminal
    regulation of, 8; different consequences of
    heterosexual intercourse, 24; as a harm for
    the young, 47; morals offenses, 54–55;
    power differences in negotiating, 47; as
    public health matter, 249; sex outside of
    marriage, human rights arguments for
    decriminalization of, 4

sexual assault: analyses of prosecutions for,
    8; failure to disclose HIV status as, 261,
    264; human rights arguments for
    criminalization of, 4; over skirt length in
    African countries, 134–36, 140, 151, 154;
    sabotage of condoms as, 265–66; in
    Swaziland, 139; victim precipitation belief
    about, 143
sexual autonomy: in African culture, 142–43,
    145; criminalization of prostitution and, 3,
    213; gender propriety and, 152; in South
    Korea, 93, 100–104; and traditional African
    values, 148, 152–53. See also sexual
    self-determination
sexual dignity, crimes against, 128. See also
    dignity
sexual exploitation: of children, in Brazil,
    127, 129; HIV nondisclosure as, 264–65;
    trafficking for, in Brazilian law, 129, 130
sexual freedom, 65–66; criminal justice
    systems and, 133; harm of sexual assault as
    denial of, 266; prostitution and, 110. See
    also sexual autonomy
sexual harassment: in Brazilian law, 128; in
    South Korean law, 95
sexuality: in Africa, intersections of race,
    culture, gender and, 145–50, 153; blackmail
    and extortion based on, 181–82; in human
    rights advocacy, 7; normative models of, 11;
    previously tolerated practices around, 45;
    public health framing of, 25; regulation of,
    2–4, 9–11, 178; social categorization based
    on, 8; South Korean legal changes
    regulating, 93–113; UHAI support for
    activism around, 173–84; young people's
    rights concerning, 50
sexual justice, in India, 185–98
sexual minorities: discrimination against,
    Indian law on, 71, 72; UHAI EASHRI focus
    on, 173
sexual orientation: bias-related violence based
    on, 76; Kennedy's decisions on, 236–42.
    See also specific topics
sexual politics, 221; for lesbians, 18; in South
    Korea, 93–113
sexual possession: in Brazilian law, 123; by
    fraud, in Brazilian law, 128
sexual rights, 2; in Brazil, 114, 125–31; of
    children, 47, 50–51
sex selection campaign in India, 186–98.
    See also sexual autonomy; sexual freedom

sexual self-determination, 9; feminist scholars on limits of right to, 99–100; gender and rights to, 100; prostitution exceptionalism and, 93, 105–13; sexual violence as infringement of, 99; society's need for morality and order vs., 100; in South Korea, 93, 94, 98–113 (see also prostitution exceptionalism); of wives, 101. See also sexual autonomy; sexual freedom

sexual victimhood: equating sex work with, 104–11; gender-specific, 110–12

sexual violation by fraud, in Brazilian law, 128

sexual violence: in Brazilian law, 118–19, 131; committed in armed conflict, 28–29; disparate punishment for, 86; distinction between sex crimes and sexual violence crimes, 100; and failures of U.S. criminal justice system, 84, 85; as gendered violence, 109–12; in India, 185; presumption of, 131; as priority for international feminists, 37; public attention to, 45–46; in South Korean law, 95, 98, 99, 104

sex work/commercial sex: analyses of, 8; in Brazil, 130–31; criminalization of, 249; East African laws targeting, 179–81; harm principle and, 73; harm production in criminalization of, 251–60; HIV epidemics and decriminalization of, 249; as morals offense, 54, 82; New York City policing practices and, 83; prostitution exceptionalism, 93, 105–13; South African courts on, 66–69; in South Korea, 108–11; United States law on, 64, 179; U.S. Model Penal Code on, 58. See also prostitution and prostitution law

sex workers: Bedford court reliance on evidence from, 255; in East Africa, 183; HRAPF legal aid to, 180; legal reforms to protect, 260; rights advocacy by UHAI for, 175–77; rights advocacy in Brazil for, 129

sex work feminists, 36–37

Silent Observer (India), 190

siloes, 7

skirt length, African conflicts over, 134–57, 175

social categories: intersection of, 8; privilege and marginalization conferred by, 8

social difference, intersectionality among frames of, 21, 22

social media, in miniskirt conflicts, 137–39

socioeconomic status, social categorization based on, 8

sodomy and sodomy laws (defined as same sex): in Brazil, 116; in Canada, 251, 259; in East Africa, 175, 179–80, 182, 183; in Europe, 59–60; gay rights campaigns centered on, 183; in India, 184; in Kenya, 175, 183–84; in Northern Ireland, 59–60; in South Africa, 67; in Tanzania, 175; in Tasmania, 60; in Uganda, 181; in the United States, 57, 58, 62

solidarity, 13, 14

South Africa: conflict over women's trousers or miniskirts in, 139; march for women's clothing rights in, 144; morals offenses in, 66–69

South Korea: antiprostitution laws and anti-trafficking campaigns in, 93–95, 104–11; discourse of liberal selfhood in, 95; financial bailout for, 95; gender and sexual purity politics in, 93–113; historic gendering of sexual virtue in, 96–100; legal reforms toward sexual autonomy in, 100–104; proposal to ban miniskirts in, 141; prostitution and sex work in, 97, 105–6, 108–11; prostitution exceptionalism in, 93, 105–13; recent Criminal Code reforms in, 93

Special Act on Sexual Violence (South Korea), 94, 99, 109

state power: and African beliefs about the human body, 148; criminal law and, 1, 2; human rights and, 11, 126; lack of rational limit on, 167; monopoly over legitimate force and, 29

states: abusive practices of, 42; child rights and, 49; criminal justice system roles of, 78–81; criminal law and role of, 52; human rights advocates' distrust of, 42, 52–53; moral judgments and, 55

State v. Romano, 64

Statute of Children and Adolescents (Brazil), 127

stigma, 168

structural inequality, 95, 206, 253

Stübing v. Germany, 60

subaltern feminist work, 21

substantive due process doctrine, 238, 239

Suresh Kumar Koushal v. Naz Foundation, 70–72, 185

Swaziland, miniskirts in, 139, 143

SWEAT v. Minister of Safety and Security, 68–69

Tanzania: law on nonnormative sexual practice in, 178; sodomy laws in, 175

theoretical incommensurability, 23

TJ (transitional justice) movement, 41–44

tolerated residuum of abuse (TRA), 29–31

Toonen v. Australia, 60

torture: in central Asia, 82–83; documenting, in East Africa, 182; in Saudi Arabia, 77, 82; sentencing for, 86

tradition, in African cultures, 134–57

trafficking. *See* human trafficking/trafficking

Trafficking Protocol, 33

Trafficking Victims Protection Act (South Korea), 105

Trafficking Victims Protection Act (United States), 35

transgender persons: Indian law on, 71; police abuse of, 76; rights for younger people, 50; U.S. public toilet rights for, 58. *See also* gender, men/women

transitional justice (TJ) movement, 41–44

transnational theory and practice: increased reliance on prosecution to vindicate rights, 39–53: morals offenses, 54–74

treason: abortion as, in France, 159–69; in criminal theory of conduct, 168

Uganda: antihomosexuality bill in, 175; criminalization of intentional HIV transmission in, 3; death penalty for homosexuals in, 3; law on nonnormative sexual practice in, 178; miniskirt ban in, 139–40, 143; pornography law in, 139, 140, 175; public order laws in, 180

UHAI EASHRI (East African Sexual Health and Rights Initiative), 173–84

UN Convention on the Elimination of All Forms of Discrimination against Women, 128

UN Declaration of the Rights of the Child, 49

UN Human Rights Committee, 234

United Nations Human Rights Committee, 60

United Nations Office for Drugs and Crime, 33, 35

United States: abortion law in, 58, 61; adult consensual incest law in, 63; adultery law in, 57, 64; age-sensitive legal regimes in, 49; anti-sex work ordinances in, 179; bigamy law in, 63; calls for recriminalization of abortion in, 9; colorblindness in, 205–6; criminal justice system in, 80–87; death penalty for killers of homosexuals in, 3; disparity of sentencing in, 86; fornication law in, 57, 64; gay movement, 235; HIV epidemic in, 17–18; incarceration of marginalized people in, 85; justice inequality in, 80–81; marriage equality in, 66; marriage rates in, 244; Model Penal Code of, 54–55, 57–58; morals offenses and privacy in, 61–66; power differences in negotiating sex in, 47; prosecution of those racially marginalized in, 13; and rise of international criminal law, 33; same-sex marriage in, 234–42, 234–44; sex work/commercial sex law in, 63, 179; sodomy laws in, 57, 58, 62; "super predator" idea in, 51; torture in, 82; Trafficking Victims Protection Act, 35; transgender persons' public toilet rights in, 48; violations of international human rights in, 84–85

University of Zimbabwe, 134–36, 142, 151

vagrancy laws: in East Africa, 174, 179; in Uganda, 180

values, pluralism of, 246

victimization, language of, 112

victims: equating sex work with sexual victimhood, 104–11; gender-specific sexual victimhood, 110–12; men as, in Brazilian law, 118–19; precipitation of sexual assault by, 143; of rape, marriage to, 117

violence: bias-related, 76; in Brazil, 126; failure of criminal justice systems and, 79–80; harm and, 253, 254; over skirt length in African countries, 134–36, 140, 143, 151; presumption of, 131; toward people in marginalized communities, 78

violence against women (VAW): call to end impunity for, 3: prosecution to "end," 44–46

virgin, virginity, 92, 116, 117, 119, 122, 123, 230

vulnerable persons, rape of, 131

war on drugs, 84, 249

welfare programs, in South Korea, 109

West African nations, model legislation addressing HIV epidemic in, 3

Wolfenden Committee, 49, 56–60, 248

women: assimilating to children, 46–47; in Brazilian law, 122, 123; in Brazilian prison population, 133; in Saudi Arabia, 76–77, 82;

skirt length conflict in African countries, 134–57; South Korean gender distinctions, 96, 98, 99, 101, 104; uncompensated labor in the home by, 27–28. *See also* lesbians, LGBTI, gender

women's autonomy: criminalization of prostitution and, 3; prosecution to "end" violence against women and diminishment of, 44–46; and sex selection campaign in India, 185–98

Women's Caucus for Gender Justice, 45–46

women's rights: in Brazilian law, 117; in criminal prostitution laws, 3; to define cultural limits of sexual propriety, 154–55; in Lebanon, 229–31; to sexual self-determination, 93, 98–113

women's rights advocacy/activism: criminalization of intentional HIV transmission and, 3; harm as rights violation and, 39;

harm principle in, 248; prostitution exceptionalism in, 94, 105; tension between mainstream human rights actors and activists, 78–79; turn toward prosecution in, 44–46; Zimbabwe skirt length issue and, 136, 137

women's rights movement: in India, 185, 189; prostitution exceptionalism and, 105–13; in South Korea, 94–98, 105, 109–11

World Conference on Human Rights (Vienna; 1993), 34, 44–45

Zambia, 140

Zimbabwe, 145; commodification of sex and the body in, 149; contraception in, 147; idea of causality in, 147–48; marriage in, 150; prostitution in, 149–50; skirt length in, 134–39, 142–44, 148, 151–55

ACKNOWLEDGMENTS

This book came into being as part of an impassioned argument among human rights scholars and advocates about their embrace or suspicion of criminal law: Will criminalization serve justice? For whom and at whose expense? Thus, our first and most abiding acknowledgment must go to the advocates tussling with and against the state, at risk of their own work, security, and even lives, in every permutation of issue and place. These arguments matter.

Out of these arguments and discussions, the idea for a book took root. We are grateful for the generous and patient support of an anonymous donor and to the scholars and advocates who initially attended the 2013 Harvard Law School meeting. Parallel projects have been launched, and we were honored to be part of consultations on this topic by actors such as the UN Office of the High Commissioner for Human Rights, Amnesty International, Creating Resources for Empowerment in Action (India), the Center for Reproductive Rights (USA), and the Sex Workers Project of the Urban Justice Center (USA), among others.

We have benefited from the advice and participation of all of the authors, as well as essential "first thinkers" and advocates such as Carole S. Vance and Sara Hossain, whose conversations informed our project. Other key thinkers such as Laura Katzive kept us focused on the intersections of gender, sexuality, and abortion policy; Sofia Gruskin's, Eszter Kismodi's, and Susana Fried's thoughts have enriched ours.

Our team of research assistants—Lauren Birchfield, Alex Hess, Zain Rizvi, Ann Sarnak, Camila Vega, Rachel Wilkinson, and Tara Zivkovic—were unparalleled in their dedication, insightfulness, and perseverance.

We thank Peter Agree, editor in chief at the University of Pennsylvania Press, and its staff for their many efforts.

As with any project that stretches both mind and time, we thank our families for their forbearance and our institutions—Berkeley, Harvard, and Yale Law Schools—for giving us support and space.